THE CAMBRIDGE COMPANION TO THE
MODERN GOTHIC

This *Companion* explores the many ways in which the Gothic has dispersed in the twentieth and twenty-first centuries, and in particular how it has come to offer a focus for the tensions inherent in modernity. Fourteen essays by world-class experts show how the Gothic in numerous forms – including literature, film, television, and cyberspace – helps audiences both to distance themselves from and to deal with some of the key underlying problems of modern life. Topics discussed include the norms and shifting boundaries of sex and gender, the explosion of different forms of media and technology, the mixture of cultures across the Western world, the problem of identity for the modern individual, what people continue to see as evil, and the very nature of modernity. Also including a chronology and guide to further reading, this volume offers a comprehensive account of the importance of the Gothic to modern life and thought.

Jerrold E. Hogle is University Distinguished Professor and Director of Undergraduate Studies and Honors in English at the University of Arizona. He is editor of *The Cambridge Companion to Gothic Fiction* (Cambridge, 2002) and author of *The Undergrounds of* The Phantom of the Opera: *Sublimation and the Gothic in Leroux's Novel and Its Progeny* (2002) and *Shelley's Process: Radical Transference and the Development of His Major Works* (1988).

D1610372

THE CAMBRIDGE
COMPANION TO THE
MODERN GOTHIC

EDITED BY
JERROLD E. HOGLE

CAMBRIDGE
UNIVERSITY PRESS

University Printing House, Cambridge CB2 8BS, United Kingdom

Cambridge University Press is part of the University of Cambridge.

It furthers the University's mission by disseminating knowledge in the pursuit of
education, learning, and research at the highest international levels of excellence.

www.cambridge.org
Information on this title: www.cambridge.org/9781107678385

© Cambridge University Press 2014

First published 2014

Printed in the United Kingdom by Clays, St Ives plc

A catalog record for this publication is available from the British Library

Library of Congress Cataloging in Publication data
The Cambridge companion to the modern gothic / edited by Jerrold E. Hogle.
pages cm. – (Cambridge companions to literature)
Includes bibliographical references and index.
ISBN 978-1-107-02356-7 (Hardback) – ISBN 978-1-107-67838-5 (Paperback)   1. Gothic
revival (Literature)–History and criticism.   2. Literature and society.   3. Modernism
(Literature)–History and criticism.   4. Postmodernism.   I. Hogle, Jerrold E., editor.
PN3435.C28 2014   809.3'8766–dc23
2014021601

ISBN 978-1-107-02356-7 Hardback
ISBN 978-1-107-67838-5 Paperback

CONTENTS

LIST OF CONTRIBUTORS

KATARZYNA ANCUTA, Assumption University, Thailand

LUCIE ARMITT, University of Lincoln, UK

ELISABETH BRONFEN, University of Zurich, Switzerland

GLENNIS BYRON, University of Stirling, UK

SUSAN CHAPLIN, Leeds Metropolitan University, UK

SHARON DEANS, University of Stirling, UK

CARLOS GALLEGO, St. Olaf College, Minnesota, USA

KEN GELDER, University of Melbourne, Australia

JERROLD E. HOGLE, University of Arizona, USA

AVRIL HORNER, Kingston University London, UK

E. L. MCCALLUM, Michigan State University, USA

JOHN PAUL RIQUELME, Boston University, USA

CHARLES SCRUGGS, University of Arizona, USA

ISABELLA VAN ELFEREN, Kingston University London, UK

MAISHA L. WESTER, Indiana University, Bloomington, USA

SUE ZLOSNIK, Manchester Metropolitan University, UK

PREFACE

This *Companion* is designed to introduce college-level undergraduates, as well as more advanced scholars and interested general readers, to many of the numerous fictional forms taken in the twentieth and twenty-first centuries by the "Gothic" mode. "The Gothic," as it is often called because it stretches across many different forms of expression, has greatly expanded its reach from the "haunted" narratives and dramas of eighteenth-century England, where it began, to encompass a wide array of constructions, from the printed and the filmed to the televised, the computer-graphic, and the cybernetic, that have become pervasive in the modern-to-"postmodern" world. Each of the fourteen brand-new essays here, all by world-class experts in the areas they treat, focuses on a specific range of works and subjects within the vast mixture that the Gothic encompasses by now, though at times some of us have found it essential to trace the roots of some modern Gothic back to earlier examples of that mode in which more recent images and issues had their beginnings. As much as we have fashioned this collection to be approached on its own, it is, in fact, something of a sequel, or companion *Companion*, to *The Cambridge Companion to Gothic Fiction* (2002), still widely available. Seeing as the modern Gothic has become so varied and global that no one book can encompass it all, we therefore refer our readers, for basic accounts of the earlier Gothic, to that collection, as well as to other introductions to this mode (see Chapter 1), and we have chosen not to treat in detail the aspects of the modern Gothic that are emphasized already in Chapters 10–14 of that *Gothic Fiction* volume.

That decision, however, still leaves a great many areas of the modern Gothic to be defined and explained in these essays, often in the context of theories of culture and interpretation (which we explain, since we do not assume our readers already know them) that have proven revealing in accounting for the features of the Gothic and its many variations. Overall, these essays show that the Gothic in all its forms is not just a haunting and unsettling – sometimes horrifying – sideshow in the development of modernity, but is in fact a distinctive conflation of symbolic figures vital for grasping the underpinnings of much of what we think of as "modern" in our world. To advance and contextualize that collective argument, this *Companion* opens with an orienting chronology of important appearances of the Gothic since it began, albeit one geared to what is emphasized in the essays themselves. Following all fourteen essays, this volume closes with both a guide to further reading and a guide to further viewing that highlight the primary and secondary texts, including films, television productions, and video games, that we believe our readers should turn to first, once they have considered our essays. These sections, like this whole collection, run the risk of not being able to encompass all the instances of the Gothic and Gothic studies that are worthy of attention. But we hope our readers understand that these added study aids are designed primarily to complement what is emphasized in the essays here, even though both sections do offer what we think are some good avenues for exploring the modern Gothic beyond the limits of this book. Indeed, all primary Gothic works of literature or visual media, as well as some major theories and studies of the Gothic, mentioned, but not quoted, in these essays are given full source citations only in these guides. The notes at the end of every chapter are reserved only for the sources of what is quoted directly in the main text or for sources essential for exemplifying what the main text claims.

One of the quandaries that these essays have faced, to be sure, is whether they should refer to the mode we examine as "Gothic" or "gothic." The use of the capitalized "G" in the past has been justified by the reference of "Gothic" to the northern Germanic tribes of the early Middle Ages who have been group-identified as "Goths" or "Visigoths," thus making these words proper names. But interpreters of the much later Enlightenment, Romantic, and modern "Gothic," our focus here, realize that even linking the Goths to medieval church architecture and religiosity, let alone narratives and dramas much closer to modern times, is really an error that looks back to the misnaming of late-medieval buildings as "Gothic" by early-modern art critics inclined to see them as "primitive" compared to neoclassic structures descended from the designs of ancient Greece and Rome. Much as "Gothic" is therefore a floating signifier that has been moved from referring to older tribes or constructs to mislabeling buildings to classifying newer forms of fiction-making, however, this collection will still refer to the ongoing conflation of symbolic features that we analyze as "Gothic," reserving lower-case "goth" or "gothic" for very local variations (such as social groups), which do not usually employ the full combination of key motifs that have come down to us from Horace Walpole's *The Castle of*

Otranto: A Gothic Story (1764–1765). "Gothic" here is akin to "Romantic" or "Enlightenment" in referring to a lasting and interconnected, if somewhat unstable, set of conflicted assumptions and aesthetic devices that has survived as recognizable from the eighteenth to the twenty-first century across many different and changing venues. The authors of these essays, after all, believe that it is the floating variability of reference in the Walpolean "Gothic" mixture of ingredients that has allowed them to survive together as powerful tools of representation and to be as symbolic as they are of undercurrents in modern life from the late nineteenth century until today.

In any case, the editor of this *Companion* is deeply grateful to everyone who has had a hand in bringing our collection about. He is grateful most of all, of course, to the fifteen other contributors here, themselves writing from around the globe and thus true international Gothicists all, who have each provided outstanding expertise and insights by distilling these into concise accounts that still define, explain, and exemplify large areas of modern Gothic (or near-Gothic) works and ranges of reference. Each of these scholars, in fact, has surpassed the normal call of duty to work graciously with the editor in crafting these essays carefully to be just right for the purposes of a *Cambridge Companion*. In addition, all of us are grateful, the editor especially, for the tireless and extensive support provided to this effort by the editor's research assistant, Peter Figler, at the University of Arizona. We also appreciate our staff associates and our fellow faculty or student supporters or mentors, along of course with our supportive families, at our different universities and in our individual lives. Ultimately, too, we are most grateful to the leadership in literary studies at Cambridge University Press – particularly Linda Bree and Anna Bond – for all the guidance, counsel, and work they have provided in enabling this further collection of studies on the richness of the Gothic and on the modern world to which this haunting mode still contributes so much.

CHRONOLOGY: IMPORTANT "GOTHIC" EVENTS

1764–1768	Horace Walpole publishes the first editions of *The Castle of Otranto* and composes (without staging) the Gothic play *The Mysterious Mother*.
1789–1797	Ann Radcliffe publishes six increasingly popular Gothic "romances," including *The Mysteries of Udolpho* (1794) and *The Italian* (1797).
1796–1797	Matthew Gregory Lewis publishes *The Monk*, followed by the writing and staging of his play *The Castle Spectre*.
1798–1800	Charles Brockden Brown publishes his American Gothic novels in Philadelphia, including *Wieland* and *Edgar Huntly*.
1798	William Wordsworth and Samuel Taylor Coleridge publish their first *Lyrical Ballads*, including some highly Gothic pieces, such as "The Rime of the Ancient Mariner."
1816	Coleridge publishes his heavily Gothic "Christabel" with "Kubla Kahn" (both composed 1797–1802); C. R. Maturin's play *Bertram* is first staged in London.
1816–1819	A "ghost-story-writing contest" proposed by Lord Byron near Geneva leads to the publication of Mary Shelley's *Frankenstein* and John Polidori's *The Vampyre*, plus indirectly to Byron's "The Prisoner of Chillon" and his Gothic tragedy *Manfred*.
1816–1820	Walter Scott publishes the most Gothic of his historical novels, from *The Antiquary* (1816) to *The Bride of Lammermoor* (1819) and *Ivanhoe* (1820).

1817	Jane Austen's satirically Gothic *Northanger Abbey* (written 1798–1799) is published with her *Persuasion* months after her death.
1819–1820	Washington Irving publishes *The Sketch Book* in New York in seven parts, which include "Rip Van Winkle" and "The Legend of Sleepy Hollow."
1820	Charles Maturin's influential Irish Gothic *Melmoth the Wanderer* appears.
1835	Nathaniel Hawthorne publishes his "Young Goodman Brown" story.
1835–1846	Edgar Allan Poe publishes *The Narrative of Arthur Gordon Pym* (1838) and a series of Gothic tales, including "Legeia," "The Fall of the House of Usher," "The Murders in the Rue Morgue," "The Black Cat," his 1844 poem "The Raven," and "The Cask of Amontillado."
1845–1847	James Malcolm Rymer's *Varney the Vampire* is serialized in England before and after the 1846 publication of Rymer's *The String of Pearls*, the "penny dreadful" that tells the Sweeney Todd story.
1847	Charlotte Brontë publishes *Jane Eyre*; Emily Brontë publishes *Wuthering Heights*.
1848–1870	Charles Dickens publishes his most Gothically inflected ghost stories and novels from *The Haunted Man* (1848) to *Bleak House* (1852) to *Little Dorrit* (1857) to *The Mystery of Edwin Drood* (left unfinished at his death).
1851–1860	Hawthorne publishes *The House of Seven Gables* (1851) and *The Marble Faun* (1860); Herman Melville publishes *Pierre* (1852) and "Benito Cereno" (1855–1856).
1861–1862	Wilkie Collins publishes *The Woman in White*, an exemplary Victorian "sensation novel," shortly before Mary Elizabeth Braddon publishes *Lady Audley's Secret*.
1871–1872	Joseph Sheridan Le Fanu publishes the vampiric "Carmilla," first in *The Dark Blue* magazine and then in his *Through a Glass Darkly* collection of tales.

1886–1888	Robert Louis Stevenson publishes his *Strange Case of Dr. Jekyll and Mr. Hyde*, which soon leads to the first London stage adaptation and becomes connected in the public eye with the unsolved Whitechapel murders associated with "Jack the Ripper" (1888–1891).
1890	Arthur Machen publishes "The Great God Pan."
1890–1894	Oscar Wilde publishes *The Picture of Dorian Gray* (twice) in London, followed by the French and English publications of his revenge tragedy *Salome* (banned from the stage in 1892, but finally first performed in Paris in 1896 with Wilde by now in prison for "gross indecency").
1892	Charlotte Perkins Gilman publishes "The Yellow Wallpaper" in *New England Magazine*.
1893	Bram Stoker publishes his Gothic story "The Squaw."
1896	Braddon publishes *The Good Lady Ducayne*; H. G. Wells publishes *The Island of Dr. Moreau*.
1897	Stoker publishes *Dracula*, Florence Marryat publishes *The Blood of the Vampire*, and Richard Heldman (as "Richard Marsh") publishes *The Beetle*.
1898	Henry James publishes *The Turn of the Screw*; Stephen Crane publishes his novella *The Monster*, reflecting both the legacy of *Frankenstein* and the ongoing problem of race prejudice in America.
1899	Joseph Conrad's semi-Gothic *Heart of Darkness* is published.
1910	Gaston Leroux publishes the novel *Le fantôme de l'Opéra* in Paris.
1915	Franz Kafka publishes *The Metamorphosis* in Austria-Hungary.
1916	James Joyce publishes his Gothically inflected *A Portrait of the Artist as a Young Man*.
1917	Virginia Woolf publishes "The Mark on the Wall."

1919	Sigmund Freud publishes his essay "The Uncanny" in Austria; Pathé Frères releases the post-World War I film *J'accuse*, directed by Abel Gance, in France.
1920	H. P. Lovecraft publishes "Nyarlothotep" to begin a series of American Gothic tales; Philips Film releases Germany's *The Cabinet of Dr. Caligari*, directed by Robert Wiene; *The Black Mask* magazine begins publishing occult and crime stories by Raymond Chandler, Dashiell Hammet, and others.
1921	Woolf publishes "A Haunted House."
1922	Film Arts Guild releases silent *Nosferatu*, directed by F. W. Murnau; T. S. Eliot publishes *The Waste Land* and Joyce his *Ulysses*, both with Gothic ingredients.
1924	E. M. Forster publishes *A Passage to India*.
1925	Universal releases a silent *Phantom of the Opera*, directed by Rupert Julian.
1928	"The Fall of the House of Usher" is first adapted to film in America by MGM, directed by James Sibley Watson, and in France, directed by John Epstein.
1931	Universal releases *Dracula*, directed by Tod Browning, and *Frankenstein*, directed by James Whale; Paramount releases *Dr. Jekyll and Mr. Hyde*, directed by Rouben Mamoulian; William Faulkner publishes *Sanctuary*.
1932	United Artists releases *White Zombie*, directed by Victor Helperin; Universal releases *The Old Dark House*, directed by Whale; Faulkner publishes *Light in August*.
1934	Karen Blixen publishes *Seven Gothic Tales* (Danish–English) under the name "Isak Dinesen."
1935	Universal releases *The Raven*, directed by Lew Landers, and *The Bride of Frankenstein*, directed by Whale.
1936	Djuna Barnes publishes *Nightwood*; Faulkner publishes *Absalom, Absalom!*

1938–1940	Daphne du Maurier publishes *Rebecca*, soon adapted as a Selznick-United Artists film, directed by Alfred Hitchcock.
1940	Richard Wright publishes *Native Son*.
1941	Warner Bros. releases *The Maltese Falcon*, directed by John Houston, based on the 1929–1930 Hammet novel, solidifying film noir; Universal releases *The Wolf Man*, directed by George Waggner; RKO releases the often Gothic *Citizen Kane*, co-written and directed by Orson Welles.
1943	RKO releases *I Walked with a Zombie*, directed by Jacques Tourneur.
1946	Universal releases *The Killers*, directed by Robert Siodmark, beginning a succession of different films noirs based on Ernest Hemingway's 1927 story of that name.
1949	Selznick-London releases *The Third Man*, directed by Carol Reed.
1950	Paramount releases Gothic-noir *Sunset Boulevard*, directed by Billy Wilder.
1952	Ralph Ellison publishes *Invisible Man*; Javanese writer Pramoeda Ananta Toer publishes the story collection *All That Has Gone*; Flannery O'Connor publishes *Wise Blood* to launch a career of southern Gothic fictions, most of them short stories.
1953	Samuel Beckett publishes *The Unnamable*.
1954	Richard Matheson publishes *I Am Legend*.
1955	*The Night of the Hunter*, directed by Charles Laughton, is released by United Artists.
1957	Hammer Studios in England begins its Gothic color-film onslaught (lasting through to 1972) with *The Curse of Frankenstein*.
1959–1960	Robert Bloch's novel *Psycho* becomes the basis for a Paramount-Universal film, directed by Hitchcock; Shirley Jackson publishes *The Haunting of Hill House*.

1960	Champs-Élysées Production releases *Eyes without a Face*, directed by Georges Franju; American International begins a Poe-based series of films with *House of Usher*, directed by Roger Corman; Eleanor Hibbert as "Victoria Holt" starts her four decades of Gothic romances with *Mistress of Mellyn*; Leslie Fiedler publishes *Love and Death in the American Novel*, establishing the Gothic as deeply woven into American writing.
1962	Warner Bros. releases *What Ever Happened to Baby Jane?*, directed by Robert Aldrich.
1963	MGM releases *The Haunting*, directed by Robert Wise, based on *The Haunting of Hill House*.
1966	Jean Rhys publishes *Wide Sargasso Sea*, a Jamaican Creole's answer to *Jane Eyre*; Leonard Cohen publishes *Beautiful Losers*.
1967	Angela Carter publishes *The Magic Toyshop*.
1968	Philip K. Dick publishes *Do Androids Dream of Electric Sheep?*; N. Scott Momaday publishes *House Made of Dawn*; Paramount releases *Rosemary's Baby*, directed by Roman Polanski, based on the 1967 Ira Levin novel; Continental releases *Night of the Living Dead*, directed by George Romero, to set a major new zombie-film standard.
1970	Kim Sŏk-pŏm publishes *The Curious Tale of Mandogi's Ghost*.
1971	Tomás Rivera publishes *... y no se lo tragó la tierra / ... and the Earth Did Not Devour Him*.
1971–1973	William Peter Blatty publishes *The Exorcist* and soon writes the screenplay for the Warner Bros. film, directed by William Friedkin.
1972	Margaret Atwood publishes her Canadian Gothic novel *Surfacing*.
1972–1973	Oscar Zeta Acosta publishes his *Autobiography of a Brown Buffalo* and then *The Revolt of the Cockroach People*.

1974	Nadine Gordimer publishes *The Conservationist* out of South Africa.
1974–1975	Stephen King starts a popular run of Gothic novels with *Carrie*, then *'Salem's Lot*.
1975	First release (by 20th Century Fox) of *The Rocky Horror Picture Show*, directed by Jim Sharman, based on the 1973 British stage musical by Richard O'Brian.
1976	MGM releases *Carrie*, directed by Brian de Palma; Anne Rice publishes *Interview with the Vampire*; Alice Walker publishes *Meridian*.
1977	Leslie Marmon Silko publishes *Ceremony*; Stephen King publishes *The Shining*.
1978	United Film releases *Dawn of the Dead*, directed by Romero; Falcon and Compass release *Holloween*, directed by John Carpenter, which, under some influence from *Psycho*, sets a new standard for the Gothic-based horror film and has helped to establish the "slasher movie" as a popular form to this day.
1979	Herzog Films releases a *Nosferatu* remake, directed by Werner Herzog; 20th Century Fox releases *Alien*, directed by Ridley Scott, to be followed by sequels (1986, 1992, 1997) and a 2012 "prequel" (*Prometheus*, directed by Scott); Peter Straub publishes *Ghost Story* (adapted for film in 1984); Angela Carter's story collection *The Bloody Chamber* also appears.
1980	Warner Bros. releases *The Shining*, directed by Stanley Kubrick; Salman Rushdie publishes *Midnight's Children*; Chart Korbjitti's novel *No Way Out* appears, followed quickly by his *The Judgment* (1981); J. M. Coetzee publishes *Waiting for the Barbarians*; Eve Kosofsky Sedgwick publishes *The Coherence of Gothic Conventions* in America, David Punter *The Literature of Terror* in England, and Julia Kristeva *Powers of Horror* in France, the stirrings of a newly burgeoning study of the Gothic in academia.
1982	Warner Bros. releases *Blade Runner*, directed by Ridley Scott, based on the 1968 Dick novel; Isabel Allende

publishes the semi-Gothic/magical realist *The House of the Spirits*; Stephen King publishes *Danse Macabre*, his nonfiction account of the cultural meanings of Gothic fiction and cinema.

1983   Catherine Lim publishes *They Do Return ... But Gently Lead Them Back*; Pira Sudham publishes the partly Gothic *Tales of Thailand*; Rushdie publishes *Shame*; Fay Weldon publishes *The Life and Loves of a She-Devil*.

1984   William Gibson publishes *Neuromancer*; Orion releases *The Terminator*, directed by James Cameron, far more Gothic than its sequels; New Line Cinema releases *A Nightmare on Elm Street*, directed by Wes Craven, setting up a succession of sequels and a 2010 remake.

1985   Cecile Pineda publishes *Face*; Anne Rice publishes *The Vampire Lestat*; United Film releases *Day of the Dead*, directed by Romero; Gloria Naylor publishes the African American *Linden Hills*.

1986   De Laurentiis Group releases *Blue Velvet*, directed by David Lynch; Maryse Conde's *I, Tabitha* is published, retelling the story of the Salem witch trials from a slave's perspective; Andrew Lloyd Webber's stage-musical version of *The Phantom of the Opera* debuts in London, directed by Harold Prince, and eventually becomes the longest-running musical ever on the West End and (starting in 1987) on Broadway in New York.

1987   Toni Morrison publishes *Beloved*.

1988   Atwood publishes her story collection *Bluebeard's Egg*; Patrick McGrath publishes *Blood and Water and Other Tales*, among the earliest of his many Gothic works.

1989   Randall Kenan publishes *A Visitation of Spirits*; Jeanette Winterson publishes *Sexing the Cherry*; Jamaica Kincaid publishes her story "Ovando"; Top Shelf Productions begins the serial publication of *From Hell*, based on the Whitechapel murders and setting a new standard for Gothic graphic novels to come.

1990   K. K. Seet publishes *Death Rites*; Su Tong publishes *Raise the Red Lantern* in China; debut of ABC-TV series *Twin Peaks*, created and directed by Lynch; Annette Cutis Klause publishes *The Silver Kiss*, signaling big growth in the teen-Gothic market; Anne Rice publishes *The Witching Hour* to begin her New Orleans Gothic *Lives of the Mayfair Witches* series; Charles Johnson publishes *Middle Passage*, an African American recasting of Poe's *Arthur Gordon Pym*.

1991   Koji Suzuki publishes his first *Ringu* novel in Japan, launching a series of sequels and film adaptations; Ma Jian also publishes her *Noodle Maker* stories; L. J. Smith begins publishing *The Vampire Diaries* (adapted as a television series starting in 2009); Angela Carter publishes both *Wise Children* and *The Virago Book of Fairy Tales*, vol. 1; Orion releases *The Silence of the Lambs*, directed by Jonathan Demme, based on the 1988 Thomas Harris novel; Vietnamese author Bao Ninh publishes *The Sorrow of War*.

1992   Rebecca Brown publishes *The Terrible Girls* stories; Morrison publishes her *Playing in the Dark* lectures; American Zoetrope and Columbia release the lush *Bram Stoker's Dracula*, directed by Francis Ford Coppola, with its "Love Song for a Vampire" by Annie Lennox becoming an international hit.

1993   Debut of *The X-Files* series, created and directed by Chris Carter, on FOX-TV; Alison Lurie publishes her *Women and Ghosts* collection; Chapman Productions and Miramax release *The Piano*, written and directed by Jane Campion, based partly on Jane Mander's *The Story of a New Zealand River* (1920); idSoftware releases the first version of the *Doom* video game, setting a new standard for game-video technology – and global popularity – using elements from the Gothic tradition.

1995   Helena Maria Viramontes publishes *Under the Feet of Jesus*; Vivian Vande Velda publishes teen-oriented *Companions of the Night*, while Mary Downing Hahn issues her similar *Look for Me by Moonlight*; Atwood publishes *Strange Things: The Malevolent North in Canadian Literature*; Lois Parkinson Zamora and Wendy B. Faris publish the important collection *Magical Realism*; Hidekai Sena's Japanese *Parasite Eve* appears; Catherine Lim publishes *The Bondmaid* to begin a series of Chinese romances.

1996   Dimension releases *From Dusk till Dawn*, directed by Robert Rodriguez; Patricia Windsor publishes *The Blooding*; Haitian Edwidge Denticat publishes her story collection *Krik? Krak!*

1997   Arundhati Roy publishes *The God of Small Things*; WB Television begins the series *Buffy the Vampire Slayer*, created and directed by Joss Whedan, based on his script for a 1992 film of that name; J. K. Rowling in England publishes the first of eight *Harry Potter* novels, containing many Gothic elements, all visually intensified in the nine films released by Warner Bros. and Heyday (2001–2011).

1998   S. P. Somtow publishes *Dragon's Fin Soup* out of Thailand; Gaétan Soucy publishes *The Little Girl Who Was Too Fond of Matches*; Maya Montero publishes *In the Palm of Darkness*; Denticat publishes *The Farming of Bones* even as Stephen King publishes *Bag of Bones*.

1999   Sarah Waters publishes *Affinity*; Fox 2000 releases *Fight Club*, directed by David Fincher, from the 1996 novel by Chuck Palahniuk; Mo Yan publishes *Shifu, You'll Do Anything for a Laugh*; Momentum releases *eXistenZ*, directed by David Cronenberg; Julia Leigh publishes *The Hunter* (adapted as a film in 2011); Paramount and Mandalay release *Sleepy Hollow*, directed by Tim Burton; Hexen Films releases *The Blair Witch Project*, directed by Eduardo Sánchez and Daniel Myrick; the International Gothic Association's journal, *Gothic Studies*, commences publication.

2000   China Miéville publishes *Perdido Street Station*; Eden Robinson publishes *Monkey Beach*; Straub publishes *Magic Terror: Seven Tales*; Mark Z. Danielewski publishes his multilayered *House of Leaves*.

2001   Charlaine Harris begins *The Southern Vampire Mysteries* with *Dead Until Dark*; El Deseo releases *The Devil's Backbone*, directed by Guillermo del Toro; Dimension releases *The Others*, directed by Alejandro Amenábar; Hong Ling's vampire story "Fever" appears.

2002   Pineda publishes *Bardo99*; Sarah Waters publishes *Fingersmith*; Rachel Klein's *The Moth Diaries* appears; Hannah Crafts' *The Bondswoman's Narrative*, a novel possibly written by a slave in the 1860s with Gothic motifs, is published for the first time; Michael Crummy publishes *River Thieves*; Dreamworks releases the Canadian film *The Ring*, directed by Gore Verbinski, based on Suzuki's 1991 *Ringu* and Japanese–Korean film adaptations of it (1998–1999); Screen Gems releases the first *Resident Evil* film, directed by Paul W. S. Anderson, setting up many sequels, all based on a Capcom video game begun in 1996, created by Shinji Mikami, and reprogrammed annually through 2012.

2003   Allende publishes *My Invented Country*; publication of the first graphic novel in *The Walking Dead* zombie series by Robert Kirkman and Tony Moore (adapted as an AMC/FOX-TV series starting in 2010).

2004   Andrew McGahan publishes *The White Earth* in Australia.

2005   Universal releases *Land of the Dead*, directed by Romero; Laura Whitcomb publishes *A Certain Slant of Light*; David Hontiveros publishes *Takod* and *Craving* from the Philippines; Duong Thu Huong publishes *No Man's Land* from Vietnam; McGrath publishes Gothic stories about New York in *Ghost Town* as a reaction to 9/11; Stephenie Meyer begins the *Twilight* saga with *Twilight* (released as a film in 2008).

2006   Touchstone releases *The Prestige*, directed by Christopher Nolan; Esperanto Films and Warner Bros. release *Pan's Labyrinth*, directed by del Toro; Vernor Vinge publishes *Rainbows End*; Pu Songling's seventeenth-century *zhiguai* stories are translated in *Strange Tales from a Chinese Studio*; Mo Yan publishes *Life and Death Are Wearing Me Out*; Kiran Desai publishes *The Inheritance of Loss*; Cormac McCarthy publishes the Gothically inflected *No Country for Old Men*, adapted on film by Joel and Ethan Coen (writers/directors) in 2007.

2007   Junot Diaz publishes *The Brief Wondrous Life of Oscar Wao*; Helen Oyeyemi publishes the magical realist-Gothic *The Opposite House*.

2008   HBO begins the series *True Blood*, created and directed by Alan Ball, based on the Harris *Southern Vampire* novels; R. Scott Bakker publishes *Neuropath*; FOX-TV begins the series *Fringe*, created and directed by J. J. Abrams, Alex Kurtzman, and Roberto Arci; Patricia Ness publishes *The Knife of Never Letting Go*; Sandrew Metronome releases the Swedish film *Let the Right One In*, directed by Tomas Alfredson, based on a 2004 novel by John Ajvide Lindqvist (which also led to an American remake, *Let Me In*, in 2010).

2009   Oyeyemi publishes *White Is for Witching*; Warner Bros. releases *Splice*, directed by Vincenzo Natali; Carrie Ryan publishes *The Forest of Hands and Teeth*, while Michael Grant publishes *Gone*.

2010   China Miéville publishes *Kraken*.

2011   Paramount releases *Super 8*, directed by Abrams, and *Hugo*, directed by Martin Scorsese.

2013   Warner Bros.-New Line releases *The Conjuring*, directed by James Wan; Chuck Palahniuk publishes the graphic novel *Doomed*.

2014   *Suburban Gothic*, directed by Richard Bates, Jr., is released by New Normal Films; the "Whitby Gothic Weekend" is announced for April 25–27 on *The Blogging Goth* site as the latest event of the *UK Gothic Festival* begun in 2012.

PART I

The Gothic and modernity

I

JERROLD E. HOGLE

Introduction: modernity and the proliferation of the Gothic

On the face of it, modernity would seem at odds with "the Gothic."
Granted, that highly mixed mode – a set of often-linked elements rather
than a fixed genre – that began in English prose fiction, theater, and some
poetry in the eighteenth century has by now crept, throughout the world yet
with many of its initial features still visible, into a wide array of media: film,
television, surreal art, comic books and graphic novels, paperback "romances" by the hundreds, computer and video games, labyrinthine Web sites in
cyberspace, popular or avant-garde music, and the actions and dress of
"goth" subcultures, not to mention parodies and self-parodies for more
than two centuries. Nonetheless, this extensive "progress" always seems
to be pulling backward too, recalling the Gothic's earlier forms, as was the
case when the Gothic as we now know it first came about. Even when
placed at some distance from, while also referring to, the time of medieval
"Gothic" architecture – a misnomer applied by later neoclassicists to the
"barbarity" of pointed-arch buildings dating from the 1100s to the 1300s,
which were wrongly linked to the fifth-century "Goths" who helped end the
Roman Empire[1] – "modern Gothic" certainly seemed a flagrant oxymoron
when Horace Walpole published his novella *The Castle of Otranto* in 1764.
He admitted as much himself in 1765 in the second edition, subtitled
A Gothic Story (the first use of that label), by way of a second preface that
defines this new mode as a "blend" of the "two kinds of romance, the
ancient and the modern."[2] The "modern" there refers to the rising middle-
class novel of that time, concerned heavily with the ideological aspirations
of the growing bourgeoisie and anchored in the values of "nature" being
"copied with success" and empirically verified "rules of probability"
governing character motivation and behavior without supernatural intervention. All of these assumptions were key to that break from older
absolutes of religion and politics that soon came to be called the
"Enlightenment," a major assertion of modernity by largely Protestant
thinkers, of whom Walpole was one. It was the elements in *Otranto* tinged

3

with the old-style supernatural, though, thereby recalling "ancient romance" (really pastiches of Shakespearean, operatic, medieval-chivalric, once-Catholic, and ancient Greek features), that then attracted and still attract the most audience interest. Hence Walpole defends them in 1765 as vital to reviving "the powers of fancy," even as he admits some of these elements to be so retrograde that readers should view them as "unnatural ... machines" now divorced from their older (and Catholic) groundings while the characters in the story must be rendered as accepting them within the belief systems of their moment. Though already a floating signifier transferred from one referent (fifth-century tribes) to another (high-medieval architecture) and then another (Walpole's hybrid), "Gothic" from Walpole on has thus come to connote a backward-leaning counter-modernity lurking in both the emerging and recent stages of modern life. This retrogression appears to undermine, and in that way "haunt," the assumption that the "modern" has left behind any regressive tendencies that might impede its progress and fulfillment.

Certainly it is those features still redolent of "ancient" romance as they are transformed in their tug-of-war with their "modern" counterpart that have lasted enough in countless variations on this "new Gothic" since *Otranto* to make us know when we are facing the Gothic today even in quite different and more cross-cultural manifestations of Walpole's hybrid scheme. Those features include (a) antiquated settings, often with obscured undergrounds harboring age-old texts, from moldering castles, graveyards, mansions/houses, and primitive wildernesses to urban and suburban under-worlds, multilayered computer programs, and aging train stations or spaceships; (b) ghostly or monstrous figures, intermixing life and death as well as other incompatibilities, that loom forth in or invade these settings, usually because of secrets from the past buried deep in memories or archives, and may be either supernatural or psychological in origin, at times even hinting at a personal or cultural unconscious; (c) central char-acters, such as Walpole's Manfred or Theodore, consequently caught between conflicting systems of belief, being pulled retrogressively toward outmoded superstitions while also being open to more progressive thinking, like the two-faced god of ancient Rome (Janus) that looks backward and forward simultaneously; (d) women specifically, such as Walpole's Isabella and Matilda, trapped and terrified in archaic patriarchal structures yet also starting to see dim possibilities for greater freedom and equality that might blur old boundaries of sex and gender; and (e) over-the-top word-patterns and images that incongruously mix "old romantic" hyperbole – including the obscure and terrifying "sublime" aroused by ruins suggestive of ghosts in Edmund Burke's *Philosophical Enquiry* of 1757[3] – with forms of quasi-realism, often joined with disruptions of standard linear narrative.

Consequently, any "light" of rational revelation in the Gothic is always countered by a fearsome chiaroscuro that mixes illumination with ominous and mysterious darkness, as well as reversals of progressive time, creating what we now know as the scary "Gothic atmosphere" that lingers on in so many forms today. These elements can be manipulated by authors, film-makers, and game creators toward an emphasis on *terror* (the frightened anticipation of potential, but uncertain, threats, as in the 1790s romances of Ann Radcliffe) or a confrontation with *horror* (visible violence, dismember-ment, and death, as in Matthew Lewis' *The Monk* of 1796), provided there is always the reassuring safety of the observer implied by the blatant fictiveness, the hyperbolic exaggeration, of the atmosphere and the situation being presented, making it all "just a story." Since the Gothic is a mixture of quite different elements and inherently unstable anyway, some fictions use only partial forms of it, employing several but not all of the above elements alongside very different conventions. Others attempt a full-blown Gothic recalibrated to the cultural fears of their own times by including all these features in some form, invoking the thoroughly Gothic, as opposed to the semi- or near-Gothic, for the many layers it offers of symbolic, as well as emotional, suggestiveness.

True, with these characteristics being somewhat uprooted, even by Walpole, from older ways of thinking that once underwrote them, they, like the word "Gothic," can be transported out of their past contexts, despite some harkenings back that always linger. Because of that mobility, they can be used to intimate, while also to disguise, conflicts between regressive and progressive tendencies, a set of widely felt, underlying, unresolved quandar-ies, in the cultural belief systems (or ideologies) of the audience at the time of each new work. That is why the scholar-critic E. J. Clery has rightly seen Walpole's inaugural "Gothic Story" as both wildly fictionalizing and suggesting – and hence exaggerating, while obscuring – a "contradiction" in the author's and his culture's thinking "between the traditional [or old aristocratic] claims of landed property and the new [more bourgeois] claims of the private family."[4] This sublimated contestation was really more frightening at the time than the ghosts and portents in Walpole's story announced specifically as "exploded now" in first preface of 1764 in an era when such vestiges of "ancient" Catholicism had become symbols mostly of emptied-out meanings. The hybridity of the Walpolean, and now the post-Walpolean, Gothic counters the surface claims of the sup-posedly greater modernity in which it continues to appear. It does so by intimating the Janus-faced nature of the unresolved pulls between older and newer systems of belief, including the resulting conflicts within or among people, which really underlies nearly all Gothic fictions constructed mainly for middle-class audiences. As David Punter, a major Gothicist, has written, it is in the Gothic that "the middle class displaces the hidden violence of present social structures," what the Slovenian theorist Slavoj Žižek calls the repressed "Real" of underlying "social antagonisms," and so "conjures them up again as past," thereby falling "promptly under their spell,"[5] using its special mixture of symbols to throw off (or "abject")[6] the conflicted underpinnings of the lives and the world that the members of the bourgeoisie want to imagine for themselves.

All the essays in this *Companion*, even so, propose to explain many of the different forms in which this Gothic mode has reappeared in more recent times by revealing how much the Gothic, despite its apparent countering of the modern, is deeply bound up with the contradictions basic to modern existence, even the "post"-modernity of more recent decades. We – all the authors here – in fact, have set out to analyze many of the manifestations in which this very paradox appears across the very late nineteenth, the twentieth, and the early twenty-first centuries. As we see it, the Gothic hints at the obscure anomalies of its times during these modern periods even more than once it did in 1764–1765 and across the six decades afterward in England, Western Europe, and America, the time and places in which the Gothic first grew into a major symbolic scheme in the West.

The philosopher-historian Charles Taylor has defined the "social imaginary" of modern life in Western cultures, "the ways in which [people during and after the Enlightenment] imagine their social existence ... in images, stories, legends, etc.,"[7] in a way that helpfully reveals the tensions underlying all of them, as we want to argue that the Gothic does as well. For him modernity, yes, is an "amalgam of new practices and institutional forms (science, technology, industrial production, urbanization), of new ways of living (individualism, secularization, instrumental rationality) and of new forms of malaise (alienation, meaninglessness, a sense of impending social dissolution)."[8] But within all of these is the profound complication, given the post-Enlightenment questioning of older certainties, that "we have changed not just *from* a condition where most people lived 'naively' " with an acceptance of supernatural intervention into perceived reality, but also "*to* one in which almost no one is capable of this," while at the same time much of the West believes that such an option remains "*one among many.*"[9] In modernity, then, vestiges of older schemes of belief, as well as newer ones, are still among the alternatives that individuals now see themselves as free, not forced, to select. They remain the kinds of grounding, ironically, that many "moderns" still long for in an increasingly less grounded and secular world. In the words of American professor Diane Long Hoeveler, this modern "imaginary" is therefore one of "ambivalent secularization." At the heart of it is a "paradox" within "the invention of the modern individual" that is caused by an "ideological split," taking many different forms, between people needing to accept "immanence," a process of everything emerging from within natural developments, including empirical perception, and the same people desiring some level of "transcendence," a causality from some agency – and a separate level of being – beyond the immediately natural or consciously human.[10] It is the hybrid Gothic among post-Enlightenment creations, we claim here, in which this unresolved undercurrent of modernity is best suggested, most forcefully symbolized, and most vividly struggled over, all under the cover of an extreme form of fiction, indeed a pastiche, that may or may not be taken seriously by audiences.

We would add, too, that this conflict in the social unconscious, which the Gothic hints at while also obscuring, enables, even more than Hoeveler describes, a "raucous, contested terrain" of struggles between ways of thinking.[11] At that level of the modern, individual or group quests for workable configurations of human psychology, class, sex and gender, race, nationality, power, law, cultural "superiority" or "inferiority," and even aesthetic form – all problems in constructing any "imaginary" of the modern self in the wake of "ambivalent secularization" – are pulled between retrograde or regressive and emergent or progressive constructions of all these, as well as between claims of "immanent" or "transcendent" causalities as realms from which solutions to the conflicts might come. It is by being extremely and eclectically fictional in a Janus-faced way, we would argue, that forms of the Gothic have become essential to the articulation of such a contentious modernity. The regressive *and* progressive nature of the Gothic has been *and remains* necessary to deal with the social unconscious of modern humanity in all its extreme contradictions spawned by its looking backward and forward so much of the time, even today. We therefore propose to trace the Gothic's now global proliferation across many of the sociocultural and aesthetic spaces that modernity has spawned under the assumption, the basis of this book, that the Gothic is endemic to the modern. After all, the ever-extending tentacles of modern enterprise are always haunted by the doubts, conflicts, and blurring of normative boundaries that the Gothic articulates in every form it assumes because, at its best, it is really *about* the profoundly conflicted core of modernity itself.

No Gothic text after the dawn of modernity, of course, can better exemplify this mode's intimations of modernity's deep tensions in a part-naturalistic, part-fantastic fiction than Mary Shelley's original

Frankenstein (1818), the most influential Gothic text ever published and the basis of numerous modern adaptations that reshape its suggestions about early-modern conflicts into "monstrous" symbols of similar or different undercurrents at later stages of history. Rearranging virtually all the "Gothic" elements of Walpole's *Otranto*[12] while anxiously reflecting the cultural quandaries of its day about science, technology, industrial production, individual initiative, and the nature of the unconscious, Shelley's Gothic story has its title character try to give shape to a post-Enlightenment humanity by fashioning a prototype of its supposed perfectibility, but also, in the same process, symbolizing in that construct some of the most pervasive conflicts troubling Western humanity after the American and French revolutions. These Janus-like tugs-of-war, inside and outside Shelley's novel, include recollections of medieval alchemy being resisted by later-eighteenth-century chemistry and the even wider debate of the 1810s over whether the source of infusible life is transcendent (from an outside electrical "light") or immanent (arising within "the minutiae of causation" visible in relations among the body parts used to compose the new humanoid being).[13] The large and swarthy end product of this morass is monstrous to Victor Frankenstein because it/he, in being the "living dead," is a stitching together of the ancient and the modern, thus incarnating conflicted modernity in that alone. In the Gothic yoking of opposites, it/he also becomes a haunting site, as well as an alter ego of his maker, in which he and we can throw off, but also behold, myriad social and psychological antagonisms underlying modernity. Among them are the need for, yet the dehumanization of, industrial workers on the part of the educated middle class;[14] an awareness of, but also a revulsion at, the white race's dependence on many different "other" ones (suggested in the creature's multicolored face);[15] the deep male need for the maternal and the feminine (as in Victor's dream of re-embracing his dead mother right after his creation comes to life)[16] set over against patriarchy's sidelining of women as science takes even giving birth away from them; and the desired separation of the producer from his product in the rising Industrial Revolution intermixed with the possibility, given the Enlightenment rooting of responsibility in every person's inner depths, that this monster's actions really carry out his creator's own preconscious desires (as we see when the creature kills Victor's fiancée and reminds us that Frankenstein unconsciously holds her responsible for the death of his mother). Why else does Victor come to feel, anticipating so much of the vampire-and-cyborg traditions in more recent Gothic, that the creature may well be "my own vampire, my own spirit let loose from the grave, and forced," like some extension of a rapacious modern entrepreneur, "to destroy all that was dear to me" in the process of being an alienated self-representation of its creator and the human race?[17]

Shelley's *Frankenstein* even plays out the conflict in the Walpolean Gothic and the modern social imaginary over the human body. Here there is a shocking concentration on the massive physicality and sexual outreach of the body and yet a desire to distance that body from people in an objectified representation of it. Both drives are intensified in the outsized creature's desire for a mate, yet also in Victor's effort to make its larger-than-normal body an othered representation of humanity away from himself and all those around him, like all the dis-embodied ghosts in *Otranto* that the creature does resemble. Here the subject (Victor again) does not really want to confront the sheer multiplicity of the grossly physical or the confusingly sexual even while raising up a model or signifier of them. This paradox is still visible in modern humanity's greater comfort with artificial and tech-nological simulations of the body than with the gross fluidity or morbidity of it. We are therefore confronting more undercurrents of modernity itself, as well as inconsistencies in Victor's personal unconscious, in Shelley's novel, both later when he destroys the body-in-process of the female crea-ture he has promised to make[18] and earlier when he hopes he can look on the visage of his male creation and find it artistically, as well as physically, "beautiful."[19] What he confronts at both moments is an inchoate mass of sensual and racial multiplicity that leads him to throw off this complex and conflicted reality, including his own homoeroticism (his attraction to the *man* he imagines he is making), into what now seems a horrifying repre-sentation of the *in*-human, even though it really embodies elemental man and nearly all of Victor's personal longings.[20] Modern humanity's use of technologies to extend and reconstruct the self and thereby estrange, and even protect, the self from itself could not be symbolized more vividly or reveal the quandaries within it more thoroughly. In the face of such capaci-ties of the Gothic so visible in *Frankenstein* and its endless reworkings, there can be little doubt that this mixed mode is modernity's dark, if fictive, "ghost," the specter within it that haunts it with hyperbolic symbols of the most underlying and unresolved conflicts between and within the modern world's constructions of human life, the body, and the world.

The Gothic, we would also claim, is about the conflicted "social uncon-scious" of modernity even when it reappears within what many critics now regard as *post*-modernity. By most accounts, the postmodern in its many aesthetic forms, compared to the modern (supposedly finished by the mid-1960s) and brought into prominence for many by Thomas Pynchon's novel *The Crying of Lot 49* (1966), openly makes "references" to "earlier styles and conventions" that assume a near-complete divorce of those signifiers from fixed meanings or older contexts; the consequence is usually "a deliberate mixing of different styles and media (often with self-referential or parodic intent)," because of their uprooted condition, along with a stepped-up "incorporation of images relating to consumerism, mass-communication, etc."²¹ This peculiar combination, as the Marxist critic Fredric Jameson has said, reveals what underlies this entire way of seeing and writing: "that aesthetic production today has become integrated into commodity production generally" in an era of global capitalism ungrounded in a single location or any agreed-on system of beliefs.²² We in this collection believe the Gothic is, first, a precursor of this counter-aesthetic and thus, more recently, a fellow traveler with postmodernity as defined above. *Lot 49* itself, it could be argued, is evidence of that fact. Its haunted 1960s heroine becomes obsessed with interpreting sporadically appearing signifiers that may hint at a one-time organization for posting letters that was possibly operative back in Walpole's eighteenth century. This system may have been taken over by a more recent one, but it may then have gone underground and continued to exist, leaving ghostly verbal/visual indicators scattered around San Francisco, a mystery that is never solved and may even have been hallucinated. This regression of layers is indicative of a late modernity where nearly everything is commodified texts looking back only to texts and where the perceptions of characters may therefore be just as ghost-like and ungrounded.²³ As the late professor Allan Lloyd Smith has shown us, such "indeterminacy" of meaning is basic even to Walpole's Gothic, since *Otranto* withdraws believability from its "ancient romance" ingredients, thereby making its ghosts signs of empty signs (of effigies and paintings more than people). The Gothic thus sets in motion "competing non-privileged narratives and contradictory discourses ['ancient' versus 'modern romance']" "to produce an uncertainty of signs [the uncertainty of the postmodern] by locating each of them within more than one interpretive framework."²⁴ One danger, to be sure, is that the Gothic as postmodern can become sheer capitalist reproductions of its emptied elements, what Jameson laments as the "airport paperback categories of the gothic and romance," void of any reference to the conflicted "underside of culture."²⁵ Several of the essays in this *Companion*, though, argue what Lloyd Smith and, quite recently, Professor Glennis Byron have found instead:²⁶ that the creative Gothic as pre-postmodern (*Frankenstein*, for example) and postmodern (in *Lot 49* and much more) uses the uprooted and circulating signs that enable capitalist globalization – frequently the ghosts of earlier specters – to give form to the fears and irresolvable conflicts now underlying that very globalization, as was the case even in Mary Shelley's time, given *Frankenstein*'s allusions to international slavery and colonization in the signs of them on the creature's face.

The modern Gothic as we analyze it here, then, both continues and enables its hyper-articulations of modernity's dark undersides by extending these in postmodern forms of Gothic, or in Gothically inflected works of postmodernism, because its symbolic features are as much precursors of the postmodern as they are deeply interwoven within the longer process of modernity's historical and aesthetic development. It is just these tendencies and cultural implications within the Gothic, it turns out, that have enabled it to proliferate in so many different forms since the later nineteenth century and to do so increasingly all around the world, making its ungrounded signifiers astonishingly adept at symbolizing many underlying conflicts within those cultures at different points in time. "Certain tropes," because they have become uprooted in the West and even the modern East, as Professor Avril Horner has said "(for example, ghosts; sacred space; ... the living dead in the form of vampires and zombies)," can now be "repeated across time and space" more than ever, "albeit inflected by different histories, cultural legacies and ideologies" at every turn. That is because these tropes are themselves repeating – and are therefore haunted by – "huge flows and shifts in various forms of energy (for example, money, information, communication systems, media empire 'soft power')," which, because these are always specters of other things, are "beyond the control of individual countries or states and thus capable of destabilizing cultures and societies as well as enriching them."[27] The Gothic, we would argue, has always had this double-edged power within modernity in general. Consequently, we propose to analyze the multimedia, cross-cultural, and international spread of the Gothic's already conflicted elements across the long historical arc during which some late-nineteenth-century undersides of the modern have given way to "modernism" and then "postmodernism" and then to what some scholars now call "globalgothic," that "tangible reaction to the distress and anxiety of a globalized system that erupts from or within public cultures across the world."[28] Some of these analyses focus on "subcultural" areas, groups of authors, or types of media within larger cultural regions or nations where the Gothic has both enacted and destabilized modernity. Other ones emphasize how and on what bases the Gothic has crossed what we have taken to be "borders" in the past, whether these be the supposed boundaries of nations, laws, races, gender norms, sexual orientations, age groups, or genres of media. Our idea is to introduce (for some) and more fully explain (for others) a great deal of what the Gothic has become as the drives of modernity have proliferated themselves, taking with them the possibilities of a mixed and unstable mode symbolic of deep conflicts that has long been and remains inextricably bound up with what it means to be "modern."

In setting out to show all this in what follows, to be sure, we have to acknowledge just how wide, varied, and boundary-breaking the spread of the Gothic has become since its initial heyday in the later eighteenth and early nineteenth centuries, when it really appeared only in Western Europe and the eastern half of America. That enormous breadth by now means that this collection can help familiarize readers with the main directions and the most important forms pursued by the proliferation of the Gothic since the later nineteenth century, a principal objective of all the essays here. At the same time, though, this *Companion* offers a foundational account of the modern Gothic as it has come to proliferate around the world to help set the stage for further explorations of the numerous forms of it that other studies can help our readers examine in more detail. Certainly we feel that the Walpolean Gothic in its earliest stages of haunting modernity through the mid-nineteenth century and even later, the time frame before the one in this collection, has been well explained in several other books, among them *The Cambridge Companion to Gothic Fiction* (2002) as well as David Punter's *The Literature of Terror* (1980, rev. 1996; see n. 5), his Blackwell *Companion to the Gothic* collection (reissued as *A New Companion to the Gothic* in 2012), and Andrew Smith's concise introduction to Gothic writing and film for the Edinburgh Critical Guides (2007, rev. 2013), to name a few of the good starting places for study after students have read some primary Gothic fictions and this collection.

Certain key tendencies or groups of works in more recent Gothic, though we do note them, are also given fuller accounts in some of these very books. In *The Cambridge Companion to Gothic Fiction*, for example, Kelly Hurley shows the striking effects on British Gothic writing through the 1930s of the theory of evolution's assault on older conceptions of the human body and mind; Misha Kavka traces the earlier stages of modern Gothic cinema up through the 1960s and 1970s, the point after which Elisabeth Bronfen here takes up Gothic films from the 1980s to 2011 (see Chapter 7 below); Lizabeth Paravinisi-Gebert traces the extensive development of the modern postcolonial Gothic primarily in the Caribbean (an unusually rich area for it), leaving this and further volumes to treat the far greater range of postcolonial Gothic in other regions; and Steven Bruhm explains the Western cultural need for the Gothic after World War II, as in the very popular horror writing of Stephen King, in terms of the modern Gothic's parallels with Freudian and post-Freudian psychoanalysis, which we are pleased to echo at certain points but feel no need to repeat at length. Also in *Gothic Fiction*, finally, Fred Botting has shown how some Gothic games, narratives, and films, especially after the 1980s, are so cognizant of signs being references only to other signs *and* being unable to shock us in the face of the graphic violence broadcast every day on television that these variations have chosen to suggest a near-future existence that may become "posthuman" (abandoning all the current norms by which we still conceive of human beings) and leave the vestiges of all belief systems evacuated of all their meanings, a potential that Botting explores more fully in his book *Limits of Horror* (2008). We feel we can be more introductory about such modern Gothic dimensions because these accounts have been so thorough in treating them. Even the newest edition of the Blackwell *Companion* so accepts the internationalization, as well as the postcolonialism, of the Gothic in recent times that we find it offering helpful separate chapters on Australian, New Zealand, and Canadian Gothic, among others, that add to the insights in this collection, though we still recommend reading ours first.

Some further dimensions of the modern-to-postmodern Gothic, meanwhile, have also been dealt with in good introductory, yet probing, accounts, so much so that we want to send our readers on to them as well once they have acquired the foundations that we strive to provide here. The whole domain of "goth" subcultures in the West, some but not all of them driven by adolescents (long-standing subjects of the Gothic, as Chapter 6 shows), do have connections to cyber-Gothic of the sort examined in our Chapter 9, but they are given such good explanations in Paul Hodkinson's *Goth* (2002) and Catherine Spooner's *Contemporary Gothic* (2006) that we invite readers to consult them especially about the "punk-goth" phenomenon since the 1960s. The Spooner book is also helpful in providing students with more detail about the several modern variations on "Gothic" visual art, and the same perceptive scholar has turned her attention to costume art in *Fashioning Gothic Bodies* (2004), the best analytical study of the modes of dress influenced by or influencing Gothic fictions from the eighteenth century up to the "undead fashion" that helps continue the vampire tradition today – one way of dealing with modern ambivalence about the body with which the Gothic, as I have noted, is so often concerned. More about the increasing relationship between the Gothic and newer forms of music, from films and television to the sounds of the "goth" milieu, meanwhile, has recently been offered in Isabella van Elferen's remarkably insightful *Gothic Music* (2012). The ever-growing "zombie" tradition in print, on screen, and in cyberspace, meanwhile, though pointedly discussed in what now follows, is given its most thorough grounding in the Gothic tradition in Kyle William Bishop's *American Zombie Gothic* (2010). For some further theorizations and effects of the Gothic's recent global diaspora beyond what several of the essays in this collection already show, we further recommend the collection *Globalgothic* (2013) as an important point of departure, especially as it launches the new International

Gothic series of books from Manchester University Press. Finally, though we do treat the counter-movements in some modern Gothic against the further losses of meaning that Botting sees, there are some recent neo-Gothic attempts at "developing the frameworks of new religious movements," signs of a rising twenty-first-century "sub-Zeitgeist" different from the ones that the older Gothic challenged.[29] For more on that development, we suggest Victoria Nelson's study of that still-unfolding trend in her provocative, though also controversial, *Gothicka* (2012; see n. 29).

Still, there are a great many important avenues pursued by the modern Gothic that we do emphasize here, and these fall into four larger subject areas that the Gothic has profoundly affected, that have affected it, and that have extended the reach of its multiplicity while building on its earlier proclivities. The remaining essays in Part I, following this opening reflection on the interconnection of the Gothic with modernity, function almost as "bookends" (one discussing earlier twentieth-century writing, art, and film, the other late-twentieth- and early-twenty-first-century Gothic) in drawing out some often-repressed undercurrents of the modern imaginary that it has taken post-Victorian continuations of the Gothic to make us see in literature and other media after 1900. On the one hand, John Paul Riquelme's piece (Chapter 2) shows us how writers from the movement of the 1910s to the 1940s that came to be called "modernism" in Europe and America, though its principal enunciators saw it as "anti-Romantic," actually found themselves employing the Gothic again and again. They did so, Riquelme reveals, to image and suggest their own questionings of the assumptions or hierarchies that were being publicly asserted alongside the expansion of industrialism, all of which seemed to dehumanize, as well as alienate, people before and after World War I. Susan Chaplin's essay (Chapter 3), on the other hand, noting the Gothic's long-standing challenges to *and* affirmations of the norms of civic and cultural laws in the West (another level of its Janus-faced nature), shows how quite recent Gothic efforts have exposed the problems in the modern era's never-ending attempts, law on top of law, to make the terms of law cover and contain every contingency.

To exemplify that new-Gothic process, Chaplin turns understandably, as others in this collection do as well, to modern-to-postmodern revisions of the vampire figure in literature and film. The vampire, to a larger extent than the more empty-headed "zombie," has overtaken versions of Frankenstein's creature as a primary symbol of later modernity's contradictions and has done so while recent Gothic has made the "undead" a semi-positive, often victimized, being in contrast to the more strictly evil blood-sucker (epitomized by Stoker's *Dracula* [1897]) in Gothic iterations that started at the time of *Frankenstein*, most obviously in John Polidori's *The Vampyre*

(1819), famously begun where Shelley began her novel too.[30] This seeming reversal of a Gothic bogey in recent years, however, even though it is imbued with fears of the modern self being "bled dry" by economics, technology, and cultural misconstructions of human multiplicity, is actually a continuation of the Gothic vampire as a figure who, like Shelley's "monster," has always suggested many undersides, and not only the worst ones, of modern human existence.[31] One of these, Chaplin reminds us, is the paradox in which its seeming "otherness" both draws law toward it in order to contain it and ends up revealing the failure of law to completely control or circumscribe a great many human tendencies of individuals or groups.

The chapters in Part II, in turn, explore late-twentieth- and twenty-first-century redevelopments of the conflict in the earlier Gothic, as we saw above in *Frankenstein*, between representing the human body by modern methods so as to explain it more deeply and keeping that same body at a "safe" distance by classifications or coverings of it that seem to contain its actual amorphousness. Avril Horner and Sue Zlosnik in their Chapter 4 show how later-modern Gothic, in the wake of feminism's challenge to received notions of femininity, has creatively explored the instability of gender and its relationship with the body much in the way contemporary thinkers have theorized at about the same time. In Chapter 5, E. L. McCallum picks up on the Gothic hints at "alternative," more recently "queer," sexualities that extend back to Walpole and even Matthew "Monk" Lewis[32] and shows how these have been expanded in some indicative Gothic texts of recent years. Such expansions *both* open up the complex contradictions (including multiple orientations) that need to be better understood in the sexualities of different bodies *and* show how such widened understandings can best be achieved in "queerings" of standard narrative and descriptive form that extend the already experimental nature of the Gothic as an unsettled and unsettling mode. Chapter 6, by Glennis Byron and Sharon Deans, also looks back in its own way to the Gothic concern with the betwixt-and-between body state of adolescence, again as early as Walpole – not surprising, since the Gothic is in some ways an "adolescent" mode caught between beliefs that are old and alternatives that are young. This chapter does so, however, by examining the construction of the modern Gothic for specifically adolescent audiences as ways of helping them (and their elders) wrestle with the contradictory inclinations in their bodies and psyches that they need to see hyperbolically foregrounded, yet kept at a distance, under the cover of "fantastic" fiction.

The essays in Part III, by contrast, all respond to the Gothic being a mixture of media from the start, recalling that it eclectically combined Shakespearean theatrics, diegetic narrative, the portrait image, and print drawings of architecture, as much as ancient with modern romance, as early as *The Castle of Otranto*. The signifiers that the Gothic has borrowed from age-old and contemporary sources, after all, have been openly torn from their older grounds to reappear often in media different from their earlier ones and to signify states of being or thoughts (Protestant and middle-class, say) far removed from their initial (once-Catholic and aristocratic) points of reference. The pieces here on Gothic and modern media therefore celebrate, even as they account for, twentieth- and twenty-first-century re-Gothicizings that move Janus-faced figurations from page to stage to screen, from the still to the moving image, and from all of these to cyberspace and the sheer simulation of computer-generated imagery (CGI, a great enabler of Gothic films and games). Elisabeth Bronfen's Chapter 7 highlights exaggerated hyper-depictions on film, usually adapted from novels, of social and psychological conflicts that really do haunt recent modernity, but primarily as these post-1970s productions bring to audience attention the spectral qualities of cinema as a medium after it has already been Gothicized, and so has haunted itself, for decades. Chapter 8, by Charles Scruggs, steps both backward and forward in the history of Gothic filmmaking to account for the surprisingly long-lasting mode of film noir, a transformation of the older "urban Gothic" still most visible in Stevenson's original *Dr. Jekyll and Mr. Hyde* (1886). As Scruggs shows, this form of Gothic, which has lasted well beyond the 1930s and 1940s, re-enacts the alienation, paranoia, and losses of secure assumptions that have turned out to haunt America after the all-shattering horror of World War I. Then, as adept as she is at explaining mod-Gothic music, Isabella van Elferen in Chapter 9 proves equally so in distilling the different forms that the cyber-and the techno-Gothic have taken on in the last several decades. These forms have first mixed established Gothic figures with ones from other mixed modes (a Gothic process in itself), she explains, and have then, more recently, reworked the hyper-imaging that results in a wide variety of media, nearly always to suggest the conflicted cultural fears and longings aroused by our increasing dependence on simulations of simulations.

Part IV goes on to close this collection with five probing essays on how, in the first place, the Gothic has crossed from its Anglo-Western beginnings into other ethnicities within the Western world, accompanied by the racial anxieties and prejudices already haunting it, and how, in the second place, the Gothic, never solidly rooted anyway, has vaulted over international boundaries: first in postcolonial writing recalling *and* resisting Anglo-Western dominance and then in very modern encounters with non-Anglo and even non-Western populations. Maisha L. Wester (Chapter 10) shows just how far back the politics of race goes in the Euro-American Gothic in order to reveal how that racism has come to be both continued and turned against itself in modern Gothic texts, now increasingly written by "minority" authors. Carlos Gallego (Chapter 11), in turn, reveals that some of the seminal modern works of Native American, African American, and Hispanic American literature have interwoven Gothic constructions with more localized forms of expression and myth expressly to render the subjugations, resistances, and self-reclamations of these so-called "subcultures" with the haunting aesthetic power that their histories deserve. Chapter 12, by Ken Gelder, then offers a thorough, yet revealingly synoptic, analysis of the most important revelations that postcolonial Gothic writing, all from regions once subjected to Anglo-Western occupation, has brought forward throughout the globe, increasingly with the help of recent advances in postcolonial theory and interpretation. In Chapter 13, Katarzyna Ancuta displays her immersion in many Southeast Asian cultures, which she shows to be as different from as they are adjacent to each other. Her account, consequently, details how imported pieces of Euro-American Gothic, never left exactly as they were, have been combined with various indigenous forms of haunting and horror to generate an astonishing cross-regional multiplicity of distinct texts and films that should not be lumped together or limited in their meanings under the current stereotypes of "Japanese Gothic." In the wake of all this, Lucie Armitt's essay (Chapter 14) occupies this collection's concluding position because it helpfully explains a juxtaposition of distinct ghostly modes currently under way and still a work in progress all over the world: the interplay of quite different assumptions, yet the off-and-on similarities and borrowings, between the unstable Gothic that began in Europe and the unstable traditions of "magical realism" that arose in Latin America but have more recently spread to India and Africa and some cross-cultural spaces in Europe and North America.

Such a conclusion is fitting because the proliferation and complexity of the modern Gothic are very much still in process and should remain open to still more cross-cultural modification in works of many different mixed media in the years ahead. Only this multiplicity, we want to argue throughout this collection, can do real justice to the malleable mode or symbolic scheme, inherently crossing between media from the outset, that is the multidimensional and Janus-faced "Gothic." Only this multiplicity, both enacted by creators and accepted by readers and audiences, can achieve and demonstrate the full range of methods by which the Gothic can reveal the undersides of modernity, with which it remains in dialogue as much in the twenty-first as it was in the eighteenth century.

NOTES

1 See Paul Frankl, *The Gothic: Literary Sources and Interpretations through Eight Centuries* (Princeton University Press, 1960), pp. 259–260.
2 Horace Walpole, *The Castle of Otranto*, ed. W. S. Lewis and E. J. Clery (Oxford University Press, 1996), pp. 9–10.
3 Edmund Burke, *A Philosophical Enquiry into the Origin of Our Ideas of the Sublime and Beautiful*, ed. Adam Phillips (Oxford University Press, 1990), pp. 54–55.
4 E. J. Clery, *The Rise of Supernatural Fiction, 1762–1800* (Cambridge University Press, 1995), p. 77.
5 David Punter, *The Literature of Terror: A History of Gothic Fictions from 1765 to the Present Day* (London: Longman, 1980), p. 418. See also Slavoj Žižek, *The Sublime Object of Ideology* (London: Verso, 1989), p. 45.
6 See Julia Kristeva in *Powers of Horror: An Essay on Abjection*, trans. Leon S. Roudiez (New York: Columbia University Press, 1982), esp. pp. 1–11.
7 Charles Taylor, *A Secular Age* (Cambridge, MA: Harvard University Press, 2007), pp. 171–172.
8 Charles Taylor, *Modern Social Imaginaries* (Durham, NC: Duke University Press, 2004), p. 1.
9 Taylor, *A Secular Age*, p. 12 (emphasis added).
10 Diane Long Hoeveler, *Gothic Riffs: Secularizing the Uncanny in the European Imaginary, 1780–1820* (Columbus, OH: Ohio State University Press, 2010), pp. 4, 16–17.
11 Hoeveler, *Gothic Riffs*, p. 12.
12 See Jerrold E. Hogle, "*Frankenstein* as Neo-Gothic: From the Ghost of the Counterfeit to the Monster of Abjection," in *Romanticism, History, and The Possibilities of Genre*, ed. Tilottama Rajan and Julia Wright (Cambridge University Press, 1998), pp. 176–210, esp. pp. 179–184.
13 Mary Wollstonecraft Shelley, *Frankenstein, or the Modern Prometheus: The 1818 Text*, ed. James Rieger (1974; University of Chicago Press, 1982), p. 47.
14 See Paul O'Flinn, "Production and Reproduction: The Case of *Frankenstein*," in *Frankenstein: Contemporary Critical Essays*, ed. Fred Botting (London: Macmillan, 1995), pp. 21–47.
15 See H. L. Malchow, "Frankenstein's Monster and Images of Race in Nineteenth-Century Britain," *Past and Present*, 139 (1993), 90–130.
16 Shelley, *Frankenstein*, p.53.
17 Shelley, *Frankenstein*, p.72.
18 Shelley, *Frankenstein*, p.164.
19 Shelley, *Frankenstein*, p.52.
20 Shelley, *Frankenstein*, p.52.
21 All according to the entry on postmodernism in the *Oxford English Dictionary* online, http://www.oed.com/
22 Fredric Jameson, *Postmodernism, or the Cultural Logic of Late Capitalism* (Durham, NC: Duke University Press, 1991), p. 4.
23 Thomas Pynchon, *The Crying of Lot 49* (Philadelphia, PA: Lippincott, 1966), esp. pp. 44–54, 162–183.

24 Allan Lloyd Smith, "Postmodernism/Gothicism," in *Modern Gothic: A Reader*, ed. Victor Sage and Allan Lloyd Smith (Manchester University Press, 1996), pp. 7–12.
25 Jameson, *Postmodernism*, pp. 2, 5.
26 See Byron in her "Introduction" to *Globalgothic*, ed. Glennis Byron, *International Gothic* (Manchester University Press, 2013), esp. pp. 4–5.
27 Avril Horner, "*The Dark Knight*: Fear, the Law and Liquid Modernity," in *Globalgothic*, ed. Byron, pp. 175–187, esp. p. 175.
28 Fred Botting and Justin D. Edwards, "Theorizing Globalgothic," in *Globalgothic*, ed. Byron, pp. 11–24, esp. p. 12.
29 Victoria Nelson, *Gothicka: Vampire Heroes, Human Gods, and the New Supernatural* (Cambridge, MA: Harvard University Press, 2012), pp. xi–xii.
30 See Jerrold E. Hogle, "The Rise of the Gothic Vampire: Disfiguration and Cathexis from Coleridge's 'Christabel' to Nodier's *Smarra*," in *Gothic N.E.W.S.*, ed. Max Duperray, 2 vols. (Paris: Houdiard, 2009), vol. I, pp. 48–70.
31 See Nina Auerbach, *Our Vampires, Ourselves* (University of Chicago Press, 1995).
32 See George E. Haggerty, *Queer Gothic* (Urbana, IL: University of Illinois Press, 2006), pp. 21–30.

2

JOHN PAUL RIQUELME

Modernist Gothic

Literary modernism has been defended and attacked for its elitism (its ostensible rejection of vernacular culture), its political valences (reactionary or progressive), and its kinship (close or far removed) to earlier and later kinds of writing (Romantic, Victorian, and postmodern). Attitudes toward the Gothic are also divergent. However little agreement there is about modernism and the Gothic considered separately, their intersection is memorable and revealing. Many modernist works are not Gothic, but modernism and the longer tradition of the Gothic converge repeatedly in writings by major literary modernists in Ireland, England, and America. The convergence occurs in first-wave modernist writings by Oscar Wilde, W. B. Yeats, and James Joyce among the Irish; Joseph Conrad, E. M. Forster, Virginia Woolf, and T. S. Eliot in England; and Djuna Barnes and William Faulkner in America, to name only a few prominent figures. This intersection occurs not just in prose narratives but in all the genres, including the literary essay. Eliot's formulations in his influential prose, as I will show below, suggest that a Gothic conjoining of opposites is central to modernism's self-understanding. As a consequence, the Gothic is far from marginal within modernism, despite the great divide sometimes alleged between ostensibly elite modernism and vernacular cultural forms.[1]

The Gothic, in fact, is deeply involved in the transition from Victorian to modernist writing, primarily because the juxtaposition of opposites characteristic of the Gothic also helps manifest the world views, aesthetic attitudes, and cultural conflicts that brought modernism into being. It even suggests the violence of modern history, which reveals itself increasingly to be a Gothic narrative of visible and hidden violence, most obviously with World War I and its aftermath. Formally, neither the Gothic nor modernism adopts the style or the assumptions of realism. Also like modernist writing, the Gothic involves a literary and cultural dynamic that challenges many entrenched cultural attitudes, often by evoking the connections between apparent opposites that a realistic style would avoid. Like the Gothic from

Frankenstein onward, by evoking the coexistence of opposites, modernist works frequently question social hierarchies bound up with a desire for human domination over nature. The conjoining of opposites also contributes to a mythic level common to Gothic and to modernism, particularly in the figuration of monsters as modern myths. Through their early adumbrations of the zombie and the cyborg, literary modernism and other arts of the time even help generate mythic monsters that still challenge prevailing notions of the human today.

Virginia Woolf (1882–1941) stated memorably in 1924 that "On or about December 1910, human character changed."[2] Although she calls the date arbitrary, she clearly means that a definitive cultural break occurred at about that time, one that we might reasonably take to be the basis for the emerging art later called modernist. But there was an important continuity as well, not incompatible with the change she perceived. It involved the persistence of Gothic narratives concerning monsters and revenge, especially *Frankenstein* and *Dracula*, which became more, not less, important and relevant. Though she did publish "A Haunted House" in 1921, Woolf may not have realized that the change she saw included the greater importance of the Gothic in the cultural imagination. One case in point, James Joyce (1882–1941), the most acclaimed modernist author of prose narratives, is not usually thought of as a writer with a strong Gothic dimension. At the very time that Woolf suggests that things changed, however, Joyce was writing *A Portrait of the Artist as a Young Man* (1916), in which the Jesuit education that the artist, Stephen Dedalus, receives is a Gothic *Bildung* (or process of education), marked by instilling fear and even terror into children and adolescents using medieval iconography. Modernism accomplished a transformation of the nineteenth-century *Bildungsroman*, which typically ends with the protagonist's successful integration into socially approved adult life. Joyce undoes that teleological process in his *Portrait* by making an intense moment of dark education central (in Part III) to the narrative of failed, or refused, integration. The woodcut reproduced in Figure 1, showing a soul in hell being tormented, comes from the widely distributed pamphlet that stands behind Joyce's depiction of the religious retreat that Stephen attends at age 16 as part of his Gothic education. Later in Joyce's career, Episode 15 (often called "Circe") of his immensely influential *Ulysses* (1922) involves an infernal, nightmarish descent, during which the dead sometimes appear to the living and address them. But Gothic modernism really starts much earlier, in the work of Joyce's Irish precursor, Oscar Wilde (1854–1900).

Although the disagreements concerning modernism's character may never be resolved, the limits of the first wave (for some the only wave) of

DESPAIR.

Figure 1: "Despair (the Sixth Consideration, for Friday)" from Reverend F. Giovanni
Pietro Pinamonti, SJ, *Hell Opened to Christians, to Caution Them from Entering into It,
or Considerations of the Infernal Pains* (Dublin: C. M. Warren, 1841).

modernism are generally accepted: 1890–1945. The latter year marks, at
the end of World War II, a break, culturally and literarily, from the decades
preceding it. The earlier year marks the emergence of Wilde as an important
author on the cusp between Victorian and modernist writing. Influential
works that he published in the early 1890s, ones that all the modernists
would have known well, constitute a clear shift from Victorian attitudes and
forms. In recognizing his role in the change that Woolf identifies as
happening later, it is worth remembering that Wilde's thinking and writing
were imbued with the coexistence of opposites. As he asserts at the end
of "The Truth of Masks" from his collection *Intentions* (1891), "A truth in
art is that whose contradictory is also true."[3] The long prose narrative
The Picture of Dorian Gray (1890–1891) and the revenge tragedy *Salome*
(1893) are important contributions in just this vein both to modernism and
to Gothic writing. The figure of the dancer, Salome, influenced Wilde's younger
contemporaries, Yeats (1865–1939) and Eliot (1888–1965), who became
preeminent modernist writers, as well as Nobel laureates.[4] Yeats' many
works involving the dancer include such dark, Wilde-inspired poems about

deadly love and aesthetic creation as "The Cap and Bells," in which the death of a jester enables a queen to dance.[5] The multiple allusions to *Salome* in Eliot's early poem, often called "The Love Song of St. Sebastian," with its intense evocation of violence between a man and a woman, indicate that Wilde's play inspired it.[6]

In the play Salome dances for her lascivious stepfather, Herod, not to please him but to revenge herself on him and on John the Baptist, whose decapitation she forces Herod to order at the cost of her own life. *Dorian Gray* also includes both destructive behavior and self-destruction, which accompany an aestheticized act of doubling. Portraits often play important roles in Gothic narratives before modernism, but in Wilde's aestheticized Gothic tale, the portrait stands in a mutually defining relation with the book itself, whose title also names the painting. The work's self-reflexivity is part of its modernist aspect, now combined with the Gothic and with the aesthetic movement. Because of beauty's central place in both works' dark plots, they are late offspring of nineteenth-century aestheticism, a cult of beauty in the arts sometimes characterized by the phrase "art for art's sake." The convergence of the Gothic, aestheticism, and literary modernism antici- pates similar conjunctions in writings two and four decades later by Eliot and by Yeats. In Eliot we encounter the linking of beauty and a violence that destroys it in passages of prose and poetry involving revenge that I will turn to shortly. There is also Yeats' conjoining of beauty and the Gothic, includ- ing the vampire, which I will treat in the closing segment of this essay concerning monsters and myth.

Wilde also wrote a revenge tragedy called *Vera, or the Nihilists* (1880) more than a decade before *Salome*. Had he lived productively into the first decades of the twentieth century, it would not have been surprising for him to write additional Gothic works that would have given modernism a more explicitly Gothic aspect than it now presents. But Wilde's career was cut short, his influence masked by the scandal over his homosexuality and his prison term. Modernist writing's Gothic character is consequently more implicit and diffuse than it might have been. Even so, the dark veins in modernism and in related forms of art of the same era reveal a continuing coincidence with the Gothic well beyond the emergence of Wilde's Gothic works at modernism's initiating moment. Those dark elements include Eliot's attention to revenge tragedy in his criticism and his poetry.

Filled with violence, including murders on the stage, that early-modern precursor of the Gothic novel was popular during the Elizabethan period, even though it was little esteemed in the nineteenth century. Blood is a central element in *Dracula* (1897), to be sure, but no more so than in many revenge tragedies. Toward the end of *The Spanish Tragedy* (ca. 1590) by

Thomas Kyd (1558–1594), the central character, Hieronymo, bites off his tongue and spews blood on the stage. By writing numerous essays and reviews that focused on revenge tragedy, Eliot drew significant attention to the form, raising its standing in the English literary canon.[7] He also alluded emphatically to specific revenge tragedies in his poems, including in the closing lines of *The Waste Land*, where he quotes Hieronymo (l. 432). Revenge tragedy even plays an important role in Eliot's seminal essay "Tradition and the Individual Talent" (1919), a kind of modernist manifesto that is among the most widely reprinted literary essays of the twentieth century.[8] In his argument against the idea that poetry is personal expression, which he identifies with Romanticism, Eliot quotes late in the essay from *The Revenger's Tragedy* (1606), frequently attributed to Cyril Tourneur (1575–1626). The passage stands out for its length, its placement, and Eliot's comments. Suggesting that these lines shed not "light" but "darkness," Eliot focuses on their "combination of positive and negative emotions" concerning "beauty" and "ugliness," in a contrast that is also a convergence. He does so as part of his argument against "the substantial unity of the soul," which he thinks stands behind Wordsworth's emphasis on the personal, the self, in poetry's creation. The inherently conflicted quality of *The Revenger's Tragedy* brings the aesthetic emphasis on beauty and the Gothic emphasis on violence and ugliness together in a way that is structurally and conceptually reminiscent of Jekyll's relation to Hyde. In presenting his modernist notion of the poet's impersonality, Eliot implies a splitting of the poet's mind into apparently antithetical aspects, beauty and its opposite, that are also intertwined. This puts the Gothic and the aesthetic at the center of modernist thought and helps make that center both dual and conflicted.

An equally important moment in Eliot's defining of modernism's character is also Gothic in its conceptual structure and implications. It occurs when he defends the seventeenth-century "metaphysical poets," such as John Donne, as precursors of modernism whose handling of language Eliot explicitly associates with writers in the revenge tradition. Eliot quotes Samuel Johnson's claim that in the metaphysical conceit "the most heterogeneous ideas are yoked by violence together."[9] Eliot accepts the description but counters Johnson's skepticism about the yoking's success by suggesting that the "metaphysicals" at their best "compelled" heterogeneity "into unity," as does every great poet in his view. The lesson for a poet of Eliot's era is the need to "force" language into new meaning from diverse material.[10] Apparently incompatible elements become fused.

Such shades of black, full of extreme contradictions, occur prominently in Eliot's poems. *The Waste Land*, for example, can be compared to

Frankenstein's monster as a creation made from damaged parts, a "heap of broken images" (l. 22) and "withered stumps of time" (l. 104). That later phrase even occurs in a section that alludes to the savagely brutal act (from classical mythology) committed against Philomel by her brother-in-law, "the barbarous king" (l. 99). No Gothic text or horror film contains a more violent act than Philomel's rape and mutilation, for which she and her sister take revenge, as in Shakespeare's most extreme revenge tragedy, *Titus Andronicus*. The beautiful and the ugly are conjoined. Vividly evoked in *The Waste Land*, though with the gory details left implicit, Philomel's narrative includes rape, adultery, incest, mutilation, infanticide, and cannibalism. The presence of any of these taboos could raise the issue of what it means to be human, of what the limits are, but together they make that question, central to Gothic writing, unavoidable.

In this particular case, the disturbing details project aesthetic creation as painful, with Philomel as a Gothic version of the Romantic bird of the imagination, the nightingale, into which she is transformed. With her tongue cut out but her voice still "inviolable" (l. 101), she again embodies the contradiction of the simultaneously ugly and beautiful. Questions reasonably arise concerning an antifeminist impulse when we see such a female victim in Eliot's poem and in many Gothic narratives. But an answer is offered through another question: How is Philomel's voice inviolable? With his note directing us to Ovid's full presentation of the myth, Eliot implicitly reminds us that Philomel communicated in a graphic way by weaving a tapestry about the violation she suffered. Her action enables her to turn the tables on her violator and to take effective revenge. Figuratively she can still speak because she has retained her ability to communicate, to choose, and to act. Similar readings are possible concerning other women in modern Gothic texts, including Wilde's Salome and Stoker's Mina Harker. Their strength and ability to act effectively contrast with the behavior of many earlier women victims in Gothic narratives, such as Emily St. Aubert, who faints regularly in Ann Radcliffe's *The Mysteries of Udolpho* (1794). These modernist Gothic representations of women project instead subversive determination and resilience.

Eliot published his last significant poem, "Little Gidding," in 1942, in the wake of the sustained German bombing of England, which included *Terrorangriff* (terror attack), indiscriminate wide-area, rather than precision, bombing. Its second section presents, as a descent into an underworld in a war-torn urban setting, a dialogue between the living and the dead concerning aesthetic creation. It is Gothic as well as Dantesque in its implications for understanding history and art as involving doubles who merge despite their antithetical states of being. Eliot admired nineteenth-century writers of dark literature, including the French poet Charles Baudelaire (1821–1867), author of the collection of poems *Les fleurs du mal* [*Flowers of Evil*] (1857); the English Victorian writer of sensation novels Wilkie Collins (1824–1889); and the American writer of Gothic tales Edgar Allan Poe (1809–1849), who was famously translated into French by Baudelaire. Eliot was also influenced by Joseph Conrad (1857–1924), some of whose narratives, most famously *Heart of Darkness* (1899), reveal the underside of civilization, or, as the title indicates, its dark heart. As I want to suggest shortly, too, Eliot's work even anticipates the emergence of the zombie and the cyborg. The living dead, infernal descents, and dialogues between the living and the dead inform memorable moments in his and other key modernist texts.

By the time *Ulysses* and *The Waste Land* appeared in 1922, making it clear there had been a literary shift warranting a label, World War I had occurred. The horrendous toll of total war on individuals and countries provided abundant evidence that history, rather than being a story of uninterrupted progress, had become (or revealed itself to be) a Gothic narrative, that is, a dystopian one with dark dissolution suggested as its undercurrent and center. It is hard to imagine a generation of writers who experienced history as Gothic not producing works that reflect the experience. Yet the kinship between history and Gothic narrative is visible earlier, beginning with the French Revolution and continuing through such violent events as the Indian Sepoy Mutiny of 1857, in which English women and children were brutally killed, with the details widely published in English newspapers. Such shocking events were reflected in various ways in Gothic narratives of their time and in later writing with a Gothic dimension. Over six decades after the Mutiny, in *A Passage to India* (1924) by E. M. Forster (1879–1970), set in India of the 1920s, an English woman undergoes a terrifying experience in a dark cave that results in a conflict between the Indians and the English colonials, who continue to be concerned about the Mutiny. The disconcerting terror in the cave is also an echo of the Mutiny.

In this same vein, the horrors of World War I have their effect on the literature of the period, as well as long after. Artists were responding to historical cataclysm, as artists a century earlier had reacted to the French Revolution. Among those who responded in the midst of the war were the English "war poets," writers who went into battle, such as Wilfred Owen (1893–1918), one of many not to return. His "Strange Meeting" links antagonists as Gothicized opposites: two soldiers from opposing sides, both dead, one having killed the other the day before, who recognize their common bond in death as they meet in an underworld that is also the trenches. The soldiers are conjoined, as are the two locales, the real trenches and the underworld, because reality has become hell. Owen's poem stands within and behind the encounter in Eliot's "Little Gidding," written during the next total war. In these related moments, the poetry of the period is Gothic in its historically specific focus on doubles in strange encounters, at once real and infernal, between opposites who cannot be clearly distinguished.

Under this circumstance of history, the boundaries of the Gothic, understood initially as a kind of popular, fantastic, and scary literary narrative, simultaneously softened and expanded. Gothic inflections became visible in the visual arts, for example in Dadaism and surrealism, which came into being during and just after World War I. The spread of the Gothic beyond literature by the transfer of Gothic literary narratives from one medium to another is also evident in early cinema. There were, for instance, numerous silent films based on nineteenth-century Gothic narratives around the time of World War I and in the decade after, including several versions of *Frankenstein*, *Dr. Jekyll and Mr. Hyde*, and *Dracula*. The American inventor Thomas Edison (1847–1931) patented the first motion-picture camera in the United States, and he produced films, one of which was the first film of *Frankenstein* (1910). Set in motion most by *Frankenstein* in the Gothic, the issue of science and technology's threatening role and character carries forward from nineteenth-century narratives of terror far into the twentieth. The most famous of the early films inspired by Gothic texts, though, is F. W. Murnau's *Nosferatu* (1922), a masterpiece of German expressionist film-making based on *Dracula*. Like surrealism, German expressionism has a dark inflection, making it a precursor to American film noir (see Chapter 8), that aligns it with Gothic writing, in this case explicitly. Released in the same year as *The Waste Land* and *Ulysses*, *Nosferatu* is a thoroughly Gothic work that is both expressionist and modernist.

The Gothic inflection in literary modernism is strong because of modern history's character, then, but also because modernist writers shared with Gothic writing of the past, especially from *Frankenstein* forward, iconoclastic attitudes toward traditional views of reason, the unified self, gender, history as progressive, and the question of what it means to be human. *Heart of Darkness* is an obvious example of a narrative that involves behavior uncontrolled by reason or proclaimed moral values, and it raises the issue of what the word "human" means with reference to black Africans as opposed to the more technological white Europeans who feel themselves to be a more highly evolved race. In Kurtz, Conrad presents an inherently riven figure, like some earlier Gothic protagonists, including Dr. Jekyll, someone who affirms society's moral principles but then commits atrocities when he is away from home. Lionel Trilling identifies Kurtz as an example of the doubling, for him an indicator of authenticity in modernity, that develops in post-Victorian attitudes toward the self, a doubling incompatible with the notion of a unified identity.[11] The apparently singular turns out to be dual and inherently self-opposing. The recognition of a dark double of an antithetical kind within the individual constitutes authenticity itself, which reacts against the delusion that surfaces reveal what is beneath them. The doubling visible in modernist writing, as in Conrad's fiction, finds its antecedent and a counterpart in the doubles of the Gothic tradition.

A related form of doubling or instability of the self involves gender crossovers, as in Wilde's writings (Dorian as a male Mona Lisa) and in *Dracula* (Jonathan Harker in the female role of victim; Mina Harker's masculine traits). Later we see such crossings in the main figures of other prominent modernist works: Eliot's Tiresias, who has lived as both a man and a woman, in *The Waste Land*; Joyce's Leopold Bloom, the womanly man of *Ulysses*; and the gender-switching, undying title character of Virginia Woolf's *Orlando* (1928). Woolf also develops the concept of androgyny in Chapter 6 of *A Room of One's Own* (1929). The individual has become, if not two, then dual. All these works bear comparison with the numerous queer or ambiguous representations of gender in earlier Gothic writing, including the lesbian vampire in "Carmilla" (1871–1872) by J. S. Le Fanu (1814–1873) and the homoerotic element of Stevenson's *Jekyll and Hyde*, among others.

Like Gothic writing, modernism regularly refuses the optimistic attitude toward the progress of culture that became important during the Enlightenment and continued in altered but recognizable form after evolutionary thinking emerged in the nineteenth century. As did Gothic writing that preceded it, by frequently presenting the coexistence of opposites, modernism questions the assumption that reason is humanity's defining element and that history is both linear and improving. Consequently, the tendency to blur the distinction between opposites in both Gothic texts and modernist ones challenges accepted hierarchies of value and power, which are difficult to maintain when the contrasts on which they depend have been undermined. Central to both the Gothic and modernism, this tendency enables them, especially when they converge, to expose problems in the hierarchical thinking at the heart of modern Western culture.

In the Gothic from *Frankenstein* onward, after all, good and evil are often presented in ways that blur the contrast and raise questions about which side particular characters are on, if the sides can even be maintained. The blurred opposition between good and evil in the Gothic also visible in some significant modernist works presents an extreme contrast to the usual

Western hierarchy of value. It undermines any absolute version of the distinction between *better* and *worse* that informs all hierarchies of value and also the concept of historical progress, in which the hierarchy is spread sequentially through time: The past was worse than the present, and the future will be even better than now. The logic of the Gothic in which modernism participates responds to that kind of thinking from the perspective of merged opposites. With *Frankenstein, Jekyll and Hyde*, and *Dracula*, Conrad's narratives challenge a Manichean vision that separates the world absolutely into polar opposites of differing value. Ultimately Conrad renders the coexistence of opposites in an oscillating way that becomes structurally characteristic of literary modernism. His narration frequently includes language suggesting something "incomprehensible" right alongside a focus on "straightforward facts," such as the need for rivets to repair a steamship.[12]

The unknowable and the knowable also combine in his writing's fluctuating perspective. We see the resemblance between apparent opposites in the narratives of *The Secret Agent* (1907), "The Secret Sharer" (1910), and *Under Western Eyes* (1911), among others. The conventional expectation in a story about crime would be that the wrongdoers and the police can be told apart easily. In *The Secret Agent*, concerning a bombing near London, however, the foreign terrorists and their sympathizers are sometimes hard to distinguish from the police. Many of the characters are connected in some way to the crime, and Verloc, who instigates it, is a double agent. This doubling and blurring suggest that criminality pertains to virtually all of society rather than only to part of it. Such collapsed oppositions can confirm the recognition that Marlow articulates in *Heart of Darkness* when he says that civilization has turned us into "the shackled form of a conquered monster"[13] but that we can, under certain circumstances, recognize the monster that we are. Gothic narratives give us that opportunity, which modernist narratives regularly provide as well.

The villains in Gothic narratives often behave monstrously but are not actually monsters. The Italian Montoni in Radcliffe's *The Mysteries of Udolpho*, for example, mistreats his wife and imprisons the protagonist, Emily St. Aubert, in a forbidding castle. But Conrad's Verloc behaves truly monstrously toward his wife and her young brother, whose death he causes. Beginning with *Frankenstein*, monsters as well as monstrous human beings have become important Gothic figures as the modern world has more fully emerged. In modernism Gothic monsters play a role that includes but goes beyond the emergence of the vampire in *Dracula*, a work that, like Wilde's writings, straddles the Victorian and the modernist. Gothic modernist texts combine in varying degrees the monsters' mythic quality, modernism's own engagement with myth, and attention to hierarchies of power related to domination of the natural world. Both myth and the response to hierarchies, modernist Gothic works remind us, involve in fundamental ways the relation of opposites.

Absalom, Absalom! (1936) by William Faulkner (1897–1962) provides a revealing example of an extended modernist Gothic narrative centered on a character whose monstrous behavior, as in *The Secret Agent*, contributes to a death and results in the family's collapse. In the history of American Gothic writing, Poe's "The Fall of the House of Usher" (1839) clearly stands behind Faulkner's story about the fall of the house of Sutpen. Faulkner had no need for a Gothic villain from Italy or Eastern Europe. Thomas Sutpen is a home-made southern Gothic figure, a self-made man whose ambition is fueled by his childhood experience in western Virginia of a black servant turning him away from a plantation's front door as white trash. As the narrative reveals in bits and pieces (like Horace Walpole's fragmented *Otranto* ghost), his complicated life history and undoing include taming the land, a hundred acres acquired from Native Americans, outside Jefferson, Mississippi, and building a mansion virtually *ex nihilo* through the physical labor that he expends himself and forces from black slaves that the townspeople consider "wild negroes."[14] He then marries and has two children with a woman from the town, as part of his attempt to build a dynasty. His design is disrupted by both the Civil War and the arrival of his biracial son, Charles Bon, from a marriage that he repudiated when he discovered that his first wife had black blood. Not revealing the kinship, Bon, a university friend of Sutpen's son, Henry, courts Henry's sister, Judith, and the narrative suggests that Henry's attraction to both Bon and his sister contributes to Henry's killing of Bon.

These are the ostensible facts presented in a linear sequence, but this novel is famous for not revealing them that way. Instead, details are filtered through several characters and emerge sporadically, some as hearsay, some as speculation, mainly by two characters trying to piece the story together around 1910, long after most of the events. The multiperspectival narration in varying, sometimes exaggerated, styles is modernist in character in the wake of Joyce's *Ulysses*. It creates a degree of uncertainty in the reader – more in keeping with the Gothic than with realism – that contradicts Sutpen's attitude of confidence and certainty. As a consequence, the destabilizing of knowledge and certainty that characterizes the Gothic becomes central to modernism as a matter of form. There are many antecedents among Gothic novels that put the accuracy of perception in question, including *Frankenstein* and *Dracula*, and between them Wilkie Collins' sensation novel *The Moonstone* (1868). Collins' novel combines the reports of different characters concerning a theft, whose solution is speculative, based on an experiment involving opium that attempts to re-enact the theft. The degree of uncertainty, openness, and stylistic flamboyance in Faulkner's narrative is, however, considerably greater than in Collins'.

Although there are no Gothic monsters in *Absalom*, structurally its narrative core is isomorphic with the narrative of *Frankenstein*, and it carries forward in modernist form the implications concerning domination and hierarchy central to the myth of Frankenstein's monster. Literary modernism was deeply engaged with myth, both classical and anthropological. Modernist authors, including Eliot and Joyce, were famously invested in classical myth's relation to the character of modern life. Joyce wrote *Ulysses* as a multilayered reworking of Homer's *Odyssey*, and when Eliot reviewed the book, he announced that Joyce, with Yeats as one of his antecedents (in, for example, "No Second Troy"), had perfected a "mythical method" that other writers would also use as an alternative to linear narrative for bringing order to the chaos of modern experience.[15] Faulkner's allusions to biblical history and to *The Oresteia* of Aeschylus (Sutpen as Agamemnon; his black daughter named Clytemnestra) are in line with this same method and basic to *Absalom*'s structure, but at least as important is the structuring of this narrative around the modern myth of Frankenstein's creature.

Sutpen is no scientist-inventor, but he does invent himself. In that self-invention, he turns himself into a monstrous being. The self-invention involves taming the wilderness and dominating the slaves who are his instruments. Both Frankenstein and Sutpen desire to control nature and to establish themselves at the top of a hierarchy of power that pertains to social relations and not just nature. The hierarchical logics of social superiority and of dominating nature are cognate, with anything below the pinnacle being an instrument or else part of nature and not considered human. Yet the conjoined oppositions permeating Faulkner's narrative undermine the hierarchy's stability. One result is that this novel's many blurred antitheses reflect the interplay of radical differences that is characteristic of Gothic. Miscegenation and incest are, for example, opposites, but in Bon's proposed union with Judith, they coincide. Henry's dual attraction adds a queer element and a doubly incestuous one. On the one hand, by replicating the story of Frankenstein and his creature, Faulkner stages hierarchical logic. Like the creature, both Sutpen and Bon have been rejected as children (because of class and racial differences, respectively) and want recognition. Sutpen is the injured party as a child and the injuring party as a parent. Like Frankenstein's creature, who has non-European features, Bon wants to be recognized as his progenitor's child and as a human being. He is willing to revenge himself on the father who rejects him if the recognition is not forthcoming.

On the other hand, because neither Sutpen nor Frankenstein will accept the defective, monstrous offspring, the struggle becomes mutually self-destructive and breaks hierarchy down. When one brother, Henry, who is white, shoots the brother who is considered black on their way back from the war to what cannot be home for either of them, they enact a Gothic meeting of conjoined contraries, like Victor facing his creature. The encounter between the brothers who are different simultaneously expresses and revokes a common bond, their actual kinship, when one comrade kills the other. They are on the same side, and they are on opposing sides. Henry's shot echoes the madness of hierarchical domination in the face of blurred levels that drives both *Frankenstein* and Faulkner's modernist Gothic narrative, both of which invoke paradigms from myths as old as Cain and Abel.

In the same year that *Absalom, Absalom!* appeared, Yeats published the first significant anthology of modernist poetry, the *Oxford Book of Modern Verse, 1892–1935* (1936). Despite the anthology's dates and focus, the initial item is Yeats' sixteen-line free-verse setting of the *prose* passage from Walter Pater's essay "Leonardo da Vinci" of 1873 that compares Mona Lisa to a vampire:[16]

> Like the vampire,
> She has been dead many times,
> And learned the secrets of the grave.[17]

By presenting this passage as an originating moment for modern poetry, Yeats clarifies the place of the Gothic monster in modernism. It stands at the intersection of the Gothic and the aesthetic in the context of the technological imperative to master nature's secrets that Leonardo represents. That intersection – in Pater, Wilde, Eliot, and Yeats – is itself revealing because aestheticism and the Gothic seem incompatible. They are, however, counterparts, like yin and yang. One light, the other dark, one focusing on beauty, the other on the grotesque, one utopian, the other dystopian, both enable culturally critical judgments by creating a distance from the habits and experiences of everyday life. By tying the monster to Leonardo's image, Pater implicitly connects Leonardo and the technological imperative with the countervailing mythic logic of conflated opposites that the vampire embodies.

By *myth* I mean a narrative that everyone in the culture knows, with varying degrees of clarity and detail, even without having read *the* text, if there is one, that first brought the myth to prominence or firmly codified it. As Claude Lévi-Strauss (1908–2009) famously argued, "the purpose of myth is to provide a logical model capable of overcoming a contradiction," "an impossible achievement if … the contradiction is real."[18] Central among such contradictions is the one between life and death, the opposites that define the character of the human as a creature aware of its own eventual dissolution but unable to understand and control its coming. The vampire, one of the supreme Gothic myths, responds to that contradiction emphatically because it is *the undead*, the phrase that was *Dracula*'s title until just before its publication, embodying simultaneously being alive and being dead, which are supposedly mutually exclusive. Composed of dead body parts yet alive, Frankenstein's creature is similarly contradictory, as is the zombie, an animated corpse that emerges as a myth under much later historical circumstances. Although the cyborg appears to be a different kind of entity because of its machine aspect, in fact, as a combination of something living and something mechanical, it too expresses the contradictory yoking of the living with the unliving. The inherently contradictory character of all these Gothic monsters understood as myths informs the strange meetings and other disturbing conjunctions in the Gothic and in modernism that challenge hierarchies of power, especially ones involving oppositions between good and bad, better and worse, human and nonhuman. As long as the human species is characterized by the mortality of its individual members, the reminder that the undead creatures provide about our permanently enigmatic dual situation, as the living-who-become-dead, works to undo the absolute oppositions used to designate some individuals and groups as more valuable, or more fully human, than others.

The Gothic monster is not only before, within, and behind modernism, I should add; it is also after modernism. Some lineaments of its future forms are visible within literary modernism and in art of the period in other media. Readers who think of Eliot as the arch-conservative of modernism may be surprised to learn that his work arrestingly projects the zombie and the cyborg long before they became common. With the phrase "mythical method," Eliot identified an inter-animating merger of classical myth and contemporary reality. But literature can also involve a generative mythical method, one that helps produce myths, as in *Frankenstein* and *Dracula*. In the closing verse paragraph of Part I of *The Waste Land*, Eliot's poem is indeed generative of mythic forms (ll. 62–66):

> A crowd flowed over London Bridge, so many,
> I had not thought death had undone so many.
> Sighs, short and infrequent, were exhaled,
> And each man fixed his eyes before his feet.
> Flowed up the hill and down King William Street

Rather than vampires, the undead beings are the living dead, what later came to be zombies, corpses that have figuratively come strangely back to life to walk the streets of London. The word "zombie," with its African Caribbean roots, had not come into English in 1922 with the meaning that it takes on later, but the concept of this kind of living/dead creature, different from the vampire, had invaded England because of World War I in newsreels and in the flesh. Eliot and his initial English readers would have recognized the image of walking wounded, both on the battlefield, moving haltingly with their damaged, bloodied limbs and heads, and at home, suffering from shell shock, ruined lungs, and lost arms and legs. The figure of the zombie comes into being as a result of technology turned against the human. Eventually, language catches up with the reality of such a Gothic history and gives these mangled creatures a name.

Eliot is not alone at the time in making art out of what modern life has made us: in effect, zombies. The first movies with "zombie" in the title come decades later, but *J'accuse* (1919) by the French filmmaker Abel Gance (1889–1981) features the living dead. Eliot and other modernists could have seen this film. One critic has even suggested that it influenced Woolf's *Mrs. Dalloway* (1925).[19] Near the film's end, in any case, dead soldiers arise in great numbers from their graves and together march across the land to their homes, where villagers are confronted with the spectacle of their dead relatives and neighbors.[20] These living dead are not violent, although the impression that they make is. When Gance remade the film in 1937, the living dead were portrayed by members of Les gueules cassées, an organization for former soldiers with mutilated faces.[21]

Following World War I, anticipations of the cyborg also began to emerge as part of the machine aesthetic of the time. After recovering from being gassed in World War I, Fernand Léger (1881–1955), for example, produced, during his career's mechanical art phase, *Le mécanicien* (*The Mechanic*, 1920), a famous painting that captures the crossover between the human and the machine by composing this human icon of technological culture as smooth geometric shapes resembling machine parts. His mechanic is a male, technological Mona Lisa for a new age. He also conceived and codirected the post-cubist, Dadaist film *Ballet mécanique* (1924), in many frames of which machines, mechanical objects, and geometrical images of body parts move as if they were dancing. The most stunning crossover between human and machine in the art of the period, though, occurred in the most admired avant-garde dance performance of its time, the *Triadische Ballett* (*Triadic Ballet*, 1922, performed provisionally from 1916),[22] by Oskar Schlemmer (1888–1943), which became identified with the Bauhaus and toured until 1929. The robotic costumes and movements evoke the mechanical quality of the human, not just the body as mechanical. In that way, they parallel Eliot's sense of the modern artist's impersonality, which he at times manifested by reading his own poems "like an actor imitating a machine."[23] Such representations are no more precisely the cyborg as we understand it now than Eliot's or Abel Gance's living dead are precisely zombies, but Léger's and Schlemmer's dancing mechanical art, which came into being during the modernist period, bears comparison with the female android exotic dancer of *Blade Runner* (1982), who calls herself Salome.

These works contemporary with literary modernism and complementary to it contribute to a Gothic recognition about Western humanity, ourselves, that confirms and extends the knowledge of our compound character made possible by the modernist Gothic. As the science-fiction writer William Gibson (b. 1948) claims, "We are already the Borg, but we seem to need myth to bring us to that knowledge."[24] By revealing the often unspoken dynamic of modern existence, the inherently contradictory myths that inform both the Gothic and modernism enable us to recognize our place in the contradictory situation of modernity.

NOTES

1 See Andreas Huyssen, *After the Great Divide: Modernism, Mass Culture, Postmodernism* (Bloomington, IN: Indiana University Press, 1986).
2 Virginia Woolf, *Mr. Bennett and Mrs. Brown* (London: Hogarth, 1924), p. 4.
3 *The Artist as Critic: Critical Writings of Oscar Wilde*, ed. Richard Ellmann (University of Chicago Press, 1969), p. 432.
4 See Frank Kermode, *Romantic Image* (London: Routledge and Paul, 1957).
5 *The Collected Poems of W. B. Yeats*, ed. Richard J. Finneran, 2nd edn. (New York: Simon and Schuster, 1996), pp. 64–66.
6 T. S. Eliot, "The Love Song of St. Sebastian," in *Inventions of the March Hare: Poems 1909–1917* (New York: Harcourt Brace & Co., 1996), pp. 78–79. See also John Paul Riquelme, "T. S. Eliot's Ambiviolences: Oscar Wilde as Masked Precursor," *The Hopkins Review*, 5 (2012), 353–379.
7 Eliot collected many of the essays in his *Essays on Elizabethan Drama* (New York: Harcourt, Brace & World, 1960).
8 T. S. Eliot, *Selected Essays* (New York: Harcourt, 1960), pp. 3–11.
9 Eliot, *Selected Essays*, p. 243.
10 Eliot, *Selected Essays*, p. 248.
11 Lionel Trilling, *Sincerity and Authenticity* (Cambridge, MA: Harvard University Press, 1972).
12 Joseph Conrad, *Heart of Darkness*, ed. Paul B. Armstrong (New York: Norton, 2006), p. 14.
13 Conrad, *Heart of Darkness*, p. 36.
14 William Faulkner, *Absalom, Absalom! The Corrected Text* (New York: Vintage, 1986), p. 27.
15 Eliot, "*Ulysses*, Order, and Myth," in *Selected Prose of T. S. Eliot*, ed. Frank Kermode (New York: Farrar, Strauss and Giroux, 1975), pp. 177–178.

16 Walter Pater, "Leonardo da Vinci," in *The Renaissance: Studies in Art and Poetry*, ed. Adam Phillips (Oxford University Press, 1986), pp. 63–82, esp. p. 80.

17 *The Oxford Book of Modern Verse, 1892–1907*, ed. W. B. Yeats (New York: Oxford University Press, 1936).

18 "The Structural Study of Myth," in *Structural Anthropology*, trans. Claire Jacobson and Brooke Grundfest Schoepf (New York: Basic Books, 1963), pp. 206–231, esp. p. 229.

19 Leslie K. Hankins, "Abel Gance's *J'accuse* and Virginia Woolf's *Mrs. Dalloway*: Re-Reading a Modernist Novel by the Light of the Silver Screen," pamphlet accompanying the DVD of *J'accuse* (Lobster Films, 2008), pp. 14–17.

20 http://www.tcm.com/mediaroom/video/197880/J-Accuse-The-Dead-Arise-Movie-Clip-.html

21 Kevin Brownlow, "The Waste of War: Abel Gance's *J'accuse*," pamphlet accompanying the DVD of *J'accuse*, p. 3.

22 http://www.youtube.com/watch?v=87jErmplUpA

23 A statement to me in February 1988 by Professor Kenneth R. Johnston of Indiana University.

24 William Gibson, "Googling the Cyborg," in *Distrust That Particular Flavor* (New York: G. P. Putnam's Sons, 2012), pp. 243–255, esp. p. 249.

3

SUSAN CHAPLIN

Contemporary Gothic and the law

The literary Gothic has, for over two hundred years, constituted one of the most sustained, if highly ambivalent, popular cultural engagements with and interrogations of the modern Western rule of law. Many critics in recent years have argued that late-eighteenth- and nineteenth-century Anglo-American Gothic fictions served to problematize the vulnerable, unstable position of subjects faced with modern forms of juridical authority now that such subjects are less predefined (by class, etc.) than they used to be. Several scholars of the Gothic have observed that it is this mode specifically that has come to articulate potently since the mid-eighteenth century something approaching the disintegration of the law's symbolic authority in contemporary Western culture. The law emerges in Gothic fictions (and, more recently, in Gothic film and TV drama) as a contaminated, limited and even perverse space: impure, perpetually unstable and at times monstrous. In the modern world, the space of law is a Gothic space.

This chapter considers the complex nexus between contemporary Gothic and the "operations, justifications and limits"[1] of law in late modernity. It argues that what is key to the relationship between modern Gothic and the rule of law is the persistent depiction within Gothic narrative, across a range of media, of the radical failure of the symbolic authority of law. This is most vividly apparent, moreover, in the mode of Gothic that has exerted perhaps the greatest fascination over the popular and literary imagination during the 1970s and since: the vampire narrative.

Desire, sacrifice, contagion, law

The mid-1970s marked a shift in the representation of the vampire that has been widely discussed by critics in recent decades. Beginning with Anne Rice's *Interview with the Vampire* in 1976, the vampire has become increasingly "human," moving from the monstrous predators of Bram Stoker (1897), Richard Matheson (1954), and Stephen King (1975) to the tortured, sympathetic and often highly romanticized "Byronic" hero-vampires of contemporary culture. While this shift has been evident in Gothic literature over several decades, it has become especially pronounced in Anglo-American popular culture across various media since the turn of the millennium, and it is through these diverse postmillennial narratives that the Gothic mode continues its interrogation of the subject's fraught relationship to modern juridical authority.

This chapter analyzes in particular the Gothic's relationship to what might be termed the *failure* of law in modern times. What is at issue here is not the failure of the law's disciplinary and regulative functions, but rather the increasing inability of law in modern societies to maintain its *symbolic* coherence. Central to this analysis is the work of René Girard on sacrifice and its complex, and often highly conflicted, relationship to modern, secular modes of governance. To introduce some of the key theoretical components of the argument, I begin with a brief analysis of an extraordinarily "Gothic" legal precedent that illuminates the connection between law and sacrifice.

In "Sacrifice before the Secular" (2009), Jonathan Sheehan considers a highly unusual case that came before the south Florida district court and ultimately the US Supreme Court in 1993.[2] The case was prosecuted under a 1987 Hialeah city council ordinance which banned, or at least purported to ban, animal sacrifice. The defendant was the Florida church of Santeria, which from time to time incorporated animal sacrifices into its worship. The church invoked in its defense the constitutional right to free religious expression under the First Amendment, claiming that the ordinance was unconstitutional insofar as it infringed on this amendment. The prosecution argued, and the Florida court agreed, that the ordinance was not unconstitutional and that animal sacrifice was therefore unlawful in the district of Hialeah; the law in question was not intended to ban *only* religious sacrifice, but *any* animal sacrifice, and thus it did not fall foul of the First Amendment. A law that was of "neutral and general applicability" was allowed to stand, even if it *might* impact negatively upon certain religious communities, so long as it did not inhibit free religious expression in general. A great deal turned upon the wording of the ordinance, which deliberately avoided the use of the term "religion"; it defined "to sacrifice" as "to unnecessarily kill, torture or mutilate an animal in a public or private ritual or ceremony not for the primary purpose of food consumption." The ordinance thus left open a space for the court to conceive of a secular form of sacrifice; that possibility, and the implication therefore that the law *was* neutral and not solely aimed at prohibiting religious ritual, allowed the Florida court to find against the church of Santeria.

The Supreme Court took a different view, though, and allowed the church's appeal. Its reasoning was as follows: Though it was possible to allow an exception to the First Amendment where a law was "of neutral and general applicability," this particular law could never in practical terms be neutral – it could only *ever* apply to practices performed within a religious context. There is no such thing as a "secular" sacrifice, and thus the rituals of the Santeria church were entitled to the protection of a neutral, secular juridical code.

Modern secular law posits itself as the agent of neutrality; this is the basis of its legitimacy in modern times. It will allow all manner of religious rituals as long as they do not violate the criminal code of a civilized country. Indeed, one of the key ideological assumptions underlying this case is that it is the law's ability to tolerate a wide range of religious practices deemed harmless, if bizarre, that marks it out as civilized, secular, and modern. Thus it appears here that while the law is prepared to protect a religious sacrificial ritual in certain circumstances, the law has decisively replaced the sacrificial principle with juridical logic. Indeed, one of the tenets of the decision was that the church's rituals are permissible precisely because they are useless ("unnecessary" in the language deployed in the case); the sacrifices have no material efficacy whatsoever and are thus harmless remnants of a primitive sacred order. Whatever occult power the church invests in these rituals poses no threat at all to the symbolic or material authority of a rational, secular law. Rituals do not disrupt juridical logic or the political stability of the state, however much they might offend certain liberal, secular sensibilities in a modern society. A neutral constitution, presiding over free religious expression in a free and diverse society, permits this eccentric expression of belief on the part of a small minority of peaceable Americans. As Sheehan argues, this case reveals the extent to which secular law has appropriated the discourse of the sacred (specifically here, the premodern juridical function of religious ritual) for itself. Animal sacrifice is permissible now (as opposed to, say, during the witch-hunt frenzies of the Middle Ages) precisely because the law judges it to be utterly pointless.

Sheehan analyzes the extent to which Western law has absorbed and nullified the sacrificial principle beginning with the institution of ancient legal codes in Greece and Rome. As these codes began to take shape, he notes, they necessitated a shift from sacrifice to law as the basis of the community's internal regulation. This shift was hardly smooth, and to facilitate the gradual triumph of law over sacrifice, it was decided that only one person should be allowed to offer sacrifice: the king. At the same time, however, the juridical authority of the king diminished, ensuring that eventually the power of law would rest with a secular body that was no longer required to perform sacrifice in order to affirm and perpetuate its authority over its subjects. This is at the heart of the Santeria judgment. Since the law no longer demands sacrifice, it no longer needs to appropriate sacred violence overtly to itself.

Sacrifice remains the hidden foundation of secular law, however, and René Girard's analysis of the ongoing nexus between law and "the sacred" is extremely pertinent to the modern Gothic's interrogation of the rule of law. What sacrifice enacts, Girard argues, is a primeval act of collective violence so destructive and traumatic that it must be repudiated by means of social and symbolic structures that ensure it is never repeated. Sacrifice and the law share this common origin in a moment of extreme collective trauma – what Girard terms "reciprocal violence" – that founds the community and structures its religious and juridical practices (the two, in early cultures, being indistinguishable). For Girard, this collective trauma is what ultimately constitutes the sacred as a mode of violence that is pro-jected outward away from the community and into the transcendental symbolic space of the divine. Through what Girard terms the "scapegoat mechanism" – the focusing of reciprocal violence on to the body of one victim who is made to bear the trauma of the entire community – violence becomes the sacred and is incorporated symbolically into juridical insti-tutions that appropriate the sacrificial function.

Sacrificial rites upon which the law is founded thus exist to control the threat of escalating reciprocal violence by diverting the violence of the community *against* the community onto the body of a sacrificial victim: the scapegoat. The scapegoating mechanism drives archaic rites of animal sacrifice through which ritual violence against the human scapegoat is diverted on to the body of the sacred animal. It was the resurgence of this archaic principle in contemporary Florida that so perplexed the US Supreme Court, and my argument here is that postmillennial Gothic, especially the vampire narrative, ties a resurgence of the sacrificial principle to a break-down of contemporary juridical authority, to what Girard calls "sacrificial crisis." In this respect, Girard makes a tantalizing point: "Violence is not to be denied," he says, "but it can be diverted to another object. Something it can sink its teeth into."[3] Reciprocal violence, then, is *vampiric*; it "sinks its teeth" into the victim designated as scapegoat by the wider community.

In nineteenth- and early-twentieth-century Gothic narratives, it is there-fore telling that the vampire is often seen to prey upon victims that in certain ways stand as ideal candidates for scapegoating according to Girard's analysis. They are vulnerable, somewhat transgressive, marginal-ized, "othered." In preying upon these "scapegoats" through highly ritual-ized (sacrificial) exchanges of blood, the vampire comes to embody and enact the sacred as a moment of extreme sacrificial violence – a violence that erupts temporarily out of the transcendental domain, becoming monstrously immanent within the community before being repudiated through a reassertion of the symbolic authority of law. Vampire fictions from the nineteenth century (Le Fanu's 1872 "Carmilla," Stoker's 1897 *Dracula*) to the mid-to-late twentieth century (Matheson's 1954 *I Am Legend* and King's 1975 *'Salem's Lot*) might be said to narrate what Girard terms "sacrificial crisis." They symbolically figure the apocalyptic return to the community of reciprocal violence through vampiric invasion and contagion.

The contemporary shift, then, from the vampire as blood-draining monster to a more humanized, even heroic, protagonist suggests a significant renegotiation of the relation between violence and the sacred *and* a potentially radical reconfiguration of the symbolic efficacy of law. For Girard, one of the defining features of late modernity is its susceptibility to sacrificial crisis. The point at issue here is not the decline of religion in the West; sacrificial crisis for Girard is not synonymous with a post-Enlightenment crisis of faith, but is defined in terms of the disintegration of a much broader symbolic authority – what Girard identifies as the "paternal function" – that previously negotiated the relation between violence and the sacred in premodern times. The collapse of the paternal function in the absence of any fully realized alternative, argues Girard, threatens the return of mimetic violence to the community. One symptom of this collapse, which will be discussed further below, is not that the law becomes necessarily less effective as a disciplinary mechanism, but that it becomes increasingly irrational and violent as it confronts the limit of its symbolic authority. It is within this context that the contemporary vampire has ceased to exist as the monstrous embodiment of a reciprocal, sacred violence that can ultimately be redirected into the order of the divine through ritualistic slaying. As contemporary vampire narratives insist, the vampire is now one of us. More than this, the vampire can be taken to represent the subject pushed toward an apocalyptic confrontation with the failure of law.

In postmillennial Gothic, communities of vampires work to sustain their own fragile order against forces, internal and external, that threaten to overwhelm and destroy them. In Stephenie Meyer's *Twilight* saga (2005–2008), for instance, the romance between Bella and Edward develops against the backdrop of the Cullen family's attempts to control their own violent impulses (which they do through the vampire equivalent of "vegetarianism," consuming only animal blood) and to protect themselves (and ultimately Bella) from other, more predatory vampires who might be said to represent the propensity for catastrophic violence inherent within the more "humanized" Cullen family itself. L. J. Smith's *Vampire*

Diaries, adapted for television in the 2010s, likewise foregrounds a community of vampires beset by conflict from within (the mimetic rivalry between Stephan and Damien Salvatore) and without (the murderous vampire Catherine and her accomplices).

Similarly, the best-selling series by Lara Adrian (*Midnight Breed*) and J. R. Ward (*Black Dagger Brotherhood*) depict tight-knit communities of warrior vampires committed to eliminating their deadly supernatural adversaries through high ritualized violence that maintains the always rather precarious stability of the vampire clan. In these novels, a special class of vampires, usually led by an exceptionally charismatic and powerful leader, emerges; it comprises heroic yet vulnerable and embattled subjects who work cease-lessly on behalf of the wider vampire community to avert annihilation. This band of brothers is a hierarchical group bonded by close fraternal ties founded upon their allegiance to their leader and upon ritual exchanges of blood that mark the vampires' belonging to this warrior class. Nevertheless, relations between the vampire brothers are often fraught with conflicts that can be understood in terms of Girard's theorization of the demise of the "paternal function" in late modernity. These communities are subject to complex systems of law, posited as having an overtly sacred origin, that exist to contain the almost overwhelming propensity toward violence that the brothers display not only toward their adversaries, but toward each other, and even at times toward their leader. Within this fraught, unstable environ-ment, the proper deployment of sacred violence becomes vital to an ongoing process of asserting and maintaining vampire law.

In Adrian's narratives, for instance, the threat to the stability of the vampire "breed" emanates from a group of renegades known as "Rogues." These are vampires who have entirely given themselves over to the "blood lust" that afflicts all vampires and which they must perpetually struggle to control. The Rogue is the outsider, the transgressor whose presence makes manifest the threat of an outbreak of catastrophic reciprocal violence. In Ward's fictions, this threat is embodied by a supernatural fraternity known as "Lessers" who display marked similarities to the vampires pledged to destroy them. They are transformed by their makers into immortal "undead"; they possess supernatural powers that enable them to predate violently upon vampires and humans, and they can only be killed by means of a blade through the heart. These monstrous predators are simultaneously "doubles" of and "others" to the strongly humanized vampire clans that ritualistically kill them, and this complex, violent dynamic reveals, through one of the most popular contemporary genres of Gothic fiction, the extent to which postmillennial vampire narrative is committed to the interrogation and negotiation of the complex link between law, violence, and the sacred.

The commencement in 2008 of the American TV drama *True Blood*, based on the popular series of novels by Charlaine Harris, marked a new departure in contemporary vampire narrative. Charlaine Harris' premise is that vampires have entered human society following the invention in Japan of a synthetic blood substitute that enables vampires to live without feeding from humans. The emergence of vampires into human communities, however, is accompanied by a good deal of hostility, and often violent bigotry, from humans, and both Harris herself and director Alan Ball play extensively with the trope of vampires as an oppressed American minority facing often extreme prejudice and seeking constitutional protection for their rights.[4] Within this scheme, there is a moment in Episode 10 of Season 1 that illuminates the importance to the Gothic of economies of law and sacrifice that appear always on the verge of catastrophic collapse. Vampire Bill Compton is called before a figure known only as "the Magister" to account for the crime of killing another vampire in order to save his human lover, Sookie. Here is an act of violence on Bill's part that threatens the stability of the vampire community; the possibility emerges of an outbreak of deadly, uncontainable reciprocal violence, a possibility that is dramatically realized in Season 3 when violence in the vampire community rapidly escalates following a series of betrayals and killings. The Magister in this instance must seek not only to punish Bill, but to calm a restless, blood-hungry crowd. The Magister thus ponders what the appropriate punishment in this situation might be and concludes that the only viable response to Bill's transgression is to require him to turn a human girl, Jessica, into a vampire in front of the mob. Jessica serves as the scapegoat whose sacrifice restores order to the vampire community. Moreover, Bill's punishment transforms him from outsider to insider. Bill has so far during his long life resisted turning a human into a vampire. He has killed humans, sometimes brutally, but he has sought nevertheless to set himself apart from the vampire community to some extent. His refusal to be responsible for creating a vampire is, until this point, the key marker of his difference, of his resistance, to the blood economy of the group. That Bill is 160 years old and still not a "maker" (the term used for a vampire who turns a human) clearly constitutes something of a joke, but also something of a scandal, to the vampire community. In becoming a maker, Bill is initiated fully into the group at the same time as his punishment stages the sacrifice necessary to re-establish group solidarity.

What threatens the community here, and what is repeatedly enacted throughout the narrative of *True Blood*, is precisely what Girard terms "sacrificial crisis," the catastrophic failure of the law to fulfill its "sacred" function to contain the contagion of violence imitating other violence. One symptom of this crisis for Girard is that the material violence of the law increases even as its symbolic coherence decreases, and to consider why this might be so, the next section evokes Slavoj Žižek's discussion of the symbolic function of capital alongside Girard's sense of a sacrificial crisis that he deems virtually synonymous with late modernity.

Law, capital, and sacrificial crisis

For Žižek, the order of law is established and maintained through the institution of a "master signifier" capable of generating and sustaining an ontological fantasy of absolute meaning and coherent, complete being. Žižek terms this master signifier the "big Other"; it can be understood as the space occupied in the symbolic order by signifiers of authority that might emerge in different cultures and epochs in the form of God, the King, the Republic, and so on.[5] In the West, argues Žižek, the symbolic space of the master signifier is disintegrating rapidly under the conditions of late capitalism because there is no longer anything that suffices to fill it; the result is the demise of the "big Other" and an inevitable collapse of meaning that suggests something similar to Girard's "sacrificial crisis." This is not to say that ordinary signifiers of authority such as nation, God, law, and so on lack symbolic importance entirely; on the contrary, the appeal to these signifiers becomes, if anything, *more* intense as society becomes more fractured and less stable. Such notions can no longer sustain a secure, coherent fantasy of power and meaning, no longer "fill in the master signifier with a particular content." If they could do that, there would be no need to make frenzied appeals to their authority; their authority would go without saying.

What is it that can account for such a failure in the order of meaning? For Žižek, postindustrial global capitalism provides the context for this crisis. The influence of global capital accounts for the form this crisis has taken, a point not sufficiently interrogated by Girard. In the following passage, Žižek compares the operation and influence of capital to that of a "meme" – any cultural element or sign that reproduces itself by non-genetic means – which uses human beings as passive agents in the process of its transmission within and across cultures:

> What is so unsettling about this notion is that we, as humans endowed with minds, wills, and an experience of meaning, are nonetheless unwitting vehicles of a "thought contagion" which operates blindly, spreading itself like a virus ... So where is the parallel with capital here? In the same way that memes [ideas, styles, or images that spread from person to person], misperceived by subjects as means of communication, effectively run the show

(they use us to reproduce and multiply themselves), the productive forces which appear to us as merely means to satisfy our needs and desires also effectively run things: the true aim of the process, its end-in-itself, is the development of the productive forces, and the satisfaction of our needs and desires is just a means towards that development.[6]

It is notable that Žižek uses the metaphor of contagion; capital seems to possess and direct the individual and the community in a manner that ensures its own expansion. There is a parallel here with Girard's account of reciprocal violence operating also in the manner of a "contagion." The imitative impulse drives individuals and communities to replicate violence in a manner analogous to the way in which the forces of production work to replicate capital on a global scale. What emerges out of Girard's analysis, moreover, is that reciprocal violence operates outside the symbolic order; it breaks open the order of representation and destroys meaning. Capital operates in a similar manner according to Žižek; it is beyond order and beyond reason, so much so that "the experience of contingency and indeterminacy as a fundamental feature of our lives is the very form of capitalist domination, the social effect of the global rule of capital."[7] This accounts for why the big Other appears to be undergoing a process of disintegration; capital drains the symbolic order of meaning, generating a radical indeterminacy that renders obsolete any claim by any particular signifier (God, Nation, Constitution, etc.) to occupy the symbolic space of the big Other. All that remains to occupy the place of the master signifier is the mad, spectral entity that is capital itself: "The spectral presence of capital is the figure of the big Other which not only remains when all traditional embodiments of the symbolic big Other disintegrate, but which even directly causes this disintegration."[8]

Anne Rice's second vampire novel provides an interesting reference point here. *The Vampire Lestat* (1985) begins with the protagonist waking in the late twentieth century after nearly sixty years of sleeping underground. After a brief period of disorientation, and in a parody of Christ's resurrection, Lestat comes fully to himself after three days. His first instinct is to feed and then to make sure he looks good: He acquires "a big black Harley Davidson," "gorgeous leather clothes [and] a little Sony Walkman."[9] He then turns to arranging his financial affairs:

By the end of the first week I had a pretty female lawyer in a downtown glass and steel skyscraper who helped me procure a legal birth certificate, Social Security card, and a driver's license. A good portion of my old wealth was on its way to New Orleans from coded accounts in the immortal Bank of London and the Rothschild Bank.[10]

The old European banks that hold Lestat's wealth and facilitate its circulation are, like the vampire, "immortal." The capital they release for Lestat is the only thing that can enable him to function within a postmodern capitalist economy. The vampire is thus tied here to processes of consumption and exchange that are beyond death, beyond national boundaries. They effectively replace the law as the means by which Lestat acquires juridical identity through the manufacture and purchase of simulations of legitimacy. Capital thus absorbs the function of the sacred and the function of the law into a spectral economy of legitimized, but not really legitimate, commodities.

Another suggestion about the power of capital and its relation to law and the sacred is offered by the key premise of *True Blood* and the novels on which it is based. Vampires in Alan Ball's television series and Charlaine Harris' *Southern Vampire* novels are able to enter the human community (to "mainstream" as they put it) by virtue of the invention of a synthetic blood substitute named Tru Blood. Given the symbolic importance of blood to economies of sacrifice, and given that the vampire has traditionally embodied and diverted the threat of reciprocal violence through the consumption and exchange of blood, the shift in these narratives from *true* blood to the synthetic drink is of considerable symbolic importance. Vampiric violence as sacred violence is absorbed into and its effects nullified by this commodity. The manufacture and distribution of Tru Blood offer an alternative means of containing and controlling the threat of sacrificial crisis. The problem is that the commodity fails entirely to avert this threat. The transformation of this sacred substance into a commodified simulation of itself is accompanied by a radical failure of juridical authority – an authority that emerges in *True Blood* as a violent, incoherent simulation of the big Other.

"I am the Authority, you idiot!"

This chapter began with an unusual recent legal precedent in which the law's relationship to sacrifice was foregrounded. An ostensibly neutral, secular law insists on its separation from the sacred and its right to adjudicate over questions of sacrifice. Sheehan considers the extent to which the law in the West has over centuries appropriated the function of the sacred in order to establish and maintain juridical authority. As the sacred loses symbolic coherence in late modernity, however, so does the law. As Jean Baudrillard argues, moreover, this crisis of authority takes a very particular form within a postmodern milieu: "Power itself," he contends, "has for a long time produced nothing but the signs of its resemblance."[11] In *True*

Blood, the vampire community across the United States is governed by a mysterious agency known simply as "the Authority." This institution never seeks to justify itself in terms of any constitutional right to rule; it simply posits itself as "the Authority." It represents itself as the origin and administrator of vampire law that in the postmodern era has dissolved into pure simulation (memes in constant circulation). The Authority is the exemplary embodiment of modern power in a society on the verge of disintegration; indeed, the Authority is both a product of and a response to the phenomenon that Girard terms "sacrificial crisis."

In *True Blood*, the consumption of the fake-blood drink replaces the sacrificial rites associated with the consumption of real blood. In Season 4 of the series, the Authority is revealed as the instigator of the drive to synthesize and commodify human blood so as to end the vampires' violent predation upon humans. The attempt to replace a violence that belongs to an old economy of the sacred with a desanguinated and desanctified commodity spectacularly fails, however, and the human and vampire communities are repeatedly driven to the brink of catastrophic breakdown. The Authority's various attempts to avert the disasters of which it is itself the cause entail strategies for the regulation of blood consumption that are forced to stretch beyond the simple manufacture and distribution of Tru Blood. The juridical enforcement of these strategies is invariably arbitrary and often incoherent and this constitutes another symptom of impending sacrificial crisis according to Girard's thesis. Juridical authority becomes unfocused, irrational, and increasingly violent.

A vivid example of the dissemblance, violence, and irrationality that characterize "Authority" in *True Blood* is given in Season 3 when the Fangtasia bar, owned by the vampire Eric Northman, is raided by a subsidiary of the Authority known as the "V Feds." "V" is a slang term for the kind of vampire blood, in a twist on conventional narratives of vampiric blood-exchange, that is traded illegally in *True Blood* as a potent hallucinogenic drug for human consumption. The V Feds exist to investigate and punish this illegal trade. Dressed in black storm-trooper uniform and led by the vampire Nan (who functions as the public face of the mainstream vampire community, the head of the American Vampire League), they violently apprehend Eric, who is charged with dealing V and interrogated by three mysterious representatives of the Authority via Webcam. Eric cannot see his interrogators, but they are briefly visible to the viewer as black-suited men with their backs to camera sat before a huge screen. They murmur inaudibly and even Nan, who is connected to them by a headphone, appears to struggle to understand them. Eric attempts to exonerate himself by implicating another vampire, Russell Eggington, in a conspiracy to overthrow the Authority and declare war against humanity. It is not clear whether he is believed, and no sentence at this point is passed. When judgment is finally delivered, it amounts to a repudiation of the Authority's involvement in any of the circumstances pertaining to Eric's arrest: "The Authority disavows any knowledge of your interview and indeed of this ruling itself. This never happened."

The Authority's enforcement of its own opaque law makes no sense, not even to Nan, who delivers its judgment to Eric with an attitude of weary cynicism. Power here loses symbolic coherence; as Žižek argues, the master signifier – the big Other that guarantees the symbolic efficiency of power – is evacuated of meaning by becoming global capital (signified here by the immense profits generated by Tru Blood and the black-market dealing of V). Institutions of power do not cease to function as disciplinary mechanisms; on the contrary, their violence often intensifies as they struggle to impose order upon increasingly fractured and crisis-ridden communities. What is lost to power, though, is its ability to sustain any kind of belief in its legitimacy. Subjects thus become not only disoriented and disillusioned in the face of power, but profoundly cynical and paranoid as regards their position before the law. What we witness here, and it is vividly depicted throughout the *True Blood* narrative, is a demise of symbolic efficiency that creates the conditions for a new form of subjectivity that can no longer take "on trust" its relation to the law. The subject can no longer believe or invest in the power of the big Other to guarantee the appearance of "reality" in the symbolic domain. Žižek is clear that the big Other is always already a symbolic fiction. What we do *not* witness here is the disappearance of a previously authentic, ontologically stable "Presence." The point is that this public symbolic master, says Žižek, "never existed in the first place, that is, the non-existence of the big Other is ultimately equivalent to the fact that the big Other is the *symbolic* order, the order of symbolic fictions which operate on a level different from that of direct material causality."[12] This "fiction" of the law's efficiency, moreover, is "strictly correlative to the notion of belief, of symbolic trust, of credence, of taking what others say at 'face value.' "[13]

The disintegration of the big Other is thus accompanied by a failure of trust, by the inability of the subject any longer to offer "a minimum of non-reflected acceptance of the symbolic Institution."[14] This disappearance of trust in the authority that regulates the symbolic order produces for Žižek subjects that are ontologically disoriented (they no longer know how to be, since the law cannot guarantee their symbolic efficiency in the public domain) and deeply cynical; their attitude to "authority" is suspicion, contempt, paranoia. These subjects are not, in a loose postmodern sense, simply "more dispersed than they were before, in the alleged good old days of the self-identical Ego."[15] The demise of the big Other deprives these subjects of the symbolic fiction that gave performative power to their actions as "subjects" in the symbolic domain. The failed fiction of the big Other, its collapse into pure simulation, thus inaugurates what Žižek terms "the order of the lie."

The new vampire world order initiated by the Authority through the manufacture of Tru Blood epitomizes the "order of the lie." Nowhere is this order more evident than in Season 4 when Bill Compton, a committed "mainstreamer" who has thus far attempted to distance himself from vampire politics, reluctantly becomes one of the Authority's key players. In what Nan describes as the "post-Russell Eggington world" (Eggington by this point has emerged as a terrorist who has threatened humanity with extinction), humans are understandably unwilling to accept that vampires are entirely satisfied with their blood substitute; the Tru Blood experiment appears to have failed and the Authority must intervene again to control blood consumption. It does so not by outlawing the consumption of human blood outright, but by prohibiting feeding only if it is caught on camera. The ideological logic behind this strategy is compelling. The Authority cannot outlaw the consumption of this sacred substance, but in an economy of simulation it does not need to: Only the spectacle matters. As "king" of Louisiana, Bill becomes responsible for implementing this law. Faced with a young vampire who has appeared on YouTube feeding from a willing human female, Bill has no choice but to order execution. As the accused is dragged off to meet the "true death," he protests that he will seek redress, that he will take his case "to the Authority." Bill responds impatiently, "I am the Authority, you idiot!" The young vampire has made the stupid mistake of assuming that there is some other "authority," some impartial public representative of a just law in whose power it is possible to believe. There is no such power. At this moment, as the accused stands before the law, there is only Bill Compton, the once conscientious "mainstreamer" turned cynical, dissembling king who here embodies the material violence and symbolic incoherence of a "sacred" law in crisis.

The Gothic has displayed throughout its history a marked preoccupation with abuses of juridical power in various forms, and the aim of this chapter has been to identify the extent to which highly popular modes of contemporary Gothic continue this engagement. To return to the Gothic's point of inception in the turbulent political, social, and juridical contexts of the late eighteenth century, we might consider the predicament of two very different Gothic protagonists – Ann Radcliffe's Vivaldi in *The Italian* (1797) and William Godwin's Caleb in *Caleb Williams* (1794) – as they struggle to make their case before the law. While Godwin's novel stands as an overt condemnation of the English ancient regime, contemporary political anxieties in Radcliffe (and in many other Gothic fictions of the period) are displaced onto the religious and juridical institutions of the Catholic Church. These displacements and projections can easily be read as anti-Jacobin hostility toward revolutionary "terrors" associated with Catholic Europe, but they are also arguably much more than this. As Claudia Johnson observes, "torture was hardly a remote affair" in England in the 1790s;[16] Radcliffe was certainly no radical in the Godwinian sense, but her fiction nevertheless interrogates the position of ostensibly "free" subjects (subjects ideologically positioned, in spite of their geographical and historical locations, as *modern* subjects, subjects of the English Protestant Enlightenment) before an unjust and opaque legal system. This malign system of law, moreover, cannot be characterized as wholly "other" to a contemporary English juridical order that had overseen the repeal of *habeas corpus* and the severe curtailment of freedom of speech and association in the 1790s. Radcliffe's Gothic manifests an "intense, if displaced, engagement with political and social problems."[17] These problems, like those foregrounded insistently by postmillennial Gothic narrative, center upon the deeply ambivalent position of the ostensibly free, modern subject before an ostensibly enlightened "Authority" that nevertheless remains grounded in and productive of terror. The contemporary Gothic, it turns out, has carried out this inclination in Radcliffe to a far greater extreme, exposing (if also fictionalizing) the failure of law in the face of rampant worldwide capitalism.

NOTES

1 David Punter, *Gothic Pathologies: The Text, the Body and the Law* (London: Macmillan, 1998), p. 19.
2 Jonathan Sheehan, "Sacrifice before the Secular," *Representations*, 105:1 (2009), 12–36.
3 René Girard, *Violence and the Sacred* (London: Continuum, 2004), p. 4.
4 For critical readings of this narrative's place within the wider tradition of vampire fiction, see *True Blood and Philosophy*, ed. George A. Dunn and Rebecca Housel (Oxford: Wiley-Blackwell, 2011), and *True Blood: Investigating Vampires and Southern Gothic*, ed. Brigid Cherry (New York: I. B. Tauris, 2012).
5 Slavoj Žižek, *The Parallax View* (Cambridge, MA: MIT Press, 2009), pp. 37–41.
6 Slavoj Žižek, *Living in the End Times* (London: Verso, 2011), p. 132.
7 Žižek, *Living in the End Times*, p. 132.
8 Slavoj Žižek, *The Ticklish Subject: The Absent Centre of Political Ontology* (London: Verso, 2000), p. 322.
9 Anne Rice, *The Vampire Lestat* (New York: Knopf, 1985), p. 13.
10 Rice, *The Vampire Lestat*, p. 13.

11 Jean Baudrillard, *Simulacra and Simulation* (1981), trans. Sheila Glaser (Ann Arbor, MI: University of Michigan Press, 1994), p. 23.

12 Žižek, *Ticklish Subject*, p. 354.

13 Žižek, *Ticklish Subject*, p. 323.

14 Žižek, *Ticklish Subject*, p. 342.

15 Žižek, *Ticklish Subject*, p. 330.

16 Claudia Johnson, *Equivocal Beings: Politics, Gender and Sentimentality in the 1790s* (University of Chicago Press, 1995), p. 121.

17 David Punter, *The Literature of Terror*, 2nd edn., 2 vols. (London: Longman, 1996), vol. I: *The Gothic Tradition*, p. 54.

PART II

The Gothic and the modern body

4

AVRIL HORNER AND SUE ZLOSNIK

Gothic configurations of gender

Work in Gothic studies over the last twenty-five years has contributed significantly to our understanding of the complexities of gender, the cultural construction of sexual identity. One aim of this essay is to offer a historical perspective on the development of ideas about gender as they have been theorized by cultural and feminist critics. Its main aim, however, is to explore how the Gothic's tendency to interrogate received ideas has resulted in memorable and often disturbing critiques of conventional thinking about gender. Moreover, our readings of some popular Gothic texts reveal that frequently they not only complement and reflect changing ideas about gender, but may also anticipate them. In order to illustrate this, in the second part of our essay we focus on the vampire, an enduring figure that demonstrates the Gothic's capacity both to represent the instability of gender categories and, in its more recent manifestations, to shore them up.

The late nineteenth century witnessed profound cultural shifts that resulted in what feminist critic Elaine Showalter has called "sexual anarchy."[1] In the popular texts of the day, many of which we would now identify as "Gothic," sexual identity and the cultural meaning attached to it appeared unstable, often monstrous, as bodies themselves refused their orthodox boundaries and became what Kelly Hurley has termed "ab-human."[2] Such bodily metamorphosis, an outward sign of the dissolution of the subject, can be found both in late-nineteenth-century works that have had a profound cultural impact and remain well-known, such as Robert Louis Stevenson's *Strange Case of Dr. Jekyll and Mr. Hyde* (1886) and Bram Stoker's *Dracula* (1897), and in those that have been recuperated as a result of academic studies in the Gothic, such as Richard Marsh's *The Beetle* (published in the same year as *Dracula*) and Arthur Machen's story "The Great God Pan" (1890). These novels and short stories demonstrate the instability of bodily identity during the fin de siècle and anticipate what Judith Butler was much later to theorize as its performative rather than essential nature. The Gothic's transgressive space provided the fictive theater where such performativity could be brought into the spotlight. Thus fiction anticipated, as is so often the case, insights derived from intellectual argument and theoretical formulation.

The Gothic, for long dismissed as the dark and dissolute underside of Romantic writing or as the popular frippery of "horrid novels" and melo-dramatic theater, was late in becoming an object of serious study. It is no accident that the rise of Gothic studies in the academy was contemporaneous with the development of feminist literary theory and criticism that emerged from second-wave feminism during the 1960s and 1970s. During these two decades feminist theorists, challenging androcentric assumptions and hetero-sexuality as a norm, fiercely questioned conventional configurations of gender. Feminism's progeny, over the next twenty years, included both gender studies and queer theory; indeed, the revival of the Gothic in aca-demic circles, marked by the publication of David Punter's *The Literature of Terror* in 1980, coincided with the rise of gender studies in the United States and the United Kingdom. This is not surprising given that the Gothic text's preoccupation with boundaries and their transgression or permeability has always extended to the demarcations of gender identity; the way in which the Gothic text frequently queries the social construction of gender and under-mines its certainties resonates exactly with the impulse in gender studies to deconstruct the social "givens" of masculinity and femininity. Both gender theorists and Gothic critics analyze culture in order to query human behavior in relation to concepts of male and female, masculine and feminine, conven-tional and transgressive. This approach derives from twentieth-century crit-ical thinking that, embracing postmodernism, abandoned the metanarratives enshrined in Christianity, empire, and the supposed fixities of gendered behavior.

Second-wave feminism was an aspect of this irreverent and energetic critique of the status quo. It prompted the publication not only of Betty Friedan's *The Feminine Mystique* (1963) and Germaine Greer's *The Female Eunuch* (1970) but also of many Gothic fictions that focus on the configur-ation of gender, such as Angela Carter's novel *The Magic Toyshop* (1967) and her collection *The Bloody Chamber* (1979), a volume that rewrites traditional tales in order to ask disquieting questions about oppression and female identity. While the work of feminist academics at this time offered intellectual analyses of gender configurations, the Gothic text, by making the normal appear "uncanny," rendered such interrogation in a vivid, disturbing, dislocating manner that still catches the reader's imagination and emotions. Both *The Magic Toyshop* and the title story of *The Bloody Chamber* revive the Gothic tale of Bluebeard. In the first, the Bluebeard story is played out in a London suburb of the 1950s in a fantastic and operatic vein. Its emphasis on the nature of female desire, on women's economic dependency, and on the home as a place of entrapment seems, in retrospect, to anticipate the work done in the 1980s by feminist theorists both in the United Kingdom and in North America concerning the position of women in Western culture. In "The Bloody Chamber," Carter explores the naive young heroine's complicity with her own oppression; the nameless narrator plays the masochist to her sadistic husband, thereby demonstrating how masochism is culturally associated with the female subject position in a patriarchal society. The narrator's self-abasement before the powerful Marquis includes an element of erotic desire that almost blinds her to her dangerous predicament. However, her exploration of the forbidden room and her discovery of the bodies of Bluebeard's previous wives bring her to her senses. The plot's denouement in Carter's version of the story disturbs conventional expectations of gendered behavior: The heroine is rescued not by her three brothers, as in the traditional folk version of the tale, but by a gun-wielding mother on horseback whose tiger-shooting past in Indo-China stands her in good stead when her daughter is about to be beheaded. Released from an imprisoning marriage, the heroine chooses as her next partner a blind, sensitive, and kind piano-tuner. In tune with the anger women felt during the 1960s and 1970s as they realized their cultural positioning as objects of the male gaze, Carter's story gives us a "new man," a more feminized construction of masculinity, as the perfect partner. The rise and popularity of Gothic fiction by women, from this period onward, perhaps owed something to the fact that the fantastic allowed women writers and readers to go beyond a reality that was both oppressive and depressing. Not surprisingly, the Gothic tale of Bluebeard was reworked by several authors in the following decades, including Margaret Atwood in the title story of *Bluebeard's Egg* (1988) and Alison Lurie in "Ilse's House" (in *Women & Ghosts*, 1994).

Alongside this Gothic creative portrayal of female economic, emotional, and sexual experience, there developed a strong academic impetus to retrieve women writers to form a newly enlarged canon of literature. This agenda, called "gynocritics" (another term coined by Elaine Showalter),[3] included the desire both to add women authors to the list of Gothic writers and to read Gothic fictions by women in new ways. Ellen Moers' *Literary Women* (1976) was a key text in this respect, not only excavating numerous women writers of the past but also containing a chapter entitled "Female Gothic," a term which then entered Gothic critical discourse. Focusing on Mary Shelley's *Frankenstein*, Emily Brontë's *Wuthering Heights*, and Christina Rossetti's "Goblin Market," Moers offers fresh readings of all three nineteenth-century works, memorably relating Shelley's novel to the author's experience of her children dying in infancy. Gilbert and Gubar's *The Madwoman in the Attic* (1979) followed Moers' agenda in retrieving many female authors lost to history and also in offering fresh readings of work by women, including Gothic texts, by focusing less on biological difference and more on gendered cultural experience. Thus Jane Austen's *Northanger Abbey*, for example, is found to harbor a palimpsest which renders it "a Gothic story as frightening as any told by Mrs. Radcliffe"[4] insofar as it lays bare the severe limits on self-determination suffered by young women in the late eighteenth century. Beneath such surface plots of love and marriage, Gilbert and Gubar argue, can be seen stories of rage and anger, with their readings reflecting something of the anger expressed politically during second-wave feminism.

French feminist theory, however, presented a challenge to such politically inspired Anglo-American criticism by charging it with essentialism. Taking their cue from Simone de Beauvoir's *Le deuxième sexe* [*The Second Sex*] (1949), the second volume of which opens with the memorable sentence "One is not born, but rather becomes a woman,"[5] French feminists queried the cultural and linguistic foundations and categories of gendered identity. Beauvoir had already argued that, in patriarchal societies, the "self" is constructed as male, with the female – representing all that is not known and understood – seen as a mysterious and threatening "Other" that is a shadow or object rather than a full subject. Developing Beauvoir's insights further, French theoretical feminists suggested that "femininity" no longer mapped unproblematically onto female bodies but could be discerned in nonlinear, transgressive modes of writing, what Hélène Cixous called *écriture féminine*, and that it could even be found in the work of some male writers – for example, as Cixous argues, that of James Joyce. During the 1980s, translation made the work of key thinkers such as Cixous, Julia Kristeva, and Luce Irigaray available to scholars working in English. By the 1990s such thinking had become absorbed into Gothic criticism: Anne Williams, for example, makes use of Kristevan theory in her *Art of Darkness: A Poetics of Gothic* (1995) in identifying and contrasting male and female plot structures. Particularly influential for Gothic scholars has been Kristeva's *Pouvoirs de l'horreur* (1980), translated into English as *Powers of Horror* in 1982; her theory of abjection continues to be used creatively by Gothic scholars as a way of understanding how Gothic texts, with their monstrous "others," represent the "throwing off" and "casting down" of fundamental instabilities and multiplicities (such as blurrings of gender boundaries) both at the level of the individual and at that of social and national identity.

During the 1990s, however, many academics who concentrated on Gothic writing by women critiqued the feminist literary approaches of the 1980s, in particular the tendency to represent female characters as passive and as victims. From the standpoint of the 1990s, such readings were seen as negatively reinforcing both conventional gender stereotypes and the idea that the plot of many women's lives was inevitably one of constraint and incarceration. It had by this time become important to see female characters in Gothic texts as autonomous, powerful, and transgressive. That word "transgressive," carrying a then glamorous resonance from the work of French psychoanalyst Jacques Lacan, gave the term "female Gothic" a new currency in the 1990s. Female Gothic, according to Elaine Showalter in 1991, could be seen as a mode of writing that corresponded to "the feminine, the romantic, the transgressive and the revolutionary."[6] French feminism, then, was an important influence in the development of gender studies which, embracing queer theory and masculinity studies in the 1990s, offered a far more nuanced critical perspective on writing and gender than had second-wave feminism. Much of the political thrust of the women's movement, however, was undermined by such developments, and Helene Meyers, for one, voiced concern that they might return us to "a phallic economy of sameness" in which the diversity of women's writing would be lost. Gothic fiction by women, she argued, is particularly important in that "its aesthetic links to both realism and postmodernism and its thematic emphasis on violence against women" enable a negotiation "between the scripts of 'male vice and female virtue' associated with cultural feminism and the 'gender scepticism' associated with poststructuralist criticism."[7]

Despite such reservations, in the 1980s and 1990s post-structuralism combined with gender studies and queer theory to produce a rejection of essentialism and a vigorous skepticism concerning the term "female Gothic." The result was a shift of focus from feminist readings to theorized readings of masculinity and homosocial/sexual desire. For example, in *Between Men: English Literature and Male Homosocial Desire* (1985) and *Epistemology of the Closet* (1990), Eve Kosofsky Sedgwick offers fresh readings of both Gothic and non-Gothic texts, focusing on their representations of homophobic mechanisms, homosocial bonding, and homosexual panic. In particular, she usefully highlights the frequency of a triangular textual relationship between two men and one woman in which the latter exists only to defuse or to distract from the powerful but socially "unspeakable" homoerotic bond between two men. Taking her cue from Sedgwick's claim that the "male paranoid plot ... always ends in the tableau of two men chasing one another across a landscape evacuated of alternative life or interest,"[8] Marilyn Butler points out that, although Frankenstein's love of Elizabeth and the creature's longing for a mate suggest heterosexual desires, these relationships are:

> thwarted by the violent deaths of both females before consummation can take place. The remainder of the third volume can be read as a blackly funny homoerotic mime, with man chasing man through a world where the loved women are all dead or far away, and no new ones appear.[9]

More recently, Damion Clark has analyzed Bram Stoker's *Dracula* in the light of Sedgwick's ideas, suggesting that it can be fruitfully reread in relation to the trial of Oscar Wilde, which took place in 1895, two years before the publication of the novel. As a homosexual Irishman, Wilde was both an outsider and a threat to British ideas of sexual and cultural normality, as indeed is Dracula. In this light, Clark sees the phallic teeth of the vampire as suggesting the threat (or liberation?) of gender reversal: "After the penetrating bite of Dracula, the women become like men in their expressions of sexual desire and the men become like women."[10] By the norms of Victorian conventional morality, this reversal is utterly taboo: The men still desire the (masculinized) women, thus revealing their repressed homosexual longings. Indeed, Clark concludes that the victorious "Crew of Light" represents the necessary closeness between men – or "homosocial bonding," to use Sedgwick's term – that is vital to the survival of patriarchy in the face of "sexual anarchy," to use Showalter's term.[11]

However, perhaps the most influential text of this postfeminist period was Judith Butler's *Gender Trouble: Feminism and the Subversion of Identity* (1990), which expounded a persuasive theory of gender as performance. Drawing on the thought of Kristeva, Lacan, and Foucault, Butler critiqued the work of feminist theorists such as Simone de Beauvoir, Joan Rivière, and Luce Irigaray in order to deconstruct the idea that sex and gender can be conceived of as distinct entities: "perhaps this construct called 'sex' is as culturally constructed as gender; indeed, perhaps it was already gender, with the consequence that the distinction between sex and gender turns out to be no distinction at all."[12] Thus Butler argues that gender is performative: there is no essential sexual identity behind the performance itself and gender has to be acted out, even unconsciously to oneself. Her argument presents gender as both fluid and unstable, always open to fresh interpretation. Her title, *Gender Trouble*, suggests that supposedly fixed categories of gender can be "troubled" by varieties of performance, some of them resistant to conventional gender roles. Influenced by Butler, new work in both gender and Gothic studies began in the 1990s to address masculinity. As is often the case, many Gothic fictions of the late 1980s and early 1990s either anticipated or coincidentally dramatized gender as performance and exposed the fragility of normative heterosexual masculinity, frequently using a combination of humour, parody, and the monstrous body in order to deconstruct received ideas about gender.

Iain Banks for example, parodically appropriating *Frankenstein* in his novel *The Wasp Factory* (1984), presents masculinity as masquerade and does so in ways that are simultaneously horrifying and comic. Banks' main character, a sadistic young boy, turns out not to have been castrated by the family dog as a child (as he has been led to believe) but to have been born a girl. We learn – but not until the very end of the novel – that a combination of hormone treatments, administered in strong curries cooked by his father, was part of a grotesque gender experiment thought up by a highly disturbed, but clever, parent who had trained as a scientist. This experiment, combined with a cultural expectation that masculinity is founded on misogyny and brutality, results in a comically ghastly character whose identity is validated through extreme acts of violence. Indeed, Frank Cauldhame's deeds include the murder of three children while a child himself. The narration of these deaths is dispassionate, but the bizarre cunning of the murderer's mind gives rise to grotesquely comic effects. The bullying cousin has a poisonous snake slipped into his artificial leg while he sleeps, the innocent younger brother is encouraged to blow himself up with a World War II bomb, and the girl cousin is swept out over the sea entangled in a giant kite, never to be seen again. The wasp factory of the title is an ornate contraption built inside an old clockface that used to hang over the Royal Bank of Scotland in the nearby town. Frank uses it as an elaborate torture chamber and arbitrary dispenser of death to his captured wasps. The desire for power and control that completely dominates him is expressed through a need to predict the future and a propensity for sadism; it also includes hatred of women and of the sea. He defines himself against women, whom he despises, and he loathes elements that are beyond his control and more powerful than he is. Frank may be monstrous in his amorality, yet he operates as a recognizable parody of masculinity. *The Wasp Factory*, a novel that shocked many readers and reviewers upon its publication, is not mere gratuitous Gothic horror. Rather, it uses horror and humor to encourage a detached and ironic perspective on the social construction of gender.

Some of Patrick McGrath's early short stories, collected in *Blood and Water and Other Tales* (1988), also offer parodic Gothic perspectives on performative masculinity. "The Skewer" challenges the phallocentric assumptions of traditional psychoanalysis, eventually revealing its dead victim to have been biologically female; in burlesque mode, "Hand of a Wanker" makes fun of the popular assumption that male sexuality is an imperative that must be obeyed, as the disembodied hand wreaks havoc in a seedy New York nightclub. In the same decade, Fay Weldon's *The Life and Loves of a She-Devil* (1983) and Jeanette Winterson's *Sexing the Cherry* (1989) highlight the instability of gender boundaries by disrupting received ideas of femininity and womanhood. Thus Weldon's "mannish"-looking Ruth Patchett, once she hugs revenge to her breast, is not only able to burn down her domestic cage and abandon her children but also eventually manages to morph into the body and wealth of her husband's mistress, the novelist Mary Fisher. In Winterson's novel, the Dog Woman is massive, hideous, and filthy, but takes pride in her physical power and her independence. Oblivious to the male gaze, she takes pleasure in rooting out corruption and hypocrisy wherever she finds them, at one point gouging out the eyes and pulling out the teeth of some canting Puritans to make her point. At the heart of the novel lies a serious message, however: Women should not allow traditional configurations of gender to limit their potential for change. In the novel's final phase, the story is continued through the eyes of a late-twentieth-century young woman who feels this seventeenth-century figure as a massive strength inside her. It is her internalization of the Dog Woman's power that enables her to become an eco-warrior. When this present-day heroine burns down a building, it is not a domestic space (as in *The Magic Toyshop* or *The Life and Loves of a She-Devil*) but a polluting factory symbolic of global capitalism. Similarly, Angela Carter's *Nights at the Circus* (1984) presents us with a freakish heroine who is over six feet tall and who has wings growing out of her shoulders. Her body's refusal to confine itself to conventional feminine proportions becomes her strength. She not only rescues men in peril but is also able to fly above conventional expectations concerning what it means to be a woman.

In the rest of this essay we shall focus on a Gothic body that has proved particularly fertile as a repository of fears concerning the instability of gender: that of the vampire, a figure that has proved itself capable of extraordinary transformations since it entered the Western literary tradition at the beginning of the nineteenth century in the wake of reports of vampirism from Eastern Europe dating from the mid-eighteenth century. Early vampire stories provided three templates: that of the grotesque (and decidedly unerotic), resurrected peasant body in Eastern European folklore; that of the handsome, degenerate, unrepentant aristocrat (for example, Lord Ruthven in *The Vampyre* by John Polidori, published in 1819); and that of the reluctant or remorseful vampire who loathes his condition (as in James Malcolm Rymer's populist *Varney the Vampire* [1845–1847]). While the first model is more akin to the now ubiquitous zombie, those of the aristocratic seductive vampire and the reluctant vampire have produced enduring fictional progeny.

For complex cultural and historical reasons, the fin de siècle was a key moment in the evolution of the vampire figure. The year 1897 saw the publication not only of *Dracula* by Bram Stoker but also of *The Blood of the Vampire* by Florence Marryat. Both novels present the vampire as an outsider: Dracula is a Transylvanian count and thus connected with what the Victorians considered the regressive superstitious culture of Eastern Europe, while Marryat's vampire, Harriet Brandt, is Jamaican, the daughter of a mad scientist and a mixed-race voodoo priestess. Both vampires eventually make their way to England, Dracula sailing to Whitby concealed in a coffin full of earth, Harriet Brandt traveling to London after staying in a Belgian seaside resort where she has taken refuge following the slaves' revolt on her home island. Whereas *Dracula* has become a canonical text, *The Blood of the Vampire* has only recently received serious critical attention. They are certainly intriguing to compare and contrast. Dracula is an aristocratic and unrepentant vampire who, like Lord Ruthven, sinks his fangs into his victims. As many critics have argued, Stoker's novel clearly articulates anxieties relating to new and threatening gender configurations (including that of the New Woman, who constantly oversteps the boundaries of conventional decorum), and the figure of the homosexual, which had become more prominent during the 1890s. Once bitten, Lucy Westenra becomes openly voluptuous and frank about her sexual desires for her fiancé, Arthur Holmwood; the blood transfusions she receives from three men fail to restore her uncontaminated self while metaphorically suggesting her repressed desire for a promiscuous sexual life. Her violent preying on children at night on Hampstead Heath provides the antithesis to late Victorian sentimentality concerning woman's "natural" gender destiny as that of loving mother. Finally, only a stake through the heart, with all the phallic connotations that carries, can render her dead, rather than undead, and restore her to the quiet passivity far more appropriate to Victorian ideas of femininity. The curious scene in which Dracula forces Mina Harker to suck at the blood oozing from his chest, likened by Stoker "to a child forcing a kitten's nose into a saucer of milk to compel it to drink,"[13] suggests an ingestion of blood and semen in an act in which Mina is both victim and protagonist and Dracula both passive and dominating, thereby thoroughly destabilizing the conventional gender boundaries of the time. It is as if the body, like gender itself, is a leaky vessel prone too easily to dilution and contamination, at least for Victorian sensibilities.

Florence Marryat's vampire female, by contrast, has no fangs and draws no blood; however, her very proximity drains her victims' life force, leaving them pale and enervated. Beautiful and lively with "lips of a deep blood colour ... her head ... covered with a mass of soft, dull, blue-black hair,"[14] Harriet easily attracts people, but those who become close to her gradually sicken and die. Like Dracula, she represents the racial "Other" but, like Lucy Westenra and Mina Harker, she also suggests the New Woman of the period, since she is financially independent and spirited. Marryat carefully manipulates reader response: When we first meet Harriet she is willful, selfish, and insensitive, oblivious to the fact that she has caused the death of Margaret Pullen's baby by constantly cradling it. An unsuitable liaison with Margaret's brother-in-law, Ralph Pullen, prompts the family doctor to step in, who explains to Harriet that she will always cause the death of those she loves. Horrified by this, she is nevertheless persuaded by the writer Antony Pullen, Ralph's brother, to marry him. Shortly after his death while they are on honeymoon, she takes an overdose of chloral in order to relieve the world of one "unfit to live."[15] By the end of the novel she has become a reluctant vampire, able to empathize with the suffering of others and recognize that she has been cursed by her genetic inheritance. Reflecting contemporary anxieties about miscegenation and the growing interest in eugenics, the novel also relates to the medical pathologizing of women at this time.

Indeed, the famous sexologist Havelock Ellis argued in 1894 that, because of loss of blood during menstruation and the naturally "thinner, more watery" nature of women's blood, they were generally anemic, a condition that led them to crave fresh blood. Hence, invalids and anemic women were encouraged to visit abattoirs during the 1890s in order to drink the blood of newly slain cattle as a tonic.[16] Superstitions about vampirism and emerging medical discourses were also reflected in Mary Elizabeth Braddon's 1896 story "The Good Lady Ducayne," which features an ancient and very rich aristocrat kept alive by her doctor through the progressive draining of the lifeblood of a series of young, penniless, female companions.[17] Given the cultural anxieties of the time concerning atavism and regression, it is not surprising, as Bram Dijkstra notes, that "It began to seem by no means farfetched to suspect the existence of vampires, and especially vampire women."[18] Indeed, Dijkstra records that as late as 1922 a senior and well-respected doctor in the United States suggested that a woman who desired sexual intercourse more than "once in two weeks or ten days" was a danger to her husband: "It is to her that the name vampire can be applied in its literal sense."[19]

This figure of the female "psychic" vampire evolved into the figure of the "vamp" during the 1920s and 1930s, the word often signifying a curious combination of boyishness and female sexual allure that was deadly to the male. Rebecca, in Daphne du Maurier's most famous novel (1938), fits this template exactly. Reconstructed through the memories of Mrs. Danvers, Rebecca signifies both femininity and masculinity. On the one hand, the housekeeper emphasizes her beauty, sensuality, and femininity by endowing her fine clothes with a metonymic significance. On the other, she stresses Rebecca's power and masculinity. What she loved in Rebecca, it seems, was her strength, her courage, and her "spirit": "She ought to have been a boy, I often told her that."[20] Indeed, throughout the novel, Rebecca's handwriting is associated with a masculine strength and an indelible authority that runs counter to Maxim's idea of the good wife. In her portrayal of Rebecca, who can be seen as the alter ego of the quietly compliant and shyly awkward nameless second wife, du Maurier draws on both the tradition of the Gothic double and the legacy of the female vampire. In so doing, she reflects widespread cultural ambivalence about the increasing power and sexual freedoms that many women were claiming during the first few decades of the twentieth century. Although Rebecca, like Harriet Brandt, is a "psychic" vampire, her identity is connoted by characteristics traditionally associated with the vampiric body: facial pallor, plentiful dark hair, and a voracious sexual appetite; moreover, like the vampire, she has to be "killed" more than once (she was shot; she had cancer; she drowned). The cultural slippages between the terms "vamp" and "vampire" are reflected not only in the unstable status of Rebecca's body (missing dead body; wrongly identified body; diseased body; erotic ghost) but also in her association with a transgressive, polymorphous activity – for Rebecca is both a heterosexual adulterer and (it is implied through her relationship with Mrs. Danvers) a lesbian. In disrupting the boundaries between masculine and feminine, dead and alive, heterosexual and queer, Rebecca represents the Kristevan abject: that which disturbs "identity, system, order," does not respect "borders, positions, rules," and represents "the in-between, the ambiguous, the composite."[21] In short, she challenges then-current definitions of gender.

It is not surprising, therefore, given the taboos that for so long surrounded same-sex desire, that the figure of the vampire has been used to explore nonheterosexual identities. Sheridan Le Fanu's story "Carmilla" (1871–1872), in which the shape-shifting Carmilla/Mircalla/Millarca tries to seduce Laura, a virginal 27-year-old who lives in an Austrian schloss with her widowed father, is generally accepted as the first lesbian vampire story in prose fiction. Laura, who falls into an inexplicable state of languor, anticipates the fate of Harriet Brandt's victims in Marryat's novel, although her ambivalent attitude to Carmilla suggests a repressed desire for a female lover that is absent from *The Blood of the Vampire*. The sense of transgressive love as both disturbing and seductive is conveyed not only through

Laura's dreams, in which Carmilla appears as a beautiful girl or black cat sinking her sharp teeth into Laura's breast, but also through Le Fanu's use of endless replication in the tale, creating a world in which (anticipating Freud's theory of the uncanny) repetition works not to confirm order and system but to unsettle them. Like du Maurier's *Rebecca*, Le Fanu's tale presents the female subject as "split" between an outwardly conforming self, which embodies a conventional respectable femininity, and an inner repressed self, full of erotic and transgressive desire. It is worth noting that, many years later, Rachel Klein was to employ Le Fanu's novella as a key intertext in her novel *The Moth Diaries*, which uses the trope of the vampire in a tale of tortured female adolescence, suggesting that the modern Gothic continues to speak to anxieties about desire and femininity.[22]

With the growth of a more tolerant attitude toward lesbian, homosexual, and transgender identities during the last quarter of the twentieth century, at least in the Western world, the figure of the vampire became a vehicle of celebration rather than abjection. Taking their cue from Sue-Ellen Case's claim that "The vampire is the queer in its lesbian mode,"[23] critics have recently focused on vampiric homoeroticism in contemporary writing in order to explore cultural constructions of gender and same-sex desire. Paulina Palmer's analysis of some Gothic lesbian fictions leads her to conclude that their authors "portray the lesbian vampire as a signifier of an alternative economy of sexual pleasure which is more emotionally intense and fulfilling than its heterosexual counterpart."[24] Nevertheless, despite greater tolerance, the identity of the lesbian and the homosexual as independent loner or member of loosely knit groups is still reflected in the individual isolation and underground networks of the vampire. Indeed in many works – such as Anne Rice's *Interview with the Vampire* (1976) – the vampire's existence is used to elicit reader and audience sympathy. In contrast with their literary forbears such as Stoker's Dracula, Rice's vampires no longer represent an enigmatic and dangerous "otherness" but are endowed with a compelling subjectivity. Louis in Rice's *The Vampire Lestat* (1985) tells his story to his interviewer, expressing vividly his conflicted feelings about his vampire existence. His vampiric "father," the charismatic and dandyish Lestat, takes on the identity of a rock star, giving contemporary rein to his performative nature. Their insecurities, as Gina Wisker has pointed out, align them with the complexities of the postmodern world.[25] In them, we see ourselves.

Rice's vampires might also be seen as reflecting late-twentieth-century cultural anxieties about sexually transmitted diseases such as AIDS and the changing nature of the family; in both the novel *Interview with the Vampire* and its film version (1994), two male vampires become adoptive fathers to

Claudia, the female child vampire. Similarly, Poppy Z. Brite's *Lost Souls* (1992) can be read as a critique of the conventional bourgeois American family unit, in which fixed gender roles combine with materialist values to produce emotional dysfunction. In creating a parallel community and an alternative family structure, based on a shared eroticism rather than on genes and inherited wealth held in common, the vampires of Brite's novel aggressively assert social, emotional, and bodily difference.[26] Gay vampire fictions of this period also often use humour to critique contemporary representations and styles of lesbian and homosexual identities, exposing their prescriptiveness and their absurdities, anticipating or reflecting Butler's argument that " 'butch' and 'femme' as historical identities of sexual style" do not reflect original heterosexual identities; instead they expose and throw "into relief the utterly constructed status of the so-called heterosexual original."[27]

Since the late twentieth century, the vampire has thus assumed a prominent role in popular culture, often as an object of desire or a fascinating icon of transgression. In *The Lure of the Vampire*, Milly Williamson explores how some girls and women use vampire style as a way of rejecting hegemonic images of femininity. Substituting black for pink, they embrace the identity of outsider, "using black to say to *others* 'I am different', 'I am unapproachable' and 'I am strong.' "[28] *Buffy the Vampire Slayer*, a highly successful television series in the 1990s, initially cast the strong woman in the role of the vampire's nemesis. In later episodes, however, the relationship has become more complex as Buffy negotiates her way between two vampire lovers: Angel, who in some respects resembles Rice's reluctant vampire Louis, and Spike, who embodies unbridled desire. It is possible to see the *Buffy* series as promoting feminism in its emphasis on community and shared power, and its director, Joss Whedon, has repeatedly said that he aims to change attitudes in the real world, especially attitudes to women.[29] However, a recent critic has pointed to *Buffy*'s Angel as the turning point that made the vampire "romance fodder,"[30] the most notable example of which is perhaps the commercially highly successful *Twilight* series. In these books and their film adaptations, we see the male vampire resurrected as romantic hero with his female counterpart, the Gothic heroine, cast in a more traditional passive mode. This might suggest that the success of the *Twilight* brand in both books and films owes something to a cultural nostalgia that, through a hyper-capitalist appropriation of Gothic devices, retrieves a reactionary agenda for gender. Disturbingly for feminist readers, Bella Swan's reasons for wishing to be transformed into a vampire herself include not only the desire to be with her vampire hero, Edward, for ever but also a terrible fear of aging: Her worst nightmare, described in the opening pages of *New Moon* (2006), is that she might see "some sign of impending wrinkles in my ivory skin."³¹ Bella is a Gothic heroine, it would seem, for the age of *post*feminism, in which "girl power" is accompanied by (and indeed feeds upon) an acute anxiety about becoming an older woman.³²

In *Twilight* (2005), Bella Swan is 17 and falls in love with Edward Cullen, a stunningly good-looking vampire who sparkles in the sunlight (which he must avoid if his vampire identity is to remain a secret) and who has special powers, such as exceptional strength and speed. The Cullen family are extraordinarily glamorous, living in a state-of-the-art house, wearing designer clothes, driving Mercedes cars, and seeking to "pass" as human. The family represents, in short, all that an adolescent girl brought up in a Western consumer society might find enticing. Indeed, the Cullens are anything but threatening and troubling, representing instead a degree of normality and social conservatism. Far from being transgressive figures, they demonstrate an adherence to conservative values, fixed in their hetero-sexual gender identities. The three subsequent novels see Bella also involved with Jacob Black, a Native American and a werewolf, who is hot to Edward's cold and to whom Bella is also attracted. Edward's erotic qualities remain ambiguous and Bella's attraction to him in some sense defies the Brontë-esque romance tradition the novel seems to embrace. It is as if Jane Eyre finds the marble-like St. John Rivers irresistible rather than the sensual and dark Mr. Rochester. The last line of *Twilight* indicates a level of masochism in Bella's submission to Edward: "And he leaned down to press his cold lips once more to my throat."³³ Finally (after several battles with other vampire groups), Bella marries Edward and produces, in great agony, a daughter who is half-human and half-vampire.

From the outset, Bella is defined by her relationship with Edward, abandoning career plans, other interests, and her female friends; her choices, in fact, reassert the values of neoconservative middle America, including its traditional configurations of gender. Edward, it may be argued, is an embodiment of patriarchal power and therefore presents a clear and present danger to Bella's autonomy. In the first novel, *Twilight*, he becomes in effect a stalker, indulging in such suspect behavior as entering Bella's bedroom at night and watching her sleep. In the fourth novel of the series, *Breaking Dawn* (2008), they marry, and her first sexual encounter leaves her scarred and bruised. It is her own susceptibility to his charisma that poses the greatest threat to Bella; as the series progresses, it becomes apparent that she needs to be protected from her masochistic sexual desires, which indeed result in a pregnancy that kills her mortal body. The assault upon her body by the hybrid fetus and the subsequent medical intervention in an attempt to save her life, followed by Edward's vampiric intervention to "change" her, are graphically described in the novel and also portrayed in the film version. Thus the "conjunction of femininity and death" explored by Elisabeth Bronfen in her 1992 book *Over Her Dead Body: Death, Femininity and the Aesthetic* is overtly displayed and, as Bronfen suggests may happen, "the uncanny convergence of femininity and death" serves "as a displaced signifier for masculinity, survival, presentation and continuation."[34] Bella's subsequent metamorphosis from susceptible human Gothic heroine to vampire, far from a process of "queering," firmly establishes her in the Cullen clan as a proud and traditional maternal figure.

Despite our liberal use of the word "transgressive" throughout this essay, then, it should be clear from this brief survey of modern vampire fiction that it is not always subversive. Some vampire stories daringly reconfigure gender in an imagining of future identities; others seem to challenge conventional configurations of gender only to recuperate normativity through exterminating the vampire and re-establishing heterosexual conventions; others firmly and unambiguously reassert traditional configurations of gender. Like the Gothic mode itself, the vampire is seductive and abject, protean and fluid, a figure that channels our uncertainties and anxieties about ourselves as the world about us – like our ideas about gender – changes from decade to decade.

NOTES

1 See Elaine Showalter, *Sexual Anarchy: Gender and Culture at the Fin de Siècle* (1990; London: Bloomsbury, 1991).
2 Kelly Hurley, *The Gothic Body: Sexuality, Materialism, and Degeneration at the Fin de Siècle* (Cambridge University Press, 1996), pp. 3–4.
3 Elaine Showalter, "Feminist Criticism in the Wilderness," in *The New Feminist Criticism*, ed. E. Showalter (New York: Pantheon, 1985), pp. 243–270.
4 Sandra M. Gilbert and Susan Gubar, *The Madwoman in the Attic: The Woman Writer and the Nineteenth-Century Literary Imagination* (New Haven, CT, and London: Yale University Press, 1979), p. 143.
5 Simone de Beauvoir, *The Second Sex*, trans. and ed. H. M. Parshley (London: Picador, 1988), p. 295.
6 Showalter, *Sisters' Choice: Tradition and Change in American Women's Writing* (Oxford: Clarendon Press, 1991), p. 129.
7 Helene Meyers, *Femicidal Fears* (Albany, NY: SUNY Press, 2001), pp. x–xii.
8 Eve Kosofsky Sedgwick, *Epistemology of the Closet* (1990; London: Penguin, 1994), p. 163.
9 Marilyn Butler, introduction to Mary Shelley, *Frankenstein (1818 text)* (Oxford University Press, 1993), p. xliii.
10 Damion Clark, "Preying on the Pervert: The Uses of Homosexual Panic in Bram Stoker's 'Dracula,' " in *Horrifying Sex: Essays on Sexual Difference in Gothic*

Literature, ed. Ruth Bienstock Anolik (Jefferson, NC: McFarland, 2007), pp. 167–176, esp. p. 172.

11 Clark, "Preying on the Pervert," pp. 171 and 174.

12 Judith Butler, *Gender Trouble* (New York and London: Routledge, 1990), p. 7.

13 Bram Stoker, *Dracula* (1897; Harmondsworth: Penguin, 1993), pp. 363 and 371.

14 Florence Marryat, *The Blood of the Vampire* (1897; Brighton: Victorian Secrets Ltd., 2010), p. 4.

15 Marryat, *The Blood of the Vampire*, p. 187.

16 See Bram Dijkstra, *Idols of Perversity: Fantasies of Feminine Evil in Fin-de-Siècle Culture* (Oxford University Press, 1968), pp. 336–337.

17 See the title story in Mary Elizabeth Braddon, *The Good Lady Ducayne* (1896; Whitefish, MT: Kessinger, 2004).

18 Dijkstra, *Idols of Perversity*, p. 338.

19 Dijkstra, *Idols of Perversity*, p. 334.

20 Daphne du Maurier, *Rebecca* (1938; London: Pan Books, 1975), p. 253.

21 Julia Kristeva, *Powers of Horror: An Essay on Abjection*, trans. Leon S. Roudiez (New York: Columbia University Press, 1982), p. 4.

22 See Rachel Klein, *The Moth Diaries* (Washington, DC: Counterpoint, 2002).

23 Sue-Ellen Case, "Tracking the Vampire," *Differences: A Journal of Feminist Cultural Studies*, 3 (1991), 1–19, esp. 2, 9.

24 Paulina Palmer, "The Lesbian Vampire: Transgressive Sexuality," in *Horrifying Sex*, ed. Anolik, pp. 203–232, esp. p. 203. See also her *Lesbian Gothic: Transgressive Fictions* (London and New York: Cassell, 1999).

25 Gina Wisker, "Love Bites: Contemporary Women's Vampire Fictions," in *A New Companion to the Gothic*, ed. David Punter (Oxford: Wiley-Blackwell, 2012), pp. 224–328, esp. p. 228.

26 See William Hughes, " 'The Taste of Blood Meant the End of Aloneness': Vampires and Gay Men in Poppy Z. Brite's *Lost Souls*," in *Queering the Gothic*, ed. William Hughes and Andrew Smith (Manchester University Press, 2009), pp. 142–157.

27 Butler, *Gender Trouble*, p. 31.

28 Milly Williamson, *The Lure of the Vampire: Gender, Fiction and Fandom from Bram Stoker to Buffy* (London: Wallflower Press, 2005), p. 153.

29 See Rhonda Wilcox, *Why Buffy Matters* (London: I. B. Taurus, 2005), p. 101.

30 Colette Murphy, "Someday My Vampire Will Come? Society's (and the Media's) Lovesick Infatuation with Prince-Like Vampires," in *Theorizing Twilight: Critical Essays on What's at Stake in a Post-Vampire World*, ed. Maggie Park and Natalie Wilson (Jefferson, NC: Macfarland, 2011), pp. 56–69, esp. p. 57.

31 Stephenie Meyer, *New Moon* (2006; London: Atom, 2007), p. 7.

32 See Diane Negra, *What a Girl Wants? Fantasizing the Reclamation of Self in Postfeminism* (London and New York: Routledge, 2008), p. 12.

33 Stephenie Meyer, *Twilight* (2005; London: Atom, 2006), p. 434.

34 Elisabeth Bronfen, *Over Her Dead Body: Death, Femininity and the Aesthetic* (Manchester University Press, 1992), p. 433.

5

E. L. MCCALLUM

The "queer limits" in the modern Gothic

The Gothic has a long history of playing with uncertainties about sexual differences, inevitable in a literature that relies on secret identities and misleading appearances. When Walpole's Prince Manfred ostensibly searches for the Isabella he feels he must marry late in *The Castle of Otranto* (1764), the reader finds suddenly that, "flushed by wine and love," he "has come to seek" her father, Frederic, in the most amorous state he will ever reach in the whole tale.[1] Accompanying this tension where sex feels undecidable is the Gothic's flirtation with, and at times its embrace of, sexual perversion – if only, more recently, as the deviation of the vampire's bite from what Sigmund Freud would call the "normal" heterosexual aim.

The relation between the Gothic and the queer, in fact, is by now a well-established aspect of this very mixed literary genre. The Gothic's hybridity – of genre, of gender, of high literature and low fiction, of artificiality and verisimilitude – turns out to be deeply bound up with its sexual politics. Hence, to understand those politics, one must read modern Gothic literature alongside its contemporary co-conspirator in queer theory. The two are interconnected by now, and so I will provide a bit of background on queer theory before I turn to the readings of literature. As the modern context of sexual politics changes, there is considerable impact on Gothic literature and vice versa. For many decades, the Gothic has inspired scholars of sexuality to examine and critique the cultural definitions of sexual difference and sexual identities, as well as the representation of sexual practices. In an age where same-sex desire is increasingly viewed as "normal" and even sanctioned by the institution of marriage, what, it must be asked anew, makes the Gothic queer?

To "queer" means to destabilize the settled and normative meaning (of a word, notion, or text), to pervert that meaning (given the etymological root of "perversion": to "turn away"), just as queer sexuality perverts or turns away from heterosexual norms. One of the most important scholars of the Gothic and queer theory, Eve Kosofsky Sedgwick, has described queer as referring to "experimental linguistic, epistemological, representational, political adventures"; she acknowledges equally, however, that at other times "queer" serves "to denote, almost simply, same-sex sexual object choice, lesbian or gay, whether or not it is organized around multiple criss-crossings of definitional lines."[2] I cite her definition because the remarkable range between "adventures" and just simply "same-sex sexual object choice" demonstrates the inherent slipperiness in defining "queer." This slippery definition comes through in modern Gothic literature as well. Alison Bechdel's highlighted definition of "queer" in her Gothic graphic memoir of 2007 – "at variance with what is usual or normal in character, appearance, or action; qualmish; put in a bad position; counterfeit" – defines the main theme in her tale of her closeted gay father, as well as giving a range of meanings to the theoretical term.[3]

As it happens, the classic Gothic has been very successfully "queered" through many insightful critical readings, like Sedgwick's, that highlight how same-sex desire is figured in Gothic tropes such as the uncanny double or in masquerade and innuendo. Yet because of the slipperiness of defining "queer," tracing the dynamics of same-sex desire in a classic text may not fully reveal what has come to be queer in the newer Gothic. The system of sexual differences in the Western world is not absolute but mutable, and it has shifted to accommodate modern identities and alliances, including the move to reclaim queer as a positive designation.

"Queer" as a term of art rather than disparagement emerges out of twentieth-century sexual politics, in particular out of the convergence of two major social movements: second-wave feminism and gay liberation. Both movements were to varying degrees made possible by Freud's psycho-analysis, which paralleled and informed the Gothic's development, as several critics have shown.[4] This correspondence is hardly surprising, since psychoanalysis itself arose in the context of late-nineteenth-century scientific inquiries into the nature of sexual feeling, and the Gothic is deeply interested in the secrets of sexuality. Beyond sex, however, psychoanalysis' interest in the unconscious, the uncanny, and the non-normal enable it to theorize some of the same phenomena that Gothic literature explores. Meanwhile, feminism flooded American society, particularly in the 1960s and 1970s (see Chapter 4), and rose to intellectual prominence in universities in the 1980s and 1990s, partly through debates about the usefulness of psychoanalysis for feminist theory. Similarly, the social movement of gay liberation, ignited in 1969 by the Stonewall rebellion and further impelled by the impact of AIDS on the gay community in the 1980s and 1990s, developed its twin in theory and criticism through the work of influential philosopher and historian of sexuality Michel Foucault, as well as that of a number of psychoanalytically oriented literary scholars. Their work embraced the fundamental insight of a third trend, post-structuralism: that all formations of culture – including things that seem to be timeless, transcendent, or absolute – are themselves fabricated in systems of signs, all of them changeable and open to new interpretations, failures, or adaptations, just as language itself is. Using post-structuralism's insights, which have provided more nuanced tools for analyzing how culture works, feminists have developed trenchant critiques of the dominant systems of sexuality and gender, arguing that modes of expressing femininity or masculinity are not innate traits but shaped by culture and experience. That shaping, however, does not mean that one can choose one's gender or sexuality at will, since our patterns of expressing sexual difference are instigated early in our lives, often at an unconscious level. These are constantly reasserted and negotiated over the course of our lives, in fact, and draw on a culturally specific vocabulary of qualities that become associated with particular sexual differences.

The binaries of heterosexual/homosexual, masculine/feminine, perverse/ normal, even subject/object, then, have all been contested, reinforced, and reconfigured in significant ways in both theory and social practice since 1960, not to mention in the centuries since the Walpolean Gothic's inception. These shifts have had an impact on the Gothic as well, since changing frontiers of social acceptability recalibrate what shocks, thrills, or horrifies. A gay marriage that would have aroused a radical frisson (if it were even comprehensible) in 1764 has by now become a conservative manifestation of same-sex desire. To address how this larger social shift speaks to the Gothic now, I have here strategically chosen a few more recent texts to examine, albeit ones at the outer limit of "contemporary," from the early 1990s. Despite the burgeoning industry of Gothic representations across media in today's culture, I focus in what follows on literary works because I want to make a claim about how form as well as content factors in to the relation between Gothic and queer.

As the lessons of feminism, gay liberation, and queer theory were digested in the 1990s, the Gothic became a rich literary source for thinking about how sexual differences are inherently relative and unstable. At the same time, however, insofar as the Gothic is still invested in some degree of conventional closure, focused on realistic styles over experimental aesthetics, or otherwise inclined to use form to stabilize meaning, it puts a limit on how much the same-sex content or gender play can radically disrupt any supposed "norms." Even some of the Gothic's most distinctively perverse themes – as in repeated scenes of female masochism – collude with sexual normalization. If queer theory disrupts stable definitions and established polarities of sexual differences, that disruption is a matter for formal analysis as much as a question of content. To what extent does claiming queer for the Gothic neutralize the challenge of queerness, the edge that thrills, so as to contain it within a conventional genre? Like the carnivalesque, where temporary inversions flirt with changes in power structures, only to reaffirm the status quo, the Gothic can serve as a release valve in the cultural system.[5] The Gothic is always already deeply woven into the norms of our Western Euro-American culture, since the Gothic aligns with psychoanalysis in prescient ways. Moreover, while the Gothic does frequently offer a feminist critique of patriarchy,[6] it also heeds capitalist norms of consumption and accumulation.[7] How do the "alternative sexualities" visible in several Gothic representations – transgressing every norm and boundary – serve to tame that strangeness, to dispel sexuality's threat to the self by grafting it onto the trauma of horror stories, in which a sort of de-distancing takes place?

By de-distancing,[8] I mean the way in which the far or strange is placed in relation to us and thus rendered less remote. That can happen on almost any scale. We see this in the way the Gothic positions us in a spectator's relation to trauma, so that, as Steven Bruhm puts it, "I may not be traumatized as an individual reader but I certainly join with the Gothic mode in *feeling like one who is traumatized.*"[9] Like Edmund Burke's "terror sublime" from which it derives, the Gothic lets us feel trauma without compromising our safety. Sexuality is also traumatic, a threat to the integrity of the self, a risk of boundlessness. That is why we have the norms of heterosexuality designed to contain it *or* the practice of psychoanalysis to cope with its complex manifestations in our lives *or* the romance novel to narrate its risk in safely fictional territory.[10] The Gothic performs the same function more darkly. But it remains important not to collapse all our mechanisms for containing breakdowns of conventional identity. What queer and Gothic have to do with each other is hardly neat. Not only are they not overlapping, but they open up gaps between them. Much as we might think they are similar in their contestation of the normal, *queer itself* is queer to the Gothic, even in Gothic fiction.

Indeed, if we look at *The New Gothic*, a major collection of contemporary Gothic fiction published in 1992,[11] we find that it features hardly any deviant queer sexuality, as if all the sexual undecidability that we find in the Walpolean Gothic were now passé – this despite its inclusion of writers who are hardly strangers to queer issues: Jeanette Winterson, Angela Carter, Kathy Acker, Anne Rice. But has the post-Stonewall era of gay liberation, lesbian feminism, and queer politics rendered same-sex desire too normal, or at least too open, to intrigue the Gothicist? Of course not; in the early 1990s, when both AIDS and queer activism were in full swing, the mainstreaming of LGBT people was nowhere near the point where it has come to be in the twenty-first century. Patricia Dunker observed that "the aggressively invigorating 'in your face' queer activism of groups such as Outrage and the Lesbian Avengers does not make lesbian and gay lives any more legible, intelligible or comprehensible to the advocates of hetero-sexual orthodoxy," and she argues that the Gothic subtleties of subversive innuendo therefore are still useful.[12] We have to ask, for whom is queer visibility important? Should the legibility of same-sex desire be limited to a particular population, or should anyone be able to read the social practices such desires engender? Not just private pleasures but public politics are at stake. Still, the omission of queer sexuality, of same-sex desires, even the minimizing of kinky transgressions like bestiality or S/M scenes in *The New Gothic* is striking. Has the new Gothic lost its edge? To pick up on the most obvious/successful example from the list of *The New Gothic* authors above, Rice's gay-themed *Vampire Chronicles* were well under way as a publishing phenomenon by this point: *Interview with the Vampire* had been out for fifteen years. But by the excerpt from *Interview* in *The New Gothic*, you wouldn't even know how gay it is.[13]

Still, if the content of *The New Gothic* turns away from queer or kinky, it is not entirely without its queer moments. Detecting the queerness of the Gothic is not necessarily about discovering the secrets in the depths of the text; it can rely on a surface reading, on what is evident right under our noses. Looking at the words on the page may tell us how queer changes in this new Gothic, or what makes this new Gothic queer. The secret – so crucial to classic Gothic – becomes something unconcealed in the text. It is not repressed by the text but produced by its very wording and suggestions, as an effect rather than a cause.

The New Gothic's editors, Bradford Morrow and Patrick McGrath, introduce their collection with the observation that "Gothic fiction ... was known by the props and settings it employed, by its *furniture*."[14] Furniture! And who really cares about furniture's atmospherics if not (as Kathy Griffin would say) the gays? This may be thin evidence indeed, relying on hoary stereotypes about the interior design flair, love of antiques, and theatrical bent of those who are "bent." But it is indicative of the indispensable indirection of the Gothic, which has always made its sugges-tions of undercurrents at least somewhat "queer" with an indirection that plays upon how suggestion and atmosphere, innuendo and setting, work together to unsettle and decenter the characters and plot events that would normally be the focus of a narrative. In other words, perversely, the context or setting of the characters' actions overshadows them in the Gothic, and this overshadowing produces another way to threaten a self's integrity, a formal one where the secondary features of narrative overtake the conventionally primary ones. This indirection is why the Gothic is hospitable to queers: As Dunker adds, "We are not always out, let alone 'in your face'. We are to be found within gossip, tall stories, freak shows, allegations, cabinets of curiosities, hints, gaps, innuendoes."[15] She might as well have included "nocturnal" and "underground" to complete the Gothic picture. I take Dunker's point less to emphasize how the Gothic is queer than how queers need the Gothic – perhaps today, more than ever. But I want to push that idea further to argue that both the Gothic and the queer need to challenge, unsettle, or destabilize reading practices, ways of knowing the world, and even our apprehension of sexuality in order to keep their edge and keep breaking conventional boundaries.

Perhaps even more on the surface, as if it were the return of the repressed, the term "inversion" haunts Morrow and McGrath's framing of the Gothic tradition, yet without explicit acknowledgment of inversion's sexual connotations, which go back to nineteenth-century sexologists using that term to describe both same-sex attraction and transgender identity (often conflating the two).[16] Let us, then, look closely at how their word choice lets queer back into a collection that had seemed to have left it out, since this kind of reading provides a model for interpreting how the Gothic and queer relate differently in the modern era. The *New Gothic* editors mark Edgar Allan Poe as the point in the Gothic's chronology where the genre turns inward, goes psychological, blurs the boundary between subjective experience and external location. Without irony, they announce that the spaces of the Gothic – subterranean passages, cellars, vaults, etc. – are each "a vivid analogue of the tomb, and each provided a site of inversion, where terror and unreason subverted consensus and rationality, where passion was transformed into disgust, love turned to hatred and good engendered evil."[17] Moreover, here the editors take as their Gothic example Matthew Lewis' *The Monk* (1796), a novel that critics have long been interested in as representing same-sex desire.[18] Blurring the line between that novel's specificity and the larger conclusions they wish to draw about the genre, the *New Gothic* editors say that "the gothic clearly delighted in moving to the dark term of any opposition it encountered. Inversion was its structural principle."[19] With this unintentionally punning claim, Morrow and McGrath quickly recoup the queerness of their word choice into a settled binary opposition: light versus dark. But in doing so the editors seem to miss the truly queer insights and perverse pleasures the Gothic tradition has afforded us: passion as both delight and disgust, love blended with hatred, the desire to penetrate another's body by sword, dagger, teeth, or penis, all blurred together in narrative acts of seduction, consumption, and murder.

Let us examine more closely the queer sense of inversion as the Gothic's structural principle. The conversion of light into darkness is just one swing of the Gothic's pendulum of horror. The classic Gothic figures rely on this conversion: The diurnal living human is transformed into the undead night-seeking vampire; the upright and holy monk is transformed into a voracious philanderer and murderer; the holy nun is revealed to be an earthly mother. But it is important to recall that duality, not singularity, has also been key in the genre – to wit, James Hogg's justified sinner of 1824, R. L. Stevenson's Dr. Jekyll and Mr. Hyde of 1886, or the uncanny double in Oscar Wilde's *The Picture of Dorian Gray* (1890–1891). So we would do well to expect a return swing of the pendulum – or even a consistent, steady movement from one side to another. A simple reversal of the normal order must find inversion again the moment that apparent equilibrium is regained. To be truly terrifying, and to be truly queer, inversion must continue to happen, or at least be always on the brink of happening. If the Gothic's structural principle is inversion, then what destabilizes or queers the Gothic is a continuous, dynamic inversion, hinging on the liminal, the crossing back-and-forth over thresholds, more than the maintenance of separate domains.

What makes the Gothic queer, in fact, is its investment in the liminal, the in-between, the brink – particularly, although not exclusively, the line between life and death, whether figured as the living dead of vampires, mummies, zombies, or similar supernatural beings, or the trope of living burial.[20] This liminality, however, is especially valuable symbolically because of its dynamic uncertainty, its irresolvability. For example, in Poe's "The Cask of Amontillado" (1846), the narrator Montresor tricks his rival Fortunato to come to his wine cellar to sample some Amontillado wine, only to entomb him in a niche in the cellar. Fortunato's being bricked into the walls is horrifying in hewing as it does to that very line between living/dead with masonry, which would seem to provide quite a final resolution to the two men's rivalry.[21] But Fortunato's sameness to the narrator and the way Montresor seduces Fortunato puts the homo in the horror. They are both noblemen, friends; they share a connoisseur's taste for fine beverages; and Montresor deploys Fortunato's own narcissism to lure him in. The interplay between the latter's recognition and failure of recognition (about being seduced) is irresolvable. Moreover, the liminality of the living burial is exacerbated by the liminality between victim and avenger. Montresor sees the insult Fortunato has ventured as a threat to his own ego integrity, beyond the slights that he characterizes as "injuries." A symptom of this threatened self-dissolution is the way the very language of the tale fragments into puns, adding insult to injury; it marks a sexual juncture, a convergence of body and sign, albeit indeterminately so.

What makes the new Gothic queer has something to do with how inverted the "old Gothic" could sometimes be. Although inarguably a nineteenth-century story, "The Cask of Amontillado" suggests that Poe is at the juncture of not just one break in the Gothic – inward and psychological, according to Morrow and McGrath – but two, the second being his turn from singularity to repetition. This turn sets the stage for the contemporary Gothic, which is frequently marked by an untimely immediacy and a changeable liminality, where inversion is not simply the structuring principle in a one-time, static sense but the repeated gesture that pushes the limits of intelligibility and blurs boundaries between supposedly distinct objects, beings, genders, and orientations. This repetition means that, rather than foregrounding space, the contemporary Gothic is distinguished by a back-and-forth relationality, full of queasiness and caveats, as well as unsettled, liminal time. To be disoriented in time can be as horrifying as any spatial threat the classic Gothic posed. The aptness of Bechdel's word "qualmish" for queer turns on its implicit appeal to the unstable body and its inherent temporality.

To grasp the queer contemporariness of Poe's tale, let us look closely at its ending. Montresor concludes his tale saying that to this day, five decades later, no "mortal" has disturbed Fortunato's tomb. The point, however, is not simply that Montresor has gotten away with murder, but that it has been a long expanse of time over which he has held – indeed conserved – Fortunato. The sadistic entombment is not unlike the marriage in Charlotte Perkins Gilman's "The Yellow Wallpaper" (1892), from which the weaker party, the subordinated female, seeks to escape. We should ask why Montresor feels he needs to claim this half century between his story and his telling of it. Why mark that time? Because that time delimits Montresor's relation to Fortunato. Montresor has engulfed Fortunato gaily. Within this horizon, he can be both murderer and witness to the trauma; he can be both homoerotic seducer and conserving necrophiliac.[22]

Another marker of time, curiously enough, comes at the beginning of "The Cask." "You, who so well know the nature of my soul," Montresor says to a second person – but when readers do not even know his name, how are we to know his soul's nature?[23] This second-person address is queerly dislocated in time and space; it opens up a negative space to the story's figures, an off-screen interlocutor, if you will, who seems to ground but also disrupts the framing of the tale. The second-person address puts an immediacy to the telling of this seduction and underscores the perverse relationship of fifty years. The tale's fetishistic and incessant interplay with narrative boundaries makes it a precursor of the new, in a way that *The Monk*'s Gothic hybridity, which reveals perversities only to reaffirm conservative polarities, never can. Such a dislocation in time is new and becomes essential to the modern Gothic.

Indeed, this dislocation in time, I would argue, is baked into the plot or structure of the contemporary queer Gothic. Let me reapproach the relation of queer and Gothic through a novel that is, on the face of it, more queer than Gothic. Randall Kenan's 1989 *A Visitation of Spirits* tells the struggle of Horace Cross, a black, gay teen from a conservative Baptist family in rural North Carolina, to come to terms with his sexuality in the face of familial expectations; as with too many gay teens, his story ends with suicide. But the novel is not exclusively focused on Horace's story. It interweaves the events of Horace's last twenty hours (April 29, 1984, 11:30 a.m., to April 30, 1984, 7:05 a.m.) with a day in the life of his much older cousin, Jimmy Greene (December 8, 1985). The two men intersect when Jimmy, who is principal at Horace's school, intercepts Horace just before he kills himself; formally, the juxtaposition of their stories lets us see the interrelations in a broader family network and the community in which they live. In this way the novel could be said to depict a community fostering the conditions that lead a promising, smart, gay youth to self-annihilation – a dark tale indeed.

The Gothic comes into play in two ways. The first is on the level of content, as Horace seeks to escape his life through sorcery, to turn himself into a hawk; instead the spell goes queer and he is possessed by a demon. The second is on the level of form: The novel dislocates us in time. This dislocation is not just prompted by how the novel offers parallel plot events between April 1984 and December 1985, one chapter from each year per section. Plenty of realist novels offer multiple or parallel time lines. But here slippages in time – between chapters as well as within a chapter through interwoven memory, dream, and fantasy – disorient us in the narrative. Form in this novel breaks up the smoothness and coherence of the realist model, whether in reveries, presented through free indirect discourse, which overlay family history with the present moment of the narrative, or as some chapters switch from prose to dramatic dialogue. The pastiche quality of the novel's form recalls and re-enacts the Gothic's generic hybridity.

The collective focus of this novel's roving perspective across family members also suggests a heavy sense of history haunting the novel, aligning it with the claustrophobia of classic southern Gothic. Moreover, as if underscoring this weight of community, two collectively focalized anecdotes frame the novel: a vivid, bloody scene of a hog killing at the beginning and a "Requiem for Tobacco" at the close. The novel blurs the boundary between individual and collective and thereby makes the Gothic storyline of Horace's possession by a demon redound upon the "straight" storyline of Jimmy Greene's everyday experience, haunted as it is by the losses not just of Horace but also of Jimmy's wife, grandmother, mother, as well as the fading ways of life in his community. Jimmy Greene becomes as Gothically unmoored as Horace, and the untimely form of both stories serves to orient us to their qualmishness and to unsettle us as readers.

In what seems to be the realist climax of Horace's storyline, where we learn of Horace's family's disapproving of his piercing his ear *particularly* because the clique of white boys he has been hanging around with had all done it, the novel asks:

> What does a young man replace the world with, when the world is denied him? True, the world was never his, but if the promise of the world, free of charge, is suddenly plopped in his lap and then revoked ... If he is given a taste of a shining city of no limits, and then told to go back to the woods?[24]

This disembodied question's lack of location marks how the very realism of the novel is always already queered by the Gothic. Who asks this? Is it Horace's free indirect discourse? Is it the narrator's? Is it Jimmy Greene's voice, bleeding in from elsewhere in the novel because he is haunted by Horace's suicide? Is it the demon possessing Horace – particularly telling because Horace went to the woods first for his spell-casting then later for his suicide? Immediately prior to this moment of questioning, there is another exchange of disembodied voice(s), although these speakers are implied to be Horace's family. Here his grandfather's voice emerges most clearly:

> I didn't raise you to run on the road with a bunch of fools, drinking and carrying on, not with black ones and my God, not with white ones ... I don't want to hear it. Look at that, to think that a grandson of mine would do a damn fool thing like that. Them white boys done took a hold of your mind.[25]

Again there is a question: How much does possession – or self-dispossession – haunt the ostensibly realist thread of the novel?

So how queer is the new Gothic, if contemporary queer experimental literature tends to the Gothic? As we return to this question, we might say that the new Gothic actually is queer not simply in its refusal of tired norms of heterosexuality, which is hinted at in Poe's "Cask," but also insofar as it challenges those systems. One way this happens is arguably in plot structure, which, as Judith Roof has claimed, has been heteronormative in Western literature.[26] This is the case not just in the ending of *A Visitation of Spirits*, which juxtaposes the violence of Horace's suicide, dispassionately and vividly described much like the hog killing at the outset, with the more diffuse blurring of his own personal memories of life (experiences of food, sex, church, school) into the collective experiences of the farming community lost to memory: Hiram Crum kicked by a mule, Henry Perry raping Lena Wilson, Ada Mae Phillips blowing out Jess Stokes ... (none of these names are characters in the book, as they only appear on the last page). But a queer plot structure also emerges in the persistent open-endedness of contemporary queer Gothic stories, the way that their plots suspend climax just before the peak, or, as in this case, perversely turn away from the expected or normal climax to a more muted, even diffuse conclusion. Rather than resolve into a soothing, conventional denouement, this story-structure leaves readers hanging at a crucial moment, effectively using plot to escalate and then truncate thrill, exacerbating our bodily response – which is, after all, key to the pleasures of the Gothic. What is new even about the stories in *The New Gothic* is how they turn temporal dislocation into a formal element, paring down standard plots, and thereby open up ways to unsettle, and perhaps even queer, the conventions of the Gothic.

Rebecca Brown's *The Terrible Girls* (1992) shows this process in action throughout its stories of queer Gothic longing that rely on this indeterminate plot structure of the contemporary story common in *The New Gothic* (although Brown's work is not included in that anthology). Brown's tales exemplify the queer new Gothic, participating in the larger trend of reworking Gothic conventions in content and form. A particularly illustrative example, "Dr. Frankenstein, I Presume," recounts the narrator, a doctor, cutting into the body of her patient, who is also the story's addressee, and taking out the heart, a candy valentine heart with changing colors and messages: pink, "You're Mine"; sky blue, "Kiss Me"; yellow, "You Belong to Me." The backstory of the pair is told though fragments of the narrator's memory, and the relation between the narrator and interlocutor is ambivalently cast as both doctor/patient and lover/beloved:

> just supposing, that you had told me the truth when you'd first come to me. Would I have believed you? ... When what you would have said, if you had ever said the truth, was that the most you'd ever been is less than human, a bloodless, heartless, pretty-faced cadaver? How did you do it, darling?[27]

The situation is both the scene of a doctor–patient interview and the retrospection of lovers at the crux, if not the end, of their relationship. The narrator's emotional investment in the patient is clear if indirectly revealed: "if you had ever said the truth" is loaded with rebuke.

The tale ends suspended as the patient on the table, who has not felt the doctor-lover's hands around her heart nor felt it removed from her bloodless body, nevertheless keeps asking: "When are you going to do it?" And the narrator recounts her immobility:

> I open my mouth to answer you, but I can't speak. I want to look away from you, so calm and pretty on the bed, but my head is locked. My arms tremble under the weight. I want to drop [the heart] but I can't let go.[28]

E. L. MCCALLUM

The arrest of the narrator's action in the story parallels formally the end of the telling. The end's stasis contrasts with the opening's dynamism, where the assistant awakens the doctor at a propitiously storm-brewing moment and they rush to the castle laboratory where the patient-lover awaits. Though clearly alluding to Mary Shelley's Gothic *Frankenstein* from 1818 (itself now read as queer for its evident male homoeroticism and same-sex reproduction),[29] the horror of the tale comes from a more realistic experience of the heartless lover, here rendered literally.

Many of the tales in *The Terrible Girls* play out across this power dynamic of the omnipotent beloved and the powerless lover, but always within same-sex couplings. The collection's first story evokes the masochism of a self-sacrificing lover who rescues – she thinks – her beloved despite public humiliation from the beloved and having to swim with the injured beloved across the river and carry her to a place safe from their pursuers. The lover is left literally in the dark, on the porch, while her beloved celebrates her return to her own sweetheart inside the house. Like the literally heartless lover, the dark side of this Gothic tale is less the threat of death, dying, and decay, which have been sanitized out of our purview in late modern Western culture, and is more the horror of the insidious ways power operates to disorient us about what comes from inside and what is externally imposed, or even introjected, from the outside. Brown's stories confront us with the horror of what we do to ourselves in our passion for others, as well as what those others do to us in their failure to recognize, engage, or return that passion. The disruption of desire – Am I loving you? Why am I loving you? – by the manipulation of power is very much a queer issue, even as it has long been a Gothic one as well from the final words of *The Castle of Otranto* to the opening chapters of *The Monk*.

While in *The Terrible Girls* the question of how power shapes our subjectivity seems to hinge on relationships across space, and thus to take us out of the temporal qualmishness that I earlier deemed key to the new Gothic, in fact Brown's stories unsettle time primarily. The longest story, "Lady Bountiful and the Underground Resistance," relies on a retro construction of time akin to steampunk. In a Victorianesque city the (female) narrator's lover has wed Lord Bountiful, elevating her out of the hardscrabble existence of the quasi-proletarian "resistance" movement and into the aristocracy and heteronormativity. With its mix of newspapers, mining elevators, workhorses, castles, and Xerox machines, the story is littered with anachronisms. The underground resistance itself exudes an early-twentieth-century revolutionary aroma, although that too is shown to be passé, since the narrator becomes the only activist left. On the face of it, this story is not so Gothic – or rather, it takes the Gothic toward the horizon it

82

shares with Orwellian, dystopian tales. But there is a mysterious bag that Lady Bountiful keeps with her, hidden on her body, a kind of abject love child begotten with the narrator or a secret body part that links her to her past. It thus resonates with other stories in the book about bags or body parts – particularly the macabre tale of a lover who cuts off her arm because she is asked for it by her beloved, who then mounts it like a trophy over the fireplace, and then loses it. With most of the stories having a claustrophobic-ally narrow present whose tight focus produces a heightened sense of fatalism when the narrator looks to the past (as the story of literally giving her lover her arm, only to regret it, illustrates), time becomes almost tangible, uniting different stories into a Gothic composite, despite their disparate subjects. The stories combine to produce a hybrid, patched-together darkness that is disturbing, queer, Gothic, and untimely. There is a sameness to their unspe-cific present that is distinctively not like the nostalgia of the Gothic of yore, but more like the insistent and vertiginous presentness of Montresor's account that we saw in Poe's "Cask of Amontillado."

The sameness of the sex of the lovers in *The Terrible Girls* produces the queer effect that Leo Bersani calls "homo-ness," an identity in which one seeks a lover for their sameness to one and the goal of union is self-shattering.[30] The sameness of "homos" is a radical form of resistance to sexual normalization, which is predicated on difference, and this resistance is usually acknowledged incompletely in the Gothic. We see this hyperbolic sameness not only in Brown, but in the similarly anachronistic Gothic texts of Sarah Waters. In the plot-crucial sameness of her protagonists Maud and Sue in *Fingersmith* (2002), the girls' origins as foster sisters tinges their own sexual congress with incest.[31] The novel's settings, with its Gothic house evocative of Edward Causabon's *Middlemarch* library in a much darker manifestation, its sadistic insane asylum, and the mean streets of London, all return us to the furniture of the Gothic. But reassuring as that furniture's stolidity is to locating us in the Gothic space as readers, here too the Gothic time is unlocatable: some vaguely past century yet with a modern sensibility.

The Gothic has always had what might be considered a queer time – the very name of the genre comes from the retrospective appropriation of medieval motifs centuries later – so it is no surprise that many contemporary Gothic tales capitalize on anachronism in ways that queer time on multiple levels. Indeed, the way that any number of contemporary vampire novels rework the undead motif into a centuries-transcending narratorial view-point offers another quasi-conventional expression of being unstuck in time.[32] But what makes such Gothic time necessarily queer?

It is not simply about same-sex desire. The lesbian vampire – particularly in Sheridan Le Fanu's "Carmilla" (1871–1872), itself indebted to

S. T. Coleridge's "Christabel" (1799–1801) – had been around for many years before the first use in English of the word "lesbian" to denote female same-sex desire in 1890. It was thus already too conventional a figure to queer the new Gothic. So let me illustrate the queer limits of Gothic in one last direction, with a beyond-lesbian vampire. Hong Ling's short story "Fever" (2001) tells of a vampire girl who is struck with a fever and takes shelter in a desolate hotel. Cruised by the check-in girl as she returns at 4 a.m., Ling's vampire is described thus:

> Combining the sharpness of the waxing moon and the softness of the waning moon, the contours of her lips, finely inlaid on her fair skin, looked like the marks of the aerial path of a red phoenix bathed in fire, speeding with irresistible momentum on an earth devoid of the color of blood, stirring up a barely controlled, barbarous, and violent blaze in its wake.
>
> This is what the young woman who filled in as a front desk clerk, her eyes still heavy with sleep, thought as the girl rushed to her room and quickly closed the door. When she sat back down in her chair and entered again the realm of sleep, she couldn't help dreaming of the fiery glow of beautifully red logs, embers still ablaze, on a ground covered by silvery snow, a glow that became unruly and turned into a wild blazing fire that scorched the surface of the earth.[33]

Here is a not atypical vampiric list of features: retreat at dawn, moon imagery, pale skin, fear of fire, rousing victims from sleep and returning them to dream, and finally the red of the vampire's lips all overtake the observing woman's impression of the vampire, tinging her view with desire. Meanwhile, the vampire in her room finds herself restless and uncomfortable apparently because of her rising temperature; she thinks back over her regrets about the women she's loved and lost and decides to "forge ahead, disregard the consequences, and test the strength of the sun." The anticipated encounter is erotically described:

> The room's window was facing the direction in which a perfectly round sun would very soon gradually rise – the bright yellow sphere that had always passed her so closely that they almost rubbed up against each other was about to float out from the bottom of her persistent line of vision. The blazing rays were on the verge of piercing her body, which was shaking and trembling uncontrollably. The vampire, not without joy, imagined the peculiar pleasure of the rays lacerating the skin.[34]

This is a queer scene indeed: perversely beyond same-sex or even inter-species sex to inter-entity erotics, made possible by a de-distancing relation to the sun. The most telling detail here is the sun's tactility.

Nonetheless – spoiler alert – this anticipated meeting is not to be. The sunrise has not been seen since the last year of the twentieth century, fifty years ago: "after the ozone layer in the atmosphere broke, the surface of the earth has been covered by a protective screen to eliminate the light in order to protect the health of the skin of the inhabitants of the whole earth," as the hotel manager tells her, before asking if she has a fever.[35] Like the half-century asserted at the end of "The Cask of Amontillado," this period of fifty years is telling. How could the vampire have become so unstuck in time as to miss this change, this gap? Does this mean she is not actually a vampire and only thinks she is? Is it just the fever?

The queerness of this Gothic story dislodges us in time. The shift in scale from love-object to the sun, which is far beyond our usual object-scale, also marks a shift in the scale of time, from planet to universe. What is new is how the haunted and inverted spaces of the old Gothic become the disorienting temporalities of the new Gothic. Moreover, queerly, in that vertiginous time, object choices change into chosen not-quite-objects. If we say that the Gothic has always been queer, then we have to understand what that untimeliness means in the contemporary writing of queer Gothic. It evolves both to traverse liminal spaces and to be held perversely within them – lingering irresolvably – in the twenty-first century.

NOTES

1 Horace Walpole, *The Castle of Otranto*, ed. W. S. Lewis and E. J. Clery (Oxford University Press, 1996), p. 108.

2 Eve Kosofsky Sedgwick, *Tendencies* (New York: Routledge, 1994), p. 8.

3 Alison Bechdel, *Fun Home: A Family Tragicomic* (New York: Mariner, 2007) p. 57; see also E. L. McCallum, "Lost in the *Fun Home*: Alison Bechdel's Gothic Queers," in *Gothic N.E.W.S.*, ed. Max Duperray, 2 vols. (Paris: Houdiard, 2009), vol. i, pp. 310–322.

4 See Steven Bruhm, "The Contemporary Gothic: Why We Need It," in *The Cambridge Companion to Gothic Fiction*, ed. Jerrold E. Hogle (Cambridge University Press, 2002), pp. 259–276, and George E. Haggerty, *Queer Gothic* (Urbana, IL: University of Illinois Press, 2006).

5 On the carnivalesque, see M. M. Bakhtin, *Problems of Dostoyevsky's Poetics*, trans. Caryl Emerson (Minneapolis, MN: University of Minnesota Press, 1984).

6 Michelle Massé, *In the Name of Love: Women, Masochism, and the Gothic* (Ithaca, NY: Cornell University Press, 1992); Diane Long Hoeveler, *Gothic Feminism: The Professionalization of Gender from Charlotte Smith to the Brontës* (University Park, PA: Pennsylvania State University Press, 1998).

7 In "Contemporary Gothic," Bruhm notes that Sedgwick argues same-sex bonding between men "is the glue that cements capitalist relations in the west" (p. 270).

8 The term (in German, "Entfernung") designates our tendency to be not only invested where we are, but connected to an elsewhere to which we relate; see Martin Heidegger's *Being and Time*, trans. Joan Stambaugh (Albany, NY: SUNY Press, 2010), pp. 97–102.

9 Bruhm, "Contemporary Gothic," p. 272 (original emphasis).

10 This view of sexuality builds on the one in Jean Laplanche's *Life and Death in Psychoanalysis*, trans. Jeffrey Mehlman (Baltimore, MD: The Johns Hopkins University Press, 1985); see also Leo Bersani's *Is the Rectum a Grave? And Other Essays* (University of Chicago Press, 2009).

11 *The New Gothic: A Collection of Contemporary Fiction*, ed. Bradford Morrow and Patrick McGrath (New York: Vintage, 1992).

12 Patricia Dunker, "Queer Gothic: Angela Carter and the Lost Narratives of Sexual Subversion," *Critical Survey*, 8:1 (1996), pp. 58–68, p. 58.

13 See the full texts of Anne Rice, *Interview with the Vampire* (New York: Ballantine Books, 1997) and *The Vampire Lestat* (New York: Ballantine Books, 1997), among others in her *Vampire Chronicles* series.

14 Morrow and McGrath, *The New Gothic*, p. xi (original emphasis).

15 Dunker, "Queer Gothic," p. 58.

16 As in Richard von Krafft-Ebing, *Psychopathia Sexualis*, trans. Franklin S. Klaf (New York: Stein and Day, 1965), and Havelock Ellis, *Sexual Inversion* (New York: Arno Press, 1975). Freud also famously used the term "inversion."

17 Morrow and McGrath, *The New Gothic*, p. xiii.

18 As in Haggerty, *Queer Gothic*, pp. 10–13 and 26–30.

19 Morrow and McGrath, *The New Gothic*, p. xiii.

20 See Eve Kosofsky Sedgwick, *The Coherence of Gothic Conventions* (New York: Methuen, 1986), pp. 128–134.

21 "The Cask of Amontillado," in *The Complete Stories and Poems of Edgar Allan Poe* (New York: Doubleday, 1966), pp. 191–196.

22 See Leland Person, "Queer Poe: The Tell-Tale Heart of His Fiction," *Poe Studies*, 41 (2008), pp. 7–30, and Elena Baraban, "The Motive for Murder in 'The Cask of Amontillado' by Edgar Allen Poe," *Rocky Mountain Review of Language and Literature*, 58 (2004), pp. 47–62.

23 "The Cask," p. 191.

24 Randall Kenan, *A Visitation of Spirits* (New York: Grove Press, 1989), p. 256.

25 Kenan, *Visitation*, p. 239 (original ellipsis).

26 See Judith Roof, *Come as You Are: Sexuality and Narrative* (New York: Columbia University Press, 1996).

27 Rebecca Brown, *The Terrible Girls* (San Francisco: City Lights, 1992), p. 98.

28 Brown, *The Terrible Girls*, p. 100.

29 See, for instance, Michael Eberle-Sinatra, "Readings of Homosexuality in Mary Shelley's Frankenstein and Four Film Adaptations," *Gothic Studies*, 7 (2005), pp. 185–203.

30 Leo Bersani, *Homos* (Cambridge, MA: Harvard University Press, 1996), p. 101.

31 Sarah Waters, *Fingersmith* (New York: Riverhead, 2002); see also *Affinity* (New York: Riverhead, 2000).

32 In addition to Rice, see Jewelle Gomez, *The Gilda Stories* (New York: Firebrand, 1991), and Octavia Butler, *Fledgling* (New York: Seven Stories Press, 2005).

33 Hong Ling, "Fever," in *Red Is Not the Only Color: Contemporary Stories*, ed. Patricia Sieber (Lanham, MD: Rowman & Littlefield, 2001), pp. 149–152, p. 149.

34 Ling, "Fever," p. 151.

35 Ling, "Fever," p. 151.

6

GLENNIS BYRON AND SHARON DEANS

Teen Gothic

Those we now describe as "teenagers" have always featured in Gothic fiction. From the unfortunate Conrad of Walpole's *Castle of Otranto* and the rather passive Emily in *The Mysteries of Udolpho* through to wide-eyed Catherine Morland in Austen's *Northanger Abbey*, flirty Lucy of Stoker's *Dracula*, and, more recently, the much-abused Regan of Blatty's *The Exorcist* (1971) and Stephen King's eponymous *Carrie* (1974), the Gothic has always had links with adolescence. Indeed, according to David Punter, adolescence, that time of disturbance, change, and growth, is integral to Gothic writing. For Punter, adolescence can be seen as a time when there is as much an inversion of boundaries as there is in the Gothic: "where what is inside finds itself outside (acne, menstrual blood, rage) and what we think should be visibly outside (heroic dreams, attractiveness, sexual organs) remains resolutely inside and hidden."[1] But perhaps this merely serves to "Gothicize" adolescents in adult eyes.

Teen Gothic, on the other hand, in the sense of fiction written about teenagers for teenagers, is a relatively recent phenomenon, and while there are earlier examples of young adult (YA) novels with Gothic overtones, such as Alan Garner's *The Owl Service* (1967) and William Sleator's *House of Stairs* (1974), the materialization of teen Gothic novels as a distinct, plenteous category really began with the emergence and popularity of vampire fiction for teenagers in the late twentieth century. Trends in YA fiction generally follow trends in adult fiction, and YA vampire fiction became popular after the resurgence of adult vampire fiction that began in the 1970s and 1980s especially with Anne Rice's *Vampire Chronicles*. Rice's reinvention of the vampire inspired a host of adult vampire fiction from the early 1990s on, ensuring that contemporary adult vampire fiction has remained on the best-seller lists ever since. This is a pattern subsequently repeated in the YA market. It would be a mistake to say that Stephenie Meyer and her *Twilight* series about teen vampires (2005–2008) were in any way at the forefront of vampire fiction for teenagers; numerous earlier examples can be found, most notably Annette Kurtis Clause's *The Silver Kiss* (1990), Vivian Vande Velde's *Companions of the Night* (1995), and Mary Downing Hahn's *Look for Me by Moonlight* (1995). These earlier YA vampire novels, however, while well known to teen readers, did not have the wider and quite astonishing commercial success of Meyer's *Twilight* saga, and it is the popularity of *Twilight* that has produced a surge of interest in teen Gothic in the twenty-first century. Unfortunately, the influence of, and the critical interest in, *Twilight* has led to a distorted view of what teen Gothic is, resulting in it all too often being excessively equated with the genre of dark romance in general.

This chapter investigates Gothic texts written for adolescents with a focus on the twenty-first century and examines what happens to the Gothic mode in the increasing gap between young children's literature and adult fiction; it looks at the ways in which, through the Gothic lens, YA literature explores and represents the teenager's relationships with issues such as sex, death, and autonomy. Gothic fictions written for young adults certainly seem to confirm David Punter's contention that the Gothic is "erotic at root"[2] and often focused on the centrality of sexuality, and so we begin by considering representations of "changing bodies" and the adolescent's burgeoning sexuality and desire for romantic relationships. We then move on to the examination of the ways in which the adolescent is shown to engage with death, and we finally consider representations of adolescent power and autonomy. We also use the terms "young adult," "adolescent," and "teenager" interchangeably throughout.

YA literature generally refers to texts that are aimed at an audience from about the age of 12 or 13 years to 18 or 19. Although there are some examples of mid-to-late-nineteenth-century fiction aimed at adolescents, such as the adventure stories of G. A. Henty, R. L. Stevenson, and R. M. Ballantyne, by and large these decidedly patriarchal British boys' stories are more concerned with empire than with adolescence, and it has only really been since the latter part of the twentieth century that the production of YA literature has become widespread. The proliferation of twentieth-century YA fiction also goes hand in hand with the socio-cultural construct of adolescence itself. Although adolescence as a social concept began to gain widespread attention with the publication of G. Stanley Hall's pioneering psychosociological study *Adolescence: Its Psychology and Its Relations to Anthropology, Sociology, Sex, Crime, Religion and Education* in 1905, adolescence as we recognize it today is primarily a mid-twentieth-century construct, and this is when books marketed to this demographic also begin to appear. Additionally, in the robust economic years following World War II, teenagers themselves gained increased economic resources and social autonomy, further increasing their market power, and literature (including film) specifically aimed at, and marketed to, adolescents therefore began to proliferate.

Delving into the dark side

Contemporary young adolescents are not culturally constrained by sex. They are bombarded with it from every angle, schooled in it and lectured on it, and have a whole genre of YA literature dedicated to it. This literature, Roberta Seelinger Trites suggests, exemplifies Michel Foucault's argument in his *History of Sexuality* (1976–1983) that Western cultures simultaneously liberate and repress sexuality. Written according to cultural norms that define teenage sexuality in terms of deviancy, they focus on control: Seeming to liberate the teen reader by showing sexual curiosity as natural, they then undercut this opening by trying to close it "with a series of messages framed by institutional discourses that imply teenagers should not have sex or else should feel guilty if they do."[3] Much YA literature, to paraphrase Foucault, constructs a science of sex devoted to the analysis and control of desire rather than the increase of pleasure.

In contrast to "realist" YA fiction, most teen Gothic novels have generally depicted sex metaphorically. For that purpose, enter the vampire. Unfettered from the restraints of overtly didactic "realist" fiction, the figure of the vampire liberates the teenager from the fairly frightening and mysterious "mechanics" of sex and simplifies matters: "sex without sex." Rather than reading novels implicitly loaded with Foucault's "science of sex," apparently devoted to analyzing, tediously, the negative consequences of submitting to teenage desire (and perhaps equating that desire with anxiety and fear), the figure of the vampire allows the teenage reader to back up a little, to explore and enjoy the nature of desire itself. This, we would argue, explains the undying appeal of the vampire for the adolescent. The vampire's desire refuses to be controlled, and adolescents view vampires as they view themselves, as ambiguous, subliminal figures.

Nina Auerbach's oft-quoted "every age embraces the vampire it needs"[4] can be read in two ways; not only does each era create its own vampire, but each age group does so too. A creature of everlasting fascination, bearing the weight of endless metaphor, the vampire nevertheless has a particular resonance with adolescents. The vampire has moved on from his monstrous late-nineteenth-century incarnation and has been supplanted by a divided and tortured figure, whose actions are a result of his physical condition (the vast majority of YA vampires are male) rather than some abstract conflict between good and evil: The adolescent in a nutshell. "Hovering between animal and angel," as any parent will attest, the adolescent therefore identifies with the repulsive, yet attractive, nature of the vampire as expressed by Auerbach.[5]

Commonly construed as a metaphor for sex, the vampire's kiss retains this promise for the adolescent; although the vampire is most often written as a sexualized predator, it is, in fact, his very sexual nature that most appeals to young adolescents. For the majority of these readers, sex is something that has not fully happened yet, but something they spend a lot of time thinking about. Through the figure of the vampire, and the sensual encounters depicted with him, the young adult reader can explore sex without sex. As Joseph DeMarco argues, "[i]t has all the trappings of sex, all the feeling of a sensual experience, but none of the real sex. Except, perhaps, in the mind of the reader."[6]

The teenage protagonist in any YA vampire novel, usually female, is frequently struggling to find her place in the world, is somehow marginalized from the mainstream, and is facing a problem, usually familial, that she feels she cannot surmount. The novels tend to trace the movement from the disintegration of the family unit to the sexual awakening of the protagonist by the vampire; death is often faced along the way, and the novels generally culminate with the protagonist establishing an identity independent from that of her parents.

Simon in Annette Curtis Klause's *The Silver Kiss* (1990),[7] for example, epitomizes the vampire as an outsider; a somewhat feral, predatory, orphaned, and isolated 300-year-old "undead" teenager, he lives on the streets and subsists on birds and rats when necessary. He is able to exercise some control (just) and need not always kill when he feeds on humans – but sometimes he does. Beautiful and seductive in a Byronic mold, Simon looks like "an angel in a Renaissance painting," is "tall and slim," has "lean, powerful muscles" and a "finely sculpted face."[8] There is nothing new, in other words, about Meyer's Edward Cullen. Echoes of this description can be found in any YA vampire novel: Male teenage vampires are always beautiful, always seductive; their irresistible glamour forcefully exerts a pull on the female heroine, who is attracted despite her better judgment. Simon's isolation for Klause mirrors that of Zoë, her heroine, who feels shut out of her family. Her mother is dying of cancer and because of this her father has little time for her. Zoë herself is conflicted by death: She has little regard for her own life, but tries to deny the inevitability of her mother's death. As Zoë becomes more distanced from her family, she becomes closer to Simon. Although Simon is dangerous and predatory, he is also desirous and desired; Zoë (and, by implication, the teenage reader) is attracted to him even though she knows he is dangerous. They are shown to consummate their relationship through the vampire's "silver kiss," where Simon kisses and feeds from Zoë. This is all too clearly written as "sex without sex":

> [S]he moaned and slipped her arms around him. It was the tender ecstasy of the kissed that he could send her with his touch. It throbbed through his fingers, through his chest, like blood through her veins. It thrummed a rhythm in him that he shared with her. She sighed, her breath came harder.[9]

Zoë enjoys this sensual experience with Simon: "But it was ... I mean, it wasn't terrible. It was ... I don't know," and Simon replies "It can be terrible ... I can make it sweet";[10] here teenage sexuality is expressed, metaphorically through the figure of the vampire, in terms of an *ars erotica* rather than Foucault's *scientia sexualis*. The knowledge of sensual pleasure, the truth about that pleasure and how it can be experienced, is being passed from an experienced master (the centuries-old vampire) to the novice (the virginal teenager).

Teenage protagonists in vampire fiction are ultimately empowered by their relationships with their respective vampires; the girls exemplify the notion of a teen sexuality in which they are active agents, where their own desire, pleasure, and subjectivity is emphasized, and in which they are allowed to make their own choices. Kerry, for example, in Vande Velde's *Companions of the Night*, refuses the vampire Ethan's "kiss," much as she desires it. Their sexual desire is generally shown to be expressed and explored metaphorically rather than being imbibed functionally and didactically, and, quite unlike Meyer's Bella, they are often empowered enough to relinquish the objects of their desire: Zoë helps the weary Simon to kill himself, reconnects with life herself, and moves forward toward being a responsible adult.

Werewolves are similarly borderline creatures – and this is just as appealing to the teenage reader. The werewolf, like the vampire, functions as an ambiguous and metaphorical manifestation of adolescent sexual fears and desires. After all, it represents both a dread of invasion and infection, even as it functions as an expression of inner desire. Traditionally, werewolves function to show the repressed "beast within" that must be destroyed in the interest of social and psychic stability. However, in YA Gothic, the werewolf has also "moved on" from "his" monstrous construction; he is no longer always regarded as cursed, is increasingly considered more alluring than monstrous, and is no longer exclusively male.

Werewolf novels that are written for boys, such as R. L. LaFevers' *Werewolf Rising* (2006), in which the protagonist, Luc, comes to terms with his changing self, tend to be aimed at the younger end of the market (12- to 13-year-olds). They emphasize the importance of "the pack" and equate the werewolf metamorphosis with the onset of puberty, the flooding of the young boy's body with testosterone. Although they deal with the discovery of the "beast within" and examine the nature of new urges, drives, and needs, they do so lightly and do not address full-blown sexual desire, focusing instead on fighting and hunting. These books are rarely Gothic in nature, and are, instead, concerned with rites of transition and the need for young boys to have adults guide them into manhood. The hierarchical and societal structure of the wolf pack lends itself well to this purpose.

When werewolf texts are written for the (slightly older) teenage female market, they certainly do deal with sexual desire and can take one of two paths: The female protagonist is attracted to a male werewolf or, more interestingly, the female protagonist is, or becomes, a werewolf herself. Although packaged and marketed as Gothic texts, the former tend to be no more than fantasy romances generally containing few Gothic elements, as in Maggie Stiefvater's *Shiver* (2009), a gentle "werewolf romance" containing minimal threat, and none whatsoever from the main werewolf himself; sex, when it occurs, is literal, sweet, consensual, and understated. Indeed, the werewolf in this category of novel appears to be somewhat tame and declawed. The latter category, however, grabs the Gothic with both hands and shows the female teenage werewolf appropriating the predatory, dominant, devouring, and sexual nature of the male werewolf and acknowledging it as her own. As the "beast within" erupts, the female protagonist recognizes, with a thrilling fierceness, that sexual/bestial part of herself which, not being socially acceptable, she has had to struggle to keep repressed.

Patricia Windsor's werewolf novel *The Blooding* (1996)[11] presents one such teenager. When Maris Pelham is transformed into a werewolf by her abusive employer, Derek Forrest – for whom she is working as an au pair and with whom she is infatuated – the transformation is expressed in highly sensual language, and we see a heroine who is more than a little complicit in her own seduction. Although Derek takes advantage of Maris' budding sexuality, he does not force Maris into becoming a werewolf; he makes her an offer: " 'If you really want something, you must be willing to go after it. If you want a change, you must make one yourself.' "[12] Furthermore, when Derek "initiates" Maris into his world, she undergoes a sexual awakening that she has unconsciously been searching for:

> A warmth began to spread over her ... She was ready for him ... His head moved onto her legs. She felt the weight of it, the heat of it ... Suddenly he pushed forward, nuzzling the soft flesh at the inside of her knee ... The bite,

stinging but tender, drew blood ... In one long shuddering tremor, she knew she had been blooded. She put her own fingers into the blood on her knee, lifted them, and smeared her cheeks.[13]

This passage unquestionably includes the metaphorical loss of the heroine's virginity (the blood is, by implication, hymenal), but rather than feeling abused, Maris appears immediately empowered by this sexual experience. There is a direct connection between the loss of Maris' virginity, her own sexual empowerment, and her transformation into a werewolf. She realizes that she has allowed Derek to "transform" her, not through some childish fairytale notion of romantic love, but rather through her unconscious desire to gain knowledge of her own sexual pleasure: "Do I love him or is this something else, an answer to an old longing, something inside me, that had always been there?"[14]

Through her transformation, Maris overthrows her perceived need for romantic love and family life and acknowledges the power of her own sexuality as her body becomes "a fierce instrument of the night."[15] Maris delights in the power of her body; she can turn into a werewolf with ease and fears nothing; she views her transformation as a blessing, not a curse: "This knowledge of who I now am plows me, deepens me, pushes me through time. I know everything."[16] While the sexual connotations of "plow," "deep," and "push" are clear, it is the "I know everything" that is the most telling, for in Maris' transformation the text neatly reverses the path that this particular werewolf tale is taking; Maris has no desire to be the abusive Derek's submissive partner/mate, and rather than fearing the beast within Derek, she prefers to relish the beast within herself. Leaving Derek dead in an English field, she returns to the United States "different in a way no one could understand."[17]

For teenagers sitting on the cusp of adulthood, sex is, like both the vampire and the werewolf, alluring yet dangerous. If we allow that the Gothic presents us with two possibilities – the transcendence of social objectification through desire or the monstrous consequences of pursuing our passions – then the Gothic figure in any of these YA novels can be seen to offer the adolescent a different choice: the possibility of subversion and transgression, or else the "safety of conformity."[18] While most protagonists are shown to reach the safe path by the novel's end, along the way they have, at least, resolved some of the inconsistencies which were plaguing them from within. They have explored the nature of their sexual desire in conjunction with the other problems that they invariably face and have delved into their dark side, usually without letting it absorb them completely.

"There is death but it is not my own"

"Perhaps the most obvious thing about death," write Elisabeth Bronfen and Sarah Goodwin, "is that it is always only represented. There is no knowing death, no experiencing it and then returning to write about it, no intrinsic grounds for authority in the discourse surrounding it."[19] As a result, they posit, "[e]very representation of death is a misrepresentation," and our analyses of such representations must demonstrate not only how they claim to represent death, but also "what else [they] in fact represent, however suppressed." Death is both abstract and concrete, we must remember; it poses metaphysical questions but is also a physical fact. In contrast to mainstream "realist" texts for adolescents, representations of death in teen Gothic fiction turn away from the universality, nonfunctionality, and irreversibility of death, all of which are delimited by the fact of our embodiment and move toward other forms of continuance, embodied or not.

While dying remains a biological inevitability in the real world, death, as represented in the fantasy world of teen Gothic fiction, is transformed into what Clive Seale has described as "an orientation towards continuing";[20] oftentimes this continuance is welcome – sometimes it is not. However, although teen Gothic fiction represents a fantasy world, it both addresses and symbolizes very real issues that teenagers have when it comes to thinking about both life and death. The ambiguity of their status in the world – no longer a child, not yet an adult – is reflected in their ambiguous relationship with death, and this fact underwrites the representation of death in teen Gothic. Indeed, death and its inevitability, as Trites puts them, are "the *sine qua non* of adolescent literature, the defining factor that distinguishes it from both children's and adult literature."[21] In "realist" books for younger children, Trites shows, death is used to demonstrate children "learning to individuate by separating from their actual or symbolic parents ... and death is portrayed as part of a cycle, as an ongoing process of life."[22] YA "realist" novels are more linear because the *Bildungsroman* formula demands a plot

> determined by the concept of growth as linear [and] death is the endpoint of that line ... Death is more than a stage in development, symbolic of a separation from one's parents; death in adolescent literature is a threat, an experience adolescents understand as a finality.[23]

This is not so in teen Gothic, where the "living dead" predominate.

If, as Punter notes, adolescence is a time when there is a "fantasized inversion of boundaries," then this is particularly evident in teen Gothic, in that supposedly "final" boundary between life and death. Death in mainstream "realist" adolescent texts is depicted as permanent, and the teenager is deemed mature when he or she accepts both the permanence of mortality and the fact that we are all, in Martin Heidegger's terms, "Being-towards-death." While many Gothic texts certainly show that teenage protagonists achieve this moment of maturation, coming to define themselves in terms of their own death, they then refute the permanence of death and/or the state of "not being" by featuring zombies, vampires, and ghosts. Whether they appear in zombie fictions such as Carrie Ryan's trilogy *The Forest of Hands and Teeth* (2009–2011), ghost fictions and dead narrator tales such as Laura Whitcomb's *A Certain Slant of Light* (2005), or any of the innumerable vampire fictions now in circulation, these Gothic figures function as both a threat to life and a promise that death is not the end. Paradoxically, then, although death is the Gothic's stock-in-trade, very few teen Gothic novels deal with actual death. "Real" death, it would seem, remains the preserve of those mainstream, didactic, "realist" fictions. We can undoubtedly argue that any narrative or "aesthetic representation of death lets us repress our knowledge of the reality of death precisely because here death occurs *at* someone else's body and *as* an image . . . There is death" thinks the reader, "but it is not my own."[24] It is this denial of the inevitability and permanence of death that we most often see highlighted in teen Gothic texts, where death, while still sometimes appearing as a threat, is not always "an experience adolescents understand as a finality."

To illustrate this paradox we need look no further than Bella Swan, the teenage protagonist in Meyer's *Twilight* series.[25] It has been argued that in her desire for the vampire Edward Cullen, Bella subconsciously desires the grave; Edward, with his pale and cool body which requires neither food nor sleep, could be likened to a corpse. But in fact the last thing Edward resembles is a corpse; corpses eventually decay and become food for the worms, and this is not true of Edward who is, and will always be, an eternal "Adonis."[26] As well as being the god of beauty and desire in Greek mythology, however, Adonis is also a dying god, an annually renewed, ever-youthful god, a life–death–birth deity whose nature is tied to the calendar. This is what Bella wants. She does not crave death, she craves stasis; she desires for herself the beauteous immortality that Edward and the Cullens all have, and, despite ambiguously thinking "[l]et me die, let me die"[27] during the pain of her inevitable transformation, she never really defines herself in terms of her own "not being." The thought is ambiguous because, on the one hand, Bella screams internally to die in order to escape the bodily pain she is experiencing at that moment in time, and, on the other, she knows she has to die "momentarily" to achieve her immortality. Bella desires immortality; she wants to be exempt from death; she also yearns to be immortal in the wider sense of not wanting to be liable to perish or decay. She wishes to be as Edward is, everlasting and unfading.

Assuredly, then, Bella is not, in Heidegger's terms, a "Being-towards-death"; she does not accept her own maturation, and she repeatedly complains about it throughout the first three books of the series. For Bella, "[g]etting older" is, indeed, "the worst that could happen."[28] Wishing to forestall the aging process, Bella constantly pleads with Edward to turn her into a vampire, but does not get her wish until Edward's hand is forced in the final book, when he has to step in and save Bella after a particularly horrific birthing scene involving a fully sentient and rapidly increasing fetus which is both eating Bella alive and breaking up her body. Naturally, here the transfiguration is viewed as positive, for, on balance, the hero has saved the heroine's "life." The inherent paradox in immortality for Bella, of course, is that she has to "die" to achieve it:

> My heart stuttered twice, and then thudded quietly again just once more.
> There was no sound. No breathing. Not even mine . . .
> And then I opened my eyes and gazed about me in wonder.[29]

This is not presented as "real" death; Bella experiences no loss of sensation or vitality, quite the opposite, in fact; she rises from her transformation with all her senses heightened. Death, when presented as immortality, is hugely desirable in Bella's eyes, and the text completely underplays the idea that this is death. Bella does not have a death wish, nor does she reject life; instead, she gains greater awareness and appreciation of the living world, and Meyer spends pages describing the extraordinary clarity of Bella's newly heightened senses. Misrepresentations of death in teen Gothic fiction can therefore function to represent the ambiguous nature of adolescent understandings of death. The study of representations of the vampire, zombie, ghost, and immortality in YA literature reveals adolescents who wish to define themselves against the inevitability of death, refuting the argument that they can only be considered mature when they define themselves in terms of their own death. Ultimately the texts have more to say about living than dying.

O brave new world

Indeed, most of the YA Gothic fictions that have had popular and widespread success following *Twilight*, and which have attracted a far wider readership than the largely predominant dark-romance *Twilight* clones, have been books focusing primarily on issues of autonomy and power. Novels such as Patrick Ness' *Chaos Walking* (2008–2010) trilogy, Michael

Grant's *Gone* (2009–2013) series, and Suzanne Collins' *Hunger Games* (2008–2010) trilogy depict protagonists who, having been torn from their parents' side too early, go on to forge strong alliances with their peer group and ultimately challenge the existing power structures. In "realist" YA fiction, Trites argues, the teenage protagonists must learn about "the social forces that have made them what they are. They must learn to negotiate levels of power that exist in the myriad social institutions within which they must function."[30] Although adolescents in such YA fiction are empowered to an extent, ultimately their individual power becomes repressed and reinscribed within the existing power structures, and the YA novel is generally found to be a genre which shows the teenager learning how to accept and live within the capitalist institutions that necessarily control and define their lives.

Teen Gothic, however, does not finally reinscribe adolescents within existing power structures. Power struggles that exist between individuals and institutions in realist YA novels generally lead to conflicts between adolescents and authority – generally a parent or parent substitute. While Gothic fiction for adolescents similarly, and often, depicts the teenager in various struggles for authority and autonomy, it does not generally perpetuate the status quo; the emphasis of Gothic fiction lies, rather, in overcoming repression and leaving ultimately empowered teenagers who do not necessarily, as Trites believes, "learn their place in the power structure" or "learn to balance their power with their parents' power."[31]

If it is Trites' argument that mainstream YA novels "teach adolescent readers to accept a certain amount of repression as a cultural imperative,"[32] then it is our argument that adolescent power is depicted in a far more positive and empowering fashion in teen Gothic texts, where power structures are shown to be challenged, compromised, and defeated. For Trites, the presence of parents in YA novels often proves problematic because they "usually serve more as sources of conflict than as sources of support. They are more likely to repress than empower";[33] this view for us, however, is captivated by a clichéd view of adolescence. Teen Gothic, conversely, is not concerned with portraying "out-of-control" teenagers rebelling against their parents, and, by extension, society, but rather reflects the adolescent's latent, and little acknowledged, fear of abandonment. Todd Hewitt, for example, the protagonist in Patrick Ness' *Chaos Walking* trilogy, is shown to have been "abandoned" twice over. An orphan from the outset, he is then forced to flee his loving adoptive family. Similarly, Caine Soren, the antagonist in Michael Grant's *Gone* series, is shown to struggle with the fact that he was the only one of twins to have been put out for adoption; he is then "re-abandoned" when all the adults vanish from Perdido Beach. By focusing on the postapocalyptic, teen Gothic thus addresses the adolescent's fear of "what would happen if" they were to suddenly lose the guidance of their parents (and/or parent substitute), as well as tackling questions of the nature of their power, autonomy, and authority within the wider world.

From Aldous Huxley's *Brave New World* (1932) and George Orwell's *Nineteen Eighty-Four* (1949) through to Anthony Burgess' *A Clockwork Orange* (1962), Margaret Atwood's *The Handmaid's Tale* (1985), and Cormac McCarthy's *The Road* (2006), there has always been a strong relationship between the dystopian novel and the Gothic tradition. The dystopian or postapocalyptic novel, where the action is taken out of the home and the present and into a wider, future world where the familiar is made strange, affords a useful scenario in which to fictionalize conceptions of adolescent autonomy. In keeping with Gothic fiction as a whole, post-disaster fiction is unlimited in its possibilities and can transgress all boundaries, supplying, therefore, a very broad canvas which, according to Kay Sambell, can be used to depict a wide range of narrative situations "dominated by authorial fears about the violent, inhumane social and political worlds young people seem likely to inherit."[34] Sambell, in agreement with many critics, maintains that post-disaster or dystopian fiction represents a future that "child readers must strive to avoid at all costs" and "didactically foregrounds social and political questions by depicting societies whose structures are horrifyingly plausible exaggerations of our own."[35] Indeed it does, but that is only to go halfway; if we look past "authorial fears" for society's future and concentrate instead on the actions of the individual protagonists in these texts, we can also read them as ultimately empowering narratives in which adolescents are allowed not only autonomy and agency, but, additionally, a say in how the world is run: a function denied to them in the "real world" of the here-and-now and a status that does not, perhaps, sit well with them. This is perfectly exemplified in Michael Grant's *Gone* series, in which, in a nod to William Golding's *Lord of the Flies*, the survivors of a nuclear meltdown are all children. Golding's children, however, were all under the age of 12, while Grant's group includes adolescents; his survivors are all under the age of 15. Although there is much infighting, violence, death, and horror along the way, the series shifts from Golding's pessimistic depiction of inevitable descent into outright savagery, and portrays instead the children, the adolescents in particular, as moving toward, rather than away from, civilization, and successfully attempting to create their own economy and government. The exploration of social possibility that these texts offer is not only the negative possibility of future disaster, therefore, but also the positive possibility of future empowerment. Their endings are usually explicitly redemptive and hopeful. Sambell criticizes such endings in children's and YA dystopian fiction. Reluctant to extinguish hope, she argues, they equivocate in delivering a moral; however, this is to concentrate too much on the purpose of the didactic nature of the dire warnings for the future of the world and not enough on the inherent message of autonomy and empowerment that are contained in the narrative process. For the adolescent reader, post-disaster fiction is not necessarily about a future to be averted but a fictionalized representation of what is already happening to them in their own world; in this respect, they are a critique of the existing social order not only in the didactic terms of the wider global issues posed by the danger of, for example, nuclear and environmental threats, but, more importantly, in terms of the adolescent's perceived lack of autonomy, agency, and their own sense of self.

As a result, the angst of adolescence can be portrayed on both a public and a personal level in post-disaster fiction, and this combination is nowhere more evidenced than in Suzanne Collins' *The Hunger Games* (2008).[36] The main protagonist of *The Hunger Games* is 16-year-old Katniss Everdeen, who lives in the postapocalyptic nation of Panem. Political control is exercised over Panem by the Capitol, a highly advanced and sophisticated metropolis. The titular Hunger Games are an annual event in which one boy and one girl, aged between 12 and 18, from each of the poorer twelve districts surrounding the wealthy and powerful Capitol, are selected in an annual ceremony called "the reaping" to compete in a televised battle to the death until only one victor remains. Initially devised as a punishment for a previous rebellion, the Games now serve as a demonstration of the Capitol's power and are used to keep the citizens of Panem subdued and in line.

When Katniss is selected at the reaping to take part in the Hunger Games, along with Peeta Mellark, she is already a protagonist coping without her parents. Her father died when she was 11, and her mother has been mentally absent ever since. From a young age Katniss has been the provider for her family, effectively both mother and father to her younger sister, Prim. Katniss has become emotionally autonomous before she should, having been forced to relinquish any dependence she may have had on her parents. She is also behaviorally and cognitively autonomous to a great extent; she functions independently, governs her own actions and behavior, and acts on personal decisions. However, while she has a sense of self-reliance, she does not believe that she has complete control over her own life because of the power structures governing Panem.

It is the Capitol's aim to have the competitors give up their autonomy and unthinkingly kill each other for the sake of entertainment, and the victor is promised a life of luxury, free of want. However, if Katniss and Peeta are to retain their individuation and independence, it is important that they resist the lure of the Capitol. Throughout the course of the Hunger Games themselves, and after many misunderstandings, each saves the other's life, and they are soon interdependent. This is not to say that either loses their independence; arguably we could say that this would have happened had either killed the other, for then they would have been fulfilling the desires of the Gamemakers and the Capitol, for whom the "real sport of the Hunger Games is watching the tributes kill one another."[37]

Although Katniss becomes aware that she could easily, in fact, be the victor in the Hunger Games, she soon realizes that in order to hold on to her own sovereignty she will have to risk death after all, but by her own choice, not at the dictate of the Gamemakers. When she and Peeta are the only surviving competitors, neither can kill the other, and they resolve, at Katniss' suggestion, to commit suicide. This is something of a calculated risk on Katniss' part. She shrewdly realizes that the Gamemakers, the Capitol, and the watching world, need "to have a victor";[38] she calculates correctly, and she and Peeta are quickly declared joint victors. For Katniss and Peeta, the suicide attempt was deemed a risk worth taking. Foucault explains how the ancient right of the sovereign body "to *take* life or *let* live" was replaced by the power of the social body "to *foster* life or *disallow* it to the point of death";[39] in this dystopian narrative, however, the development works in the reverse, and the power of the social body "to *foster* life or *disallow* it to the point of death" is seen to be replaced by the power of the sovereign (the Capitol) "to *take* life or *let* live." Although the Gamemakers may be deemed to have "let" Peeta and Katniss live by declaring them both victors, they could not make them take each other's life, and as such both of them have defeated the system. Additionally, Katniss and Peeta would have been happy to go through with the suicide, for they were putting themselves outside of any power structure, sovereign, social, or political. The Capitol makes it clear that it sees this as an act of rebellion, and the people of Panem come to view Katniss as the face of rebellion. Peeta and Katniss return home to support their families, with extra food rations granted in perpetuity; however, they are now adolescents who, having learned the importance of intelligence and autonomy, cannot return to live happily within the family home. They have transcended their dependence on family and community to reach a higher stage of development, and, wittingly or not, they are now revolutionaries; they are not seen to turn their backs on family and community, but rather to use their increased autonomy and power to bring about change on their behalf.

Teen Gothic texts focusing on power and autonomy generally depict protagonists who lose their parents suddenly (as opposed to rebelling against them) and are plunged into difficult situations. While they do overcome their loss, and gain an increasing sense of self and autonomy, this is not achieved by independently going forward in a state of complete self-reliance, but by forming new relational ties and undertaking greater social commitment. When the protagonists have the opportunity to return to their family, for example in *The Hunger Games* and *Gone*, they refuse to do so, not because they have been in any particular conflict with their parents, but because they have successfully become autonomous individuals and to return now to the family fold would be regressive. The texts have therefore addressed a key adolescent fear and shown that it can be overcome.

According to Trites, "adolescent literature seems to delegitimize adolescents ... even though the surface intention of most YA novels is ostensibly to legitimize adolescence."[40] She argues that adolescent literature is an institutional discourse which "serves to simultaneously empower readers with knowledge and to repress them by teaching them to accept a curtailment of their power."[41] In teen Gothic, the reverse is true. Teen Gothic texts bestow upon the adolescent an alternative viewpoint which allows them to see the world in a different way and crucially allows them to escape the didactic and instructive nature of "realist" texts. As such, the adolescents depicted in contemporary teen Gothic are also quite distinct from the adolescents represented in most Gothic fictions written for an adult audience. They are by no means the often passive beings of earlier Gothic fictions who tend to lack agency, autonomy, and any real control of their own lives, and who end up either dead, like Matilda and Conrad, or ensconced in a "suitable," economically viable, marriage, as do Emily and Catherine. Nor are they demonized simply for being adolescents in the manner of much later Gothic fiction, from *Dracula*'s Lucy, staked and stamped for her promiscuity, to Regan and Carrie, both literally demonized largely for being adolescents.

The protagonists in teen Gothic are shown to be adolescents negotiating the balance between an emerging sense of self as a competent individual, on the one hand, and a transformed, but continued, feeling of connection with significant others, on the other, and this emerging sense of self and autonomy is shown to be accompanied by an equally increasing awareness of their own personal power. Unlike depictions of sexuality in "realist" texts, which generally show the teenager disempowered by the consequences of their sexual actions, depictions of sexual desire in teen Gothic are most often positive, allowing teenagers to reappropriate their desire from institutional discourse. Misrepresentations of death in teen Gothic function to argue against death being the inviolable authority in adolescent literature and dispute the notion that adolescents can only be considered mature when they define themselves in terms of their own death. Consequently, teen Gothic yet again presents us with adolescents who do not succumb to institutional discourse. Finally, in contrast to "realist" fiction, gains in adolescent power and autonomy in teen Gothic are not subsequently repressed and reinscribed within existing power structures, but quite the reverse: The protagonists are generally shown to take control of their own destinies and, in due course, change their environment. Teen Gothic therefore forestalls the determination of issues that are considered to be relevant to adolescents by institutional discourse, and, by opening up an alternative window through which to view the world, allows adolescents to explore, question, and decide for themselves what it really means to be a young adult in contemporary society.

NOTES

1 David Punter, *Gothic Pathologies: The Text, the Body and the Law* (London: Macmillan, 1998), p. 6.
2 David Punter, *The Literature of Terror*, 2nd edn., 2 vols. (Harlow: Pearson, 1996), vol. II: *A History of Gothic Fiction from 1765 to the Present Day*, p. 191.
3 Roberta Seelinger Trites, *Disturbing the Universe: Power and Representation in Adolescent Literature* (University of Iowa Press, 2000), p. 88.
4 Nina Auerbach, *Our Vampires, Ourselves* (University of Chicago Press, 1995), p. 145.
5 Auerbach, *Our Vampires*, p. 131.
6 Joseph DeMarco, "Vampire Literature: Something Young Adults Can Really Sink Their Teeth Into," *Emergency Librarian*, 24:5 (1997), pp. 26–28, p. 27.
7 Annette Curtis Klause, *The Silver Kiss* (1990; London: Corgi, 1999).
8 Klause, *The Silver Kiss*, pp. 32 and 96.
9 Klause, *The Silver Kiss*, p. 127.
10 Klause, *The Silver Kiss*, p. 127.
11 Patricia Windsor, *The Blooding* (1996; London: Hodder, 1997).
12 Windsor, *The Blooding*, p. 189.
13 Windsor, *The Blooding*, p. 199.
14 Windsor, *The Blooding*, p. 212.
15 Windsor, *The Blooding*, p. 214.
16 Windsor, *The Blooding*, p. 214.
17 Windsor, *The Blooding*, p. 279.
18 *The Gothic in Children's Literature: Haunting the Borders*, ed. Anna Jackson, Karen Coats, and Roderick McGillis (New York: Routledge, 2008), p. 13.
19 Elisabeth Bronfen and Sarah Goodwin, "Introduction," in *Death and Representation*, ed. S. Goodwin and E. Bronfen (Baltimore, MD: The Johns Hopkins University Press, 1993), p. 4. The citation in the next sentence comes from p. 20.
20 Clive Seale, *Constructing Death: The Sociology of Dying and Bereavement* (Cambridge University Press, 1998), p. 1.
21 Trites, *Disturbing the Universe*, p. 118.
22 Trites, *Disturbing the Universe*, p. 118.

23 Trites, *Disturbing the Universe*, p. 118.
24 Elisabeth Bronfen, *Over Her Dead Body: Death, Femininity and the Aesthetic* (Manchester University Press, 1992), p. x.
25 Stephenie Meyer, the *Twilight* series (London: Atom, 2005–2008).
26 Meyer, *Twilight* (London: Atom, 2005), p. 277.
27 Meyer, *Breaking Dawn* (London: Atom, 2008), p. 349.
28 Meyer, *New Moon* (London: Atom, 2006), p. 9.
29 Meyer, *Breaking Dawn*, p. 356.
30 Trites, *Disturbing the Universe*, p. 3.
31 Trites, *Disturbing the Universe*, p. x.
32 Trites, *Disturbing the Universe*, p. 55.
33 Trites, *Disturbing the Universe*, p. 56.
34 Kay Sambell, "Carnivalizing the Future: A New Approach to Theorizing Childhood and Adulthood in Science Fiction for Young Readers," *The Lion and the Unicorn*, 28 (2004), pp. 247–267, p. 247.
35 Sambell, "Carnivalizing the Future," pp. 247–248.
36 Suzanne Collins, *The Hunger Games* (London: Scholastic, 2008).
37 Collins, *The Hunger Games*, p. 214.
38 Collins, *The Hunger Games*, p. 418.
39 Michel Foucault, *The History of Sexuality*, vol. 1 (1976), trans. Robert Hurley (London: Penguin, 1998), p. 138.
40 Trites, *Disturbing the Universe*, p. 83.
41 Trites, *Disturbing the Universe*, p. 140.

PART III

The Gothic and modern media

7

ELISABETH BRONFEN

Cinema of the Gothic extreme

Although cinema, born on the eve of the twentieth century, came late to Gothic culture, its proximity to the spectacle of the supernatural has turned it into the natural successor of a literary tradition concerned with ghosts, revenants, and demonic forces. As Martin Scorsese reminds us in his film *Hugo* (2011), Georges Méliès (1861–1938) was the innovator of this coupling because of his ability to adapt the theater of magic to the new medium of film. With his penchant for fairies, demons, and other marvels, for both journeys into unknown lands and chilling adventures in haunted houses, Méliès instigated the relation that film was to have with the Gothic, given the emphasis of both on an experience of the world beyond rational comprehension. As in Gothic fictions, the affective power of the cinematic image feeds on our willingness to believe in, and be moved by, apparitions of light and shadow cast on a white screen in a darkened room (like the black words on the white page of a Gothic novel or the projected specters in the lantern-show "fantasmagorias" of the eighteenth and nineteenth centuries).

Indeed, the charm of cinema depends on the viewer transforming an actual two-dimensional screen into a spectral three-dimensional world whose appearance is still the effect of the film being projected onto a white surface. Images imprinted on celluloid (or now digital cyberspace) that seem to come alive and whose movements render palpable an immaterial world hover between the actual and the imaginary, the present and the past. Neither the actors nor the locations where they perform are really present; they are perceptible only as remnants of a location that once existed. Although what we see and hear took place when the film was being shot, the world the actors move in is purely immaterial. We, in the audience, are really partaking in a shared experience of ghost-seeing. Giving shape as it does to an absent world, cinema's power of reanimation, however, is quite fragile. Even as people and scenes that were shot in the past are brought back to life, this uncanny reappearance heralds a subsequent revanishing.

Once the screen has again gone dark and the lights come on in the theater, the film's images disappear. The special relation film art has to the Gothic is thus both thematic and formal. Adapting plots, sets, and characters from its literary predecessor, Gothic cinema, precisely because it confronts us with uncomfortable realities yet also makes them ghostly, both calls up and keeps safely distant anxieties and forbidden desires deep in our culture and psyches. It thus uses the screen as a conceptual space where, by virtue of an embodied, yet also spectralized, performance, concerns that profoundly trouble a specific cultural moment can be addressed and worked through under the guise of seeming fictional.

At the same time, by viscerally staging vampires returning from the dead, human bodies transforming into their monstrous other, or grotesque creatures that exist only in fantasy, Gothic cinema self-consciously speaks to its own technical apparatus. Producing a double of the world it represents, the art form of film is involved in a hallucinatory enterprise, rendering tangible not actual but possible experiences. Gothic cinema, in fact, foregrounds the spectrality of the film medium by undercutting all semblance of "realistic" verisimilitude, seeming to open a passage between the spiritual beyond and the material here. Telling stories based on blurring the boundary between life and death, human and animal, flesh and machine, these films speak to the uncanniness of their own mode of communication as it gives imaginary tangibility to what is physically absent. By addressing unresolved cultural concerns too, Gothic cinema evokes a past in the name of a future where persistent fears might possibly be put to rest. On screen, however, these distinct time zones and states of mind become inseparable, giving shape again to disturbing apparitions that sustain the tension between ghostly reappearance and an anticipated revanishing. The special relationship cinema has to the Gothic is thus first and foremost grounded in the gesture of haunting that they both enact.

It's a strange world

Blue Velvet (1986) offers a good point of departure for a discussion of the specifically postmodern version of Gothic cinema this essay focuses on, a postmodernism that deals with an increasingly more violent, technological, deceptive, and conflicted world by taking to new extremes the kinds of haunting that Gothic films have always achieved. The opening scene of David Lynch's picture introduces the incursion of violence into the ordinary everyday that will render Lumberton, a clichéd rendition of small-town America, suddenly uncanny. As a dark blue velvet curtain, swaying in the breeze, transforms into the bright blue sky over a row of suburban homes, each enclosed by a white picket fence, a red truck drives across the screen, with a fireman waving to us. Then, out of the blue, the elderly Mr. Beaumont, suffering a stroke while hosing down his backyard, falls to the ground and the camera penetrates below him into the earth, until, in an extreme close-up, it comes upon a group of bugs digging their way through the soil. Something lies beneath the surface of this home-town idyll which insists on erupting into our field of vision. Indeed, we have a perfect cinematic rendition of Freud's suggestion that the uncanny is the frightening experience of the return of repressed material within what we call "home": "*Heimlich* is a word the meaning of which develops in the direction of ambivalence, until it finally coincides with its opposite, *unheimlich*," disclosing the uncanny as being a subspecies of *heimlich*, the homely.[1] Although such experiences draw attention to something which ought to have remained hidden but has suddenly come to light, the prefix "un-" signals the indelible link between something long known and the strangeness negating that surface but also underlying it.

In German, the word "uncanny" (*unheimlich*) explicitly links the onslaught of the strange to the actual home (*Heim*), so that the domestic family space is both the original position from which the uncanny develops and the target of its onslaught. Occurrences of the uncanny hint that the home was always already split in itself, familiar and strange, safe and dangerous, and it is precisely this dark inversion of the ordinary that *Blue Velvet* celebrates. Once Mr. Beaumont's son Jeffrey has returned home from college to run the family business while his father is recovering from his stroke, he draws out three interlinked arenas of Gothic violence that trouble surface normality. Seeking to investigate a drug-related crime, Jeff finds himself drawn into a sadomasochistic game with the nightclub singer Dorothy Vallens, who forces him to acknowledge a perverse side to his sexual desire he had so far kept unconscious. Moving into her nocturnal underworld, he is also confronted with the sadistic violence embodied by the gangster Frank Booth, who functions as the obscene counterpart to the fallible father of the opening scene. Refiguring the rite de passage common in the Gothic fiction of Ann Radcliffe, the film's script has Jeff destroy this demonic figure of underworld crime so as to contain his own prohibited sexual drives. Yet the opening scene also locates violence in primordial nature, a Real beyond and beneath all surface representation. By also drawing attention to the frailty of the human body, it introduces mortality as a further destructive threat to the familiar safety of quotidian life.

Lynch's world is clearly allegorical, foregrounding the forces of temptation and destruction in the proverbial garden American culture has erected in the wilderness. The actual historical moment of 1986 is translated into a mythic geography that descends from canonical American texts such as Brockden Brown's *Wieland* or Hawthorne's "Young Goodman Brown." Yet the homage Lynch pays to this tradition deploys a significant gender reversal. While it is Sandy, the daughter of a local police detective, who initially provides Jeff with clandestine information about the nightclub singer, he is the one to step into the shoes of the classic Gothic heroine. His curiosity will repeatedly bring him into situations of danger, compelling him to walk down dark corridors and enter forbidden rooms in search of the key to a mystery which is as much about the crime he seeks to solve as his own perverse desires. Once he has embarked on his quest to save Dorothy from her evil oppressor, his entire world transforms into a hallucinatory dreamscape in which he becomes an accomplice in the sadomasochistic game connecting all three characters. He explains to Sandy, "I am seeing something that was always hidden, involved in a mystery and it's all secret." As the boundary dissolves between his fantasies and what he experiences in the underworld of Lumberton, both the obscene violator and the violated woman emerge as distorted versions of himself.

Lynch takes the Gothic tradition to an unusual extreme most, though, in the self-conscious artifice of his cinematic language. What renders this prototypical American small town uncanny is first the excessive sharpness and intense color of the images of Lumberton even during the day. The initial images of *Blue Velvet* signal to us that this is not a realistic representation of provincial life, but a recycling of our nostalgic fantasy of 1950s suburbia. Lynch also deploys an eerie undercurrent of sound to mark the visual transitions between the ordinary world and its dark inversion. In a scene early on in the film we see Jeff, who, having picked up a human ear he found lying in the grass, has decided to pay Detective Williams a visit. As he walks along the street at night, we hear a ghostly rustle on the soundtrack, then a close-up of the ear is superimposed over his body, and, as the camera moves into the dark void at the center of this ear, the sound submerges us into its cavernous emptiness while our hero fades from the visual frame. At various points in the film, a similar break with realism, marking the unbridled intrusion of fantasy into the ordinary, uses the close-up of a burning flame, pairing it with the distortion of human voices and bestial growls. While, on the soundtrack, "Blue Velvet" and other 1950s pop songs support the nostalgia for an earlier time, the repeated superimposition of strangely warped sounds onto the ordinary soundscape intimates the primordial world of unrestrained instincts only barely contained by the codes of cultured behavior, then as now.

As in so many classic Gothic texts, at the end of Jeff's voyage through Lumberton's underworld, order is restored. Yet Lynch maintains his tone of excess, undercutting the very idyll he reinstalls. As the camera slowly pans away from the inside of Jeff's ear in the final scene, we find him blissfully sleeping in the safety of his own backyard. Sandy's voice, calling out that lunch is ready, wakes him. It could all have been his dream. As he joins her and Aunt Barbara in the kitchen, he finds both women staring at a robin perched on the windowsill. Earlier on in the film, Sandy had told Jeff of a dream in which thousands of robins, suddenly set free, flew down on the darkened world, bringing with them a blinding light of love. Once Aunt Barbara notes in disgust that this particular robin is holding a live bug in its beak, Sandy, smiling cannily, reiterates Jeff's line from the prior scene: "It's a strange world." Providing apparent closure to excess, the editing moves from a close-up of the robin to shots of yellow tulips and red roses behind a white picket fence and the red fire truck, which, along with the bugs, had been part of the film's opening tableau. Having panned back up into a bright blue sky, it ends where it began, with the blue velvet curtain swaying in the breeze.

The forces of evil may have been contained, but the disturbing story the film projection called forth remains as a memory trace. Part of the Gothic formula postmodern cinema inherits is the repetition-compulsion that promises a return of the repressed on which our fantasies rely. Another aspect of this legacy is the conviction that the Gothic serves a symbolic negotiation of personal and collective fears, confronting us with troubling concerns under the guise of seeming fiction. By bringing the dark inversion of small-town America to the screen, *Blue Velvet* tries to identify the criminal violence and sexual excess riddling 1980s culture, even while, as Fredric Jameson suggests, it illuminates the failure of this attempt because it reduces "itself to the recombination of various stereotypes of the past."[2] What the aesthetic gesture of recycling finally achieves is that by pairing the haunting of a primordial Real with the haunting of previous cinematic representations of it, a transhistorical strangeness within the ordinary is retained on screen.

Types of Gothic creatures

In the expressionist style of Weimar cinema, the collective shock of World War I was successfully refigured in Gothic film narratives. *The Cabinet of Dr. Caligari* (1920), *Dr. Mabuse: The Gambler* (1922), and *Nosferatu* (1922) use madness, criminal magic, and the invasion of a foreign vampire to offer mythic resolutions to the sustained shell shock of the postwar era. During this haunted interwar period, Hollywood also produced film adaptations of canonical Gothic texts. Four versions of *Dr. Jekyll and Mr. Hyde* appear between 1911 and 1941. Both James Whale's *Frankenstein* and Tod Browning's *Dracula* premiere in 1931, while Poe's tales of horror are variously brought to the screen (among others, "The Fall of the House of Usher" twice in 1928 by James Sibley Watson and John Epstein; "The Raven" by Lew Landers in 1935). Yet, even though the Gothic is prevalent in the period that marks the rise of the Hollywood Studio System, as Misha Kavka notes, "there is no delimited or demonstrable genre specific to film called the Gothic."[3] Instead, it hovers as an umbrella concept above categories like suspense, terror, horror, and the spooky. Keeping that in mind while moving historically beyond the classic Hollywood period as well as the occult films of New Hollywood such as Roman Polanski's *Rosemary's Baby* (1968), William Friedkin's *The Exorcist* (1973), and Steven Spielberg's *Close Encounters of the Third Kind* (1977), this chapter will now map the postmodern appropriation of a Gothic extreme. The lack of clear genre definition means it will speak about films that deploy a Gothic sensibility in the sense of a particular attitude toward pervasive problems of postmodern existence. The Gothic film gesture is one of rendering intellectual and socio-cultural crises in excessive visceral, as well as visual, terms.

It is fruitful at this point to recall that, because the extreme marks the position furthest from a designated center, as a stance it involves having no fixed position. As the center shifts, so, too, does the gesture of destabilizing categories that have evolved around it. If, then, in its attempt to contest the norm, any extreme position must repeatedly begin anew, it is the rhetorical gesture of this repetition which postmodern Gothic cinema foregrounds. I have isolated three sets of Gothic creatures – spectral ghosts, doubles, and, as a cluster, zombies, aliens, and cyborgs – to discuss how a blurring of the distinction between bodies and belief systems continues to *reflect* and *reflect on* cultural anxieties which remain unfinished business in Western culture. Part of their Gothic legacy is that these films offer up stories about how troubling events from the past, once they have been played through again on screen, come to be resolved. As they refigure traditional stories of revenants and vampires, these films are often themselves haunted by the other art forms from which cinema emerged in the course of the nineteenth century: literature, photography, and magic theater. Furthermore, by keeping the cultural legacy of Gothic haunting alive, but in a cinematic way, these films keep enacting a process of repetition. While playing to the need for mythic solutions to unsolvable antagonisms of postmodern existence, Gothic cinema keeps showing that such containment is nothing more – but also nothing less – than a protective fiction. Watching it, we continue to be haunted by both the reality and the fictionality of haunting itself.

Ghosts of the past

Stanley Kubrick's *The Shining* (1980), still considered to be one of the scariest movies ever made, thrives on a repetition-compulsion in more than one sense. At the beginning of the film, the writer Jack Torrence, about to take on the job of winter caretaker at the Overlook Hotel, discovers that his predecessor ran amok and killed first his family and then himself. Drawn into a bond with this phantom Charles Grady, Jack will attempt to repeat the history of paternal violence that has come to be contained at the site of this luxury resort once it is cut off completely from the rest of the world by a snow storm. Yet, from the start, several types of haunting are at issue, apart from the echoes of Stephen King's 1977 novel of the same name. Ever since Jack came home drunk one evening and, during a violent scuffle with his son, dislodged the boy's shoulder, Danny has "the shining." Upon his arrival at the Overlook, Danny is thus the first to have visions recalling the actual paternal violence that took place there. He sees torrents of blood flooding the corridors as well as the two Grady children, revenants that have been resurrected from death, as mangled corpses. These preternatural visions encode his justified fear of his father's proclivity to brutality even while they also serve as portents. Because Danny is in tune with monstrous specters of the past, warning him of what will happen if he remains, he is able to devise an escape for himself and his mother.

Jack, in turn, becomes the target of two separate types of haunting. On the one hand, the phantom Grady he converses with in the ballroom functions as an embodiment of his repressed murderous instincts. Under the influence of his suggestion, Jack's own mental breakdown accelerates. With an axe in his hand, he too becomes obsessed with the idea of destroying his family. Read in this way, the phantom Grady is less an occurrence of the occult than the externalized embodiment of Jack's mental anguish (the uncanny), erupting into the open after having been restrained. From his wife, Wendy, we discover that, after hurting his son, Jack had stopped drinking so as to prevent further abuse. The abandoned hotel can be read as the stage where a tendency to violence can be re-encoded as the onslaught of demonic possession. At the same time, the Overlook also serves as a force field that draws Jack in so that he might take on the part that spirits of the past have designated for him. The ballroom, transporting him into a past world where he can be served alcohol unavailable to him in the present, emerges as a place of spectral residue. For those emotionally attuned to such a passage, the past inhabits the fabric of the present to assure that its spirit is kept alive. As Grady explains to his successor, "you were always the caretaker here." Jack's hallucinations thus also raise the issue of the transhistorical spirit of male violence, seamlessly moving from one body and one era to the next. The ballroom thereby serves as the stage where personal histories of domestic brutality intersect with America's history of violence. The elegant world of leisure Jack returns to in his hallucinations is set in the prohibition era, when alcohol-related crime had its heyday, indicating that this historical moment has also left its traces in the contemporary world.

In both cases, the Overlook functions as what Michel Foucault has called a heterotopia – a disorderly countersite to the normal that actually exists, reverse-mirroring and contesting the ordinary world.[4] Here, instead of writing his novel, Jack transforms into the medium through which forbidden fantasies of domestic destruction can again occur. Once he has begun to explore his new uncanny home, his son Danny, in turn, becomes the medium through whom the victims of paternal violence speak. The father's attitude to the Gothic experience is thus diametrically opposed to that of his son. While Jack is drawn further and further into hallucinations of a past he prefers to his actual present (equated as it is with the myth of sovereign paternal power), Danny treats these as portentous signs meant to help him abandon this arena of spectral visitations. Yet the Overlook Hotel is also a heterotopia in another sense, given that it critically reflects on cinema itself. The notion of "a shining" is what connects the represented story with our position as spectators. If the hotel renders visible traces of things that happened in the past, so, too, does the film screen; like those characters who have the shine to them, we, too, are privy to these apparitions. In the rooms of the hotel as well as in the cinema, a traumatic history of violence, both personal and collective, is shown to inhabit the fabric of the present. The temporal loop played through by the story is reduplicated so well that, on screen, our present is shown to fold into a transhistorical past, whose force, though ultimately contained by the narrative, can resurface in our field of vision even more violently than before.

Kubrick's Gothic extreme thus plays to the power of possession in both senses of the word. The past, as unfinished business, takes hold of the film's characters as it takes hold of us, presenting itself to us as a cultural legacy we cannot *not* acknowledge. At the end of *The Shining*, Danny has successfully lured his manic father into the heart of the maze outside in the park while cannily covering his tracks as he surreptitiously finds his way out. Yet the final shots of the film move from Jack's upper body, frozen to death in the snow, to a photograph hanging on the wall inside the hotel. Here too, standing in the center of a group of hotel guests that fill the frame, he is frozen in a gesture of acclaim, his right hand forever waving to us. The picture bears the inscription, "Overlook Hotel, July 4th Ball, 1921." This final shot takes a film narrative about a failed writer back to cinema's own beginning in photography. The spirit of violence has been contained in the double sense of the word. Although in death Jack's murderous desire has been restrained, his survival as a photographic image suggests that this demonic force has also been preserved. In the logic of Gothic cinema, it can always be released again, even if only in the shape of apparitions when we again watch *The Shining*. This final shot references the actual history subtending the film's fictional narrative only obliquely, and yet the frozen image of Jack's smiling face offers its own portentous warning to us that male violence will not go away simply by our supposing it a thing of the past.

Trouble with the double

The uncanny double, giving shape to a fascination with the division and changeability of the modern self, is predicated on a different blurring of the boundary between imagination and reality. As Mladen Dolar notes, by confronting the subject with a living image of himself, this particular Gothic creature produces two contradictory effects. On the one hand, the double "arranges things so they turn out badly for the subject."[5] On the other hand, because he commits transgressive acts and indulges in an obscene enjoyment the subject would never allow to himself, the double also "realizes the subject's hidden or repressed desires." A narcissistic dialogue with the self is played through, which is dangerously pleasurable because it is predicated on screening out the reality of the external world along with the symbolic laws regulating it. Yet even as the subject is drawn ever more into the world of his fantasies, he realizes that he must fight against the phantom embodiment of his egotistic desires. The uncanny self-duplication ends in a final showdown, in which, because he was unaware that "his only substance and his very being were concentrated in his double,"[6] the subject, by killing his adversary, kills himself, as in most versions of *Dr. Jekyll and Mr. Hyde*.

With *Fight Club* (1999), based on a 1996 novel by Chuck Palahniuk, David Fincher refigures this standard Gothic narrative on the eve of the twenty-first century so as to address a cultural crisis in masculinity beyond the older one of *The Shining*. His nameless hero, played by Edward Norton, gives birth to an imaginary friend in order to break out from the constraints of postmodern consumer culture. With Tyler Durden (or rather *as* him), he founds a fight club, where he and his band of like-minded brothers can indulge in unbridled masculine aggression. Their brutal fights in the cellars of forlorn buildings seem invigorating because these offer a correction to the effeminacy dictated to them by their jobs in the service sector of corporate America. The creation of an imaginary double allows the Norton figure to abnegate responsibility for this enjoyment of primitive masculine drives. He can tell himself that Tyler, not he, is the leader of an alternative masculine corporation that soon takes the anger these young men feel toward late capitalist culture to another level. The house he moves to on Paper Street becomes the training camp for a private army, planning to blow up the financial district of San Francisco – uncannily anticipating the attack on New York's World Trade Center by several years.

Significant are the two changes Fincher introduces into the standard doppelgänger plot. On the one hand, he reconceives the figure of the young woman, who, as the spoiler of the narcissistic dialogue between the subject and his double, must be gotten rid of. His Marla Singer, unlike her literary predecessors, resiliently pits her bemused gaze at Norton's self-delusions. Contesting the hallucinations he insists on submerging himself into, she embodies the voice of a reality principle that will not go away. On the other hand, Fincher refigures the obligatory showdown in such a way that his hero, by successfully resisting the fatal lure of the double, is shown to take on responsibility for his actions. Having failed to prevent the attack on the financial district which, as Tyler promises him, will bring them one step closer to economic equilibrium, the Norton figure comes up with a ruse whereby he can at least put an end to his dangerous hallucinations. He has reached the top floor of the building from which he and his gang have a view of the target of their imminent assault. The ethical turn Fincher introduces into the traditional plot is that his hero turns the gun not on his double but on himself, viscerally accepting the consequences of his fantasies. Willing to perform an excessive act of self-mutilation, in which the head as site of the imagination and the Gothic creature it has produced coexist, results in Tyler's vanishing in thin air, just as Marla enters the scene. Having relinquished his imaginary friend, our hero can finally acknowledge a love that moves beyond narcissism as he watches the spectacular collapse of the buildings. It is a form of waking up. And yet a moment of self-reflexivity is retained. The glass window in front of which this newly formed couple stands is itself a screen. The spectacle of the buildings collapsing against a nocturnal sky celebrates cinematic hallucination taken to an extreme.

The Prestige (2006), in turn, based on a different reconception of the uncanny double in Christopher Priest's 1995 novel, offers its own self-commentary by returning to the magical theater from which cinema emerged. Christopher Nolan exceeds the standard plot by introducing two types of reduplication. Set in London on the eve of the twentieth century, the story revolves around the vicious competition between two magicians, Robert Angier and Alfred Borden (who is made to look like Georges Méliès in his projection of doubles via film-magic). Each makes use of a double for an act in which the magician first disappears, only to reappear at a different location in the theater. Borden's illusion feeds on a natural doubling of the body. He has an identical twin with whom he shares both the stage and his private life as husband and father. This secret bond serves a narcissistic satisfaction. It allows the two men to successfully dupe their audience as well as Borden's wife, who only slowly comes to realize that the woman assisting her husband on stage is also his mistress. To keep up the illusion, his twin is even willing to cut off two fingers on his left hand once Borden loses them in an accident.

Angier, in turn, ups the ante on his rival by having a scientist build him a demonic machine using electric energy, not to transport bodies but rather to reduplicate them. This is a kind of magic placed deep in the Real, presenting the Gothic supernatural as the toxic inversion of scientific progress. To sustain his illusion, Angier must get rid of the double after each act, and so he has the body on stage fall into a water basin placed beneath the trap door, in which, because Angier has had it locked, he drowns, while the reduplicated self reappears high up in the gallery of the theater. Desperate to discover his rival's trick, Borden's double breaks into this secret space beneath the stage, where, unable to save the drowning man, he is caught by the police, tried for murder, and found guilty. Having a twin proves fortuitous for Borden, however, because after the execution of his double, he can confront the man who set this trap for him. In the warehouse in which the tanks containing all the corpses of Angier's duplicates are stored, Borden turns the classic showdown to his advantage. He can shoot his rival with impunity, since his twin has already sacrificed his life for a crime that not he but Angier committed.

What is extreme is not just the restorative turn that Borden's tragic recognition takes on the level of the narrative, but also the self-reflexive commentary in the film itself. At the beginning of *The Prestige*, Nolan uses parallel editing to cut between (a) the magical performance during which Borden's twin is caught beneath the stage of his rival and (b) an older magician (Cutter) as he is explaining to Borden's daughter the three acts to every magic trick. The first act is "the pledge." A magician shows you something ordinary and asks you to inspect it to convince yourself that it is, indeed, normal. The second act involves a "turn" in which the magician takes the ordinary something and makes it do something extraordinary. "You may want to know the secret but you won't find it," Cutter assures the young girl, because "you don't want to really know. You want to be fooled." A third act, called "the prestige," is necessary to complete the magic. What disappeared is brought back. This is, of course, also a definition of the magic of cinema itself.

At the end of the film, we return to this scene of instruction, only now the parallel editing moves between Cutter, speaking to the young girl, and Borden, committing the murder for which his twin unjustly received the death penalty. As Cutter finishes, the daughter finds the father whom she thought to have been executed, now returned to her, fulfilling the prestige. The film, however, ends in the warehouse with the tanks containing all of Angier's drowned doubles. As we backtrack in the narrative to just before the reunion of father and daughter, Cutter's voice-over repeats the final point of his instruction; only now he is addressing us. We are the ones who do not really want to work out the secret because our enjoyment is predicated on a wish not to know. "You want to be fooled," he assures us as the screen goes black. The narrative restitution that reunites a father with his daughter is uncannily linked to Nolan's own comment on cinema as a sustained game-playing with the dangers of the double, which do not disappear with the end of the film.

Zombies, aliens, and cyborgs

A different recognition is at issue in George Romero's *Dead* films, given that these reconceive the zombie tradition from early 1940s films in more recent political terms. Over the decades, the plot structure has remained constant, revolving around a group of people thrown together in a situation of crisis, seeking to stay alive. While this band of fugitives fends off the onslaught of the dead who have returned from their graves, a second set of predators comes into play: bloodthirsty hunters and military personnel out on a rampage. And while the zombies, slowly moving in hoards as if in a collective trance, terrify us with their unremitting drive to satisfy their hunger for flesh, Romero equally shocks us with the ease whereby gunmen can take them out by giving them a head shot. Survival, we are compelled to realize, is nothing other than one side of a two-sided death drive. Extreme are not only the graphic representations of zombies biting into and devouring living bodies, with blood splattered all over the scene. Equally acute is Romero's persistence in adjusting this narrative to the political issues driving a given decade. When *Night of the Living Dead* first came out in 1968, his audience was more than familiar with search-and-destroy missions in Vietnam and could immediately see the connection between local militia and US combat units. They could readily associate the sound of helicopters and the dehumanized language of the sheriff ordering the extermination of the zombies with the news coverage they were seeing daily on TV.

One decade later, Romero's *Dawn of the Dead* (1978) taps into the contemporary malling of America. Consumed by consumer culture, the zombies here return to the shopping center in which two members of a SWAT team and two journalists seek shelter because that is the one aspect of their former life the zombies have retained. As the Caribbean-American policeman explains to his terrified partners, these zombies are driven by the place itself. Astutely recognizing that these zombies are merely an uncanny reflection of ordinary consumer confidence, he laconically adds: "they're us, that's all." More recently, Romero's *Land of the Dead* (2005) offers a Gothic refiguration of the Bush era's encouragement of social irresponsibility on the part of the wealthiest of the nation. The zombies now offer a monstrous representation of the disenfranchised poor, excluded from the privileges of social prosperity, relegated to the other side of a walled city, and thus uncannily recalling New Orleans after hurricane Katrina. Striking back, they have turned the city into a war zone, and yet, once again, Romero's political point is an insistence on mutual recognition. At the end of the film, the hero could kill Big Daddy, the African American zombie who has been leading his troops in their successful attack on politicians who turn a blind eye to the suffering of others. But Riley chooses not to, explaining to his fellow survivors, en route with him to the Canadian border, "they're just looking for a place to go, same as us."

In Romero's *Day of the Dead* (1985), the scientist who studies zombies in an effort to domesticate them is called Dr. Frankenstein by the military protecting him, indicating a debt to Mary Shelley's student of the occult. Focusing not on a patchwork of dead body parts but, like *Day of the Dead*, on the design of cyborgs, Ridley Scott's *Blade Runner* (1982) speaks even more directly to postmodernity's anxiety regarding research on artificial intelligence. In contrast to zombies, who fall monstrously short of what is considered human, the replicants manufactured by the Tyrell Corporation represent human perfection, and, in the year 2019, show us where genetic engineering might lead. These posthuman bodies radically destabilize the notion of the human. Only a complicated test can distinguish them. Furthermore, Tyrell's newest model, Rachel, has successfully been implanted with false memory so that she herself is convinced she is human. Adjusting the Frankenstein story to the late twentieth century, Scott's film gives more extreme agency to his artificial creations. The narrative allows Roy, the leader of the band of replicants who have returned to earth to demand more life from their maker, to destroy his creator. Then, like Shelley's monstrous creature in the final passages of the novel, he, too, is given the most poetic lines of the film as he accepts his death.

True, in a manner far more conciliatory than its literary predecessor, Scott's cinematic adaptation imagines a future world in which humans and machines can coexist. Deckard, the title character, though, whose job is to terminate rogue replicants (although he may be one himself), chooses to flee with Rachel instead. After all, what postmodern cinema draws from the Gothic is a fear that the notion of the human may or may not be sustainable. Yet a far more sinister critique of the ethics of scientific research surfaces in the *Alien* trilogy of films. Like Romero's zombie pictures, these stories also revolve around a group of people who must defend themselves against the onslaught of an enemy, monstrous in that it takes the idea of the brute animal to an extreme by intermixing it with mechanical parts and enabling it to disappear into spacecraft technology. In these films too, the battle is fought on two sides. On the one hand, Lt. Ripley, a scientist sent by the Weyland-Yutuni Company to discover life-forms on other planets, repeatedly fights against the destructive Alien Queen her spaceship unwittingly stumbles upon in *Alien* (1979). On the other hand, Ripley is equally forceful in her struggle against the company that seeks to make use of the lethal force of this creature for its biological-weapons program. Once more, the Gothic serves to explore the toxic underbelly of rational knowledge not only taken to an extreme, but also coupled with the sinister interests of the military-industrial complex.

At the same time, this series of films pointedly refigures the Gothic heroine. Though Ripley is driven by feminine curiosity, she is everything but vulnerable. Instead she herself becomes uncanny, infusing the body of the resilient female warrior with a maternal instinct. Shelley's *Frankenstein* criticizes a masculine will to create that appropriates the maternal function without taking responsibility for the consequences. The *Alien* trilogy, in turn, plays through postmodern anxieties regarding the monstrous potentials of maternity by offering excessively visceral depictions of the engendering of supersized killer creatures, which (in contrast to Shelley's creature) no longer even resemble humans. Ripley engages this fear about her own body when she, the good double to the vicious Alien Queen, brutally jettisons her enemy from her spaceship at the end of *Aliens* (1986). She then fuses these two sides even more acutely in *Alien³* (1992) when, having discovered that she herself is the host for a baby Alien Queen, she throws herself into a cauldron of burning lead to prevent the company from taking possession of her monstrous progeny.

A more appealing resolution to the murky interface between scientific research into nonhuman life-forms and America's military interests can be found in *Super 8* (2011), a Gothicized homage to Steven Spielberg's *E.T.* (1982) in which J. J. Abrams is unusually self-reflexive regarding the power of cinema to disclose cultural anxieties. His small band of high-school students, who, in the summer of 1979, witness an alien escaping from a secret Air Force convoy, do so while shooting a zombie movie. Joel and his friends are able to unravel the mysterious disappearance of fellow towns-people because they are "movie smart" when it comes to supernatural occurrences. Their education in Gothic films has even endowed them with an attitude toward extraterrestrial creatures more complex than the brute force deployed by the military. In his blind effort to recapture the escaped creature, the Air Force officer in command has not only had everyone evacuated, but also allowed his troops to open fire, transforming this small town into a domestic war zone. Joel, the central character, by contrast, has respect for the distraught creature. He has discovered that the Alien's blind will to destroy is merely a reaction to the cruel treatment it has experienced at the hands of the Air Force, which has tortured it for scientific purposes. In fact, its predicament is meant to remind us of what would have happened to E.T. if he had actually fallen into the hands of NASA rather than having made his way back safely to his spaceship with the help of friendly humans.

If showing compassion for the monstrous other is the lesson Abrams has learned from Gothic cinema, his *Super 8* builds on this idea to intervene in the culture of conspiracy that emerged after 9/11, in which repressive reactions against terrorist threats to international security have turned the monstrous into the fallout that comes with globalization. Like Mary Shelley, who, in contrast to her egotistic scientist, recognizes the dignity of her creature, the showdown between Joel and the Alien in a subterranean cave is based on acknowledging alterity. Rather than fleeing in terror, the boy walks directly toward his attacker and, explaining that he knows bad things have happened, assures it that it still has the chance to live. The sublime final moment of the film celebrates a third position between destroying the foreign other (be it zombie, cyborg, or alien) and self-destruction. Back on the main street of their devastated hometown, Joel and his friends watch in rapture as the Alien, having finally completed the reparation of his space-ship, takes off as E.T. did. Soon the sparkling lights of the gigantic structure are nothing more than a faint glitter in the nocturnal sky. With this image, Abrams offers his own homage to the special affinity which cinema, as a site for experiences of alterity (be this horror or ecstasy) has always had to the Gothic. The performance of boundary transgressions Gothic cinema thrives on has steadily maintained its ethical intent. We are compelled to take note of the real consequences which, in the worst and best case, imagining the possible – and even the impossible – can ultimately have.

ELISABETH BRONFEN

NOTES

1 Sigmund Freud, "The Uncanny" (1919), in *The Standard Edition of the Complete Psychological Works of Sigmund Freud*, ed. and trans. James Strachey, vol. XVII (London: Hogarth, 1955), pp. 219–252, p. 226.
2 Fredric Jameson, "Historicism in *The Shining*" (1981), in *Signatures of the Visible* (New York and London: Routledge, 1990), pp. 82–98.
3 Misha Kavka, "The Gothic on Screen," in *The Cambridge Companion to Gothic Fiction*, ed. Jerrold E. Hogle (Cambridge University Press, 2002), pp. 209–228, p. 209.
4 Michel Foucault, "Different Spaces," in *Aesthetics, Method, and Epistemology* (London: Penguin, 1998), pp. 175–186.
5 Mladen Dolar, " 'I Shall Be with You on Your Wedding Night': Lacan and the Uncanny," *October*, 58 (1991), pp. 5–23, p. 11.
6 Dolar, "I Shall Be with You," p. 11.

8

CHARLES SCRUGGS

American film noir

Film noir – that dark, shadowy, grim, mysterious, and largely city-based form of filmmaking – attained worldwide prominence with the 1941 film of Dashiell Hammett's novel *The Maltese Falcon* (1930).[1] Most critics argue that this kind of film adapted features of what had established itself as the "urban Gothic" in literature by the 1930s and would fully blossom as film noir with the coming of World War II. Actually, though, the mainly American inspiration at the root of film noir stems from World War I, the Great War (1914–1918), a war which the historian George Kennan has called "the seminal catastrophe of the Twentieth Century."[2] It is the fact and aftermath of this war, I want to argue here, that brought about the revision and deepening of the urban Gothic that we see in film noir in its most classic forms in the 1940s, 1950s, and 1960s, and indeed in extensions of it to this day. For instance, is not the title of the recent zombie film *World War Z* (2013) a reference to World War I, as though "A" leads naturally to "Z"? Both wars – one fictional, the other real – underscore a Gothic theme of human beings turning into grotesques, ghouls, or monsters. Hence George Romero's *Night of the Living Dead* (1968) is both a zombie movie and a dark take on American life as the living dead look for their victims in the suburbs. The reality of World War I could be just as bizarre. Photographs of surreal, gas-masked soldiers emerging from the poisoned fog of the trenches in World War I became dramatized in film noir as sinister figures walking down black, wet streets, through labyrinthian alleys and the ubiquitous fog. The literary and cinematic perception of what that war meant led to the Gothic interplay of dim light and ominous shadows that the French critic Nico Frank was the first to name "film noir" in 1946.

This war, in addition to the ravages of World War II, after all, is the background to Harry Lime's remark to Holly Martins (Joseph Cotton) in the very strong Gothic-noir film *The Third Man* (1949) as these two Americans "look down" upon the Lilliputian world below from atop a Ferris wheel in Vienna. From Lime's perspective, the human beings seen from above are only "dots," insignificant to his plans for getting rich quick. He sells adulterated penicillin on the black market, killing hundreds, mostly children, each day. In other words, he is replicating in microcosm the enormous carnage of the Great War. One theme that emerged from this war is that our fabled moral compass is a fiction. Making the naive Martins and the unscrupulous Lime Americans is not accidental. Lime echoes the American war profiteers of World War I (e.g., "Daddy" Warbucks in *Little Orphan Annie*) and Martins, as a writer of dime-novel westerns, reluctantly comes face to face with the Gothic world of hideous secrets in war-torn Vienna. Screenwriter Graham Greene also wants audiences to make a connection, not only between the Vienna of World War I and that of World War II, but with the internationalism that the Great War began for the United States, despite its surface isolationism of the 1920s and 1930s. Before the Great War, Vienna was the center of the vast but unstable Austro-Hungarian Empire, the location of a government that made the crucial decision to punish Serbia for the assassination of Archduke Ferdinand. This was the catalyst for the war, leading to the downfall of the empire itself, and resulting in a weakened Austria annexed by Hitler only twenty years later (1938), one so weak that it opened itself to an unscrupulous underworld of black-marketing and profit-taking. Historical events like this one have convinced many historians that both World War I and World War II should be considered together as a "thirty-year war" (1914–1945), and I believe that *The Third Man* shows why that should be so, even as it highlights how film noir as a mode is rooted in issues stemming from World War I.

Before the Great War, American space, as it had in the past, appeared limitless. From Alexander Hamilton's *Federalist* paper no. 9 (1788) to Hector St. John de Crèvecœur's *Letters from an American Farmer* (1781) to Frederick Jackson Turner's Frontier thesis (1893), open space was the key element in the concept of American "exceptionalism," the belief that America, as a nation, was different from other nations. Although the Frontier was declared closed in 1890, Turner implied that American ideals, created by open space, could be transported to other nations. Despite the emergence of the United States from World War I relatively unscathed and wealthy (New York replaced London as the banking center of the world), American space seemed to shrink, primarily because of the transformation of the nation into a security state in which paranoia replaced dialogue. Three texts after the war also helped shut down a prewar optimism, especially among intellectuals. Freud's famous essay on "The Uncanny" (1919), Georg Lukács' *The Theory of the Novel* (1920), and D. H. Lawrence's *Studies in Classic American Literature* (1923), all deeply concerned about what had happened to the Western world, appeared within five years of the war's official end and had a profound effect on film directors, especially the émigrés from Europe who adapted German expressionism on film to the American film-noir style.

To show all this, I want to focus on Ernest Hemingway's story "The Killers" (1927) and four cinematic adaptations of it. This story illustrates two Gothic themes that find their way into film noir: the shrinkage of American space into an increasingly built-up world filled with threats in its narrow alleys and deepened shadows *and* the eruption of the past into the present that calls into question the American small town as the country's most valorized space. Put another way, in film noir, the existential void of "no man's land" replaced what Herbert Croly called *The Promise of American Life* (1909). Thus the urban Gothic in noir cinema could be both darkly claustrophobic and terrifyingly vast and empty, much as the fear-based sublime can be in Edmund Burke's *Philosophical Enquiry into the Origin of Our Ideas of the Sublime and the Beautiful* (1757). Applied to the small town, the Gothic motif is different from the "revolt from the village" movement that we associate with other American literary texts before and after the Great War (e.g., Sinclair Lewis' *Main Street*, 1920). In the "revolt from the village" scheme, American intellectuals flee the small town because of its confined, puritanical space, sometimes going abroad to recreate their own village world in Paris. The film noir view of the outmoded village is different. It does not satirize the village but rather exposes its dark center. It debunks the American myth of the village as the great, good place by revealing its Gothic past.

Another valorized spatial image within American mythology is the idea of home. Hemingway's story not only shatters that idea but foreshadows the absence of home as a refuge in film noir. "Although there are occasional houses in film noir," in the words of Vivian Sobchack, "there are hardly any homes." Film noir's dominant spatial images are "mean streets," rooming houses, cafes, motels, and cocktail lounges, but almost never homes.[3] This cinematic detail coincides with a post-World War I sociological fact. The census-takers of 1920 told Americans that they were now an urban culture, no different in this respect from their European counterparts, and that fact, coupled with American imperialism before the war (over Hawaii, Cuba, the Philippines, Latin America), would fuel a new conception of American society. Veterans of World War I Raymond Chandler and Dashiell Hammett would write for the newly created *Black Mask* (1920), a pulp-fiction magazine that featured hard-boiled detective fiction and whose settings were the modern city and its sinister underworlds. Similarly, James M. Cain and Hemingway, both World War I veterans as well, would also write stories about modernity that would become the inspiration for some of the greatest films noirs of the 1940s. It is this succession of cultural developments that would set the stage for both "The Killers" in print and all the films noirs that followed.

The carnage of the Great War was of a magnitude never seen before. As Christopher Clark has recently remarked, "the conflict that began that summer [1914] mobilized 65 million troops, claimed three empires, 20 million military and civilian deaths, and 21 million wounded. The horrors of Europe in the Twentieth Century were born of this catastrophe."[4] It is worth noting that Stanley Kubrick, one of film noir's great directors (*Killer's Kiss*, 1955; *The Killing*, 1956; *The Shining*, 1980), never made a World War II film but made a brilliant one about World War I: *Paths of Glory* (1957), a film shot in black and white, which connects the nightmarish landscape of the war to the bureaucracy that perpetuates it. Later he would make another war picture about Vietnam, *Full Metal Jacket* (1987), depicting a war that according to Robert Hughes on BBC television was America's World War I.[5] This film was in part a send-up of *Sergeant York* (1941), a Hollywood vehicle that celebrated not only the backwoods sharpshooter Alvin York but the pastoral America of his young manhood. In the film, this American hero of World War I picked off German soldiers as though they were wild turkeys. In *Full Metal Jacket*, the sniper is a young girl, protecting her home, and holding off a squad of Marines until finally wounded, taunted, and killed.

World War I, then, would shape the ideological conflicts of the new century and would define the nature of all the wars that followed. In terms of the political scene, the war triggered both the Russian Revolution (1917) and the Irish Rebellion (begun in 1916), but the "shock of the new" that came as the biggest awakening was the horror of modern warfare: machine guns, mustard gas, tanks, airplanes, and guns so monstrous that they blew people to bits. This technological "sublime" was the dark side of the Industrial Revolution, what Robert Hughes has called "industrialized death" ("Powers"). The phrase "missing in action" first appeared in World War I, as did "shell shock," and the fears at home about both would not go unnoticed in film noir, especially the resulting sense of the individual as cannon fodder (devalued, insignificant, inconsequential – what Harry Lime calls "dots").

Gregory G. Pepetone has written perceptively about the influence that this "War of Horror," as he has called World War I, has had on popular culture, especially upon American monster movies such as *Frankenstein* (1931), *The Invisible Man* (1933), and *The Wolfman* (1941).[6] But I would like to differ with him on one point, that "the impact of the Great War, which shattered European culture, was less so to American culture."[7]

Although the United States did not enter the war until 1917 and its military forces were "over there" for only eighteen months, American society underwent a radical transformation. At home, the war created the "surveillance state" that at first sanctioned the Ku Klux Klan and supported the suppression of dissent and the censorship of the press. The state also created the Bureau of Investigation, the future FBI. The failure of Wilson's "Fourteen Points" at the Treaty of Versailles (1919) also coincided with the Red Scare of 1919, a terrible irony in that Wilson had urged toleration of, and self-determination for, nation-states on the international scene and then sent to prison or had deported those who expressed negative opinions at home. This harsh treatment of dissidents resulted in the labor strikes and terrible race riots of that same year, the worst in American history up to that time.[8] All these factors created an atmosphere of paranoia, violence, and terror that was reflected in the stories published in *The Black Mask*.

Later, the Depression period of the 1930s would be linked to this wartime atmosphere in films such as *Black Fury* (1935) and *Fury* (1936), but most especially *I Am a Fugitive from a Chain Gang* (1932). This picture begins with a decorated World War I veteran returning home only to find out that the real war is "over here," not "over there."[9] Unable to find a job in Depression America and falsely accused of a robbery, he ends up on a brutal southern chain gang from which he twice escapes. At the end of the film, he is shellshocked and alienated from a country that is no longer home. The film's final scene is especially chilling, one of the most shocking in American cinema. After his second escape, James Allen (Paul Muni) disappears into the vast unknown for a year, only to emerge at the home of his former socialite fiancée. Stunned by his appearance and erratic behavior, she asks how he "lives." As he disappears into the shadows out of which he came, his final words are "I steal."

The film ends with these words, leaving a portrait of a veteran who is homeless and on the run. This theme of homelessness was underscored in the same year *I Am a Fugitive* was released by a historical event: the march on Washington by the Bonus Army, jobless World War I veterans, who wanted their promised bonuses immediately rather than on the promised date of 1945.[10] These warriors who fought for their country "over there" would be brutally attacked, and some killed, by the same army at home to which they formerly belonged. This theme of the United States as "another country" also appeared in several Hemingway stories in the 1920s, especially "Soldier's Home" (1925), a story of domestic and national alienation that would be resurrected not only in the brilliant post-World War II film *The Best Years of Our Lives* (1946), but in many post-Vietnam cinematic narratives such as *Born on the Fourth of July* (1989), *Home of the Brave* (2006), and *Stop-Loss* (2008).

The philosophical basis of "homelessness" in American film noir is Freud's postwar essay on "The Uncanny," an essay often referred to by literary scholars (along with Julia Kristeva's 1980 spin on Freud's essay in *Powers of Horror*) as articulating the psychological basis of Gothic fiction. Georg Lukács' *Theory of the Novel* also focuses on the same theme but in a different context, literary and historical rather than mental and familial. Lukács, for instance, argues that the novel is an "expression of ... transcendental homelessness" in which the traditional epic, because of changing economics and the newer beliefs that arose to explain them, metamorphosed into "a world" of many more unknowns "that has been abandoned by God."[11] Lukács intends his thesis to refer to the history of the novel, but, given the date of his book's publication (1920), his thesis seems even more appropriate to World War I than to the seventeenth century.

It is Freud, however, who most links the uncanny with World War I and (by extension) with film noir. Freud never mentions war neuroses in "The Uncanny" (although he would point to them in his equally famous essay published in 1920, "Beyond the Pleasure Principle"), but it is there by implication in his exegesis of the German word *heimlich*. Freud notes the double meaning embedded within the word: that which is both "familiar" and "unfamiliar." In German *heim* means "home," and the derived adjective, *heimlich*, means that which is "home-like" or "familiar," as are spaces within the home such as the kitchen or the parlor. But the home also contains spaces "concealed from sight," such as the basement or the attic, the "unfamiliar."[12] In his analysis of the source of dread, Freud uses the house as a metaphor for the human psyche, which like the house contains spaces once familiar but now buried and hidden because associated with some trauma. Those repressed spaces, however, can return unexpectedly, without warning, terrifying us because we do not understand their source. James Whale, the director of both *Frankenstein* (1931) and *The Bride of Frankenstein* (1935) and himself a Great War veteran, would avail himself of Freud's ideas in *The Old Dark House* (1932) in which the haunted house full of lunatics becomes a metaphor for those ancient empires and their doddering rulers who sacrificed their young during World War I. The house's mad patriarch is 102 years old and his equally mad oldest son is determined to burn down the house and everyone in it. The film is reminiscent of one of the most celebrated of postwar German expressionist films, *The Cabinet of Dr. Caligari* (1920). Its narrator turns out to be a madman in an asylum for the insane and, compounding the irony, the tale he tells is of an evil doctor who murders by proxy but who in "real life" is the director of the asylum, or so it seems. The asylum itself, the film implies, contains not only a tale told by an idiot but a director who is himself mad and a murderer, a metaphor for those who ran the war and those who fought it.

In his essay, Freud was investigating not only the unconscious mind but also the terrors of history, the terrors released by the war itself. In his classic text *The Great War and Modern Memory* (1975), Paul Fussell quotes an aged veteran who recalled his experiences in the trenches in similar terms: "In fifty years I have never been able to rid myself of the obsession with No Man's Land and the unknown world beyond it. This side of our wire everything is familiar and every man a friend; over there, beyond their wire, is the unknown, the uncanny."[13] Did this man know Freud's essay? It is probably just the opposite: Freud no doubt listened to those returning from the war and drew his own conclusions that modern technology created a new kind of Gothicism in which the "familiar" before 1914 (planes, trains, automobiles as symbols of progress) became the source of dread, the "unfamiliar." No man's land is a phrase that remains in common parlance to this day, but it really refers to what was once a pastoral landscape (e.g., the poppies in Flanders fields), now transformed into the devastated, grotesque landscape of barbed wire, machine-gun nests, and mustard gas hovering like fog in the alien trenches. This industrialized wasteland appears again and again as a setting in film noir: *The Maltese Falcon*, *This Gun for Hire* (1942), *The Naked City* (1948), *Night and the City* (1950), *The Third Man*, *Panic in the Streets* (1950), and *The Big Combo* (1955), among others.

Americans at home experienced the landscape of the "unfamiliar" in terms of modern technology that was used to spy upon them. In a brilliant, though unfinished, essay called "The State," published posthumously in the same year as "The Uncanny," Randolph Bourne described the state's "health" as dependent upon keeping people in a constant condition of anxiety, terror, and dread: "War," he said with bitter irony, "is the health of the State."[14] During peacetime, Bourne argued, the state lies dormant, but once war is declared it arises like Lazarus from the grave to swallow up the government and its citizens who then act with a single voice and with a monolithic force, as does Fritz Lang's automaton in his film *Metropolis* (1927). This monster then proceeds to stifle all dissent, coercing its citizens to act in total concert. The flag as a symbol replaces the country with its diverse ethnic strands and classes, and it is used as a club to create fear and hatred of a demonized other. Blind loyalty replaces civil liberties and freedom of speech, as the state becomes an all-seeing eye like some grotesque Cyclops.

This cultural setting affected a whole generation of filmmakers. Pepetone notes that directors such as Fritz Lang, James Whale, and later Robert

Siodmak, Otto Preminger, and Billy Wilder were émigrés who grew up with the cultural memory of the Great War.[15] Wilder, director of the powerful *Double Indemnity* (1944), was asked by an interviewer if World War I and German anti-Semitism during the 1930s shaped his "dark" outlook on life. Wilder responded tellingly: "I think the dark outlook is an American one."[16] What he likely means is that Wilder's European experience gave him the insight to perceive the "dark" side of the American experience. This could also be said of D. H. Lawrence, who wrote of Fenimore Cooper's *Leatherstocking* novels of the nineteenth century that "the essential American soul is hard, isolate, stoic, and a killer. It has never yet melted."[17] This last sentence especially suggests that Lawrence saw a connection between the horrors of American history and those of the postwar era. In 1920, President-Elect Warren G. Harding wanted American society after World War I to return to "normalcy," but Lawrence suggests that "normalcy" is the Gothic killer on the American scene that has never gone away. As Julia Kristeva has argued, it is one thing to "throw off" that which the human being does not want to acknowledge (the "abject") but quite another to cast away "the corpse . . . a border that has encroached upon everything. It is no longer I who expel, 'I' is expelled."[18]

Just two years after Lawrence published *Studies in Classic American Literature*, Hemingway published his own take on the "essential American soul" and the "corpse" that cannot be expelled in his brilliant short story "The Battler." This Gothic tale of the past erupting into the present was part of his hybrid cycle of short stories *In Our Time* (1925). In that collection, Hemingway saw violence as endemic to "our time," as he juxtaposed World War I stories with stories of violence set in America, especially in "The Battler," in which he reversed the master–slave relationship, much as did Melville in "Benito Cereno" (1855–1856). Perhaps it was this latter story that Malcolm Cowley was thinking of when he linked Hemingway with those "haunted and nocturnal writers" within America's literary tradition: Poe, Hawthorne, and Melville.[19]

"The Battler" is an ironic title, since Hemingway depicts a world in which there is warfare but there are no winners. Young Nick Adams has been riding the freight trains and has received a blow from a brakeman that gives him a black eye, but this is only a prelude to his initiation into a darker kind of violence, a nightmare on a larger scale. He stumbles upon a camp in which he meets an aging boxer, so beat up from the ring that his face looks "like putty in color."[20] Taking care of him is a seemingly benevolent "negro" named Bugs: very polite, very deferential, but vaguely sinister. The two ask Nick to share a meal with them, but when the boxer, Ad Francis, asks Nick for a knife to cut the bread, the atmosphere changes.

Bugs tells Nick not to give Ad the knife, and Ad, instead of directing his hostility toward Bugs, threatens Nick. Without any warning or hesitation, Bugs clubs the boxer with a blackjack. Although he pretends to be protecting Nick, there seems to be some kind of malicious delight in the act, some form of ancient retribution for an ancient crime. Nick leaves this troubled setting in a daze as if he had been the one hit by the blackjack. There is even a hint in this story of Kristeva's "corpse" that cannot be thrown off. Ad confesses that he is crazy but says that Nick has never been "crazy." Bugs responds ominously: "he's got a lot coming to him."[21] Some of it already has, as Nick has just caught a glimpse into the "corpse" of American history that will not go away.

A camp can be a temporary shelter. It can also be a prison in which life is reduced to "bare life."[22] In "The Killers," though, Hemingway exposes the American small town as only that, a shelter whose fragility can be revealed at any moment. In this story, two urban thugs, comically dressed like cinematic bad guys, appear out of nowhere at a small-town diner and change the atmosphere of the diner into one of terror. Those in the diner – Nick, George, and Sam (the black cook) – discover that the gangsters are there to kill the Swede, whom they have never met, "to oblige a friend."[23] The story's complexity resides not only in Nick's horrified reaction to the event – that such a thing like murder for hire could happen, and in his small town – but also in his awareness that in America after World War I there is no place safe from violence and that the Swede passively accepts his fate. It is for this reason that Robert Penn Warren argues that the story is about Nick and his "discovery of evil," not about the "killers" or the Swede. Yet Warren raises an interesting question: If it is Nick's story, then why is the story named "The Killers"?[24]

The history of film noir in adapting "The Killers" attempts to answer that question. The story's various adaptions keep suggesting that the "killer" or "killers" can be anyone and any thing in American society because, as Lawrence saw, "the essential American soul … is a killer." Each filmic interpretation shifts its Gothic focus, but taken together they blur the boundaries between film noir (roughly 1941–1952) and the neo-noir that came later. The cinematic versions of Hemingway's story start with the story itself and its origins in World War I; then each subsequent version is not only an interpretation but adds to an accumulated Gothic vision of America. What constitutes the Gothic in these films is the incremental repetition of telling and retelling the same story whose total effects create an alien landscape, reminiscent of "no man's land" from the Great War. The "seminal catastrophe" of the Great War is like a snowball rolling downhill that acquires more layers from the Depression and World War II. The films of the 1940s and early 1950s are not simply the result of the technological sublime of 1914–1918 or the surveillance state of 1917–1919. These films are the culmination of several historical moments, for behind these films lies the troubled history of the republic itself over several decades after 1914–1918, as D. H. Lawrence saw when he analyzed America's literary past.

Hemingway's story "The Killers" was twice made into films with that title (1946 and 1964) and then twice again with different titles: *Out of the Past* (1947) and *A History of Violence* (2005). In the 1946 version, the first twenty minutes dramatize the whole Hemingway story; the rest is then a flashback that explains what Hemingway chose to leave a mystery: the thing the Swede (Burt Lancaster) did to get "in wrong." This omission was deliberate, for Hemingway came to believe that "you could omit anything if you knew that you omitted and the omitted part would strengthen the story and make people feel something more than they understood."[25] This observation also helps explain the style of noir, especially its Gothic effects, because the artifice of more shadow than light, wet streets, multiple reflections (mirrors), deep focus (with its emphasis on background and foreground in the same frame), and "restless and unstable" space can just as readily make viewers "feel something more than they [understand]." The sometimes melodramatic plots of these films are one thing, but the cinematography is another. As Hemingway said of his story "Big Two-Hearted River," it was about coming home from World War I "but there was no mention of the war in it."[26] This is true of his story "The Killers" and true of its cinematic sequels. What was "omitted" was what the cinematic techniques and settings still conveyed: Home was not the home depicted in the sentimental World War II films such as *The Human Comedy* (1943), *The Very Thought of You* (1944), and *Since You Went Away* (1944).

If the 1946 film tried to explain what the Swede as ex-boxer did "wrong," the film's stylistics say that no one can explain it, that the Swede's anguish is beyond explanation. The 1964 version shifts its attention to one of the cold-blooded killers, Charlie (Lee Marvin), who is determined to find out who hired him and why a man would just wait to die without any resistance. As he discovers, a woman was involved, but what unsettles his cool is the recognition that there is a mystery that cannot be explained. Unhinged by this conundrum, he loses his focus as a killer, making himself vulnerable to a villain he would ordinarily have for breakfast. In the final scene, in which he is dying, the rifle falls from his hand, and he pathetically pulls out an imaginary gun, having only his fingers with which to shoot. His impotence links him with the very man, Johnny North (John Cassavetes), he set out to kill.

At the heart of both film versions of "The Killers" is the femme fatale, Ava Gardner in 1946 and Angie Dickinson in 1964, but, as Mary Ann Doane has noted, the femme fatale in film noir is not always so easy to define: "she harbors a threat that is not entirely legible, predictable or manageable,"[27] a potential carried over from the darkly sinful women of the eighteenth-century Gothic, such as Laurentini in Radcliffe's *The Mysteries of Udolpho* (1794) and Matilda and the Bleeding Nun in Lewis' *The Monk* (1796). The female threat is particularly emphasized in *Out of the Past*, which again rewrites the Hemingway story. In this version, director Jacques Tourneur doubles the film's femme fatale, Kathie Moffat (Jane Greer), with her black maid, Eunice Leonard (Theresa Harris). Suddenly race and racial history add to the story's complicated narrative about fall guys, bad women, and corporate crooks.

The story begins with a killer coming into a small California town, Bridgeport, looking for Jeff Bailey (Robert Mitchum), who is not at the car garage he runs but relaxing with his small-town girlfriend by a pastoral lake amid the stunningly beautiful Sierra mountains. Just as he is describing to her the "home" he wishes to build by a cove "over there," the Kid (Dickie Moore), his deaf-and-dumb helper, signs with his hands that someone is looking for Bailey. That someone is really his past catching up with him, but, as the sign language suggests, that past is coded, mysterious, a Chinese box in which the past resurfaces to expose the petty viciousness of the small town, the corrupt politics of the big city, and the racial mystery that underlies it all. Kathie may be a bad girl, but she too has her story – as does Eunice – and those two stories have both shattered the myth of American space that points to the possibility of home, now with the added ghost within that space of the dark past that once enslaved African Americans and kept discriminating against them through and after World War I.

All four film versions of this story begin with the same "normalcy." Ordinary life, the films say, is very good – but fragile and easily shattered. In the story's most recent film treatment, *A History of Violence* (2005), the Swede is recast as Joey Cusack (Viggo Mortensen), who was once a part of the mob scene in Philadelphia but now runs, under the name of Tom Stall, a respectable family restaurant in a small town in Indiana. He is married with two children and has assumed the persona of a modest businessman who loves his wife, children, and community. By the end of the movie, violence permeates everything, including the small town.

The movie begins with the killers invading the town, thinking that knocking over Stall's restaurant will be easy pickings and discovering to their horror that Joey has not forgotten his violent past. He kills both of them, thereby becoming a local hero, but the act brings him to the attention of people in Philadelphia he thought he had left behind. As killers, they travel to the small town, and what follows is more mayhem, including the revelation of the hidden violence within his hitherto pacifist son and his devoted wife. After Joey has murdered his own brother and his gang of thugs in Philadelphia, he returns home to face his bewildered family. The final shot is not comforting: Both wife and husband have to face their new selves. They have reinvented themselves, but not in line with the American dream. In her excellent study *Murder Most Foul*, Karen Halttunen notes the number of real-life "gothic narratives of family murders" in nineteenth-century America. She argues, as does this film, that the "domestic-gothic represented the family as the site of dark mysteries and unspeakable horrors."[28]

The "domestic-gothic" is made strikingly clear and given a new twist in black director Carl Franklin's brilliant take on "The Killers" called *One False Move* (1992). Like Spike Lee and John Singleton, Franklin has reworked the noir formula to place the emphasis on where it belongs, on *noir*. He is especially adept in revising the pastoral metaphor, especially the image of the southern garden. It may have been a heaven for some, but, as Toni Morrison shows in her novel *Beloved* (1987), it was a nightmare for others. Indeed, the "false move" in the title of Franklin's film is at first deceptive. The opening scenes imply that the drug murders in LA are the crimes that should concern us, that this film set in LA, with its cinematic history of films noirs, will be a thriller in which the streetwise detectives – the one black, the other white – will track down urban criminals. Even more misleadingly, the movie appears to be an interracial "buddy" movie like *Lethal Weapon* (1987) and *Die Hard* (1988). But Franklin has his two LA cops follow the trail of clues to the small town of Star City, Arkansas, the place where, we discover, the real crime has occurred. Here the situation in Hemingway's story is reversed. The two who enter the small town are not killers but two self-assured, streetwise police officers who confront their own naiveté at the same time as they uncover the primal crime in American history, what Lawrence called the "essential American soul."

Franklin's aim in this revisionist film noir is to jolt us, Gothically, into recognizing that the horrific past is a continuing presence in American life. And he does this brilliantly through reworking the image of the femme fatale. Although Leila Walker (Cynda Williams) plays a part in the drug deal gone bad in LA, her history begins in Star City. Raped as a teenager by Dale Dixon (Bill Paxton), the town's sheriff, she left her son in Star City when she began her life of crime. Her homecoming turns out to be horrific, one that even shocks the big-city cops who have assumed all along that Dale is no more than a country bumpkin and that the worlds of LA and Star City are light years apart. By the end of the movie, however, Franklin shows us that in traveling south from LA we have simply returned to the first "fallen" city, the one founded by the fratricide Cain, who in black folklore turned a ghastly white when confronted with the enormity of his crime.

As all scholars of the American Gothic have acknowledged, Leslie A. Fiedler in *Love and Death in the American Novel* (1960) has pointed especially well to "the savage colored man" (African, Native American) as a source of the Gothic in American literature.[29] As *Out of the Past* and *One False Move* illustrate, film noir is popular culture's continuation of Fiedler's thesis that "behind the gothic lies a theory of history, a particular sense of the past."[30] What the Great War did, of course, was to open the door to a renewed interest in American history and American letters. It is no accident that the Melville revival began in 1921 with Raymond Weaver's biography of Herman Melville and his 1924 edition of Melville's last manuscript, *Billy Budd*. As Melville saw in "Benito Cereno," American history, if looked at closely, was frightening not only in terms of its terror but also as the banality of evil: the slave trade as everyday commerce. Moreover, as Justin D. Edwards notes, the crimes within America's past are not limited to the African presence: "gender, homosexuality, incest, genocide, rape, war, murder, religion, and class" are also " 'proper' subjects of the nation's Gothic literature."[31] Over time, the same has become true of film noir and neo-noir.

The Great War, of course, officially ended in 1918, but its aftershocks (e.g., the war between Greece and Turkey, the counter-revolution in Russia) continued into the 1920s. In 1919, the Treaty of Versailles was signed in a room known as the Hall of Mirrors, an architectural image that would become a visual metaphor in film noir (e.g., *Phantom Lady*, 1944; *The Dark Mirror*, 1946; *The Lady from Shanghai*, 1947) for the multiple perspectives that this kind of neo-Gothic cinema brought to bear on America's past and present. This sense of mystery at the heart of the American Gothic is the opposite of American melodrama. Linda Williams has argued that American melodrama begins, and wants to end, in a "space of innocence" which is almost always the idea of "home." The idea of "home" is what gives melodrama its "moral legibility." "The 'main thrust' of melodramatic narrative," she insists, "is ... to get back to what *feels* like the beginning."[32] Film noir reverses this pattern. The "beginning" may be Pandora's box just waiting to be opened, as this peculiarly Gothic kind of cinema brings back the recurrent American nightmares that become especially acute in modern memory after all the changes set in motion by the Great War.

NOTES

1 Paul Schrader, "Notes on Film Noir," in *Film Noir Reader*, ed. Alain Silver and James Ursini (New York: Limelight, 1996), pp. 53–64, p. 54. See also Foster Hirsch, *The Dark Side of the Screen: Film Noir* (Cambridge, MA: Da Capo Press, 2001), p. 10.
2 See Belinda Davis, "Experience, Identity, and Memory," *The Journal of Modern History*, 75 (2003), pp. 111–131, p. 111.
3 Vivian Sobchack, "Lounge Time," in *Refiguring American Film Genres: Theory and History*, ed. Nick Browne (Berkeley, CA: University of California Press, 1998), pp. 129–170, p. 138.
4 Christopher Clark, *The Sleepwalkers: How Europe Went to War in 1914* (New York: Harper, 2012), p. xxiii.
5 Robert Hughes, "The Powers That Be," Episode 2 of *The Shock of the New* (London: BBC, 1980; Ambrose Video DVD, 2011).
6 Gregory G. Pepetone, *Gothic Perspectives on the American Experience* (New York: Peter Lang, 2003), pp. 95–108.
7 Pepetone, *Gothic Perspectives*, p. 101.
8 David M. Kennedy, *Over Here: The First World War and American Society* (New York: Oxford University Press, 2004), pp. 75–92; Christopher Capozzola, *Uncle Sam Wants You: World War I and the Making of the American Citizen* (New York: Oxford University Press, 2008), pp. 143, 201–205.
9 See both *I Am a Fugitive*, dir. Mervyn LeRoy, and *Heroes for Sale* (1933), dir. William Wellman, both from Warner Brothers.
10 David M. Kennedy, *Freedom from Fear: The American People in Depression and War, 1929–1945* (New York: Oxford University Press, 1999), p. 92.
11 Georg Lukács, *The Theory of the Novel: A Historical-Philosophical Essay on the Forms of the Great Epic Literature* (Cambridge, MA: MIT Press, 1990), pp. 41, 88.
12 Sigmund Freud, "The Uncanny," in *Collected Papers*, trans. Joan Riviere, vol. v (London: Hogarth, 1949), pp. 368–407.
13 Paul Fussell, *The Great War and Modern Memory* (New York: Oxford University Press, 1975), p. 79.
14 Randolph Bourne, *The Radical Will: Selected Writings 1911–1918* (Berkeley, CA: University of California Press, 1977), p. 360.
15 Pepetone, *Gothic Perspectives*, p. 102.
16 Robert Porfirio, "Interview with Billy Wilder," in *Film Noir Reader 3: Interviews with Filmmakers of the Classic Noir Period*, ed. Robert Porfirio, Alain Silver, and James Ursini (New York: Limelight, 2002), pp. 101–119, p. 101.
17 D. H. Lawrence, *Studies in Classic American Literature* (Garden City, NY: Doubleday, 1951), p. 73.
18 Julia Kristeva, *Powers of Horror: An Essay on Abjection*, trans. Leon S. Roudiez (New York: Columbia University Press, 1982), pp. 3–4.
19 *The Portable Malcolm Cowley*, ed. Donald W. Faulkner (New York: Penguin, 1990), p. 317.
20 Ernest Hemingway, "The Battler," in *The Complete Short Stories of Ernest Hemingway: The Finca Vigía Edition* (New York: Scribner, 1987), pp. 95–104, p. 99.

21 Hemingway, "The Battler," p. 100.
22 Giorgio Agamben, *Homo Sacer: Sovereign Power and Bare Life* (Stanford University Press, 1995), pp. 37–38, 65–67.
23 Ernest Hemingway, "The Killers," in *The Complete Short Stories*, pp. 215–222, p. 218.
24 Robert Penn Warren, "The Killers," in *Understanding Fiction*, ed. Cleanth Brooks and Robert Penn Warren (New York: F. S. Crofts, 1943), pp. 306–325, pp. 316–317.
25 Ernest Hemingway, *A Moveable Feast* (New York: Scribner, 1964), p. 75.
26 Hemingway, *A Moveable Feast*, p. 76.
27 Mary Ann Doane, *Femmes Fatales: Feminism, Film Theory, Psychoanalysis* (New York: Routledge, 1991), p. 1.
28 Karen Halttunen, *Murder Most Foul: The Killer and the American Gothic Imagination* (Cambridge, MA: Harvard University Press, 1998), pp. 168–169.
29 Leslie A. Fiedler, *Love and Death in the American Novel*, rev. ed. (New York: Stein and Day, 1966), p. 160.
30 Fiedler, *Love and Death*, p. 136.
31 Justin D. Edwards, *Gothic Passages: Racial Ambiguity and the American Gothic* (University of Iowa Press, 2003), p. i.
32 Linda Williams, *Playing the Race Card: Melodramas of Black and White from Uncle Tom to O. J. Simpson* (Princeton University Press, 2001), pp. 19, 28.

9

ISABELLA VAN ELFEREN

Techno-Gothics of the early-twenty-first century

The Gothic is changing. Its haunted visions adapt to the speed of techno-logical development. Our monsters no longer look and sound like robots: They are biotechnological life-forms, speaking holograms, or omniscient computer networks. Simultaneously, we nostalgically hark back to tech-nologies and monsters of yore and integrate them into our technologically enhanced daily life. We make "authentic" Instagram snapshots with our mobile phones, we buy cuddly toys shaped like H. P. Lovecraft's horrible Cthulhu online, and we post messages about both activities on Facebook, hoping our friends will "like" them. As technological advances reshape our fears and our desires, new techno-Gothic modes arise. This chapter charts the ways in which early-twenty-first-century technological developments transform Gothic fiction and film. It argues that the hybridization of Gothic with horror, science fiction, dark fantasy, new weird, and steampunk leads to three new techno-Gothic genres: singularity Gothic, cloud Gothic, and weird Gothic. Each of these, in turn, renews one of the building blocks of Gothic itself: spectrality, liminality, and metaphysical speculation.

Singularity Gothic / new specters

Cultural responses to late-twentieth- and early-twenty-first-century techno-logical developments have produced three new Gothic specters. All three focus on cybernetics, the merger of human and machine-based being. First, there are stories about all-too human machines: artificial intelligences which, in the tradition of *Frankenstein*, seem to have acquired human characteristics such as independent cognitive skills, creative agency, or emotion. Second, an increasing group of Gothic narratives addresses the (bio)technological enhancement or modification of the human body or mind, leading to the incorporation of the machine-based (or the machinic) into the human. The third technological specter is perhaps the most terrifying one: the techno-human hybrid in which technological and human provenance have been amalgamated into a new type of being, the indistinguishable Third that is neither Self nor Other but an uncanny blend of both.

The specter of the sentient machine is a familiar figure in Gothic and science-fiction reflections on technoculture. The shape it acquires depends on the type of techno-anxiety that is being projected onto it. The early twenty-first century was predicted to become the era of "the technological Singularity" by mathematician and science-fiction (SF) writer Vernor Vinge. In 1993 Vinge described the scientific developments that would, in his eyes, inevitably lead to the genesis of "entities with greater than human intelligence."[1] Technological evolution would then endorse the survival of the most intelligent, and human being as we know it would cease to exist. Vinge envisioned that the technological singularity could be established in a number of ways. The most well-known of these scenarios features independently thinking and acting artificial intelligence (AI): sentient robots, androids, or cyborgs. The exponential growth of AI technology since the late twentieth century has thus far produced various types of machinic sentience, but in spite of Vinge's predictions none of them qualify as "superhuman": while IBM supercomputer Watson won television's *Jeopardy* in 2011, proving that computers can extract cognitive solutions from data, other applications such as the robot vacuum cleaner show that independent machinic agency has a long way to go before it matches that of humans.

Despite the fact that no one will feel threatened by a robot that fails to hoover their house, though, practical obstacles do not stop Frankensteinian anxieties from being addressed in popular culture. This type of singularity is envisioned as able to destroy human life in numerous films: a "new order of intelligence" causes nuclear war in *The Terminator* (1984), for instance, and intelligent machines make human life impossible in *The Matrix* (1999). Invariably these nightmare visions of the future are depicted in Gothic imagery, with bleak landscapes painted in dark colors, humans surviving in subterranean labyrinths, and trauma and paranoia driving their psychology.

The portrayal of the sentient machines themselves has undergone significant changes over the last few decades. Between the 1960s and the 1980s, singularity had a comfortingly machine-like face. The robots C-3PO and R2-D2 in the first *Star Wars* trilogy (1977–1983) are paradigmatic. Made of metal, with rusty bits and bleepy voices, this pair of machines was cute rather than frightening. Arnold Schwarzenegger's Terminator appears to be uncannily human, but the famous 1984 scene showing the removal of his "human" skin and eye unmasks him as a robot with a metal skeleton and laser vision. Although these early technohumans were discomforting, they failed to evoke the uncanniness that Ernst Jentsch describes as the intellectual uncertainty stirred when inanimate objects appear to be sentient.[2] Because the *Star Wars* robots and Schwarzenegger's Terminator were explicitly portrayed as machinic, viewers were unlikely to be discomforted by the uncanny suspicion that they were watching a form of AI more intelligent than humans. Lacking such uncanniness, these very machinic machines may occur in popular imagination as monstrous Others, but are less convincing as figurations of the Freudian uncanny, the familiar-unfamiliar. In many cases, such representations of AI represent what Vinge calls "a bogeyman out of the twentieth century."[3] Rather than being nightmarish, this form of singularity is now even used for comedic effect: In the BBC's *Little Britain* (2003–2006), the sentient machine is not uncannily intelligent but obnoxiously ignorant – "computer says no."

Reversing the principle of machines that become more and more human, bio- and nanotechnological developments are increasingly geared toward the becoming-machine of humans. As a result, speaking robots have been replaced by technologically enhanced human bodies, from prosthetic limbs to android beings. Vinge envisioned that such interfaces could increase user intelligence to a superhuman level; similar ideas inspired early cyborg enthusiasts such as Katherine Hayles, who welcomed the post- or trans-human idea of a social interaction that is not restrained by physical limitations. The technologically enhanced human received an equally enthusiastic fictional welcome in cyberpunk, a genre combining techno-enthusiasm with punk's do-it-yourself cultural aesthetics into posthuman hacker utopias. Like early robot fiction, cyberpunk maintains a clear boundary between man and machine. William Gibson's *Neuromancer* (1984), for example, features androids and AI as well as a "Turing police" trying to protect (enhanced) humans from technological singularity.

Other narratives obscure the boundaries between humans and machines, allowing the shadow sides of technological progress to take center stage. Darth Vader, the dark counterpoint to the comfortably distinctive humans and robots in the 1977–1983 *Star Wars* trilogy, is an unsettling blend of both. A Gothic figure arising from the liminal space between two opposed poles, he is operated by "the dark side of the Force." Different from clearly distinguishable robots like R2-D2, technohumans such as Vader blur the boundaries between man and machine, so much so that it becomes impossible to tell where biology ends and technology begins. Cloaked in black, his face hidden by a grim metal facade, and with two separate actors portraying his body and his voice, Vader testifies to the cultural fear that the technological enhancement of humans may destabilize the very fabric of human ontology. This second type of singularity-inspired specter explores the Gothic implications of biotechnological simulacra. It highlights the anxiety stirred when, as Jean Baudrillard has argued, the "simulation of simulation" – creating, in this case, a simulacrum of human intelligence – reveals "that the real is no longer real."[4] This anxiety is made explicit in clone fiction, which features the mechanical reproduction of the human body and mind. Inevitably, readers and viewers of such narratives are led astray by the lifelike appearance of human simulacra: Clones like the Agent Smiths in *The Matrix* films are only distinguishable when they appear in groups. Precisely the fact that clones appear in multitudes marks the ontological loss they signify. In Gothic representations of biotechnological singularity, the juxtaposition of body and no-body reveals the omnipresence of nobody.

The impossibility of proving the existence of reality as theorized by Baudrillard[5] is an increasingly important theme in singularity Gothic narratives. More and more of these narratives center on the specter of technohuman hybridity. The ontology of this third specter of singularity is hard to pin down – is it technological or is it human? How can it be both? – and its representation is accordingly ambivalent. The hybrid is uncannily unmonstrous, underplayed, and therefore all the more frightening. The representation of androids in the *Alien* films enacts the development from the first to the second to the third specter of singularity. Ash in *Alien* (1979) is identified early on as both synthetic and suspect; the android Bishop featured in *Alien³* (1992) evokes Ripley's prejudices against droids but acquires the role of good guy; finally, Call in *Alien Resurrection* (1997) is only revealed as an android in the second half of the movie and only because she made the mistake of being superhumanly good – "no human is so humane," notes Ripley. The fear that we might not be able to recognize technological singularity is exploited in many narratives, of which Philip K. Dick's *Do Androids Dream of Electric Sheep?* (1968) and its cinematic rendering, *Blade Runner* (1982), are famous examples. A more recent exploration of this theme appears in Vinge's novel *Rainbows End*. The book's main antagonist is an entity appearing only as two different holograms, Mr. Rabbit and the Mysterious Stranger, medial projections of a singularity that cannot possibly be identified as human or nonhuman. This specter of ontological absence rings uncomfortably familiar to contemporary readers as it addresses a deeply rooted fear: that they themselves have similarly started to get stripped of humanity. Our Facebook self is a human–technology hybrid and also a spectral representation with its own intelligence and interactions – but a representation of and interaction with *what*?

As science progresses and the borders between (bio)technological and human entities become more blurred, fictional scenarios darken. One strand in recent singularity Gothic represents humans as passive victims of technological developments that push forward independently of human interference. Defenseless against the violence of viral technology, humans are infected and become raging zombies in such films and video games as the *Resident Evil* franchise (games 1996–2012; films 2002–2012). Renewing the apocalyptic visions from *The Terminator* and *The Matrix*, this type of scenario revives the fear that singularity will end the human era.

Alternatively, humans are portrayed as evil geniuses that collaborate with such destructive technologies. As new Dr. Frankensteins setting out to betray human ontology, scientists in Gothic films such as *Splice* (2009) employ biotechnological engineering to create hybrid beings. The outcome of these efforts, of course, is catastrophic, as the child, Dren, is a monstrous mixture of incompatible parts that attempts to kill her parents. With its dark inversion of the parenting instinct, the film magnifies a key fear in Frankensteinian narratives: that of our progeny as a double of our own darkest side, with technological monstrosity as the karmic return of human *hubris*. *Splice* thus exposes human nature itself as the sublimation of the Freudian uncanny, that which we would like to be unfamiliar but which is, in reality, horrifically familiar.

The monstrous babies Fred, Ginger, and Dren in *Splice* are born out of an organic machine simulating human birth, but each time mother-machine and child-creature first flatline and then produce a heartbeat. Like Frankenstein's monster, these babies are born out of death, their creators sparking sentient life out of a lifeless machine. Again the film follows the convention of the Frankensteinian narrative, in which the birth machine – even if it is called Mother (*Aliens*) or Father (*Alien Resurrection*) – is emphatically presented as a technological matrix, nonhuman, machine-only. The monsters these machines produce, therefore, always remain comfortably Other, and the technological superchild of singularity Gothic remains reassuringly spectral. *Splice* is no exception to these conventions. As the product of human hubris and technological agency, the child, Dren, is an inhuman monster.

Different from other stories in the genre, however, *Splice* also offers room for a rather more controversial question: the idea that the real terror is the parenting instinct itself, that the real hubris might be to think that creation and procreation are the ne plus ultra of human nature. Would Dren have been a monster if she had been born of man and woman instead of woman and machine? The answer is not as easy or as natural as we would like it to be. Mother, Elsa, and father, Clive, are governed by the uncontrollable drive to create, love, and nourish their unknowable progeny even if that drive displays all the tropes of vulgar Freudianism: mirroring, oedipal longing, the trauma of the primal scene, castration desires. *Splice* suggests that biological determinism is the photo negative of technological determinism. Its proclaiming of procreation as the goal of human nature is just as fatalistic as predicting the technological ending of the human era. What is regarded as the most "natural" part of human nature may drive us to annihilation faster than technological or biological singularity. Perhaps it is not our spawn that is hideous, but the hubris from which it sprang. Thus, as a thoroughly Gothic singularity narrative, *Splice* leaves the viewer with the possibility that the urge to procreate may be the most profound version of the Freudian death drive.

As divergent as the technohuman specters discussed here are, they all represent coexisting nightmare visions of the possibility that technological developments will erase the distinction between humans and machines. In order to maintain this distinction, singularity Gothic hauntingly repeats one ontological question: What is human Being? Fiction offers many possible thought-experiments in answer to this question, but none of them settles the ongoing anxiety. The most often probed theory is the idea that humanity is distinguished by its capacity for emotion. Data's deeply felt desire for human emotions in *Star Trek: The Next Generation*, the failing of empathy tests in *Do Androids Dream of Electric Sheep?*, and Dren's adolescent rollercoaster of emotions in *Splice* all question the exclusively human claim to feeling. In similar ways, the romantic notion that art and music are unambiguously human territories has been challenged in fiction and popular culture, from Kraftwerk's musical robots to the thundering techno-beats in *The Matrix* and cyber-Gothic subculture.

A recent addition to singularity Gothic is inspired by the rise of neuro-biology, which claims that not even consciousness is a defining human characteristic. Like emotion and artistic creativity, it is finally only the product of a chain of chemical reactions. R. Scott Bakker's novel *Neuropath* (2008) tests this claim. Its main antagonist is a brilliant neuroscientist-come-serial killer who manipulates his victims' brains in such a way that committing the most gruesome of murders drives them to orgasms of laughter or sexual ecstasy. *Neuropath* leaves the anxious reader with the suggestion that perhaps to be human is essentially to be a "manipulating machine."[6] The Gothic specter, as ever, lies within: The fear that machines may become sentient marks the dreadful realization that humans already are sentient. It is not technological but human Being that is uncanny.

Cloud Gothic / new liminal zones

Next to the specters that represent the fear of technological singularity, techno-Gothic fiction also creates new liminal zones representing the anxieties surrounding the pervasive nature of technology. In the era of networks, mobile interfaces, immersive video games, and augmented reality apps, the terror of a single artificial intelligence is coupled with the fear that the environment in which we move may itself acquire sentience. The Internet hive mind is a global network between humans and machines that has become a familiar nonhuman partner in day-to-day life. Consequently, the permanent connectivity of computers, mobile devices, and human users in social networks has inextricably intertwined virtual and physical worlds. Even closer to the idea of an environment that is sentient is the unremitting generation and exchange of (user) data between machines in the so-called "Internet of Things," which hardly requires human intervention and remains invisible to most users. Our everyday surroundings, in short, are saturated with black-boxed data clouds. The environment is already awake, and it inspires the creation of new liminal zones in techno-Gothic fiction.

In his discussion of genre hybridization between horror, Gothic, new weird, and dark fantasy, Roger Luckhurst employs the notion of "zone" as a metacritical space that marks out fictional content as well as generic hybridization.[7] Many contemporary Gothic narratives can be identified as zone stories. In the virtual data clouds of *The Matrix* films, the interactive zones of horror video games, and the alternate realities of the television series *Fringe* (2008–2013), zones do not only appear as narrative settings but they also mark the genre hybridization of SF, possible-worlds fiction, and Gothic liminality. This specific blend can be identified as the second new techno-Gothic genre: cloud Gothic. It is typically set within a techno-logically created heterotopia, which may range from ubiquitous computing to virtual, augmented, or parallel realities. Like the technohuman specters discussed earlier, the artificial ontology of these realities becomes progressively undetectable for narrative personae and audiences alike. While singularity Gothic made the distinction between machines and humans increasingly difficult, cloud Gothic blurs the boundary between the "natural" and technological realities in which these machines and humans operate.

While early portrayals of clouds such as the Borg in *Star Trek: The Next Generation* (1987–1994) present a networked hive mind that was easily distinguishable by ear or eye, later ones explore the possibility that cloud technology may mislead human perception. Films such as *The Matrix* and *Inception* (2010) feature alternate realities blending virtual-reality (VR) technology and the neuropsychology of the human mind. These films portray cyberspace as the "consensual hallucination" of "unthinkable complexity" envisioned in Gibson's *Neuromancer.*[8] Their heterotopias are created by technology that interferes with the human perception of reality by way of direct brain interfaces, so that the human senses are unveiled as unstable and manipulable rather than objective channels of perception. In Vinge's novel *Rainbows End*, technology's interference with reality and perception is even more pervasive, making the boundaries between natural and technological reality even harder to distinguish. The book features a far-reaching type of network technology creating "an all-encompassing cloud of knowingness,"[9] a world of sentience that overlays every aspect of life. Here it is not even necessary to plug into a VR matrix or dream software. Epiphany Wearable is a piece of incorporated augmented-reality (AR) software, a contact lens that enables people to chat in words and images, surf the Web, use phantom keyboards, and play games; instead of learning to read, children in this book "learn to wear."[10] Users can buy an expensive gaming add-on called "real feeling,"[11] which produces life-size monsters "drenched in slime – real, smelly slime."[12] One of these monsters, the Mysterious Stranger, has plotted to take over the world by way of data compiling. It wants to collect the world's knowledge by scanning and then shredding every book, thereby turning the resulting data cloud into an enormous virtual library.[13] When the main characters get lost between the various layers of reality presented to them – the design of this library, the "on" and "off" switches of their Epiphany Wearable, and the floating contents of the ghost books – *Rainbows End* becomes a zone in Luckhurst's definition: It narrates liminal zones within liminal zones that also straddle the literary zone between SF and the Gothic.

The notion of a sentient environment taps into various conspiracy theories, whose paranoid anxieties are aided by the black-boxed root structures of technology itself. The interpenetration between power-hungry globalized capital and information networks is a recurrent theme in this type of fiction. In *The Matrix*, *Inception*, and *Rainbows End*, omnipresent, omniscient cloud networks are deployed as a panopticon by domineering organizations and businesses. Such networks, in which network technology is the surveillance and disciplinary device of corporate capitalism, are able to produce a far-reaching form of what Gilles Deleuze has described as "societies of control."[14] This aspect of cloud Gothic's liminal zones is by no means only a figment of paranoid imagination. Facebook, for instance, offers a capitalist panopticon whose cloud crowd control almost equals that described in fiction. It is a mobile and location-aware network that knows where we shop, what music we listen to, what our friends do, where we go on holiday. Facebook's software contributes to what is referred to as "Big Data," the vast cloud of user data that is generated every minute of every day by the Internet of Things, the communication between PCs, Web sites, smartphones (a familiar singularity specter), electronic payment methods, social networks, entrance passes, and many more. The sentient cloud already controls us, and most of the time we are unconscious of its presence. Corporate research reports describing it have titles that are uncannily similar to those of dystopic cloud Gothic stories, as in the case of "Computers to Acquire Control of the Physical World."[15] Resistance is no longer even futile, it is irrelevant.

The interactive VR technology of video games is no less pervasive. With the popularization of games, the intrusion of medial reality into the day-to-day world has not only become a voluntary option, but has also been commodified into one of the most profitable areas of the experience economy. As computer graphics, sound, soft- and hardware become ever more sophisticated, the virtual reality of games presents an ever more credible alternate world. The development of kinetic interfaces allows players to participate physically in gaming reality, which thereby becomes an integral part of, rather than an alternative to, ordinary reality. Next to the Internet, smartphones, and digital television, gaming VR is just another component of the omnipresent cloud of ubiquitous computing.

Gothic games offer a playful exploration of the liminal zone between reality and its virtual double. With their supernatural elements, haunting and murder, dark graphics and spooky soundtracks, psychological horror games (PHGs) are Gothic in design as well as gameplay. Geared toward the implicit terror of haunting presences rather than toward the explicit horror of slaying chainsaw-carrying zombies – as in survival horror games – the strategies for performing these games are deeply Gothic. They aim not only to evoke the player's fears but also to play with and upon them. These games, with titles like *Call of Cthulhu: Dark Corners of the Earth* (2005) and *Amnesia: The Dark Descent* (2010), typically contain sections in which gameplay is interrupted by "insanity effects." In these disturbing chapters, the game's main character is revealed as psychologically unreliable, often because of past trauma: Insanity effects influence the avatar's stability by way of visual and sonic "hallucinations" or the occurrence of paranormal events. More importantly, insanity effects also test player psychology by explicitly breaking the fourth wall, the boundary between gaming reality and the player's physical surroundings, via seeming corruptions of the interface, suddenly blurry graphics and distorted soundtracks, and an ostensibly failing console that appears to delete saved games or to have crashed. While PHG gameplay aims to psychologically undermine the player by blurring the distinction between external and internal terror, that effect is technologically established by the annihilation of the illusion of objective perception and its supposed grounding in reality and sanity. These games epitomize the uneasy realization that our own unstable subjectivity is a constituent factor of contemporary cloud reality.

Gaming technology increasingly influences film narratives and aesthetics also. Films such as *Inception* and the *Resident Evil* series are designed as cinematic games, complete with title menus, labyrinthine surroundings, various levels of adventure or fighting difficulty, and 3-D special effects. David Cronenberg's cinematic exploration of gaming in *eXistenZ* (1999) reaches beyond the level of mere design. This film's plot centers on a corporately developed biotechnological gaming interface, a combination of software and wetware that is plugged directly into the player's nervous system to optimize gaming immersion. *eXistenZ* is not simply a film about a game; it is also a test of the limits of fiction-within-fiction that extends to a reality within a reality within a reality. It directly challenges the idea that human perception has any relation to reality, suggesting that the entire world may be a technologically created and/or consensually hallucinated liminal zone.

It is no coincidence that almost all the narratives discussed here end with the question of whether we – narrative personae as well as their audiences – are in virtual or actual reality or whether corporate businesses are using cloud technology to control our world and our perception. It has become impossible to prove the existence not just of reality, but of the simulacrum itself, now that reality is no longer opposed by virtual reality but turned into augmented reality (which is a curious concept in itself). Cloud Gothic uncannily doubles a culture in which everyone has their own customized AR app. VR comes prowling into our own spheres, turning the whole world into a phantom space. A particularly astute game studio makes AR ghost hunts in which players are to locate ghost holograms in their own surroundings with the help of their smartphone. In these games, virtual space overlaps actual space, fictional space overlaps factual space, perception is inflected by imagination, and cloud technology facilitates their navigation. The name of the company: Haunted Planet Studios.

The idea that perceived reality does not necessarily coincide with the actual or even the only reality has long been the main theme of "possible worlds" fiction. This strand of writing explores the possibility of infinite parallel or hypothetical worlds in its storylines while simultaneously endorsing a metafictional reflection on fiction's own world-building potential. In this typical zone literature, which blends SF, fantasy, and Gothic narrative strategies, fiction appears as an endless proliferation of narrative pathways in which readers may affirm any of the available universes at any given time. *Fringe* is a possible-worlds television series that revolves around the alternate realities theorized in quantum physics. This focus enables interesting metafictional variations. *Fringe*'s quantum universes evoke the fear that alternate realities might be scientifically proven and might represent a version of reality that perception cannot confirm. They stir the unpleasant feeling that "we are not alone," accompanied by invisible, otherworldly doppelgängers.

As Slavoj Žižek argues, however, quantum physics itself should be regarded as a form of fiction. Its formulas are representations of a physical reality, but this reality is an unreachable infinity beyond representation and imagination: the unattainable Real described by Jacques Lacan. Moreover, the formulas of quantum physics are so complex that they no longer signify anything concrete, let alone the Real. Thus, in Lacanian terms, the Symbolic order of representation has been reduced to empty signifiers, "a senseless formula" that has no relation to anything but itself.[16] Not only do quantum narratives like *Fringe* make their audience explore the idea that there might be other realities next to their own; they also test the baffling thought highlighted by Žižek that that very reality may be part of an endless rhizome of fiction and virtualization spreading in all directions.

The essentially hypertextual structuring of this (fictional) reality in possible-worlds fiction and film underlines the kinship between literary, cinematic, and gaming virtual realities. The fact that in games one can swap worlds, travel back in time, and choose one's own narrative trajectory illustrates the virtualizing potential of any fictional world-building. More importantly, Tanya Krzywinska and Esther McCallum-Stewart have argued that the tension between the limitless possibilities of game technology, on the one hand, and the restrictions of those possibilities by gameplay and interface technology, on the other, foregrounds precisely the relation between virtuality and the Real.[17] Žižek stresses the difference between VR, a permutation of the Symbolic aimed at imitation or simulacrum, and the Deleuzian notion of virtuality proper, which he defines as "the reality of the virtual (which, in Lacanian terms, is the Real)."[18] Gaming VR, like possible-worlds fiction, offers a metafictional view of the unthinkable infinitude of virtuality, and precisely because of its unimaginable vastness it may offer a glimpse of the Real. Psychological horror games push precisely this point. By creating liminal zones between virtual and actual realities as well as between perception and imagination, they tear slits in the Symbolic order of representation, forcing the player through the wormholes of her Imaginary projections, threatening to expose the Real – which Žižek describes as the unbearable actualization of fantasy.[19]

The uncanniness of cloud Gothic thus lies in technology's constant threat to actualize any part of its infinite virtuality at any time: the discomforting awareness that ubiquitous computing may undo the Symbolic and may force us to discern the abyss of the unknowable Real. It is unsurprising that, besides PHGs, many other cloud Gothic narratives present the human mind as the most liminal of realities. In *Inception*, for example, technology cannot influence the "limbo" of "unconstructed dreamspace," which consists of a "raw, infinite subconscious [*sic*]" only, a desolate, haunted plane painted in bleak colors. Aided by its own dependence on mediality and fictionality, cloud Gothic keeps articulating the same haunting suspicions, the same discomforting questions pertaining to the ontology and epistemology of technoculture: What is reality and how can I know it? It provides no answer to these questions; it merely insists on them and leaves its audience to ponder their implications. On some other side of some reality, the character Peter Bishop remarks to "Fauxlivia" Dunham that "Real is just a matter of perception."[20]

Weird Gothic / new metaphysics

Technological ontology and epistemology disclose the impossibility of proving human Being and reality. The techno/human gaze bounces off the hollow looking glasses of singularity and cloud Gothic. Behind their opaque surfaces, the Real remains looming. Fantasy – in Žižek's words "The 'real Real', the horrifying Thing"[21] – is safely tucked away in the zonic omnipresence of the Symbolic.

But there is a third techno-Gothic genre that is able to reach beyond the Symbolic order of the first two. Written in a style so baroque that it could crack any mirror, and describing monsters so unspeakable that they escape even the most elaborate metaphors, weird Gothic is able to rip open the Symbolic orders of technology. Thus, amid the evacuated zones of technoculture, a cosmic call resonates through the shards of fictionality: the call of H. P. Lovecraft's Nyarlathotep, crawling chaos, crying out to "the audient void."[22] *Ex nihilo*, virtual, and yet a suggestion of the Real, its numinous sway spawns a metaphysics of absolute Otherness. These new metaphysics are addressed in weird Gothic, a genre that overlays the technohuman contemplations of the twenty-first century with the abhuman aesthetic of weird fiction and the technostalgia of steampunk.

The new weird's urban possible-worlds fictions present a dizzying blend of weird, fantasy, SF, horror, and Gothic tropes playing out in a virtually infinite number of convergent schemes: labyrinthine alternate realities and intricate doublings, baffling surrealism and grotesque phantasms, freaks of nature and monstrous machines, physics and metaphysics, transgressive horror and sublime terror, the familiar turned unfamiliar and the reverse. In its moments of radical untechnology, new weird becomes weird Gothic, which is related to the other techno-Gothics through its seeming negation of the technological anxieties that are their key subject matter. China Miéville's *Kraken* (2010), for instance, speaks of a tentacled God rising up from the deep waters for a cosmically anticipated apocalypse, its metaphysical omnipotence rendering scientific and corporate conspiracies against it stupidly fruitless. Weird Gothic's theme is the splendor of the numinous, which it portrays as sublime nonhuman, nontechnological beings far outside the reach of human perception. Technology is portrayed as a mere instrument, an extension of man's (feeble) efforts to touch upon such divine powers. In contrast to the pleasantly recognizable specters of singularity, weird monsters, as Miéville argues, put Otherness back into its primal zone of "implacable alterity."[23] This type of arch-Otherness dwells only in the Real beyond representation, which, in its constant actualization of unknown mysteries, surpasses physics as well as metaphysics. In awe of the unspeakable Real that cloud Gothic threatens to expose, weird techno-Gothic expresses a longing for infinite virtuality.

As baroque in style as the new weird and popularized in the same decades around the turn of the twenty-first century, steampunk is characterized by a transcendent technostalgia, mixing nineteenth- and twenty-first-century technologies, that overlaps with weird Gothic's untechnology. Like new weird, steampunk seems to negate the anxieties regarding technological beings and realities expressed in other techno-Gothic genres. Steampunk's motto is "Love the Machine, Hate the Factory," which, like new weird's working-class programme, urges a rethink of the technological control of society discussed above. With its nineteenth-century setting and therefore removed from contemporary society, Stephania Forlini argues, steampunk has the critical distance to reconsider the social and philosophical implications of changing relations between humanity and technology.[24]

In their negation of technological anxiety, both types of weird Gothic invert the techno-Gothic modes of singularity and cloud Gothic. This new mixture of genres nostalgically looks back to when the first specter of singularity was the future. The Victorian machines in Miéville's novel *Perdido Street Station* (2000) and the automaton that appears in the film *Hugo* (2011) are supremely recognizable as nonhuman, and their portrayal privileges the aesthetics of steampunk appearance over their uncanny implications. These bogeymen "out of the twentieth century" represent not fear, but the Gothic nostalgia for fear. They long for a time when belief systems assumed that humans were still humans, machines were still machines, the Other was still the Other, and the unattainable Thing still dwelt in the safely ungraspable realm of the Real.

Cloud Gothic's technological realities become weirdly inverted too. Weird Gothic narratives often feature untechnological or technostalgic universes conjured up by steampunk machines, such as the quantum telegraph that is used to communicate with "the other side" of quantum reality in one of *Fringe*'s weird moments. In the 2003 film *The League of Extraordinary Gentlemen*, both singularity and cloud Gothic are inverted. *The League* is a thematic blend of steampunk, Gothic, fantasy, SF, and weird within a medial mash-up of fiction, film, and comics. An amorphous group of adventurers including Captain Nemo, Dorian Gray, Mina Harker from *Dracula*, Dr. Jekyll/Mr. Hyde, and Allan Quatermain from H. Rider Haggard's novels embark upon a heroic journey against the evil genius of one "M." This M, who is later revealed to be Professor Moriarty, intends to clone each of these heroes in order to gain world power. This plan must be stopped because the cloning process – so the characters' own traumas and demons tell them – will make the evil buried in them prevail over their good. The irony would be exquisite if Hollywood aesthetics had not flattened it out: The reproduction of already-twice-remediated fictional characters must be prevented because the heroes would risk losing their "aura," their authentic humanness (whatever that may be). Within the liminal zone of virtual-reality-within-virtual-reality (cloud Gothic), the film thus evokes the specter of technological sentience (singularity Gothic). But it does so in an almost desperate way. This new simulacrum *must* be connected with Evil so that the League can reach the safe conclusion that there still is a core of humanity in the copy of the copy of the phantom and that there still is a reality in the remediation of the remediation of the mediation. With its characters clad in brass and khaki, then, *The League* expresses a profound nostalgia for an adventure that is no longer possible: that of transgressing the borders between man and machine, good and evil. In its nostalgia for these borders – the curious nostalgia for an absolute Other – weird Gothic imagines plots that cloud and singularity Gothic avoid.

The Construct Council in *Perdido Street Station*, a malevolent hive mind originating from a mutated computer virus, presents a typically weird twist on singularity and cloud Gothic. It amalgamates references to well-known technologies from both subgenres into untechnological sublimity. Its original main frame is a difference engine in Babbage style, a huge copper-and-brass steam engine with endlessly noisy pistons, screws, and valves.[25] Its roaming avatars, however, fail to grasp the mysteries of life and cosmos. Though animating dead human bodies, they lack human imagination, emotion, and psychology:

> I am a calculating machine that has calculated how to think. I do not dream. I have no neuroses, no hidden depths. My consciousness is a growing function of my processing power, not the baroque thing that sprouts from your mind, with its hidden rooms in attics and cellars.[26]

This cloudy non-Thing is sublime in its failure, in its not-approaching of humanness, let alone the numinous evil it aspires to; it is a mundane instrument of corporate control. Moreover, its emphatically intertextual construction stresses the impotence of the Symbolic, of conventional signs supposedly referring to objects. The virtual reality of fiction and of technology alike can never reach the numinous and does not even allow a glimpse of the Real.

In an analysis of the distinctions between weird and Gothic, China Miéville identifies an opposition between the always-already of hauntology and the unprecedentedness of the weird. Because weird is about the Absolute Unknown, Miéville insists, it is diametrically opposed to the hauntological. Because it is unprecedented, it is ontologically unhaunted, like the Construct Council's avatars, and therefore "if anything ab-, not un-, canny."[27] Sublimely Other as the cosmic monsters of the weird may be, they are verbal reflections of the unspeakable. Weird Gothic needs an infinity of hyperbolic overstylizations and canny neologisms in order to describe the unspeakable. Precisely this painstakingly eloquent speechlessness, Fred Botting contends, engenders an "unnaming" that "[shreds] the screens protecting reality."[28] Approaching the unreachable and unthinkable Real in retrograde motion, weird Gothic may reach beings and realities that singularity and cloud Gothic do not even consider.

This last technogothic strand thus ultimately inverts the very questions that the first two ask. What is *nonhuman* Being? What is *un*reality, and how can I know it? Weird Gothic does not flee the unspeakable Thing but attempts to discern it beyond man/machine and real/virtual dichotomies. Impossibly, its gaze is returned:

> The fact of the Weird is the fact that the worldweave is ripped and unfinished. Moth-eaten, ill-made. And that through the little tears, from behind the ragged
>
> edges
> , things are looking at us.[29]

Weird Gothic thus marks the impossible return of the Real. With its renewal of Gothic metaphysics, techno-Gothic comes full (Möbius) circle. While singularity Gothic's specters personify the fear that technology undoes human ontology and cloud Gothic's uncanny zones suggest that technology has replaced the epistemology of the reality we inhabit, weird Gothic offers a cosmogonical vision of the horrifying Thing of the Real emerging from the tentacles of fiction.

NOTES

1 Vernor Vinge, "The Coming Technological Singularity: How to Survive in the Post-Human Era," *Whole Earth Review*, 81 (1993), pp. 88–95, p. 88.

2 Ernst Jentsch, "On the Psychology of the Uncanny," in *Uncanny Modernity: Cultural Theories, Modern Anxieties*, ed. Jo Collins and John Jervis (Houndmills: Palgrave Macmillan, 2008), pp. 216–228.

3 Vernor Vinge, *Rainbows End: A Novel with One Foot in the Future* (New York: Tom Doherty, 2006), p. 201.

4 Jean Baudrillard, *Simulacra and Simulation*, trans. Sheila Glaser (Ann Arbor, MI: University of Michigan Press, 1994), pp. 12–13.

5 Baudrillard, *Simulacra and Simulation*, p. 21.

6 R. Scott Bakker, *Neuropath* (New York: Tom Doherty, 2008), p. 308.

7 Roger Luckhurst, "In the Zone: Topologies of Genre Weirdness," in *Gothic Science Fiction, 1980–2010*, ed. Sara Wasson and Emily Alder (Liverpool University Press, 2011), pp. 21–35, p. 25.

8 William Gibson, *Neuromancer* (London: Gollancz, 1984), p. 67.

9 Vinge, *Rainbows End*, p. 160.

10 Vinge, *Rainbows End*, p. 146.

11 Vinge, *Rainbows End*, p. 51.

12 Vinge, *Rainbows End*, p. 55.

13 Vinge, *Rainbows End*, p. 172–175.

14 Gilles Deleuze, "Postscript on the Societies of Control," *October*, 59 (1992), pp. 3–7.

15 Paolo Magrassi, Angelo Panarella, Nigel Deighton, and Geoff Johnson, "Computers to Acquire Control of the Physical World" (Gartner Advisory, 2001), www.gartner.com/id=341674

16 Slavoj Žižek, *Organs without Bodies: On Deleuze and Consequences* (New York: Routledge, 2004), pp. 102–103.

17 Tanya Krzywinska and Esther McCallum-Stewart, "Digital Games," in *The Routledge Companion to Science Fiction*, ed. Mark Bould (London: Routledge, 2009), pp. 350–361, pp. 359–360.

18 Žižek, *Organs without Bodies*, p. 3.

19 Žižek, *Organs without Bodies*, p. 95.

20 *Fringe*, Season 4, Episode 3: "Do Shapeshifters Dream of Electric Sheep?"

21 Žižek, *Organs without Bodies*, p. 102.

22 "Nyarlathotep," in *H. P. Lovecraft: The Complete Fiction*, ed. S. T. Joshi (New York: Barnes and Noble, 2011), p. 121.

23 China Miéville, "M. R. James and the Quantum Vampire: Weird; Hauntological: Versus and/or and and/or or?," *Collapse*, 4: *Concept Horror* (2000), pp. 105–128, p. 113.

24 Stephania Forlini, "Technology and Morality: The Stuff of Steampunk," *Neo-Victorian Studies*, 3 (2010), pp. 72–98, p. 72.

25 China Miéville, *Perdido Street Station* (London: Macmillan, 2000), pp. 242–243.

26 Miéville, *Perdido Street Station*, p. 477.

27 Miéville, "M. R. James," p. 113.

28 Fred Botting, "More Things: Horror, Materialism and Speculative Weirdism," *Horror Studies*, 3 (2012), pp. 281–303, pp. 290, 286.
29 China Miéville, "Afterweird," in *The Weird: A Compendium of Strange and Dark Stories*, ed. A. and J. VanderMeer (New York: Tor Books, 2012), pp. 1113–1116, p. 1115.

PART IV

Multicultural and global Gothic

10

MAISHA L. WESTER

The Gothic and the politics of race

While scholars have listed a number of reasons for the Gothic genre's prevalence in the British and American traditions – particularly its capacity to be a consistent resource for the disguised expression of challenges and anxieties facing a given culture at a given moment – one of the most striking reasons for the genre's popularity has proven to be its function as a discourse on the terrors of racial otherness and racial encounter. Gothic novels have used racial others to shore up the normative " 'human as white, male, middle class, and heterosexual' at times when the desired certainty of this standard was being called into question by rapid changes."[1] Hence British Gothic literature often reveals xenophobic impulses in its frequent turns to monstrosity. Nor is this phenomenon restricted to Britain. Indeed, the Gothic is one of the main discursive genres in the United States, as established most by Leslie Fiedler in *Love and Death in the American Novel* (1960) and Toni Morrison in *Playing in the Dark* (1992), precisely because it is a genre loaded with ghostly "monsterizings" of racial otherness. More importantly, British Gothic texts such as Bram Stoker's "The Squaw" (1893) and American Gothic tales such as H. P. Lovecraft's "The Picture in the House" (1921) and "Facts concerning the Late Arthur Jermyn and His Family" (1921), which I will discuss further below, articulate the ways in which these racialized discourses are not just about the presence, horror, and transgression of the racial other in a predominantly white world, but also about anxieties over the potential that the other brings for the cultural and racial degeneration of British and American citizens.

The Gothic's mutable monsters, then, reveal panicked discourses about racial difference on top of many other cultural anxieties. On the one hand, Judith Halberstam correctly announces the multiplicity of symbolic suggestions that function conterminously in Gothic fiction, proclaiming that "meaning runs riot" in such novels.[2] At the same time, Halberstam is compelled to note how often these riots of meaning include issues of racial otherness. In fact, as H. L. Malchow explains in *Gothic Images of Race in*

Nineteenth-Century Britain, Gothic fiction and racial discourses were intertwined and influenced each other continuously across the nineteenth century. The Gothic monster, while a grotesquerie of multiple and incompatible meanings, is thus also an "economic form in that it condenses various racial and sexual threats to nation, capitalism, and the bourgeoisie in one body."[3] Consequently, the Gothic is particularly rife with "the language of race hatred" until "race becomes a master signifier of monstrosity and when invoked ... blocks out all other possibilities of monstrous identity."[4] As we shall see, there is a long and complex history that developed this trend in the genre. I also want to show, however, that some counter-versions of the Gothic have arisen too in recent years to reverse this trend by reworking the principal features of Gothicism itself.

British xenophobia and American Africanisms

Race in Britain during the nineteenth century, especially over the last half of it, was not a simple issue of skin pigmentation. Rather, as Louis S. Warren has shown, the term "race" signified cultural as well as physical attributes.[5] This range of meanings, accompanied by an anxiety in Western culture over what bodies might signify beyond themselves, was in part a response to the stretch of the British Empire and the consequent drive to define and affirm quintessential English identity over against such a multiracial expanse. Culturally, the English wanted to be considered racially distinct from the Italians, for instance, almost as much as from Africans. Consequently, in a great deal of nineteenth-century British Gothic, the monster was an all-encompassing racial other and in that way a contrast to proper Englishness. Even the Scottish and the Irish were depicted in fiction as entirely different races; compared to the British, they were outsiders whose immigration to London brought hungry and contaminating hordes that threatened the normative whiteness of the English race.

Such prejudices are apparent in both the Sawney Bean tales of the 1840s and the story of Sweeney Todd, which exemplify the ways racial others were used to provide a contrast to Englishness. Indeed, "Sawney Bean" is not only a tale of burglary and cannibalism on the Scottish Highlands; it is also the tale of a savage and inept Scottish government, one which proves to be the political equivalent of the very fiends it is hunting. Descriptions of the Scottish throughout the story are so beastly that the Scottish seem another race entirely. *The String of Pearls* (1846), the Gothic penny dreadful in which the Sweeney Todd story first appeared, is even more telling about ideologies of racial difference. Todd is portrayed as a racial monster evoking stereotypes of the Irish other as descending, cannibalistic hordes. That this murderous Irishman is meant to be read as racially other is immediately apparent when Todd is said to look like "some Indian warrior with a very remarkable head-dress."[6] Like the Scots who are marked as a different race well before the end of "Sawney Bean," Todd's Irishness is not understood as ethnic difference but as the monstrosity of a debased level of being.

Pervasive xenophobia invariably inheres in such ideologies of race and foreignness. The racism inherent in much Gothic literature of the late nineteenth century is rooted in an imperialist fantasy of the colonial other coming to "our land."[7] Racially colored stories of vampirism became particularly popular in Britain during the last third of the nineteenth century "when issues of 'unfair' economic competition, immigration of 'the unfit,' and race degeneration featured prominently" in the publications of popular and political culture.[8] Bram Stoker's *Dracula* in particular illustrates British cultural angst over the racial other's successful infiltration of society, as well as the late Victorian era's "obsession with racial degeneration and imperial decline."[9] As Sawney Bean, Sweeney Todd, and (as we will see) Stoker's own version of Poe's black cat illustrate, former slaves and Irish and Scottish immigrants threatened national collapse from within through their supposed contamination of the country's racial homogeneity.

While a variety of well-known British Gothic fictions are stalked by racial otherness, *Frankenstein*, as early as 1818, illustrates a particular anxiety over a racialized other whose monstrosity also includes suggestions of sexual perversion. Mary Shelley's monster conflates popular racial images of the Negro, first of all, most of which emphasized the black's overwhelming strength and general repulsiveness. In addition, *Frankenstein* draws on the growing threats of revolution, particularly the rise of the black Jacobins in Haiti and the abolitionist struggle to end the slave trade in England. It is thus surprisingly easy to see the novel as a reflection of the growing issue of race in political debates. *Frankenstein*'s creature, after all, is a composite of both sides of the antislavery debate, at once childlike and unjustly wronged, but also governed by a rage and destructiveness whose depths seem a result of both an oppressive environment and his or its innate temperament. As H. L. Malchow argues, the conundrum over the source of the creature's monstrosity recalls depictions of slaves in the antislavery debates, depictions featuring "excitable" Negroes whose potential for awesome destruction seems unique to their physiology even while it can be attributed to their circumstances. Furthermore, both sides of the debate at this time were infected by the notion of black duality: The black was at once anxious to please but equally quick to anger and to reach a state of extreme violence. All of these descriptions and issues prove applicable to *Frankenstein*'s monster, a creature who is moved to bloody vengeance by the injustice of his creator, who is childlike and innocent in his first months, and whose monstrosity – while understandable in light of the treatment he receives in various social encounters and in Victor's determination to first abandon and then destroy him – seems nonetheless to stem from some unfathomable reservoir.

But *Frankenstein*'s monster is like the black slave in ways other than social environment; he also resembles the slave in terms of his physiology and his sexual threat. Common descriptions of blacks emphasized their great strength and "simian dexterity."[10] The monster illustrates similar capabilities as he traverses the Alps by leaps and bounds, becoming not only sinister and grotesque in his appearance, but larger, darker, and more powerful than Victor. At the same time, popular discourse had imbued blacks with an excessive amount of libidinous energy that was usually threatening. The initial scenes of the monster's birth – in which Victor awakens in bed to find the monster towering over him – even suggest a rape threat against Victor, one which becomes more explicit in the monster's rape-like killing of Elizabeth, Victor's fiancé. As such, the monster conveys a sexuality which, all at once, is aberrant in itself and threatens miscegenation.

Like their British counterparts, American Gothic works reveal their own conflicts among discourses over the racial other in American society. Allan Lloyd Smith has rightly rooted the American Gothic in the anxiety engendered by the struggle between the ideals of reason and a sense of the inherent perverseness in the early American settlements.[11] Toni Morrison's series of essays in *Playing in the Dark* provides both an expansion upon and a critique of this notion. If Americans were concerned with a sense of inherent perversity that threatened their reason, it was because the very economic system of the country undercut its Enlightenment ideals. The constitution of the new republic offered equality and liberty to most by denying it to every other group save whites of European descent. For Morrison, every scene of slavery's brutality therefore offers an illustration of the battle between reason and perversity as slave masters worked hard to convince themselves that the savagery was "out there." The lashes dealt the slave, ideologically interpreted, are "not one's own savagery; repeated and dangerous breaks from freedom are 'puzzling' confirmations of black irrationality; the combination of . . . beatitudes and a life of regularized violence is civilized; and . . . the rawness remains external."[12] The presence of the slave body consequently provided a vehicle for defining the opposite of identity as the failure to achieve the ideals of reason, allowing writers to conceptualize and project their brutal failures onto another – or, more precisely, a racially othered – body. Morrison calls this body the "Not-Free, Not-Me" of American culture, since this othered body is made to enact all of the deviances and failures the "rational" body denies. The other thus becomes monstrous and unfathomable, necessitating the whippings it receives.

Perhaps one of the clearest examples of that racial otherness in the American Gothic occurs throughout the works of Edgar Allan Poe, an author who later provided one model for Lovecraft's politics and art.[13] Poe's novel *The Narrative of Arthur Gordon Pym of Nantucket* (1838) displaces and reimagines an exploration of the American South and an encounter with its black denizens by recasting them as devious, murderous islanders called the Too-Wits who seem remarkably like slaves in revolt against their (would-be) white masters. The Too-Wits occupy the Island of Tsalal, which is located in the southernmost region of the world. All too clearly, the geography of the island marks it as a symbolic representation of the American South; Pym identifies the island by a ledge that "bear[s] a strong resemblance to corded bales of cotton."[14] The natives of this southern land are extremely black; the Too-Wits are of "the ordinary stature of Europeans, but of a more muscular and brawny frame, their complexion a jet black, with thick and long woolly hair." Even their teeth are black, and "their lips" are "thick and clumsy."[15] Like *Frankenstein*, Poe's novel picks up on popular racial descriptions of the day in emphasizing the Too-Wits' strength and prowess. They are also seemingly ignorant, simplistic, and savage. Yet the novel reveals the Too-Wits' ignorance as a mere mask because they stage an attack upon Pym's unsuspecting white companions. In the end, the relationship between the islanders and the white crew of the *Jane Guy* suggests that this attack represents more than just the hidden threat the loosed black body poses; the Too-Wits' betrayal is actually a kind of slave uprising.

Poe extends this meditation on savagery to the hybrid in his text, Dirk Peters, and thereby depicts the consequences of an unstable color line where the border separating black from white has not been policed. The horror of Peters, his disturbing features, is a product of his miscegenation. His strength and brutality engender bloody violence, and his "demonic" body resembles the features of the Too-Wits, who are marked by racial hatred. Likewise Peters recalls myths of the racial others' threatening libidinous energy. For instance, Peters saves Augustus – Pym's friend and confidant – from a mutiny and keeps him in his chambers much like a pet. During the mutiny, while Pym is still trapped below, Peters often visits Augustus in his chambers, sometimes holding strange conversations with him and at other times leering at Augustus. Peters' attempts at affection not only recall the psychological intimacy initially established between Pym and Augustus but also illustrate how this intimacy seems "queer" and made dangerous when shared by the racial other.

While many of these representations of monstrous otherness stem from xenophobic fears, it is also important to remember that these discourses are never about the actuality of the racial other. Indeed, "the other is never simply the other"[16] but a product of the mechanism of projection within the process of abjection as Julia Kristeva has defined it, a casting away and abasing of the inconsistencies within the projectors themselves. In other words, the genre's monstrous others are an articulation of white humanity's own schizoid psyche. Often, when we think of the return of the repressed on the national scene – the hidden narratives of the oppressed and disenfranchised haunting our tidy narrative – the primary focus is on the psychological, rather than the social. And yet we should not ignore the ways that psychological journey into the dark night of the soul has been metaphorized through use of minority bodies. Pym's and Augustus' homosocial bonding, for instance, becomes harmless and innocent, despite its overtones of homosexuality, in contrast to the sexual threat that Peters poses. Peters thus provides a method for understanding the difference between aberrant and normative (that is, white) homosocial interaction. Similarly Nathaniel Hawthorne's "Young Goodman Brown" (1835) depicts a forest haunted by savage Indians, yet the savagery of these people primarily acts as a barometer for measuring the warped souls and histories of Brown and his ancestors. Likewise, though typically understood as a lament against slavery, Herman Melville's "Benito Cereno" (1855–1856) is ambivalent in both its depictions of evil slave-holding whites and treacherous enslaved blacks. As in *Frankenstein*, the peculiar dynamics within this text suggest that, on the one hand, white evil creates its own monsters and thus the treachery of the black slaves may be understood as a reflection of white villainy. Yet, on the other hand, the extremes of black violence – since one of the more striking scenes is of the bloody rage of a nursing black mother – imply an innate tendency to commit that violence and thus mark racial difference once again.

Understanding the abjective othering of such anomalies in the British and American Gothic has proven invaluable for rethinking these texts' anxieties about the cultural decline of the nation and its subjects. Gothic fiction was popular at the turn of the nineteenth into the twentieth century, as I have suggested earlier, because it functioned as a site where the national imaginary could represent and work through the dangers of racial decline posed by waves of immigrating and liberated racial others. Yet the same fictions also reveal how notions of an Anglo-Saxon race in decline as a consequence of contaminating racial encounters disguise a more disturbing truth: that the "superior" Anglo-Saxon race must throw off its own differences within itself to mask the aberration and degeneration that was always present in it and keeps threatening to erase the gap between the "proper" white subject and its subjugated others. Consequently, certain later Gothic stories, influenced by Poe and others, pointedly illustrate the ways in which the monstrous other is not as foreign to or atypical of British and American culture as the national body wants to believe.

Stoker's black cat and Lovecraft's white apes

While much has been made of the way Poe's "black cat" in his 1843 story of that name is really a metaphor for American slavery, there has been relatively little discussion of the comparable ways in which Bram Stoker's "The Squaw" (1893) portrays issues of racial otherness and vengeance for British readers. This text betrays acute anxiety over the consequences of a cross-racial existence, even as it too worries over the possibility of cultural decline. The story portrays an encounter between several different groups – Native American, British, and, given its setting, German – brought together by a body Toni Morrison would define as an "Africanist presence": an angry black cat determined to avenge the death of one of her kittens. The narrative also emphasizes the monstrosity of its racial others by highlighting particularly monstrous females of color. The female figure of the title, an Apache squaw, proves unspeakably savage in her drive for revenge. Elias, an American cowboy, recounts how "no man, white or Injun, had ever been so long a-dying under the tortures of the Apaches. The only time I ever see her smile was when I wiped her out."[17] The suggestion that the woman excels in the "tortures of the Apaches" implies that this tribe is inherently prone to human torture. Even more disturbing is the fact that, though a mother, she only smiles when she dies; the incongruity between the moment and her reaction emphasizes her horrific nature. Indeed, so horrible are her crimes that Elias never describes what she does in her torture of her victim, only that she stalked the man for over three years.

What is unspeakable in Elias' recounting of the Apache squaw's tale is implicit in the text's account of the black cat's vengeance. Like the woman, the cat seeks revenge for the death of one of her kittens, which implies that the squaw, like the cat, may have abandoned other children for the sake of vengeance. The text's comment that the cat is driven by "a blind unreasoning fury"[18] that renders her grotesque also reflects back on the Apache woman, who trails her victim for years. Like the woman, too, the cat stalks her victim, becoming more Gothically monstrous the longer she stalks Elias: "Her green eyes blazed with lurid fire, and the white, sharp teeth seemed to almost shine through the blood which dabbed her mouth and whiskers."[19] Most distressing is the consequent treatment her slain kitten's corpse receives; the mother, in her rage, does her dead kitten repeated violence, as she keeps trampling the poor corpse while trying to reach Elias. Furthermore, the cat, like the Apache, becomes a torturer, using one of the devices in the torture museum to kill her victim.[20] That the cat stands in for the Apache woman is perhaps most evident in Stoker's title. While it implies that this is a tale about a Native American, the bulk of the text is devoted to the violation and revenge of the black cat. Indeed, Elias twice refers to the cat as "the squaw"[21] and observes that she's "got on all her war paint" just before she kills him.[22] Thus the black cat becomes the squaw of the title even as, due to her coloring, we may assume the cat signifies other racial bodies as well. Both mothers become especially horrible in their violence and "dark" violations of stereotypes of feminine docility.

While "The Squaw" clearly renders the racially other body monstrous, what is even more important in the story is its concern over cultural and racial degeneration. We cannot ignore the behaviors of the two white men in the text or the narrative's prolonged descriptions of a German torture chamber. Elias seems to be a rendition and critique of William Cody, also known as Buffalo Bill, with whom Stoker became acquainted in 1886. Buffalo Bill's Wild West Show toured America and Europe between 1897 and 1916; as in *Dracula*, the show articulated how "the frontiers of racial encounter were invested with the possibility of degeneration and the necessity of race war."[23] While Cody was optimistic about the ways conquest and expansion could and would secure the "destiny of white people," Stoker's texts frequently illustrate a gloomier view, suggesting that frontiers could be "almost as dangerous to the race as vampires themselves."[24]

In "The Squaw," Elias is something of a degenerate and violent buffoon. For instance, just before accidentally killing the kitten, Elias notes that "I wouldn't hurt the poor pooty little critter more'n I'd scalp a baby."[25] Elias' vernacular proves telling, for it not only references stereotypes of Americans as inarticulate but also reveals the ways in which Elias has been influenced by Native American culture, implicit in his reference to the notion of scalping. Furthermore, Elias' own hyper-macho yet masochistic behavior is as much responsible for his death as the cat. Complaining that "I've not had a show fur real pleasure in this dod-rotted Continent, where there ain't no b'ars nor Injuns, an' where nary man goes heeled," Elias insists the museum keeper shut him up in the Iron Virgin.[26] This passage is noteworthy not just for its low-class dialect, but for the violence and cultural degeneration it alludes to. The conjunction between the bars and the "Injuns" suggests Elias misses not only alcohol but also the rowdy and violent environment of the bar itself where he is just as likely to find and fight antagonists as he is on the plains where he might find "Injuns." His thirst for violence is further inferred from his complaint that few men carry weapons, a point made explicit in the phrase "goes heeled." Thus, while the cat and the Apache woman both crave bloody vengeance, Elias proves equally problematic, if not more so, in his unwarranted hunger for violence and conflict.

Importantly, this story's prolonged portrayal of German torture chambers and devices suggests that what confronts the British Europeans is not so much an issue of cultural contamination but the reality that they are violent and degenerate themselves. Britons at the turn of the nineteenth and into the twentieth century viewed their cultural and political traditions as derived from ancient Germanic tribes, and by 1887 historical writing about the origins of British institutions was dominated by theories postulating German origins.[27] Thus Stoker's story, while seemingly set in a foreign environment, is really a return to the origins of British culture. Significantly, the entirety of the story views Germany from the Torture Tower, described as the most interesting place in the city.[28] Moreover, the Tower is profoundly Gothic, filled with "incarnate darkness" and "devices for man's injury to man."[29] The Iron Virgin in it – the method of Elias' torturous death – is particularly emblematic of tradition, seeing as it was "handed down [for centuries] as an instance of the horrors of cruelty of which man is capable."[30] In marking the Iron Virgin as both a supreme monstrosity and an aspect of inherited tradition, Stoker's text worries that white Europeans may be – or become – as horrific as any Apache squaw or black cat.

Many of H. P. Lovecraft's weird tales, written decades later in America, similarly worry over the degeneration of the white race to such an extent that they suggest "hysterical prejudices" even more extreme than Poe's or Stoker's, in the words of J. M. Tyree.[31] Time and again Lovecraft's fictions are situated in populations that are debased by ancient traditions and practices as well as tainted bloodlines. "The Picture in the House" (1921) particularly rotates around an encounter with a backwoods man who has descended into cannibalism. The story begins in Hawthornian fashion, positioning "the carven mausolea of the nightmare countries . . . the moonlit towers of ruined Rhine castles" and "the scattered stones of forgotten cities in Asia" against "the ancient, lonely farmhouses of backwoods New England; for there the dark elements of strength, solitude, grotesqueness, and ignorance combine to form the perfection of hideousness."[32] Like Stoker, too, Lovecraft locates the horrible and alien within white society, thereby worrying over civilization's decay and a monstrosity primarily associated with racial otherness. Indeed, like many of Hawthorne's texts, this story emphasizes the constraints of civilization and the chaos that arises when bodies are released from such constraints. Thus the people of the area descend from ancestors who sought freedom in the wilderness only to develop "dark furtive traits from the prehistoric depths of their cold Northern heritage."[33] But, as in Hawthorne, these people are not truly alone in the wilderness; they are located in the Miskatonic Valley, a name meant to reference a Native American history and populace. Thus, while Lovecraft worries that such degeneration is natural to whiteness, he implies that it is influenced by minority populations and traditions.

What Lovecraft's texts worry over most, though, is the degeneration and devastation caused by racial miscegenation. His texts consistently reveal "an intense hatred for mixed and hybrid forms of culture that cities in general and New York in particular represent, embody, sustain, and champion."[34] For example, the "nightmare cult" of Cthulhu worshippers in "The Call of Cthulhu" (1928) is made up of "mixed-blooded, and mentally aberrant types" including "negroes and mulattoes, largely West Indians or Brava Portuguese from Cape Verde Islands."[35] Such groups prove ideologically and genetically contaminating, producing peculiar urges in white bodies. The backwoods cannibal of "The Picture in the House" develops his taste for human flesh not from his ancestors, but from a book of carvings illustrating Africans "with white skins and Caucasian features."[36] Similarly, miscegenation produces physically misshapen and socially aberrant individuals in "Facts concerning the Late Arthur Jermyn and His Family" (1921). Jermyn's ancestor marries a creature from the Congo, a "white ape of some unknown species, less hairy than any recorded variety, and infinitely nearer mankind."[37] That this "white ape" is meant to metaphorize Africans is apparent not only in this text's repeated emphasis on the Congo and the question of warfare between African tribes, but also from the reference to the images of the Congolese Africans with Caucasian features in "The Picture in the House." Furthermore, the representation of blacks as humanoid apes repeats certain pseudo-scientific ideologies about the nature of blacks during the late nineteenth and early twentieth centuries. Such science held that African (American) blood was not only different from that of whites, but that beings with such blood were "close to the apes, physically grotesque and displayed brutish customs along with their bestial appearance."[38] Lovecraft repeated this notion to certain friends in letters, commenting on the "sensation of brushing past 'hideous negroes that resemble gigantic chimpanzees in the city subway.' "[39] Thus the "white ape-goddess" that was Arthur Jermyn's great-great-great-grandmother is, in fact, a miscegenated African.

The progeny spawned by the ape-goddess' marriage to a white man inevitably prove degenerative. The Jermyns "never seemed to look quite right,"[40] and generations of them repeatedly prove corrupt. Philip, the son from the first generation of offspring, though mentally stable, is "peculiar," densely stupid and given to brief periods of "uncontrollable violence."[41] Further descriptions of Philip's frame – "small, but intensely powerful, and ... of incredible agility" – recall the rumored apish abilities of blacks. Philip notably continues the line of miscegenation by marrying a gypsy before abandoning his family and disappearing into the Congo. Philip's son, Robert, is marked by a "weird Eastern grace despite certain oddities of proportion"[42] and is equally obsessed with Africa. Robert succumbs to madness, but not before producing three children, two of which are mal-formed and never publicly seen.[43] So heinous is the miscegenation in this family that it produces murderous madness in each of the people who discover it. Robert, for instance, kills his children and attempts to kill his grandchildren before committing suicide. Arthur likewise commits suicide after uncovering the corpse of his ancestor, the white ape goddess. At the very least, each Jermyn illustrates a disastrous obsession with Africa which hints at an attempt to uncover the problem of their bloodline. Alfred literally grapples with his heritage, choosing to train and box an African "gorilla of lighter colour than the average."[44] The determination results in Alfred's brutal death after he loses his temper in the middle of a boxing match and savagely seizes and bites his gorilla opponent.[45] Ultimately, the generations of miscegenated Jermyns prove as incapable of managing their finances as they are obsessed with Africa. The lesson is that miscegen-ation produces disastrous consequences on multiple levels for multiple generations.

Stoker's "The Squaw," then, illustrates a presence and use of the racial other typical of the British Gothic; the story also exemplifies the ways in which the racial other functions largely as a reflection of the anxieties the British subject has about itself. In a similar vein, the recurrent horror of Lovecraft's American texts is the decline of white civilization in deference to a savage, non-white society that the thin crust of civility strives to keep down.[46] Time and again, hybrid populations and cultures provide the central horror of Lovecraft's tales. The terror in "The Horror at Red Hook" (1927) flows not just from the slums but from " 'a maze of hybrid squalor,' ... the 'seas of dark, subtle faces,' the 'oriental' nightmare of an exotic, teeming port."[47] "The Shadow over Innsmouth" (1936) gains its uncanniness from the narrator's encounters with the hybrid populace. While some critics read the story's conclusion as an acknowledgment that in the future "hybrid people and cultural forms may be recognized as the norm,"[48] the shudder-inducing ending suggests that such miscegenation is a source of anxiety for the text and its author as they look to the future.

Such fear of racial others in the Gothic tradition does not end in the early twentieth century, but has been continued to the present day throughout the modern tradition of horror literature. Peter Straub's *Ghost Story* (1989), for example, is haunted by black jazz and a black trickster figure, each of which serves as a peculiar manifestation of the shape-shifting villain of the text. Stephen King's novels are particularly plagued by odd manifestations of Africanist characters. Indeed, one of his most recent and most troubling Gothic novels, *Bag of Bones* (1998), centers around a villainous black presence in exploring how the terror of a small town is connected to a history of racial violence and oppression. The source of the haunting stems from the brutal gang rape and murder of a black woman and her young daughter. However, the text reveals that this victimized woman is the villain of the story, as innocent white men, children, and families fall prey to the curse she utters before her death. She is depicted as a monstrous ghost victimizing present generations of innocent white men who are the inheritors of the crime: *They* have to be saved from *her*. Moreover, the solution to all of the horror is not exposure, not reparation, not even a decent attempt at redemption. The solution is to unearth the unmarked grave of the woman and her daughter and to pour lye over their bones – in other words, to erase evidence of the history and crime with a substance that is usually white. So at the end of the story the root of horror and evil is a vengeful black woman who accosts generations of innocent white men and their children, and the only solution is to erase all evidence of her narrative, suffering, and life. All too clearly, the racial anxieties and abjection at the heart of Stoker's and Lovecraft's works have lasted long past the dawn of the twentieth century.

African American Gothic: a retort

While white British and American Gothic writers employ metaphors of monstrosity and animality to meditate upon the place and nature of the racial other, African Americans have appropriated just such Gothic tropes to counter these very discourses. Indeed, beginning with some American slave narratives of the nineteenth century, black writers have revised this very genre's features to insist upon their own humanity and the horror of being defined as the other. Modern to postmodern texts such as *Of One Blood* (1902), *Cane* (1923), *The Street* (1946), and *Beloved* (1987) use the Gothic to articulate the peculiar complexity and horror of being black in America. Richard Wright's novel *Native Son* (1940), in fact, illustrates African American writers' use of the Gothic particularly well. Here "the gothic represents the old consciousness of capitalism."[49] Although James Smethurst defines *Native Son* as an "anti-gothic novel," we must note the ways the novel is "like most Gothic texts … obsessively intertextual,"[50] directly speaking to and revising several major Gothic works, specifically Poe's "Black Cat" and the 1931 film version of *Frankenstein* directed by James Whale. As in Poe's text, Wright's Bigger Thomas is plagued by a cat, which threatens to betray his crime as he attempts to hide Mary Dalton's body in the basement; this cat, however, is explicitly white and doubles for the hyper-white figure of Mrs. Dalton. Both cat and woman present spectral presences in the text which haunt the already troubled Bigger. Mrs. Dalton is repeatedly described as ghost-like as she blindly wanders the halls of the Dalton home. In the scene of Mary's death, her figure is so terrifying, as she stands nearly luminescent in the doorway to her room, that Bigger accidentally smothers Mary in an attempt to silence her, lest his presence be betrayed. Significantly, the haunting of these two white figures becomes a metaphor indicating the uncanny and alienating "white supervision of the black subject," a machinery which the reader sees in force throughout the text in the form of the police, the press, the law, and mass culture at large.[51]

Like Frankenstein's monster, Bigger Thomas is a created monster. More specifically, Bigger, transformed into an unnatural other because of his appearance, is born out of racial injustice and social inequity, much as social inequity and maltreatment are responsible for the monster's fiendish behavior in *Frankenstein*. Wright specifically gestures toward Shelley's text by reproducing a scene from the 1931 film. Bigger's nightmarish flight across the rooftops of Chicago and final stand-off with the police at the water tower recalls scenes from Whale's *Frankenstein* in which the villagers pursue the monster to the windmill before burning it and him down.[52] Hence, while critics hesitate to read Wright's novel as Gothic, it turns out to be littered with the Gothic topoi: "pre-monitions, curses, prophecies, spells, the subterranean, paintings, veils, trap-doors, demonic possession, graves, returns from the dead, skeletons, hauntings, ghosts, confinement, doubles, gothic mansions, visions, conspiracies, premature burial, and so on."[53] Wright manipulates the genre's tropes to speak back to it, even as he resists participation in it, precisely to implicate the racist and classist socio-economic laws governing racial relations in the United States.

Alice Walker's *Meridian* (1976) likewise seems non-Gothic at times, but also gives way to Gothic turns. Walker situates a Gothic story early in her narrative, using it as a commentary upon imagined versus real horrors. In the story, the Sojourner tree marks the place where a slave woman named Louvine buried her tongue after her master tore it out as punishment for telling horror stories to the white plantation children, one of whom has died of fright. Even the descriptions surrounding the birth of this tree are Gothic. Louvine pleads for her severed tongue while "choking on blood," then buries it on an ominous day "when the sun turned briefly black."[54] The tree therefore grows into a gigantic gravestone marking ancestral ground, which is the burial of the ancestral tongue and the reverberating silencing of the ancestral voice. While the white child dies of fright from Louvine's stories, the text's devotion to Louvine's gruesome punishment marks her trauma as the real horror. Half recalling Wright's narrative, which returns to earlier Gothic texts to revise their sense of horror, true terror in Walker's text stems from the torments and oppressions suffered by generations of black women.

More specifically, the story is a comment upon the horror of being exiled into silence. The master clearly silences Louvine's "blood-curdling" horror stories because they come from *her* familial and cultural tradition. Her first stories were ones she remembered from Africa; she only "made up new, American stories when the ones she remembered . . . had begun to bore."[55] By silencing her, Louvine's master prevents her from engaging in her cultural heritage and passing it on. He likewise prevents the further melding of her African heritage with her new American culture. Louvine is prevented from weaving new African American stories with more African characters embedded in Southern-influenced landscapes and plots. Most importantly, this punishment prevents Louvine from creatively engaging in the discourse that typically marks and uses her body as a signifier of monstrosity. At the same time, though, Louvine's literal body reaffirms her as a haunting grotesque other. Possessed of peculiar looks, with "a chin that stuck out farther than it should" and wearing "black headrags that made a shelf over her eyebrows," she becomes a "local phenomenon in plantation society because it was believed she *could not* smile."[56] Yet her Gothic stories serve as a means to prevent her utter marginalization to the realm of bizarre spectacle. The white children value her creativity, engaging with her as an intellectual being and recognizing her for the products of her mind. Denied voice, Louvine becomes a mute, grotesque object that continues to speak volumes about repressed history.

Even so, it is Toni Morrison's novel *Beloved* (1987) that best illustrates the African American reworking of the Gothic tradition. At once a ghost story and a neo-slave narrative, the novel is also an African American refusal to give "way to imaginary terror" and a decision to ground fear "in the stern realities of life" within the historical "boundaries of time."[57] While the novel opens with an encounter with the supernatural, such encounters are hardly the source of disquiet in the text, for, as Sethe calmly explains to Paul D., the ghost is merely the presence of her deceased baby in the midst of a tantrum. Sethe's motherly relationship with the ghost immediately dismisses it as a source of terror in the text, just as Baby Suggs' observation that "Not a house in the country ain't packed to its rafters with some dead Negro's grief"[58] resituates the supernatural in the mundane. Instead, the source of terror in the text stems from the realities of slavery. While Sethe reacts with calm to the baby ghost and her bloody rampages, she shudders at memories of being lashed and forcibly suckled by slave masters. Indeed, Gothic tropes of torture, murder, rape, immolation, living burial, and madness all occur as parts of narratives of slavery, not as part of the supernatural. Thus, as in the writings of Wright and Walker, the Gothic in *Beloved* becomes a way of both mystifying and symbolizing the living nightmare of racial oppression.

Later Black writers continue in the Gothic tradition while also writing retorts to specific white American Gothic texts. Charles Johnson's *Middle Passage* (1990) rewrites sections of Poe's *Narrative of Arthur Gordon Pym*. Likewise, Matt Johnson's novel *Pym* (2012) is an explicit continuation and retelling of Poe's earlier text. Nor are strictly African Americans the only ones to revise the Gothic tradition in this way. For instance, Maryse Conde's *I, Tituba* (1986) retells the story of the Salem witch trials from the perspective of the actual slave who supposedly taught the girls witchcraft. Even more striking is that this tale tells that story by revising several major Gothic texts, including Hawthorne's *The Scarlet Letter*. Similarly, Jamaica Kincaid reimagines the colonial conquest of Hispaniola in terms of native encounter with a rotting fiend in her short story "Ovando" (1989). Writers across the Black Diaspora have deemed the racial discourses within the Gothic worth contesting, knowing full well that the genre has traditionally proven rife with xenophobic utterances and abusive Africanisms. Yet, and perhaps most importantly, these discourses do not and cannot exile the black writer from the genre. Instead, the Gothic's complexity makes it a valuable vehicle for articulating the peculiar tribulations of racial otherness itself.[59]

NOTES

1 Jerrold E. Hogle, "The Gothic Crosses the Channel: Abjection and Revelation in *Le fantôme de l'Opéra*," in *European Gothic: A Spirited Exchange, 1760–1960*, ed. Avril Horner (Manchester University Press, 2002), pp. 204–229, p. 205.
2 Judith Halberstam, *Skin Shows: Gothic Horror and the Technology of Monsters* (Durham, NC: Duke University Press, 1995), p. 2.
3 Halberstam, *Skin Shows*, p. 3.
4 Halberstam, *Skin Shows*, pp. 18, 5.
5 Louis S. Warren, "Buffalo Bill Meets Dracula: William F. Cody, Bram Stoker, and the Frontiers of Racial Decay," *American Historical Review*, 107 (2002), pp. 1124–1157, p. 1127.
6 James Malcolm Rymer, *Sweeney Todd: The String of Pearls* (New York: Wordsworth Editions, 2010), p. 2.
7 Halberstam, *Skin Shows*, p. 15.

8 H. L. Malchow, *Gothic Images of Race in Nineteenth-Century Britain* (Stanford University Press, 1996), p. 127.
9 Warren, "Buffalo Bill Meets Dracula," p. 1127.
10 Malchow, *Gothic Images of Race*, p. 18.
11 Allan Lloyd Smith, *American Gothic Fiction: An Introduction* (New York: Continuum, 2004), p. 65.
12 Toni Morrison, *Playing in the Dark: Whiteness and the Literary Imagination* (Cambridge, MA: Harvard University Press, 1992), p. 45.
13 J. M. Tyree, "Lovecraft at the Automat," *New England Review*, 29 (2008), pp. 137–150, p. 137.
14 Edgar Allan Poe, *The Narrative of Arthur Gordon Pym* (New York: Penguin, 1999), p. 160.
15 Poe, *The Narrative of Arthur Gordon Pym*, pp. 163, 172.
16 Robert Miles, "Europhobia: The Catholic Other in Horace Walpole and Charles Maturin," in *European Gothic*, ed. Horner, pp. 84–103, p. 85.
17 Bram Stoker, "The Squaw," in *The Omnibus of Crime*, ed. Dorothy Sayers (New York: Payson and Clarke, 1929), pp. 1048–1059, p. 1051.
18 Stoker, "The Squaw," p. 1052.
19 Stoker, "The Squaw," p. 1051.
20 Stoker, "The Squaw," p. 1059.
21 Stoker, "The Squaw," pp. 1052, 1058.
22 Stoker, "The Squaw," p. 1058.
23 Warren, "Buffalo Bill Meets Dracula," p. 1127.
24 Warren, "Buffalo Bill Meets Dracula," p. 1129.
25 Stoker, "The Squaw," p. 1050.
26 Stoker, "The Squaw," p. 1058.
27 Warren, "Buffalo Bill Meets Dracula," p. 1141–1142.
28 Stoker, "The Squaw," p. 1050.
29 Stoker, "The Squaw," pp. 1054, 1055.
30 Stoker, "The Squaw," p. 1050.
31 Tyree, "Lovecraft at the Automat," p. 140.
32 H. P. Lovecraft, *The Call of Cthulhu and Other Weird Stories* (New York: Penguin, 1999), p. 34.
33 Lovecraft, *The Call of Cthulhu*, pp. 34–35.
34 Tyree, "Lovecraft at the Automat," p. 145.
35 Lovecraft, *The Call of Cthulhu*, p. 153.
36 Lovecraft, *The Call of Cthulhu*, p. 37.
37 Lovecraft, *The Call of Cthulhu*, pp. 22–23.
38 Allan Lloyd Smith, " 'This Thing of Darkness': Racial Discourse in Mary Shelley's *Frankenstein*," *Gothic Studies*, 6 (2004), pp. 208–222, p. 211.
39 Tyree, "Lovecraft at the Automat," p. 137.
40 Lovecraft, *The Call of Cthulhu*, p. 15.
41 Lovecraft, *The Call of Cthulhu*, p. 16.
42 Lovecraft, *The Call of Cthulhu*, p. 16.
43 Lovecraft, *The Call of Cthulhu*, pp. 16–17.
44 Lovecraft, *The Call of Cthulhu*, p. 17.
45 Lovecraft, *The Call of Cthulhu*, p. 18.
46 Tyree, "Lovecraft at the Automat," p. 145.

47 Lovecraft, *The Call of Cthulhu*, p. 144.
48 Tim Evans, "A Last Defense against the Dark: Folklore, Horror, and the Uses of Tradition in the Works of H. P. Lovecraft," *Journal of Folklore Research*, 42 (2005), pp. 99–135, p. 125.
49 James Smethurst, "Invented by Horror: The Gothic and African American Literary Ideology in *Native Son*," *African American Review*, 35 (2001), pp. 29–40, p. 31.
50 Smethurst, "Invented by Horror," pp. 29, 31.
51 Smethurst, "Invented by Horror," p. 34.
52 Smethurst, "Invented by Horror," p. 32.
53 Smethurst, "Invented by Horror," p. 32.
54 Alice Walker, *Meridian* (New York: Pocket Books, 1976), p. 44.
55 Walker, *Meridian*, p. 43.
56 Walker, *Meridian*, p. 42.
57 Hannah Crofts, *The Bondwoman's Narrative* (New York: Warner Books, 2002), p. 132.
58 Toni Morrison, *Beloved* (New York: Penguin, 1988), p. 5.
59 For more examples, see Maisha L. Wester, *African American Gothic: Screams from Shadowed Places* (New York: Palgrave Macmillan, 2012).

II

CARLOS GALLEGO

The Gothic in North American "subcultures"

The interplay in Gothic fictions of alternate realities, unrepresentable and horrific truths, and the repression and disenfranchisement of those who suffer their identities as "others" (based on categories like race, class, and/ or gender) is by now an accepted Gothic norm,[1] as shown in Chapter 10. Literary critics from Leslie Fiedler to Justin D. Edwards, in particular, have long seen "the American gothic as intimately tied to the history of racial conflict in the United States."[2] However, as Edwards reminds us, this coupling is not exclusive, since other forms of marginalization, like "gender, homosexuality, incest, genocide, rape, war, murder, religion, and class," need to be equally considered "as 'proper' subjects of the nation's gothic literature."[3] Consequently, my aim in this chapter is to extend this established critical conversation by underscoring the intricacies underlying the relationship between the Gothic and American minority literatures that are – for rhetorical purposes – grouped under the term "subcultures." The "sub-" prefix is intentionally utilized with two specific purposes in mind. First, it is intended to group the authors and works in question under the umbrella term of American ethnic/racial minority literatures; second, it is meant to highlight the importance of traditional Gothic themes particular to these minority literary traditions, such as the monstrosity associated with racial/ethnic difference and the subsequent terror or repulsion it inspires. In order to present my argument succinctly, I focus on select Gothic texts and the psycho-political anxieties about existence, knowledge, and teleology represented in this ever-expanding genre, especially as it is reimagined within an American and minority literary context.

The anxieties in question are motivated not just by existential angst but also by more universal, unconscious apprehensions concerning possible realities that transcend the comforts of our "known" and familiar existence. This sensing of the metaphysical is usually referred to as an intuition within the Gothic tradition: the sensing of ghosts or spirits that point beyond the horizons of physical existence to a different plane of being, complicating the materialism of Enlightenment science. This tension leads to unsettling doubts – do we really know what we know, and/or are there certain truths we would rather not acknowledge? – which in turn create an ontological anxiety regarding the truth of human being: What is it, and is its truth tied to physical existence? In other words, is there a direct correlation between the truth of our humanity and the accidental idiosyncrasies that constitute our physical selves? Such questions have historically given rise to psychological and political anxieties that undermine the integrity of individual identity while threatening the legitimacy of the nation-state. If we are uncertain of what constitutes reality, how can we be certain of being the individuals or nations we understand ourselves to be? The spectral difference posed by an intuited otherness within the self – best captured in the Gothic theme of the monstrous double – seems to undermine the reliable consistency that defines identity and legitimates the ego as the center of reason. After all, the anxieties resulting from such doubts form a central part of Freud's psychoanalytic theory and were represented as inherent to human experience years earlier in Gothic works ranging from Poe's "William Wilson" (1839) to Stevenson's *Strange Case of Dr. Jekyll and Mr. Hyde* (1886).

Within the American Gothic tradition, this interest in a presence that threatens the foundations of identity was expanded in the nineteenth century by such American authors as Melville ("Benito Cereno"), Hawthorne (*The Scarlet Letter*), and Perkins Gilman ("The Yellow Wallpaper") to include social, political, and cultural tensions, thereby representing how majority interests often supersede the welfare of minority populations deemed "inferior," in the process portraying the methods by which "others" (as opposed to a majority "standard") are created. These authors highlighted the anxieties associated with maintaining an uncorrupted and enlightened "American" identity, creating the groundwork for the historical critique characteristic of American Gothic. Accordingly, this mixed genre quickly became a favorite among authors interested in foregrounding the marginalization and disenfranchisement of whatever and/or whoever is considered too different to be integrated into the majority: the unassimilable and thus expendable others who are classified as subhuman, if not monstrous, and treated accordingly, as exemplified in the strategic genocidal violence against Native Americans, the institutionalization of African American slavery and its Jim Crow legacies, and the ongoing domestication of women in general.

The historical critique built into the Gothic is equally applicable to American racial/ethnic minority literatures, as evident in the classification "minor." Usually expressed in terms of identity confusion and a socio-political powerlessness stemming from cultural difference and misrecognition, the aforementioned psycho-political anxieties characteristic of the Gothic are equally present in African American, Chicana/o (Mexican American), and Native American literary works. The following sections show how these psycho-political anxieties manifest themselves in American minority literatures, as well-known Gothic themes are reimagined in a specifically American racial/ethnic literary context. Of importance is the confluence between these different "minority" literary canons and how certain shared traits and concerns allow for their more general and collective classification as "subcultures." The distinctiveness of these subcultures also demands specific theoretical approaches unique to particular situations, which in turn demonstrates the various forms that a psycho-political anxiety can take. Again, these anxieties are interchangeable and often overlap, so strategic generalizations, as well as textual examples, are foregrounded to highlight the important issues at stake in pairing the Gothic tradition with the American subcultures in question.

The time-proven and Gothic-friendly theories of psychoanalysis and Marxism facilitate this task, since they speak to both the psychological anxieties over the undermining of individual and collective identities and to the political fears surrounding an excessive, unassimilable, and uncontrollable difference. Not only do both of these traditions cite Gothic literature in order to exemplify specific points – Marx alludes to vampires as representative of capitalism's exploitative tendencies, while Freud relies on E. T. A. Hoffman's tale of terror "The Sandman" to explicate his theory of the uncanny – but they also offer insights into psychology, philosophy, and political economy that have proven highly influential, as Leslie Fiedler has shown most of all,[4] in the development of central Gothic themes. Moreover, both theories are known for challenging fundamental premises of Enlightenment thinking, such as rationalism, individualism, and the assumed equality characteristic of democratic-capitalist societies. In short, the critiques inherent in these theories have long aligned them with Gothic literature, which is also defined by its problematization of certain assumptions regarding scientific reason and certainty, puritanically disciplined morality, and narratives of progress.

The two sections that follow examine certain psycho-political anxieties that are both typical of the Gothic and uniquely represented within an American racial/ethnic minority literature. The first section examines the epistemological and historical-political anxieties surrounding the eradication of cultural traditions through modernization – specifically modernization as the realization of Enlightenment progress – represented in Native American and African American works. The main concern in this section is how Euro-American Enlightenment notions of teleological history and progress accommodate, or fail to accommodate, tradition-based but subordinated cultures that function according to different historical-epistemological paradigms. The second section investigates the psychological anxieties that emerge from identity confusion – specifically the tension between ideologies of physical appearance and the truth of human being – as expressed in Chicana/o literature. Here the main focus is on how marginalized individuals are forced to negotiate their self-perception or identity in a social order that rejects them as subhuman and how their eventual existential awakening challenges their classification as monstrous or unnatural. These examples help demonstrate how the anxieties associated with the Gothic tradition regarding ontology (questions of being), epistemology (questions of knowledge), and teleological progress (questions of history) get truly reconceptualized in a racial/ethnic/American literary context.

Modernization and its discontents

On December 29, 1890, the inevitable clash between the "modernization" embodied in European and American settler expansion throughout the United States and the traditional cultural practices and lifestyles of Native American tribes throughout the country came to a tragic and bloody climax as US cavalrymen were ordered to fire upon hundreds of Lakota Sioux men, women, and children who had surrendered and camped near Wounded Knee Creek on the Lakota Pine Ridge Reservation in South Dakota. In many respects, this historical tragedy is characterized by misunderstanding, not only in terms of the conflict's supposed origins – a dispute regarding Black Coyote's refusal to surrender a rifle he had rightfully purchased to the cavalry – but more so for the violent intersection of epistemological paradigms, one that viewed nature as an end (Native American) and another that perceived nature as a means (Euro-American).[5] At stake was the idea of civilization itself – of progress, enlightenment, and modernization – at least in the minds of US agents like James McLaughlin, who viewed resistant Native Americans like Sitting Bull as obstacles to progress. As Heather Cox Richardson notes, McLaughlin reported that "there were 'malcontents' at the agencies who refused to accept modernity and were trying to hold their people back ... slowing down the Indians' progress," thereby suggesting that "[removing] a handful of traditionalists like Sitting Bull would end all the trouble."[6]

The epistemological confrontation underlying the clash at Wounded Knee is best captured in the misunderstandings surrounding the tradition of the

Ghost Dance. Cox Richardson defines this Native American tradition and its importance in the following terms:

> The Ghost Dance promised to bring back the world of game and plenty that had been theirs before the coming of whites ... [And even though the] Ghost Dancers never hurt their non-Indian neighbors and few settlers paid them much attention ... Republican political appointees did. Incompetent and frightened by the Indians, they interpreted the religious enthusiasm as tremors of an approaching war.[7]

It is evident from the Ghost Dance's purpose that retribution for unjust wrongs is an essential component of the ceremony, thereby lending credence to politicians' fears regarding an "approaching war." Since this conflict was already occurring, both sides were highly conscious of another potential clash, with each side preparing for it according to the dictates of their respective paradigms. On the one hand, the US cavalrymen, thinking themselves agents of modernity, prepared their technologically advanced weaponry, ready to defend further progress and civilization in the name of reason and Enlightenment. On the other hand, the Lakota Sioux's preparations adhered to a more traditional world view, one untainted by the abstractions of science, markets, private property, and other European Enlightenment concepts. Instead, they confronted the US cavalry by affirming both their human dignity and their right to refusal in the simplest of terms: "We are people in this world."[8] Never having recognized the Sioux as "people" worthy of modernity, the US cavalry dismissed this proclamation and attacked. As the massacre began, the Ghost Dancers, using their "special shirts" as protection, responded to the weapons of modernity – to the rifles and bullets – with song, magic, and tradition: "Short Bull told his followers that these shirts would be imbued with magic. He promised his followers that the special shirts would protect them from the guns of the soldiers sent to stop the Ghost Dance."[9]

The historical-epistemological tensions underlying the Wounded Knee Massacre not only highlight a violent clash of cultures and world visions; the haunting irreconcilability of these paradigms becomes one of the key features of Native American and other racial/ethnic minority literatures. Classic – and often Gothic – works, especially N. Scott Momaday's *House Made of Dawn* (1968) and Leslie Marmon Silko's *Ceremony* (1977), foreground protagonists contending with internal struggles brought upon them by modernization and their attempts to integrate into contemporary American society, usually at the cost of their cultural traditions and identity. These internal struggles bespeak the difficulties of assimilation, which itself serves as the ultimate surrender to the paradigmatic defeat foretold at Wounded

Knee. The loss of traditional cultural practices and the world views they reinforced is represented as so irretrievable in Native American literature that it usually takes the form of an impossible material reality: a ghostly figure or ghost story like the Ghost Dance itself. In *House Made of Dawn*, the violent intersection of modernity and Native American cultural traditions is seen in Abel's (the main protagonist's) confrontation with a mysterious, indeed ghostly, albino figure whom he murders in a moment of drunken "madness," while in *Ceremony* this epistemological tension is represented in terms of haunting narratives, specifically different narrative styles rather than completely different types of stories, thereby suggesting something more akin to a paradigm shift than a clash. Stated in Gothic terms, Momaday's novel depicts the collision of world visions in terms of murder, ghosts, and spectral figures, whereas Silko's text focuses more on ghost stories and their effects. Despite this difference in focus, both novels underscore the devastating consequences of modernization and the need for balance between the violence inherent in Euro-American notions of progress and the respect for environmental and communal harmony advocated by traditional Native American beliefs and practices.

In *House Made of Dawn*, Abel is introduced as a victim of modernization, stumbling drunkenly off a bus and into his grandfather's arms, returning to the reservation just after having completed his service in World War II. Abel's drunkenness functions as the most obvious symbol of modernity's negative effects on Native Americans throughout the novel. Representing a failed attempt at self-medication, Abel cannot drown out the alienation he suffers as a consequence of his military service. Moreover, Abel's alcoholism blinds him to the cyclical reality of his self-destruction, thereby inhibiting both his "return home" and his cultural reconciliation. His inability to integrate into modern society or reconnect with his traditional culture – long a problem for European Gothic heroes, as in Matthew Lewis' *The Monk* (1796) – leaves him in existential limbo, suffering an internal turmoil that culminates with the murder of the mysterious albino following the latter's exceptional performance in a traditional Native American ceremony. While Abel seems out of place during the festival, the albino man amazes spectators with his horsemanship, smearing Abel with the blood of a rooster as he stands watching. Later, after drinking, Abel encounters the albino man in town where, after some discussion, he kills him.

Abel's seemingly inexplicable act of murder serves as the main problem in the novel, as it causes him to be institutionalized and transplanted to Los Angeles, two experiences that intensify his alienation. The second half of the novel addresses Abel's experiences in Los Angeles, which bring him close to death, and his attempt to return home and reconcile with his cultural past. Since readers never have access to the albino man's words or thoughts, despite his centrality to the novel's plot, he functions similarly to other famous Gothic characters that are equally marginalized within a text but play a major role in the story's development, such as the madwoman from Jamaica in Charlotte Brontë's *Jane Eyre* (1847). Like Brontë's mysterious character, the albino man serves as a kind of doppelgänger, or double, to the main protagonist. Although represented as Abel's direct opposite – an opposition embodied in their differing skin colors – the mysterious albino man serves as a mirror in which Abel sees a version of himself that is more authentically engaged with his cultural traditions.

To view the albino man as Abel's opposite, one must read his symbolic significance as literally being skin deep, with his whiteness being an embodiment of the Euro-American racialized notions of progress and modernity that have destroyed Abel's identity. Consequently, the albino man's performance at the Native American festival – coupled with Abel's existential angst – presents an overwhelming threat that reminds Abel of the modernization he despises and is attempting to escape/forget. Moreover, Abel seems mocked because of his disconnection from cultural traditions, since it is, after all, a man with white skin who outperforms him at the festival. As such, Abel's actions can be read as retribution, as the revenge of the defeated Native American paradigm against its oppressive white world. In the novel, Abel's revenge is seen as so tragic and pathetic that it is understood socially as the act of a mentally disturbed individual, its political consequence and motivation completely out of place in a modern world. Seen in this manner, Abel's killing of the albino man represents an embarrassment to Euro-American modernity, a blatant example of Native Americans' inability and/or refusal to integrate into contemporary society, as the character Tosamah, an "educated" Native American living in Los Angeles, explains:

> They gave him every advantage. They gave him a pair of shoes and told him to go to school. They deloused him and gave him a lot of free haircuts and let him fight on their side. But was he grateful? Hell, no, man. He was too damn dumb to be civilized. So what happened? They let him alone at last. They thought he was harmless. They thought he was going to plant some beans, man, and live off the fat of the land. Oh, he was going to make his way, all right. He would get some fat little squaw all knocked up, and they would lie around all day and get drunk and raise a lot of little government wards. They would make some pottery, man, and boost the economy. But it didn't turn out that way. He turned out to be a real primitive sonuvabitch, and the first time he got hold of a knife he killed a man. That must have embarrassed the hell out of them.[10]

As an integrated subject of modernity, Tosamah views Abel's crime as epitomizing a failure, his failure to accommodate a new epistemology ("too damn dumb to be civilized") and participate in historical progress ("a real primitive sonuvabitch"). Abel's institutionalization and rehabilitation therefore represent modernity's safety net and totalizing logic, implementing programs precisely for individuals like Abel so that they may be accounted for despite of (or due to) their dysfunction.

When viewed in the legalistic terms of modernity that Tosamah ascribes to, Abel's killing of the albino man constitutes a crime that must be explained, categorized, and punished under the law (always a problem in Gothic works, as noted in Chapter 3 above). Whether one views the albino as representative of the Euro-American conquest or the universalized citizen of a post-Enlightenment society, his murder frames Abel as a tragic hero – similar to several Gothic ones, as in Charles Brockden Brown's *Edgar Huntly* (1799) – who commits a wrongful act for rightful reasons. However, if the albino man is viewed in terms of a Gothic double, one that not only implies the obvious racialized mirroring of opposed paradigms (Native American versus European) but also suggests a potential metaphysical symbolism, then the albino man's doppelgänger effect can take on a completely new significance, especially when considering that *House Made of Dawn* ends and begins with Abel attempting to reconcile his alienation by engaging in the ceremonial practice of running with his dead ancestors. In other words, the novel begins and ends with ghosts, with Abel himself ambiguously represented by the end as inhabiting a space somewhere between life and death.

If *House Made of Dawn* is read as a ghost story, then the mysterious albino man's importance can be reinterpreted as metaphysical and Abel's crime as spiritually redemptive rather than politically tragic. Viewed in this manner, the albino man's white skin is less a representation of racial politics and more indicative of a metaphysical state – that of the undead. Consequently, as a ghostly figure in a Gothicized story, the albino man's murder can be understood as spiritual-cultural rather than racial-political. He represents a dead culture that refuses to die, which explains his superlative ability in the ceremonial practices, despite his white skin. He does not symbolize the intrusion of the white man's world in this context but rather a dying Native American culture desperate for a place in the modern world. His murder can thus symbolize the impossibility of this reconciliation – these two worlds can never embrace – or Abel's attempt to keep a dying culture alive by negating (indeed murdering) a negative (a ghost). Either way, Abel's motivation can be ascribed to a life-affirming epistemology, as his negation of a negation (I cannot allow my culture to die) makes his act as much redemptive as it is criminal. This paradox seems to coincide with Abel's perception of the killing as "the most natural thing in the world," since, in his oversimplified reasoning, the white man's whiteness is transparently political, making his murder the logical conclusion to an inevitable confrontation: "He had killed the white man. It was not a complicated thing, after all; it was very simple."[11]

What Abel does not understand is that the albino man's whiteness is indicative not only of racial, epistemological, and cultural difference, but also of a radical and misunderstood sameness. While Abel is confident that the albino man must die – "They must know that he would kill the white man again, if he had the chance, that there could be no hesitation whatsoever ... A man kills such an enemy if he can"[12] – he cannot articulate the reasons why. His inability to explain himself seems appropriate in a novel that centers on the secret, if not unattainable, knowledge possessed by the dead. All we know as readers is that Abel does not overcome his alienation until he transcends the limitations of the material world in a ghostly manner. At the novel's conclusion, he falls "in the snow" as he runs, covering himself in its whiteness, only to notice that, like the mysterious albino man, his words do not produce sound: "He was running, and under his breath he began to sing. There was no sound, and he had no voice; he had only the words of a song."[13]

This Gothic representation of whiteness in *House Made of Dawn* encapsulates both difference and sameness: a dualism that originates with the Enlightenment epistemological paradigm and its accompanying racial politics, one which reinforces superficial anatomical differences while masking the radical sameness of human existence. This tension can also be found in other Native American works, among them Silko's *Ceremony*, and African American classics such as Ralph Ellison's *Invisible Man* (1952). In *Ceremony*, for example, the protagonist, Tayo, is afflicted by a similar type of post-traumatic stress disorder as Abel, as he is also a World War II veteran returning to life on the reservation. Unlike Abel, however, Tayo suffers from actual bouts of depression, hallucinations, and psychosomatic episodes. Alcohol does not drown his sorrows, so he is compelled to seek traditional medicine men for a remedy. Silko constructs her novel around the ceremonies Tayo must complete in order to heal, which entails a renewed attention to old stories and storytelling that recasts the long-standing Gothic penchant, prominently exemplified in Mary Shelley's *Frankenstein* (1818), for stories within stories within stories.

Tayo's cultural awakening occurs upon his realization that narratives construct the realities we experience and that the sickness of the modernity he suffers is in essence a story that he needs to purge, which explains his vomiting fits throughout the novel. Finding and telling the proper story in the correct manner is the essence of ceremony, which functions as a type of healing practice in traditional Native American rituals. Thus *Ceremony* can be read as a type of metanarrative, a narrative about narratives as is *The Castle of Otranto*, especially with the two prefaces attached to it by 1765. In this context, modernity is not represented as a historical inevitability but rather as a narrative among various narratives. As Betonie, a medicine man, explains to Tayo, whiteness – as a metaphor for modernity – is another form of witchery that was created by ancient (indeed quite Gothic) "witch people from all directions," including but not limited to "witches from all the Pueblos." Consequently, to believe in a white world as dominating a Native American world is to surrender to an ideology of evil that achieves power by implementing false differences among humans:

> "That is the trickery of the witchcraft," he said. "They want us to believe all evil resides in white people. Then we will look no further to see what is really happening. They want us to separate ourselves from white people, to be ignorant and helpless as we watch our own destruction. But white people are only a tool that the witchery manipulates; and I tell you, we can deal with white people, with their machines and their beliefs. We can because we invented white people; it was Indian witchery that made white people in the first place."[14]

Betonie then explains to Tayo that the evil associated with "white people" is in actuality a witchcraft at the heart of primal human existence, a narrative born of a contest that unleashed a horror story that "cannot be called back."[15] This reworking of the "primal crime" basic to the European Gothic helps Tayo realize that the ill effects of modernity that he suffers are side effects of a narrative gone wrong and that the cure to his sickness lies in ceremony, in finding the right narrative and articulating it in the correct manner. Silko thus implies that the discontents of modernization, although impossible to undo, can still be altered to have a different effect. *Ceremony*, as a narrative of parallelisms, gradations, and repetitions, uses Gothic motifs to communicate a political statement that *House Made of Dawn* only suggests: Racial difference is superficial, and the alienation attributed to Euro-American society is simply the latest symptomatic consequence of an ongoing narrative of progress, which is actually regressive (and, in that sense, Gothic) and has been acted out by people since the beginning of time. The problem of alienation is as old as the story of alienation. Consequently, whiteness is not a racial category but rather a logic or narrative that, among others, functions according to a thinking that separates subjects from objects and that is celebrated by some as the backbone of modernization, as Cox Richardson suggests in her depiction of McLaughlin at Wounded Knee; there is an evil that sees "no life ... only objects" and to which the "world is a dead thing."[16]

Similarly, in Ellison's *Invisible Man*, the epistemological tensions between cultural traditions and modern notions of progress are represented as racialized in order to subvert the values associated with racist thinking. The dialectic of difference and sameness is so interwoven throughout the text that it produces a haunting effect on the characters. The unnamed African American narrator, for example, is troubled by a recurring nightmare he has had since childhood in which his grandfather too honestly states the racialized catch-22 of modernity: "Keep This Nigger-Boy Running."[17] Since the narrator attempts to assimilate into modern society through a Ben Franklinesque ethic of self-improvement, the dream serves as a Gothically haunting riddle (like the walking portrait-ghost in *Otranto*) that he fails to comprehend until adulthood. The novel develops as a play on this dream, with the narrator engaging modernity through various means in an effort to overcome his alienation. The dream is nightmarish because it is a joke on the narrator, since the answer is embedded in the dream itself: The alienation the narrator experiences is not strictly a consequence of his racial otherness. The key words in the dream are not "Nigger-Boy" but "Keep" and "Running," which underscore the so-called "rat race" that undergirds and interpellates us all as subjects of modernity.

Ellison's literary genius lies in undermining racial differences in a novel defined by its portrayal of racial alienation. The text is full of parallelisms and subtleties that complicate the assumed hierarchy of racial difference, from the doppelgänger relationship between Norton and Trueblood to the drops of black paint required to make optic white the whitest of all white paints. Ellison highlights the hidden interconnections between Anglo-Americans and African Americans by calling attention to the ideologies that utilize racial difference to determine human value. Even the pseudo-scientific thinking of the Brotherhood, which claims to be beyond the influences of ideology, ascribes to a pervasive racist logic, which prompts the narrator's eventual disenchantment and departure from it. The haunting nature of the narrator's nightmare thus lies in its universality rather than its racialization. In other words, *Invisible Man* makes it clear that the alienation the narrator experiences is a direct consequence of modernity and not simply of the isolated effects of racism. Thus the novel ends with one of the more famous haunting lines in literature, one that explains why it is upheld as a major work in various literary canons, including African American, modernist, and twentieth-century American: "Who knows but that, on the lower frequencies, I speak for you?"[18] The novel's ending suggests a radical interconnectivity or universalism between the narrator and the reader, a suggestion that reframes the haunting nightmare in a completely different way: We are all potential victims to the alienating effects of modernization; we are all versions of a "Nigger-Boy Running," the haunting primal figure. As with Silko's *Ceremony*, Ellison's *Invisible Man* demystifies race as an ideology that only perpetuates the alienating effects of modernity; as such, racial difference, while having real, material effects in the world, is founded upon a false narrative, very much like the forged will behind the hauntings in *Otranto*, which Horace Walpole himself labeled the first "Gothic story."

However, the Gothic allure of Ellison's masterpiece is not found only in its symbolic representation of modernization and its discontents. As the narrator explains in the opening lines, the story's seemingly supernatural appeal lies in the main protagonist's invisibility:

> I am an invisible man. No, I am not a spook like those who haunted Edgar Allan Poe; nor am I one of your Hollywood-movie ectoplasms. I am a man of substance, of flesh and bone, fiber and liquids – and I might even be said to possess a mind. I am invisible, understand, simply because people refuse to see me … When they approach me they see only my surroundings, themselves, or figments of their imagination – indeed, everything and anything except me.[19]

The novel goes on to playfully associate the narrator's invisibility with his racialized identity as an African American, referenced in the above passage with the pun "spook." As the title implies, the narrator's lack of recognition renders him a ghost despite his material existence. The horror of his situation is not that people cannot see him but that people choose not to recognize him as an equal and fully human being. Thus, rather than being a ghost in the Gothic tradition of Poe, a science-fiction fabrication, or a Hollywood production, the narrator's invisibility ironically stems from his material visibility. In other words, the fact that people do not see him is not due to some supernatural or scientific reason but rather to the simple fact that, as he is a black man in the United States, people choose not to see him and so make him a Gothic haunting specter of an especially revealing kind. The genius of Ellison's opening lines is that they establish and clarify a long-standing theme within Gothic literature: That which is deemed too different to be assimilated, in this case racial difference, is framed as monstrous or, in the case of *Invisible Man*, too irrelevant to be acknowledged. This reframing of difference as otherness, and of otherness as horrific or monstrous, also turns out to be a central Gothic theme in Chicana/o literature.

Monstrosity and the same difference of the other

The disenfranchisement and marginalization of difference is not unique to Anglo-American culture or its accompanying literary canon. Within the already mentioned subcultures, there are numerous examples of othering that reproduce the classifications of subhuman and monstrous. One such example appears in David Johnson's reading of the novel *Face* (1985) by Cecile Pineda.[20] In a 1991 essay on that novel, Johnson finds that Pineda's failure to market herself as a Chicana author, or *Face* as a Chicana novel, is indicative of assimilationism, an attempt to de-ethnify her work as a means of de-ethnifying herself, repressing her unique cultural difference in favor of an assimilationist ideology.[21] Though I disagree with the identity politics underlying Johnson's reading, I do agree that *Face* represents the potentially horrific nonidentity that underlies human being – the minute and infinitesimal but utter *difference* that characterizes our relationship to reality, our own bodies, and each other – as well as the remarkable capacity for overcoming confinement to one's status that emerges from such a nonidentity. In that way, it is comparable to other Gothic classics from *Frankenstein* and *Jekyll and Hyde* to Franz Kafka's *The Metamorphosis* (1915). Consequently, I do not read the novel as invested in the triumph of racial/ethnic identity, but rather in its failure and in the willpower required to endure the difficult truths that emerge from this failure. *Face* is therefore less valuable as an ethnic narrative that either rejects or embraces notions of assimilation or multicultural difference and more valuable when it is seen as contributing to a literary tradition – which might indeed be called "modern Gothic" – that includes Kafka, Ellison, even Samuel Beckett, authors that Pineda acknowledges as highly influential on her work.

Because of its remarkable narrative, it is important to note that *Face* is based on true events. In a sort of preface to the novel, Pineda explains how "*Face* started out as a filler story in the back pages of a 1977 newspaper."[22] She confesses that the

> story [she] read there gripped [her] in ways [she] could not begin to understand. Without a doubt, [she] said to [herself], such a remarkable story will appeal to some novelist who will discern meanings in it so powerful that the story will act as a catalyst for a memorable work of fiction.[23]

However, years passed and the "memorable work of fiction" never appeared until *Face*. Consequently, the text must be read as being more than a simple novel, as it challenges us, like other Gothic fictions, to think of this impossible story as necessarily possible.

The story's truth value is clearly established in the novel's prologue, which consists of an excerpt from a speech given by an unnamed doctor during the "Twenty-fifth Annual Meeting of Plastic and Reconstructive Surgery in Rio de Janeiro":

> On March 21, 19—, as he raced down a path in the outlying hills of the Whale Back, a man lost his footing. His fall from the footholds cut into the rock high above the bay left him unconscious and terribly mutilated.

He was taken, still unconscious, to a charity hospital where he lay for some time wrapped in bandages. His wounds eventually healed, but because he could not afford even meager social security payments on his barber's salary, public assistance refused him funds for surgical reconstruction.

In the Whale Back, the slum district where he had a shack, no one wanted to deal with him anymore. His face was no longer recognizable, even to his friends. He came and went mostly at night. He scavenged for food in the garbage cans of luxury districts. He survived by begging. He became known to his neighbors as a bruxo. He was feared, despised, but not ignored: they stoned his shack, and later set it on fire.

By September 21, he had disappeared. He was to board a bus at the Rodoviaria depot for Rio de Pedras and was not seen again in the Capital.

You may ask what this man was doing all this time he was in hiding ...[24]

Recasting not just the creature in *Frankenstein* but the title character of Stephen Crane's "The Monster" (1897), *Face* goes on to describe the details of exactly what this man does while in hiding, offering flashbacks of how he came to be a fugitive from humanity. It is, like many of Kafka's tales, a fantastic yet ordinary story: that of a man who has the unlucky experience of suffering an accident and remaining permanently scarred as a result of it. The banality of such an experience is evident in its role as a "filler story" in the back pages of some local newspaper. Yet, as in Kafka's *Metamorphosis*, this is not a simple tale of misfortune. There is a particularity to Helio Cara's (the protagonist's) story that manages to astound, to challenge conventional notions of what is possible and real. This sense of astonishment comes from the fact that Helio takes it upon himself to reconstruct his countenance, grafting sections of skin from his chest and sewing them to his face, thus slowly rebuilding one of humanity's most essential signifiers in an act that recalls the stitched and multicolored face of Frankenstein's creature in Shelley's novel.

A crucial moment takes place when Helio views himself in the mirror for the first time after his accident. At the clinic, during the middle of the night, he rises out of bed for the first time, fumbling for a light switch in the darkness, and sees himself:

In the sudden light, someone stands weaving before him on unsteady legs, something without nose or mouth, eyes dark purple splotches, sealed almost shut, particles tattooed onto the skin.

His groin goes hot.

Not me! Not me! His voice gargles in his throat. No sound comes, no sound at all.[25]

Helio faints and, while unconscious, recalls the details of his catastrophic fall. Later, he would also "remember sensing that something had changed";

he would remember "feeling nothing, nothing, at all," not recalling "any lapse," and that this "absence [is what] ... frightened him the most."[26]

Helio's alienating experience in front of the mirror recalls Jacques Lacan's psychoanalytic theory about the mirror stage of human development, particularly his notion of *méconnaissance* or misrecognition.[27] In this early work, Lacan explains how alienation structures the development and socialization of human beings. For him, the subject's notion of "identity" is a necessary misrecognition (*méconnaissance*) that enables him/her to function both existentially and symbolically in the world. This necessary misrecognition originates with the infant's perception of his/her image in the mirror as being an extension of his/her agency, as somehow being "real." Psychoanalysis teaches that alienation is not the unique consequence of racial, economic, or even sexual oppression but rather a defining characteristic of human existence. Though we may attempt to resolve our alienation through various attachments (like ideologies), we will ultimately fail to fully compensate for the existential lack caused by the process of socialization.

The mirror scene in *Face* offers an interesting Gothic inversion of Lacan's theory, since Helio, in a kind of Jekyll and Hyde manner, refuses to identify with the image in the mirror, claiming that the image represented is "not me, not me." Though correct in rejecting the false reality of the mirror's image, Helio's negation is not a response to the specular fantasy of self but rather a predictable reaction to the horrifying alterity or difference reflected back at him, making his cry of "not me" paradoxically correct and incorrect. On the one hand, it negates the fantasy of identity associated with the mirror stage, yet on the other hand it creates a distance between Helio and the truth of his humanity. This distance emerges because Helio ascribes to an ideology that conflates one's humanity with physical appearance, in this case the face. This is certainly expected, since he is fired from his job and abandoned by his girlfriend, an act he monstrously avenges by beating and raping her. He loses his humanity because he fails to recognize that its truth lies beyond his grotesque facelessness. His grotesqueness reveals a fundamental human sameness that undermines the ideological differences that define our respective identities. He discovers that what makes one human cannot be found in the accidental physical traits associated with anatomical differences, such as those attributed to race and gender. Like a terrifying void or abyss, Helio's facelessness functions as a blank page, capable of reflecting back the innumerable possibilities of human being to those that have the courage or misfortune to encounter him. Much like Frankenstein's creature or Gregor Samsa, Helio must first overcome the violence that accompanies his difference before realizing the truth that defines his humanity, a truth that cannot be reduced to ideological notions of identity based on categories such as race, class, and/or gender.

The ontological anxieties represented in *Face* are not uniquely attributable to Chicana/o identity – even its portrayal of identity confusion or ambiguity, traits theorized by writers and critics like Gloria Anzaldúa and Juan Bruce-Novoa[28] – as they are also found in the works I analyze above. For example, the unnamed narrator in Ellison's novel constantly wrestles with his identity, while Abel's view of the albino man as a monster who needs to be killed is indicative of his lost humanity, just as Tayo's PTSD is symptomatic of a personal and collective existential crisis. Moreover, the epistemological and historical anxieties regarding modernity found in works like *House Made of Dawn*, *Ceremony*, and *Invisible Man* are equally present in *Face*, as demonstrated in Helio's relationship to the medical and governmental institutions that refuse him reconstructive surgery but also assign him an uncomfortable mask for the sake of comforting those "normal" human beings who may come in contact with him. Within the world of modernity, Helio's unfortunate accident renders him too different to be human.

As I hope I have demonstrated, these ontological, epistemological, and historical anxieties are as present in the American racial/ethnic literature of the era after 1945 as they are in classic Gothic texts. The fears and anxieties surrounding the fragile separation of difference and sameness, identity and otherness, barbarism and civilization are central to both literary traditions, which explains why the questions these texts pose – like the narrator's dream in *Invisible Man* – continue to haunt us as readers and members of a diverse human race.

NOTES

1 For examples, see Allan Lloyd Smith, *American Gothic Fiction: An Introduction* (New York: Continuum, 2004), and *The Gothic Other: Racial and Social Constructions in the Literary Imagination*, ed. Ruth Bienstock Anolik and Douglas L. Howard (Jefferson, NC: McFarland, 2004).

2 Justin D. Edwards, *Gothic Passages: Racial Ambiguity and the American Gothic* (University of Iowa Press, 2003), p. xvii.

3 Edwards, *Gothic Passages*, p. xvii.

4 In *Love and Death in the American Novel*, rev. ed. (New York: Stein and Day, 1966), esp. pp. 23–61, 128–161.

5 See Heather Cox Richardson, *Wounded Knee: Party Politics and the Road to an American Massacre* (New York: Basic Books, 2010), pp. 266–268.

6 Cox Richardson, *Wounded Knee*, p. 127.

7 Cox Richardson, *Wounded Knee*, p. 15.

8 Cox Richardson, *Wounded Knee*, p. 266.

9 Cox Richardson, *Wounded Knee*, p. 180.

10 N. Scott Momaday, *House Made of Dawn* (New York: Harper & Row, 1968), pp. 148–149.

11 Momaday, *House Made of Dawn*, p. 102.

12 Momaday, *House Made of Dawn*, pp. 102–103.

13 Momaday, *House Made of Dawn*, p. 212.

14 Leslie Marmon Silko, *Ceremony* (New York: Penguin, 1986), p. 132.

15 Silko, *Ceremony*, p. 138.

16 Cox Richardson, *Wounded Knee*, p. 135.

17 Ralph Ellison, *Invisible Man* (New York: Vintage, 1990), p. 33.

18 Ellison, *Invisible Man*, p. 581.

19 Ellison, *Invisible Man*, p. 3.

20 Cecile Pineda, *Face* (San Antonio, TX: Wings Press, 2003).

21 See David E. Johnson, "Face Value (An Essay on Cecile Pineda's *Face*)," *Americas Review*, 19 (1991), pp. 73–93.

22 Pineda, *Face*, p. xiii.

23 Pineda, *Face*, p. xiii.

24 Pineda, *Face*, p. 3.

25 Pineda, *Face*, p. 19.

26 Pineda, *Face*, p. 19.

27 See Jacques Lacan, *Écrits*, trans. Bruce Fink (New York: Norton, 2002), p. 309.

28 See Gloria Anzaldúa, *Borderlands/La Frontera: The New Mestiza* (1987), 5th edn. (San Francisco: Aunt Lute Books, 2012), and Juan Bruce-Novoa, *Retrospace: Collected Essays on Chicano Literature* (Houston, TX: Arte Público Press, 1990).

12

KEN GELDER

The postcolonial Gothic

It is not hard to imagine the violent processes of colonization, as it takes possession of new worlds, in Gothic ways. Elleke Boehmer does exactly this when she characterizes the colonizer as a vampire draining the people whose country it occupies: "From the day the colonizer takes possession till the day he reluctantly departs ... his activities connote the extraction of the very stuff, the life-blood, from those – the colonial other – who have absolutely nothing other than abject life in abundance."[1] Audiences for the *Twilight* novels and films (2005–2012) will be familiar with this kind of historical association, with vampires arriving like the early conquistadors, killing Indigenous Americans and then remaining on American soil – because colonization does not always mean the colonizer will eventually depart. Colonialism in fact suggests settlement and governance *after* colonization, and colonial settlers often stay for a very long time. This is the end product of imperialist policies of discovery, invasion, and trade, after all, which, from the fifteenth century onward, have seen "civilized" nations like Spain, Portugal, France, Holland, and Britain claim ownership over the rest of the world.

As they made their way into unknown lands, colonizers also produced their own Gothic narratives of adventure and exploration. Patrick Brantlinger has called these narratives imperial Gothic. Among their key themes is the horror of "going native," of being possessed and transformed by local customs and beliefs (as writers imagine them) to the extent that one is no longer recognizable as "civilized." For Brantlinger, the "invasion of civilization by the forces of barbarism or demonism" is a typical narrative trajectory in imperial Gothic stories.[2] It is found, for example, in Joseph Conrad's *Heart of Darkness* (1899), as the narrator Marlow journeys deep into Africa in search of a trader named Kurtz who, utterly overwhelmed by his surroundings, has gone mad. Deeply implicated in the imperialist project, Conrad's novel has been central to the development of postcolonial criticism since the early 1980s. The critic Edward Said was especially interested in the way Conrad linked the "idea" of imperialism with the conquest-adventure narrative. A Palestinian American, Said also shared a predicament with this transnational novelist: that of living and writing in exile, culturally dislocated and slipping "in and out of worlds."[3] Thanks to Said, we now routinely talk about a "postcolonial Conrad." But Said also returned to earlier novelists to uncover less overt imperialist connections. His account of Jane Austen's *Mansfield Park* (1814), for example, draws attention to the buried links there between Sir Thomas Bertram's English property and his slave plantation in Antigua in the Caribbean. "Perhaps then Austen, and indeed, pre-imperialist novels generally," Said writes, "will appear to be more implicated in the rationale for imperialist expansion than at first sight they have been."[4] We now also talk of a "postcolonial Austen," as critics reveal connections between domestic life in English fiction and the trade routes (including the slave trade) of empire. The editors of *The Postcolonial Jane Austen* (2004) rightly note that postcolonial criticism "calls for an engagement that is attentive to all forms of relations of domination."[5] What we now call the postcolonial Gothic has the same critical purpose, and its narrative forms have similarly revisited English and European novels to expose and dramatize the "relations of domination" buried within them. It is therefore not surprising that, in many postcolonial Gothic narratives, the focus is on the possession of the "civilized" by the local characteristics of those once-unknown and now-colonized places.

The best-known example of this is Jean Rhys' *Wide Sargasso Sea* (1966). Rhys was born in Dominica, an island in the Lesser Antilles in the Caribbean. Christopher Columbus gave Dominica its name in 1493; by the time Rhys' novel was published, however, Dominica was postcolonial but not yet post-colonial, the hyphen here marking the moment after the departure of a colonial power. Rhys' mother was a Creole, a term used in some parts of the Caribbean to refer to mixed-race people who are accepted as white. The fraught position of Creole identities in the Caribbean no doubt made Rhys attentive to any presence it had in earlier literature. A peripheral character like Bertha Mason – the hidden-away "madwoman in the attic" in Charlotte Brontë's *Jane Eyre* (1847) who turns out to be Rochester's Creole wife – must therefore have seemed especially significant. Rhys called Bertha Mason an "impossible monster," as if she is unleashed and repressed simultaneously, a sort of absent presence in the novel. In April 1958, she wrote:

> I've read and re-read *Jane Eyre* ... The Creole in Charlotte Brontë's novel is a lay figure – repulsive which does not matter, and not once alive which does. She's necessary to the plot, but always she shrieks, howls, laughs horribly, attacks all and sundry – *off stage*. For me ... she must be right *on stage*.[6]

Wide Sargasso Sea completes this critique by giving Bertha Mason a history as a white Creole in Jamaica in the turbulent 1830s. It is set shortly after a brutally suppressed slave uprising on the island at the end of 1831 (at a time when black slaves made up over 80 percent of the island's population) and the subsequent 1833 Slavery Abolition Act, which abolished slavery across much of the British Empire. *Wide Sargasso Sea* thus writes a postcolonial predicament into Brontë's 1847 Gothic novel, situating Bertha Mason in a historicized Caribbean location and defining her through a highly racialized set of relationships that sees her increasingly possessed by others even as she is dispossessed of her place – and her name and identity.

In *Wide Sargasso Sea*, Brontë's character is called Antoinette Cosway. Her mother, the Creole daughter of a slave owner, tries to keep her privileged position on the island by marrying Mr. Mason, a plantation owner with properties across the Caribbean including Antigua, rather like Sir Thomas in *Mansfield Park*. But emancipated blacks are in a rebellious mood, resenting the privileges of the Creoles. Early in the novel, Antoinette's family home Coulibri is burned to the ground, a postcolonial anticipation of the Gothic scene at the end of Rhys' novel – and a scene that occurs "off stage" in *Jane Eyre* – when Antoinette, now Bertha, burns down her husband's English home, Thornfield Hall. Her Creole identity means that she is neither slave nor white; emancipation passes her by, and privilege eludes her. She is not even Jamaican, since her mother comes from Martinique. Her dispossessed, hybridized position – tied to the declining fortunes of the Caribbean "plantocracy" during this time – makes her a fascinating figure for postcolonial criticism. Along with Edward Said, Gayatri Chakravorty Spivak has been foundational to postcolonial thought, and her 1985 essay on *Jane Eyre* and *Wide Sargasso Sea* ponders the predicaments of Rhys' character. For Spivak, Rhys "rewrites a canonical English book ... in the interest of the white Creole rather than the native."[7] But who is the "native" in this novel? Even Tia, the black servant girl who plays with Antoinette but who later rejects her as the slaves rebel, is not quite a "native": her mother, the novel tell us, "was not Jamaican."[8] Although she is interested in Creole identities, Spivak is more concerned with the representation of the native or "subaltern" (a term originally used by the Italian Marxist Antonio Gramsci to refer to subordinate, politically excluded classes of people). What roles do subalterns play in the postcolonial literature of privileged social groups? How much agency do they have? Can subalterns speak, or are they always already spoken for by their colonizers? The illiteracy of subaltern classes becomes especially important as a means of excluding them from self-representation. For Spivak, Antoinette's family nurse, Christophine, is therefore more significant than

Antoinette herself. Christophine is "tangential" to the novel, but she is in fact the first character to speak. Brought over from Martinique, she is displaced and "commodified"; as Antoinette's mother explains, "She was your father's wedding present to me."[9] Nevertheless, she invokes her illiteracy defiantly: "Read and write I don't know," she tells Rochester. "Other things I know."[10]

For Spivak, those "other things" remain obscure, turning Christophine into the point at which the novel marks "the limits of its own discourse."[11] It cannot know what Christophine – the "native" – knows. For Benita Parry, however, Christophine's knowledge of obeah, a form of Caribbean folk spirituality, makes her "mistress of another knowledge dangerous to colonialism's official epistemology and the means of native cultural disobedience."[12] The colonization of the Caribbean had in fact marginalized local religious beliefs and practices precisely for these reasons. Obeah was prohibited in Jamaica in 1760, following the violent slave uprising known as Tacky's Rebellion, and has more or less remained a marginalized religious practice ever since. In Haiti, voodoo – or vodou, as it is locally termed – was similarly linked to slave insurrection, personally associated with Jean-Jacques Dessalines, the Haitian-born revolutionary who fought the French and led his country to independence in 1804, declaring Haiti the first "black republic." Joan (Colin) Dayan notes that Dessalines was "believed to have been a vodou adept – and in some stories, sorcerer."[13] After he was murdered in 1806, Dayan writes, "popular vengeance turned Dessalines into matter for resurrection," so that he came to acquire "unequaled power in the Haitian imagination": effectively becoming "a *lwa kreyol* (Creole god)."[14] Despite (or perhaps because of) its radical anticolonial associations, vodou has often been seen as something that prevents Haiti from becoming modern, connecting it to a mythologized "darkest Africa" and narratives of degeneracy.

But it is also a site of fantasy and longing, where the possibilities of resurrection and regeneration sit uneasily alongside memories of servitude – something we find expressed through the vodou figure of the zombie. During the 1930s, a number of French surrealists became ethnographically interested in vodou, visiting and working in Haiti; André Breton visited at the end of 1945, regarding Haiti as a place of struggle and energy that, far from being antimodern, promised a revolutionary future. Two years earlier, the French-born director Jacques Tourneur had released his evocative RKO Studios horror film *I Walked with a Zombie*, exploiting vodou's Gothic connotations for Western audiences. Tourneur's film is another postcolonial Gothic rewriting of *Jane Eyre*, comparable to but different from *Wide Sargasso Sea*. It is not interested in Creole identities, for example. A Canadian nurse, Betsy, travels to the Caribbean island of San Sebastian to look after Jessica, the wife of a plantation owner, Paul Holland. Jessica is a white colonial version of Bertha Mason, but she seems to have become a zombie, a punishment, perhaps, for her romantic affair with Holland's brother. The film takes its characters on a suspenseful expedition to a vodou ceremony in a remote part of the island, a familiar trope in imperial Gothic narratives. But Betsy is shocked to find that Holland's mother, Mrs. Rand, is presiding over the ceremony; it was Mrs. Rand who had placed the vodou curse on Jessica. *I Walked with a Zombie* takes its characters on a journey into the "heart of darkness," but what it reveals there is the whiteness of the colonizer. Even so, this is not exactly an affirmation of colonial power. The Rand family fall apart under the influence of vodou and a mother's jealousy; like *Wide Sargasso Sea*, this film plays out the last gasps of a Caribbean "plantocracy."

The proximity of a postcolonial (or post-colonial) country to its colonial past – the way the folk beliefs of the latter, say, continue to inhabit and shape the former – is of much interest to the postcolonial Gothic, and in Caribbean literature it is often given a symbolic power derived from the region's violent colonial history. Edwidge Danticat is a Haitian-born writer who, at 12, joined her parents in New York (where she was educated), following a migration route shared by many others from her region, including the Dominican-born author Junot Diaz. For Diaz and Danticat, the absent parent is therefore a key feature of their stories, producing both trauma and longing for the child – another trope often found in the postcolonial Gothic, as we shall see. Danticat is the editor of *Haiti Noir* (2011), a collection of stories about a place where the color "noir" has a long, complicated cultural and political history. In her introduction, she evokes the Haitian politician and ethnologist Jean Price-Mars, a champion of Haitian negritude and a defender of vodou as a cultural practice: "Forget trying to rewrite the great works of French literature on which you had been raised, he exhorted the Haitian writers of his time. Turn to Haitian life and history and folklore and find your inspiration there."[15] But Danticat is postcolonial, not anticolonial; her work takes up this nationalist challenge, but it also responds to the transnational, diasporic predicaments for Haitians as they migrate to the US mainland and elsewhere. At the same time, her writing immerses itself in Haiti's violent colonial past. Her Gothic novel *The Farming of Bones* (1998) returns to the so-called Parsley Massacre of 1937 when, under the orders of Dominican military strongman Rafael Trujillo, around 20,000 Haitians living on the Dominican border were slaughtered.

Junot Diaz, in turn, has written about the terror of Trujillo's regime and its profound influence on Dominican life in *The Brief Wondrous Life of*

Oscar Wao (2007), as if that regime were both the natural and the supernatural consequence of the discovery and colonization of the New World itself, which is where this novel begins:

> They say it came first from Africa, carried in the screams of the enslaved; that it was the death bane of the Tainos [the Indigenous people of the Antilles and Bahamas], uttered just as one world perished and another began; that it was a demon drawn into Creation through the nightmare door that was cracked open in the Antilles. Fuku americanus, or more colloquially, fuku – generally a curse or a doom of some kind; specifically the Curse and the Doom of the New World ... No matter what its name or provenance, it is believed that the arrival of Europeans on Hispaniola unleashed the fuku on the world, and we've all been in the shit ever since.[16]

Haiti's troubled relationship with Dominica also traumatizes characters in Danticat's elegant stories. In "Nineteen Thirty-Seven" (1996), the narrator's mother visits Massacre River to mourn at the border dividing Haiti "from the Spanish-speaking country that she never allowed me to name."[17] The narrator of "Between the Pool and the Gardenias" (1996) is an orphaned Haitian maid who is well aware that her wealthy Francophile employers distinguish themselves from the folk beliefs of her country: "It's that voodoo nonsense," they say, "that's holding us Haitians back."[18] The maid finds the decomposing corpse of an abandoned baby girl and claims it as her own, naming it Rose. A Dominican gardener on the property treats her with contempt – "The Dominican and I made love on the grass once, but he never spoke to me again"[19] – and then calls the authorities, accusing the maid of killing the child with vodou magic. The final lines offer a frozen Gothic moment, an intimate symbolization of the Haitian maid's postcolonial condition: "We made a pretty picture standing there. Rose, me, and him. Between the pool and the gardenias, waiting for the law."[20]

The postcolonial Gothic can also be as much about dead children as it is about missing parents, since it wonders about links to a colonial past that have been lost or displaced just as much as it imagines *post*-colonial futures that do not (yet) exist. As it does so, it turns domestic experiences of loss into symbolic accounts of lives that are simultaneously independent and hopelessly enslaved or exploited, as if these two conditions are now difficult to distinguish. Questions to do with legitimacy – one's right to occupy one place and not another, the origins of one's claims on property and the lives of others, one's capacity to possess something or to be dispossessed of something – are also paramount in the postcolonial Gothic. As we have seen with Spivak's subaltern, legitimation is a matter of representation. Who can legitimately represent others? Whose claims – and rights – are noticed, and whose are ignored? When we think about the postcolonial structures of power and recognition, who signifies, and who does not? In a speech in Dakar, Senegal, in 2007, French President Nicolas Sarkozy infamously remarked that "the African has never really entered into history."[21] This is, of course, a colonial perception rather than a postcolonial one, wiping an entire people out of the narratives that colonial powers write for themselves. It is also, we might say, a *white* view of history: This is what produces, and limits, its power and capacity for recognition. But are novels written by whites in Africa itself any more accommodating? In his 1988 *White Writing*, J. M. Coetzee remarks on how Africa is routinely imagined as a "dark continent" rather than, say, a "new world" or an "earthly paradise."[22] Narratives about white settlers on African farms – an early example is Olive Schreiner's *The Story of an African Farm* (1883) – are therefore a reconfigured version of the genre of the pastoral, a way of illuminating the "dark continent" for its settler-colonials. But the "white pastoral," as Coetzee calls it, comes to depend on "the occlusion of black labor from the scene," in which "the black man becomes a shadowy presence."[23] As in Sarkozy's view of history, black Africans are excluded from white pastoral, even though they are there; they occupy the kind of position we have seen with Bertha Mason in *Jane Eyre*, a sort of absent presence. As a result, Coetzee argues, the "literature of the white pastoral" itself occupies a space that is " 'outside' history,"[24] a fantasy space that played out its protracted death throes as racial segregation in South Africa – apartheid – slowly came to an end.

Nadine Gordimer's *The Conservationist* (1974) – published not long after the United Nations identified apartheid as a crime against humanity – marks a Gothic turning point for the white pastoral genre. Mehring is a wealthy South African industrialist who owns an outlying farm, employing black labor to run it. But the discovery of the corpse of a black man on his property, one that refuses to remain buried in the ground, is the trigger for the unraveling of Mehring's taken-for-granted sense of ownership, mastery, and belonging. The white pastoral is soon swallowed up by Gothic imagery as the farm itself is buried under the weight of historical change: "Something heavy has dragged itself over the whole place, flattening and swirling everything."[25] Gordimer's novel allegorizes its postcolonial African predicament, as Coetzee's fiction has also often done. In *Waiting for the Barbarians* (1980), Coetzee traces out the mental disintegration of a powerful white settler, a servant of the empire, the Magistrate. Heavily influenced by Franz Kafka, Coetzee applies his allegory in exact Gothic terms as the "civilized" Magistrate finds himself drawn to a "barbarian" girl held in custody. In Coetzee's fiction, South African colonialism is simultaneously racialized and gendered. White men exploit, black women are exploited. The Magistrate knows this very well, acting out his sexual mastery over the girl – "Did I really want to enter and claim possession of these beautiful creatures?"[26] – even as he makes himself postcolonial through his "sympathy" for her enslavement. In the postapartheid novel *Disgrace* (1999), Coetzee reconfigures his gendered account of postcolonial relations, as a South African academic, David Lurie, seduces one of his students and is subsequently dismissed from his post. Afterward, Lurie moves in with his daughter, Lucy, on her farm on the Eastern Cape. The novel then stages one of the Gothic horrors of African settler life – and the white pastoral – when several black men break into the farm, attacking Lurie and raping Lucy. This is a particularly postcolonial Gothic horror, recasting an older colonial fear of black men raping white women; it is also a hysterical inversion of the colonially legitimated narrative of white mastery over black women (itself recast in *Waiting for the Barbarians*). All of these narratives violently breach the racial segregations of apartheid and provoke the possibility of a further horror for white settlers, that of miscegenation, the mixing of races that were supposed to remain apart. What makes *Disgrace* distinctive here is Lucy's decision, after she becomes pregnant, to keep her baby, as if she has somehow embraced the realities of her colonial past *and* postapartheid future.

The postcolonial Gothic can certainly activate the traumas that result from a character's experience of loss and displacement after colonialism. Such is Antoinette's experience in *Wide Sargasso Sea* as she is distanced from her home and homeland. But in these white South African novels, the opposite happens. It is not displacement that triggers a Gothic effect, but *settlement*: the very fact of imagining that one is at home. The injustice of colonialism oppresses these white settlers, and their homesteads and properties are unable to protect them from its violent legacies. The prolonged, lingering effects of colonial history also haunt, and shape, the Indian novel in English, the novels of Salman Rushdie and others that have allegorized India's postcolonial condition for Western readerships.[27] Rushdie's Gothic fantasy *Midnight's Children* (1981) takes the partition of India in August 1947 into two separate states – Pakistan and India – as its point of origin, a political act that announced the end of British rule in the subcontinent and the beginning of India's post-colonial modernity. The novel then allegorizes this division through the different lives of the Muslim infant Shiva and the illegitimate, hybridized Anglo-Indian child Saleem, both born at midnight (at the moment when partition becomes official) but secretly swapped at birth, Gothic doubles who are condemned to play out the opposing forces of destruction and creation. For Neil Ten Kortenaar, "Shiva is Saleem's dark shadow; he cannot be denied but cannot be fully acknowledged either";[28] because of this, *Midnight's Children* is both an expression of faith in a modern, post-colonial nation and a chronicle of its dissolution. The Indian novelist and political activist Arundhati Roy's *The God of Small Things* (1997) came in the wake of Rushdie's novel, similarly situating itself in the framework of earlier British writing about India, including E. M. Forster's *A Passage to India* (1924). Set in Kerala, this novel meanders toward a transgressive climax involving incest between a twin brother and sister and a sexual relationship involving their mother Ammu and a Dalit, Velutha. Velutha's dwelling is given an overdetermined allegorical identity as a "History house" and is located at the novel's center even though it is a remote, peripheral place. The journey to this house is also a journey into "the Heart of Darkness,"[29] with the novel reminding us again that both the imperial Gothic and Conrad's novel are never far away here – except, in this case, Velutha is a figure of the subaltern. *The God of Small Things* melodramatizes its sense of colonial history, allowing it to overwhelm its characters, driving them apart in some cases and producing illicit intimacies in others.

Settler nations like Canada, New Zealand, and Australia can also be understood as postcolonial even though they are not republics like India or South Africa or Haiti; that is, they have not gone through the violent processes of independence that would characterize them as "post-colonial" in its hyphenated form. Indeed, all three of these settler nations are still constitutional monarchies, owing their allegiance to the British crown. Even so, their more recent literatures can be identified as postcolonial, and they have also produced their share of what we can now recognize as postcolonial Gothic. It can seem as if the journey into the Canadian north is a journey *out* of history, a way of undoing one's connection with Canada's colonial past and tying it instead to an epic struggle for survival in a remote, inhospitable – and often fatal – place. The Canadian critic Northrop Frye thought that Canadian poetry was characterized by a

> tone of deep terror in regard to nature ... The human mind has nothing but human and moral values to cling to if it is to preserve its integrity or even its sanity, yet the vast unconsciousness of nature in front of it seems the unanswerable denial of those values.[30]

Here, Canada is lifted out of its colonial framework and attached to what we would call the Gothic sublime ("the vast unconscious of nature"), signifying something that obliterates all traces of the "human." The celebrated Ontario-born writer Margaret Atwood is one of a number of Canadian writers who have since developed this sense of the Canadian north as Gothic sublime. In a 1995 collection of four lectures, she writes that "popular lore, and popular literature, established early that the North was uncanny, awe-inspiring in an almost religious way, hostile to white men, but alluring: that it would lead you on and do you in; that it would drive you crazy, and, finally, would claim you for its own."[31]

In fact, around the time Frye was writing about Canadian poetry, Atwood (who was one of his students) published several books that consolidated this myth of Canada as hostile wilderness – but situated it in the framework of colonial historical narrative. A collection of her essays, *Survival* (1972), traces a history of Canadian literature that folds the elemental aspects of wilderness into the sheer fact that "Canada is a colony," linking it to Gothic chronicles of settler life with their "tumbled-down houses and deserted farms" and the recognition that "other people are 'here' already, natives who are cooperative, indifferent, or hostile."[32] In her unusually haunting novel *Surfacing* (also 1972), Atwood gives a Gothic response to the complexity of Canada's postcolonial condition. An unnamed, troubled female narrator – an English-speaking Québécois – goes on a journey, with her lover and two married friends, to her parents' abandoned cabin on an isolated island in Quebec's far north. She is haunted by the loss of an aborted child, but she is also mourning the death of her mother and searching for her missing father, who had become interested in ancient Indigenous rock-drawings. The journey north works to distance the narrator from her sense that the United States is spreading its influence and investments through Canada like a new empire. "The future is in the North, that was a political slogan once," the narrator says; "when my father heard it he said there was nothing in the North but the past and not much of that either."[33] *Surfacing* is a kind of ghost story, but it also traces out its own version of the "heart of darkness" trope as the narrator abandons her lover and friends and increasingly immerses herself in the Canadian wilderness, leaving the cabin to become primal and animal-like, stripping naked and taking a blanket with her until "the fur grows" and making a "lair near the woodpile" with leaves and branches.[34] It mobilizes an anti-American politics as part of its investment in a Canadian nationalism, yet it also slides back and forth between these differences and others, among them the French and English in Quebec, an older and younger Canadian generation, and settler Canadians and Indigenous Canadians, with the latter again as a kind of absent presence in the narrative.

The focus in postcolonial Canadian Gothic fiction on what Spivak had called the "native" can be clear-eyed in some cases and blurred, even nonexistent, in others. An example of the former is an early novel by the renowned Canadian songwriter Leonard Cohen, *Beautiful Losers* (1966). This wild, stream-of-consciousness narrative has profoundly influenced

Canadian postcolonial writing, even though it has been neglected in critical commentary. It is never discussed in Justin D. Edwards' useful study of *Gothic Canada* (2005), yet it seems to haunt this book, with Edwards using a line from Cohen's novel – "I felt it was the end" – as an epigraph for his final chapter.[35] One of the narrators of *Beautiful Losers* is researching the Indigenous Canadian tribal group to which his wife, Edith, belongs; but Edith has committed suicide and the narrator is in turmoil. As if to fill his loss, he converses with a Mohawk woman from the seventeenth century, Catherine Tekakwitha, who survived smallpox in childhood and was baptized as a Catholic by Jesuit missionaries, becoming a devout religious figure of chastity and miracles. "In the gloomy long house of my mind," the narrator writes, "let me trade wives, let me stumble upon you, Catherine Tekakwitha, three hundred years old, fragrant as a birch sapling, no matter what the priests or plague have done to you."[36] *Beautiful Losers* plays out an early version of a postcolonial settler's crisis of identity, preoccupied by the effects of colonization on Indigenous communities almost to the point of inertia. Indigenous Canadian writers have quite a different investment in the Gothic, however. Eden Robinson's *Monkey Beach* (2000) is much more empathetically affiliated to place, unfolding on the Haisla reservation of Kitamaat in northwest British Columbia. The young narrator Lisa, a Haisla woman, is well aware of her colonial history, which has something in common with Catherine Tekakwitha's: "We stayed in this village at the bottom of the Kitimat River until about 1893, when the Methodist missionary George Raley established a rival village on an old settlement site in present-day Kitamaat Village. Convents moved there when they became Christianized."[37] *Monkey Beach* reconnects Lisa to the world around her, both natural and supernatural; it especially allows her to communicate with ghosts from her family and from local traditions. It is an example of an Indigenous postcolonial Gothic novel that works *against* a character's experience of loss and displacement through colonization, tying Lisa even more closely to her territory and her heritage.

The problem with postcolonialism, however, is that it rarely resolves conventional distinctions between belonging and displacement – or, to rephrase this in terms of the postcolonial Gothic, between possession (which may also suggest being possessed *by* something) and dispossession. This is true for both Indigenous people and settlers, even though the consequences of this irresolution play themselves out in different ways, not least because Indigenous losses are so much greater, while settlers have gained so much more. Even so, settlers can record their own sense of dispossession as they migrate (some by choice, some under duress) to new lands. We have already seen Atwood's "tumbled-down houses and deserted farms," emphasizing the darker side of a triumphant colonialism that imagines settlement as something permanent. For another writer from Ontario, Alice Munro, displacement and belonging seem to coexist. "The part of the country I come from," she has said, "is absolutely Gothic," as if this is the only way to express the irresolvability of this condition.[38] Drownings, burials, lost parents, abandoned homesteads, visitations: These are the key tropes of the postcolonial Gothic in settler Canadian fiction, which can either return to the haunting violence of colonial contact with Indigenous people – as Michael Crummey's *River Thieves* (2002) does, for example – or forget about them altogether. The French Quebec novelist Gaétan Soucy's *The Little Girl Who Was Too Fond of Matches* (2002) does the latter, but it also estranges settler Canadians from themselves. A teenage girl, Alice Soissons, narrates the story, which begins with the suicide of her father. Alice's brother is simple-minded, and it turns out that her twin sister Ariane is chained to a wall in a shed beside their huge, ruinous house, where her mother's corpse is also visible in a glass box. The story unfolds like a deranged folk tale, as Alice – pregnant with her brother's child – goes into town, perhaps for the first time in her life, to try to work out how to bury her father. Curious about her, the townsfolk investigate her property and raise the question of inheritance. "If it should happen that we could no longer live on our land," Alice says, alarmed by all this outside attention, "where the devil would we go, I ask you?"[39] Soucy's novel is a fantasy about settler dispossession, the loss of the father, and the end of property ownership. Alice may know nothing about Indigenous Canadians, but she is nevertheless able to imagine that she shares their predicament: "Hordes would come to us from the village, ignorant of our customs ... and they would dispossess us entirely."[40] Her position in the novel is, in fact, structurally comparable to that of Antoinette in *Wide Sargasso Sea*, since she loses the privileges of her former position. She is also Gothic in precisely the same way, unable to claim the status of a "native" but equally unable to assimilate into settler life.

Postcolonial Gothic narratives often chart the ways in which the taken-for-granted categories of "native" and "settler" end up colonizing each other; the Gothic effect is the result of insisting at the same time on their irreconcilable differences. Because of this, such narratives can generate conflicting and often highly charged readings. The New Zealand-born director Jane Campion's film *The Piano* (1993) returns to the 1850s when a Scottish woman, Ada, and her daughter, Flora, arrive as settlers on the west coast of New Zealand's north island to join Ada's sexually repressed husband, Alisdair Stewart. *The Piano* is another example of a postcolonial rewriting of a canonical British novel, owing a great deal to Emily Brontë's *Wuthering Heights* (1847) in both its setting and the turbulent romance it traces between Ada and a local settler, Baines. For Campion, the "wild beaches" of New Zealand in her film are "a kind of colonial equivalent to Emily Brontë's moors," a transplanting of *Wuthering Heights* to the antipodes.[41] But her film also draws on a colonial New Zealand novel, Jane Mander's *The Story of a New Zealand River* (1920), another "heart of darkness" narrative about a woman, Alice, and her daughter, who journey up river to meet Alice's husband-to-be Roland and a man to whom she becomes attracted, David Bruce. Much of the critical response to *The Piano* has focused on Ada's muteness, her predicament as a woman in a turbulent colonial space, and the significance of her piano. For Laleen Jayamanne, Ada is linked to the kind of Gothic sublime the film inherits from *Wuthering Heights*: "the Gothic woman needs the appropriate *mise en scène*, a haunted house, a desolate moor, or an 'untamed' colonial land, the space of alterity within which to explore her constitutive generic nature."[42] This is also a "postcolonial sublime," since it involves "not a complete obliteration of identity but rather a moment when the secret of identity as constituted by difference is disclosed."[43] Baines is crucial to this experience in *The Piano* as a settler who is closely associated with local Maori: He is someone who has, to a degree at least, "gone native." But other critics have been troubled by the film's portrayal of Maori characters, who remain in the background, juxtaposed to the settlers but also accommodating them and even aiding their arrival. For Rosemary Du Plessis and Geoff Fougere,

> It is Maori men who transfer Ada's luggage and the piano from the wild of the beach to the fragilely tamed settlement. It is Maori who facilitate the [closing] departure of Ada, Flora, and Baines, the piano incongruously strapped to the *waka* [canoe], visually deconstructing the opposition between the imported and the indigenous.[44]

Indigenous New Zealanders are shown to help a colonial settler's white wife pursue her romance with a settler who is not-quite-native, a task that runs the risk of burying the postcolonial politics of the film under the weight of Ada's Gothic transition from culture to nature.

Various transactions and disjunctures between the "imported" and the "indigenous" – between settlers and natives – play themselves out in Australian versions of the postcolonial Gothic too. The Indian-born postcolonial critic Homi Bhabha has talked about the way colonial governance came up against the problem of "mimicry," where the official process of assimilating the native triggered colonial anxieties about the native as "almost the same but not quite."[45] In settler countries like Australia, however, mimicry can flow in the other direction and have much more profound consequences. When might settlers themselves claim to be "indigenous"? In Andrew McGahan's *The*

White Earth (2004), an orphaned boy goes to stay with his uncle, John McIvor, at Kuran House, a large ruined homestead on a once-great cattle station. This is an Australian version of South Africa's white pastoral, with McIvor insisting on his rights of possession but expressing them as if he were a "native": "We can have connections to the land too, our own kind of magic. The land talks to me. It doesn't care what colour I am, all that matters is that I'm here."[46] But *The White Earth* is set in the 1990s, when a series of legal rulings in Australia enabled the official recognition of Indigenous claims to land and title. The novel charts a history of colonial racism – and a postcolonial denial of that history – that identifies Kuran House as built over Aboriginal bones. But it also triggers a kind of white panic as McIvor's grip on his property weakens. An apocalyptic vision overtakes him and the homestead catches fire, collapsing in upon itself toward the end, rather like the dramatic climax to Edgar Allan Poe's "House of Usher."

The White Earth is a postcolonial Australian ghost story that activates the effects of something buried – the violent history of colonization, the repressed recognition of Indigenous claims to land – and then unleashes this into modern settler life, which is itself then possessed and dispossessed ("unsettled") by these knowledges. Ken Gelder and Jane M. Jacobs have noted that postcolonial ghost stories flourish precisely at those moments when contemporary Australians are asked to remember something they have forgotten or denied or attempted to extinguish. In Australian cinema, examples include Tracey Moffatt's *BeDevil* (1993), Margot Nash's *Vacant Possession* (1996), and Ray Lawrence's *Jindabyne* (2006). Here, the act of recollection, staged as an excavation or a journey into some remote place, is itself enough to trouble the usual distinctions between present and past, settlers and natives, the "imported" and the "indigenous."[47] In Julia Leigh's *The Hunter* (1999) – made into a film in 2011 – a man is employed by an unidentified overseas company to travel to Tasmania to find and kill the last remaining Tasmanian tiger, or thylacine. In fact, the last thylacine died in captivity in 1936. But the extinction of this native species brings with it a strange desire to see it once more, to imagine (or wish) that it still lives. As he goes deeper into the Tasmanian wilderness, the hunter slaughters one native animal after another. The thylacine seems remote from him, impossible to find, yet he is also increasingly preoccupied by it, haunted by the "luminous creature," imagining that it is both nowhere and everywhere:

> And now in the chill open night he allows himself a fantasy: Is there an entire tribe of tigers – so crafty that they have avoided the human gaze for years, and – oh, an underground tribe of tigers – perhaps that wombat burrow over there is a tunnel leading to a complex maze, an Atlantis …[48]

The hunter's project connects him to the earlier violence of colonization and white settlement, as he recognizes when he stumbles across "a ring of blackened stones, and he imagines they might have been laid by the local Aboriginal people, in the years before they, the full-bloods, were almost driven to extinction."[49]

The Hunter is a novel about a white man who is literally imported into Tasmania – an introduced species, we might say – to extinguish a native species. In the process, however, he becomes feral, finally making himself comfortable in the thylacine's lair, lining up the creature's bones "like fence posts"[50] as if he is now at home, just like a settler. Leigh's novel is worth comparing to Atwood's *Surfacing* in this respect. Indeed, by playing out a series of traumatic transactions between introduced, native, and feral species, *The Hunter* also places the postcolonial Gothic in a broader ecological paradigm. Graham Huggan and Helen Tiffin have been critical of the fact that "the postcolonial field is inherently anthropocentric (human-centred),"[51] since colonization brings with it not just the destruction of the lives (and ways of living) of Indigenous people but also the destruction of habitats, forests, rivers, and species. The word "ecology" comes from the Greek *oikos*, literally, the study of a dwelling place, a home. But can an introduced species – like settlers (colonials, migrants, etc.) – ever be fully or properly at home? Introduced species are both home-building and habitat-destroying. *The Hunter* historicizes this process of colonization, but then represents it in an uncanny way. As the hunter himself is possessed by the native species he is employed to exterminate, he is also radically estranged from it. The Gothic sublime returns here, since the hunter's immersion into the natural world of the thylacine is precisely what reminds him most of its inalienable difference. In a certain sense, we are still in the vicinity of the imperial Gothic, since this is another narrative about a man who literally "goes native." What makes *The Hunter* a postcolonial Gothic novel – or rather, an "eco-postcolonial" Gothic novel – is its realization that the "native" is now something it can only imagine and be haunted by. It is preoccupied by the thylacine, but, to recall Spivak's comment about Christophine in *Wide Sargasso Sea*, it also knows that this enigmatic native species marks "the limits of its own discourse."

NOTES

1 Elleke Boehmer, "Foreword: Empire's Vampires," in *Transnational and Post-colonial Vampires: Dark Blood*, ed. Tabish Khair and Johan Höglund (London: Palgrave, 2012), pp. vii–ix, p. vii.
2 Patrick Brantlinger, *Rule of Darkness: British Literature and Imperialism, 1830–1914* (Ithaca, NY: Cornell University Press, 1988), p. 230.

3 Edward Said, *Culture and Imperialism* (London: Vintage, 1994), p. 421.
4 Said, *Culture and Imperialism*, p. 100.
5 *The Postcolonial Jane Austen*, ed. You-Me Park and Rajeswari Sunder Rajan (Abingdon and New York: Routledge, 2004), p. 3.
6 Jean Rhys, *Letters, 1931–1966* (London: Deutsch, 1984), pp. 156–157.
7 Gayatri Spivak, *A Critique of Postcolonial Reason* (Cambridge, MA: Harvard University Press, 1999), p. 130.
8 Jean Rhys, *Wide Sargasso Sea* (London: Penguin, 1997), p. 7.
9 Rhys, *Wide Sargasso Sea*, p. 8.
10 Rhys, *Wide Sargasso Sea*, p. 104.
11 Spivak, *A Critique*, p. 129.
12 Benita Parry, *Postcolonial Studies: A Materialist Critique* (London and New York: Routledge, 2004), p. 22.
13 Joan (Colin) Dayan, *Haiti, History, and the Gods* (Berkeley, CA: University of California Press, 1996), p. 23.
14 Dayan, *Haiti*, p. 30.
15 *Haiti Noir*, ed. Edwidge Danticat (New York: Akashic Books, 2011), p. 13.
16 Junot Diaz, *The Brief Wondrous Life of Oscar Wao* (London: Faber and Faber, 2008), p. 1.
17 Edwidge Danticat, *Krik? Krak!* (New York: Vintage, 1996), p. 33.
18 Danticat, *Krik? Krak!*, p. 95.
19 Danticat, *Krik? Krak!*, p. 96.
20 Danticat, *Krik? Krak!*, p. 100.
21 See Ibrahima Diallo, *The Politics of National Languages in Postcolonial Senegal* (Amherst, NY: Cambria Press, 2010), p. 186, n. 7.
22 J. M. Coetzee, *White Writing: On the Culture of Letters in South Africa* (New Haven, CT: Yale University Press, 1988), p. 2.
23 Coetzee, *White Writing*, p. 5.
24 Coetzee, *White Writing*, p. 11.
25 Nadine Gordimer, *The Conservationist* (London: Bloomsbury, 2005), p. 294.
26 J. M. Coetzee, *Waiting for the Barbarians* (London: Vintage, 2004), p. 49.
27 See Amit Chaudhuri, *Clearing a Space: Reflections on India, Literature and Culture* (Witney: Peter Lang, 2008), pp. 113–121.
28 Neil Ten Kortenaar, *Self, Nation, Text in Salman Rushdie's Midnight's Children* (Quebec: McGill-Queen's University Press, 2004), p. 44.
29 Arundhati Roy, *The God of Small Things* (London: Flamingo, 1997), p. 309.
30 Northrop Frye, *The Bush Garden: Essays on the Canadian Imagination* (Toronto: House of Anansi, 1971), p. 225.
31 Margaret Atwood, *Strange Things: The Malevolent North in Canadian Literature* (Oxford: Clarendon Press, 1995), p. 19.
32 Margaret Atwood, *Survival: A Thematic Guide to Canadian Literature* (Toronto: House of Anansi, 1972), pp. 35, 124, 17.
33 Margaret Atwood, *Surfacing* (London: Bloomsbury, 2009), p. 5.
34 Atwood, *Surfacing*, p. 198.
35 See Justin D. Edwards, *Gothic Canada: Reading the Spectre of a National Literature* (Edmonton: University of Alberta Press, 2005), p. 165.
36 Leonard Cohen, *Beautiful Losers* (Melbourne: Text Publishing, 2011), p. 23.
37 Eden Robinson, *Monkey Beach* (New York: Knopf Canada, 2000), p. 194.

38 Coral Ann Howells, *Alice Munro* (Manchester University Press, 1998), p. 13.
39 Gaétan Soucy, *The Little Girl Who Was Too Fond of Matches* (London: Flamingo, 2002), p. 87.
40 Soucy, *The Little Girl*, p. 95.
41 Miro Bilbrough, "*The Piano*: Jane Campion interviewed by Miro Bilbrough," *Cinema Papers*, 93 (1993), pp. 4–11, p. 6.
42 Laleen Jayamanne, *Toward Cinema and Its Double: Cross-Cultural Mimesis* (Bloomington, IN: Indiana University Press, 2001), p. 31.
43 Jayamanne, *Toward Cinema and Its Double*, p. 41.
44 See Harriet Margolis, "Introduction: 'A Strange Heritage': From Colonization to Transformation?," in *Jane Campion's* The Piano, ed. Harriet Margolis (Cambridge University Press, 2000), pp. 1–41, p. 21.
45 See Homi Bhabha, *The Location of Culture* (London and New York: Routledge, 1994), pp. 85–92.
46 Andrew McGahan, *The White Earth* (Sydney: Allen & Unwin, 2004), p. 181.
47 See *Uncanny Australia: Sacredness and Identity in a Postcolonial Nation*, ed. Ken Gelder and Jane M. Jacobs (Melbourne University Press, 1998), p. 42.
48 Julia Leigh, *The Hunter* (Melbourne: Penguin, 1999), p. 118.
49 Leigh, *The Hunter*, p. 57.
50 Leigh, *The Hunter*, p. 160.
51 Graham Huggan and Helen Tiffin, *Postcolonial Ecocriticism: Literature, Animals, Environment* (Abingdon: Routledge, 2009), p. 3.

13

KATARZYNA ANCUTA

Asian Gothic

At first glance, the search for Asian Gothic may seem like a quest doomed to failure. Faced with the multiplicity of languages and cultures, races and ethnicities, as well as religious, philosophical, and political viewpoints encompassed by the continent, one feels instantly humbled. Contrary to Europe, Asia never experienced any grand-scale cultural movements that would affect the entire continent, such as the European Renaissance or Romanticism, with many of its countries opting for relative isolationism instead. Although Asia spawned civilizations that predated other human settlements, only Japan experienced modernism roughly at the same time as Europe, while in 2013, nine Asian countries still remained on the United Nations' list of the least developed countries (LDC) of the world. To complicate things even further, while some Asian countries were subjected to colonization, others had colonial appetites themselves. Despite that, discussions of colonialism in Asia are commonly limited to the contrasting of the European center and the Asian periphery, ignoring for the most part intra-Asian territorial conflicts and power struggles, whose influence on local cultural production is often left unexamined.

By acknowledging that both the process and the outcomes of colonization are traumatic experiences capable of producing haunting narratives, postcolonial studies have successfully relocated the discussion of the Gothic outside the narrow boundaries of its Anglo-American foundations. Yet the postcolonial model is not always useful when discussing Asian cultural output, since European presence on the continent was certainly not the only molding force at work. Postcolonial theory may have found a fertile ground in Indian literary studies, but it has done little to account for the widespread Indian influence in Southeast Asia, whose roots predate the British Raj by thousands of years. Similarly complicated is the case of Japan and China, with their turbulent histories, their share of aggression and victimization, massive cultural heritage developed in isolation, and their complex adaptations of "Western" modernity. As if this was not enough, we must also remember that many Asian countries are culturally, linguistically, and ethnically diversified on a scale unknown in the West, which, for obvious reasons, makes any cultural study particularly challenging.

Locating the Gothic in Asia is therefore a complex undertaking that requires proceeding with caution. Given that the term itself is a foreign import, lacking equivalents in most Asian languages, it is easily dismissed as referring to an aesthetic or a set of values alien to indigenous cultures. Out of all the Asian countries, only Japan has attempted to semi-internalize the label, but the Japanese term *goshikku* refers mostly to nonliterary pop-cultural manifestations of the Gothic, such as in the Gothic Lolita (*gosu rori*), a Japanese street-fashion style based on Victorian-era clothing. Occasionally the term is also used to market pulp horror fiction, which, interestingly, in some cases is not even categorized as "literature." Other than that, the use of the word "Gothic" in Asia is chiefly limited to its architectural connotation, which, naturally, adds further confusion.

Most pioneering studies of Asian Gothic are also too limited. They tend to focus on Japanese or Indian literature, taking as their point of entry Japanese modernism and Indian postcolonial experience. Invigorating as such studies may be for the Gothic scholarly community, they inevitably pose two questions: Is there a difference between a "postcolonial" reading of a text and a "Gothic" one? More importantly, how can we convince local literary historians and critics that a "Gothic" reading of a text considered an important representative of national literary heritage is not a blatant example of Western cultural imperialism and an attempt to belittle its value? After all, we have to remember that the term "Gothic" is either unknown or misunderstood by a great majority of Asian scholars.

The idea of a focused approach, aiming to "discover" specifically Chinese, Japanese, or Indian Gothic may seem desirable from a marketing point of view. As long, however, as the concept of "Gothic" remains seen as a Western import and its analysis relies exclusively on Western methodologies, little will change in the way it is perceived in Asia. The pan-Asian approach advocated here calls for a change in the methodology in order to localize the "Gothic" within the existing Asian paradigms rather than to impose an alien label. This approach stresses intra-Asian connections and cultural influences, shared Asian heritage, philosophical and religious world views, beliefs, and values. It investigates the development of local forms associated with popular "Gothic" contexts, such as supernatural narratives; it promotes a nongeneric understanding of Gothic and attempts to develop a methodology that could be applied to studying a variety of texts; and, finally, it resets the traditional boundaries of Gothic through the application of new methodologies based on Asian philosophies and viewpoints.

With this in mind, I would argue that the search for Asian Gothic should be a three-directional quest: a re-examination of classic texts from the perspective of existing theories about the Gothic; an investigation of the concept of the Gothic from the perspective of self-defined Asian Gothic authors; and a recategorization of some contemporary pop-cultural forms, such as film, music, manga, anime, visual arts, or street fashion as "Gothic," leading to a further appropriation of the term by various Asian cultures. All of the above can only be achieved if we abandon the narrow understanding of the Gothic as a distinct literary genre and opt for a more flexible and multidisciplinary use of the term instead.

While it is possible to find Asian texts that closely mimic or expand upon the established Gothic forms, unsurprisingly, their authors often tend to be scattered outside their homelands and Western-educated – or they have been exposed to the genre through very personal literary fascinations. Writers such as S. P. Somtow, David Hontiveros, Tunku Halim, Edogawa Rampo, or Catherine Lim all fit this category. Their writing often embraces supernatural topics, at times incorporating references to classic Gothic texts, and the Gothic reading of their works needs no justification. Seen as products of popular culture and promoted chiefly for their entertainment value, their books may be marketable but are seldom treated as "serious" literature in their country of origin, and their position within the local literary scene is seen as marginal.

At the same time, Asian literatures abound in examples of fiction whose authors embrace the Gothic on an unconscious level and without any intention to follow the specific demands of the genre. Writers such as Chart Korbjitti, Su Tong, Mo Yan, Natsuo Kirino, or Duong Thu Huong are concerned with describing the violence of everyday life, exploring darker contexts of social and political oppression, gender and class inequality, and historical trauma. Their works are often considered part of the native literary canon and as such encouraged to be read and taught in ways deemed appropriate by the national ministry of culture and local academics. Given the predominant Asian misconception that the term "Gothic" is synonymous with cheap paperback horror fiction, a Gothic-inflected reading of such texts may meet with considerable opposition in their country of origin, particularly if it disregards local contexts.

With this in mind, I propose to highlight a selection of literary and cinematic texts that can help us take the first step in our exploration of Asian Gothic. For the sake of simplicity, my discussion of Asian Gothic is limited to South, Southeast, and East Asia only, three geographical territories whose cultures share a long-standing, intricate connection. The choice of texts or authors should by no means be treated as definitive, but rather seen as a springboard for finding the perceptions and ideas that will allow us to Gothicize our reading of Asian texts or perhaps Asianize our understanding of the Gothic experience.

Living with the spirits: Asian supernatural Gothic

The Gothic has always thrived on its connection with the supernatural. Ghosts, vampires, werewolves, zombies, and a plethora of other monstrosities have all been cast to play the part of Gothic villains, and, more recently, Gothic heroes, whom, thanks to a multitude of culturally informed readings, we have come to see as epitomizing racial, class, or gender differences. But ever since rationalism triumphed in eighteenth-century Europe, all the instances of the supernatural have been relegated to the realm of the marvelous in mainstream Western culture. The same, however, cannot be said about Asia, where the process of modernization did not necessarily mean the eradication of older spiritual beliefs. As frequently portrayed in books and films, Asian ghosts have no problem adapting to the demands of the modern world and its new communication technologies, abandoning their graveyards and crumbling mansions for the sake of the high-speed railway, commercial elevators, mobile telephony, or the Internet. But, more importantly, outside the province of fiction, supernatural powers help maximize business profits, play a part in politics, and accompany practically every significant lifetime event, most of which are rarely complete without their share of animistic rituals and the presence of a fortune-teller or two.

The attitude of the living toward ghosts and spirits is also significantly different in Asia. True, most supernatural narratives are likely to evoke feelings of fear, and occasionally pity, when dealing with the ghost of a wronged person. For the most part though, Asian ghosts and spirits are seen as protective, especially when understood as ancestors and land deities, and the typical relationship they foster is that of negotiation. Respected and obeyed, ghosts and spirits are meant to be asked for favors and appeased with offerings. Regardless of its scientific advancement, gross national income, dominant religion or philosophy, there is no Asian country without its spirit shrines and shamans. As a Thai popular saying warns, "you may not believe, but never offend the spirits."

This obviously complicates our usual psychological reading of haunted narratives, since not every ghost in Asia must necessarily speak of repression or past trauma. Many Asian ghosts and spirits, moreover, take forms considered alien or bizarre in Western culture, so there is no doubt that the "Gothic terrors" of those tales may escape nonlocal audiences. When, in 1998, Hideo Nakata's film version of *Ring*, inspired by the 1991 novel by

Kōji Suzuki, had the ghost of Sadako crawl out of a TV set and into the hearts of horror fans worldwide, the world went crazy over Asian long-haired vengeful spirits. Soon after that, however, the fans began to complain about the apparent repetitiveness of Asian ghost movies. Interestingly, while few have ever objected to the aesthetics of vampire fangs or werewolf claws, the simple observation that Asian cultures abound in depictions of female long-haired ghosts (e.g., Japanese *onryō*, Malaysian *pontianak* or *langsuyar*, Indonesian *kuntilanak*, Thai *phii tai thang klom*) proved too much to handle.

Despite their individual characteristics, Asian female spirits are relatively easy to inscribe into Gothic narratives. Their stories are those of madness and suicide, rape and murder, of death either in childbirth or during a botched abortion. While alive, these spirits were often mere playthings of powerful men, since a woman is powerless in a patriarchal society where her chief virtue is obedience. In death female spirits turn to rage and vengeance, but, interestingly, remain fiercely loyal to the men they used to love and are eventually subdued by male (religious) authority. One of the most archetypal stories of such unlucky women turned into vengeful spirits is that of Thai Mae Nak, a lovelorn ghost of a faithful wife who died in childbirth while her husband, Mak, was away at war. Upon the husband's return, Nak resumes her wifely duties, at the same time terrorizing the villagers to prevent them from telling Mak that he has been sharing his household with a ghost. Exorcised by a famous monk who, according to one version of the story, removes part of her skull and entombs her in a clay pot, Mae Nak's spirit has never really been put to rest. Her tale, told and retold by generations of Thais, has been turned into a poem, a novelette, a play, a radio drama, a musical, an opera, a cartoon, and about thirty movies and TV series, including at least two films in 3-D. In real life, its heroine, elevated to the rank of a local deity, continues to receive daily offerings from crowds of devotees at her shrine in Bangkok's busy district of Phra Khanong.

Then there are those spirits whose Gothic potential is at times more difficult to grasp. Many of them are dualistic creatures, or shape-shifters, like those whose bodies can split or grow extra organs at will. In Thailand, *phii krasue* is said to be just a head with glowing entrails floating in mid-air. A similar spirit can be found in Cambodia (*ap*), Laos (*kasu*), and Malaysia (*penanggalan*). In Indonesia, local "witches" known as *leaks* are said to be capable of the same transformation, and in the Philippines, rubbing *manananggal* oil on one's body is meant to cause the torso to grow bat-like wings and separate from its lower half. Filipino *aswangs* (a very extensive supernatural category to which *manananggal* belongs) are said to be capable of sprouting long tongue-like protrusions from their mouths that allow them to suck unborn babies out of their mothers' wombs. They are also known to transform into pigs or black dogs, or appear as a human doppelgänger.

Traditional ghosts and spirits, whose exploits belong for the most part to the oral lore, have experienced a sudden revival in the works of contemporary authors of the region, frequently reappearing as modern hybrids of old and new ingredients to allow for their transition into the present. In his collection of stories *Dragon's Fin Soup* (1998), S. P. Somtow, a Thai author known for his contributions to the world of American zombies, werewolves, and punk-rock vampires, is as likely to politicize his *phii krasue* by making her the sister-in-law of the Thai prime minister ("The Lottery Night") as to use her to explain an extraterrestrial invasion ("Fiddling for Water Buffaloes"). David Hontiveros blends Filipino folklore with Western pop-cultural Gothic elements. In his novella *Takod* (2005), the corrupt mayor of Mapayapa is found to be a power-hungry *aswang*, mobilizing his (or in fact her) army of hybrid monstrosities, including the golem-like *tikbalang*. The demon is defeated with the help of the *pelesit*, or *polong*, an inherited homunculus spirit that serves its master. Hontiveros' *Craving* (2005) incorporates the Malay and Filipino beliefs in *pontianak*, *langsuyar*, and *tianak* into a haunting story of pregnancy fears somewhat reminiscent of Ira Levin's *Rosemary's Baby* (1968).

Another prominent Asian supernatural form is the baby spirit. Known by many names (*kuman thong* in Thailand, *toyol* or *tuyul* in Malaysia, *xiaogui* in Taiwan), such spirits are procured through a grisly ritual involving grilling human fetuses and entombing them in a clay jar. Baby spirits are meant to be fed and entertained by their adoptive parents, and in return they are expected to bring them fortune and protect them from evil. Far from being purely a literary invention, such magical objects can be acquired for a price even today. In 2012, a British man of Taiwanese origin was arrested in Thailand with six roasted human fetuses, which he purchased for £4,000 and intended to sell online for six times the price. If convicted, the culprit was expected to spend up to a year in prison and pay a fine of 2,000 Baht (£40), which suggests that the offense was not seen as particularly grave.[1]

The *kuman thong* made its first literary appearance in the Thai epic *Khun Chang Khun Phaen*, which developed as an oral tale during the Ayutthaya period (1350–1767) and was then revised, adapted, and expanded by numerous authors including Khru Jaeng, Sunthorn Phu, King Rama II, and Prince Damrong (with the first standard edition published in 1917–1918). The story focuses on the competition between two men, Khun Phaen (handsome and adventurous but poor) and Khun Chang (down-to-earth and rich but ugly), over a beautiful woman, Wanthong, who is ultimately put to death by the king as a punishment for not being able to choose her husband. Khun Phaen's lucky strike begins when he convinces one of his lovers to make him the guardian of their son. The unfortunate lady is unaware that Khun Phaen intends to begin his parenting by slicing her in half and frying the unborn fetus to create a powerful talisman, known as the "golden boy," or the *kuman thong*. Obtained in such a gruesome way, the spirit son of Khun Phaen is bound to serve and protect him whenever his father requires it.

Though recognized as the calling card of Southeast Asian black magic, "golden boys" can also be found in other areas of Asia. Some forms of the supernatural, however, tend to be more geographically constrained, for instance the *yōkai* in Japan, a large group of mythical creatures popularized in Japanese art and folklore. Some are surprisingly humanlike; some resemble animals; there are also those that look like inanimate objects. One particular group of the *yōkai*, *tsukumo-gami* are reanimated everyday objects believed to be granted a soul on their 100th birthday. A specifically Chinese form of the supernatural, *jiang shi*, has been popularized in the West courtesy of Hong Kong martial arts comedies as "the hopping vampire." The *jiang shi* stories are supposed to have originated from the practice of hiring Taoist priests to transport the corpses of relatives who died far away from home, which they apparently achieved by teaching the dead how to hop on their own feet. East Asia is also the home of fox spirits, such as the Chinese *huli jing*, Japanese *kitsune*, or Korean *kumiho*, all sharing the similar characteristics of shape-shifters, most likely to take on the form of a young beautiful woman and seduce men to feed on their flesh. All of these creatures have found their way into works of fiction.

One of the earliest examples of Asian supernatural literature – excluding the ancient Sanskrit epic *Ramayana* (fifth century BC), whose stories of gods and demons proved profoundly influential throughout South and Southeast Asia – are the Chinese "accounts of the strange" or *zhiguai*. *Zhiguai* came to prominence in the period of Six Dynasties (AD 220–589), and their tales of supernatural encounters could be seen as creative examples illustrating the rules regulating the relationship between the living and the dead. The most acclaimed *zhiguai* stories appear in the *Liaozhai zhiyi* collection of Pu Songling (1640–1715), translated in parts as *Strange Tales from a Chinese Studio* (2006). Here we find accounts of seductive foxes, wandering spirits, and ghostly possession. In "Fox Enchantment," a young gentleman is thrilled to discover a beautiful girl asleep in his bed but foolish enough to ignore a bushy tail between her legs, which in the end costs him his life. In "The Painted Skin," another gentleman is bewitched by a green-faced ghoul wearing the skin of a beautiful maiden. After the ghost tears his heart out, the man's wife has to bear great humiliation in order to restore him to life.

Zhiguai stories have inspired countless works of fiction and been retold in movies and television dramas. Films based directly on the writing of Pu Songling, such as *A Chinese Ghost Story* and its two sequels (dir. Siu-Tung Ching, 1987, 1990, and 1991), *A Touch of Zen* (dir. King Hu, 1971), or several versions of *Painted Skin* (returning in 2008 in a blockbuster version dir. Gordon Chan, Andy Wing-Keung Chin, and Danny Ko), effectively defined the standards of Hong Kong supernatural filmmaking. Echoes of *zhiguai* can also be found in the works of modernist writers, such as Lu Xun, and are not unusual for more contemporary authors, like Su Tong, Mo Yan, Zhang Yueran, or Yu Hua, whose books have been listed as examples of magical realism but, given the authors' penchant for the macabre, could clearly be of interest to Gothic scholars.

Su Tong's novella "Raise the Red Lantern" in a collection with the same title (1990) tells the story of Lotus, a young woman forced to become the fourth mistress of a rich merchant after her father's suicide. Lotus spends her days squabbling with the remaining three wives and becoming morbidly obsessed with a disused well rumored to contain the bodies of all the murdered wives in the Chen household caught committing adultery. In her dreams she is frequently visited by their ghosts: "As soon as she thought that, she really seemed to see a pale white hand, dripping wet, reaching out to cover her eyes from the unfathomable depths at the bottom of the well."[2] Indeed, such harsh punishment is meted out to the third mistress, Coral, for her trespasses, which in the end drives Lotus to madness. Supernatural elements in Mo Yan's novel *Life and Death Are Wearing Me Out* (2006) are determined by its narrative of reincarnation. The novel's main protagonist, Ximen Nao, a landowner executed during Mao's Land Reform Movement, is introduced to us in hell, suffering torture at the hands of Lord Yama, king of the underworld, and his henchmen. Unable to break him, Lord Yama allows him to return to earth, and Ximen Nao finds himself back in Northeast Gaomi Township reborn as a donkey. Ten years later, after the donkey has been dismembered and eaten by a gang of starving citizens, he returns again as an ox, and then again as a pig, a dog, a monkey, and finally as a hemophiliac boy with a large head, the narrator of the story. Although both Su Tong and Mo Yan remain strongly rooted in realistic writing, supernatural themes and motifs manage to seep into their works on numerous occasions.

Chinese stories of the strange are also quoted as the influence behind the early Japanese tales of the unusual. Supernatural stories, adapted from Chinese fiction or inspired by Japanese folklore, frequently incorporating

Buddhist teachings, developed into a genre, known in Japanese as *kaidan-shū* ("tales of the strange and mysterious"), whose golden age culminated in the Edo Period (1603–1868). Some of the most influential *kaidan* stories can be found in *Ugetsu Monogatari* (*Tales of Moonlight and Rain*, 1776), written by Akinari Ueda (1734–1809). One of Ueda's classic tales, "Homecoming," tells the story of a long-absent husband returning home to his wife, waking up the next morning to a realization that he shared his bed with a ghost. The story, inspired by a tale from the medieval text *Konjaku Monogatari* (*Tales from the Past*), "How a Poor Man Left His Wife," was later reworked by Lafcadio Hearn as "Reconciliation" (1900) and spawned several film adaptations, such as *Ugetsu Monogatari* (dir. Kenji Mizoguchi, 1953) or *Kaidan* (dir. Masaki Kobayashi, 1964). The obsessively jealous Lady Rokujo from another medieval manuscript, *Genji Monogatari* (*The Tale of Genji*), is often credited as the prototypical female vengeful spirit, perhaps the most recurring type of ghost in the region.

Ghosts and spirits continue to haunt contemporary Japanese fiction, even if their depictions have changed. Kōji Suzuki's *Ring* novels (1991–2005) enhanced the traditional concept of a vengeful spirit by merging it with the popular urban folklore story of a cursed viral video. In Hideaki Sena's biomedical horror *Parasite Eve* (1995), the invasive creature is composed of the mitochondria cultured from the cells of the main protagonist's dead wife. A more traditional approach to ghosts can be found in Taichi Yamada's *Strangers* (1987), which depicts the relationship of a lonely middle-aged man, Harada, with the ghosts of his dead parents. As the man grows weaker with each visit to his spectral home, his new girlfriend, Kei, begs him to let go of the past. It is only after an intervention of his friend that Harada learns that his love affair with Kei is similarly flawed. On the first night they met, after Harada refused to invite her to his apartment, Kei committed suicide and soon after became a grudge-bearing spirit herself.

Japanese vengeful spirits have become international horror celebrities through their cinematic incarnations as wronged women (*JuOn*, dir. Takashi Shimizu, 2002), lost children (*Dark Water*, dir. Hideo Nakata, 2002), and elemental hybrids (*Ring*, dir. Hideo Nakata, 1998). They appear to be well integrated into modern-day media and communication technologies haunting computers (*Ghost System*, dir. Toshikazu Nagae, 2002), the Internet (*Pulse*, dir. Kiyoshi Kurosawa, 2001), and mobile phones (*One Missed Call*, dir. Takashi Miike, 2003). Hence, if we are to look for more extreme examples of fiction imitating reality, we need to turn our attention to Singapore.

Singaporean multiculturalism extends into the country's supernatural lore – an amalgamation of beliefs and superstitions interlacing Chinese ghost stories with Malay magic. The main protagonist of Sandi Tan's *The Black Isle* (2012), Cassandra, seems to epitomize that attitude. A Chinese immigrant with the name of a Greek prophetess, Cassandra communicates with the spirits and, with the help of Malay necromancy, engages their services to rid the island of its Japanese invaders. After the war, Cassandra's skills are enlisted by the prime minister, who wages a private war against the supernatural. But interestingly, it is the ghosts who have the last word and confirm their ownership of the island.

Singaporean ghost stories circulate widely through oral lore, and this specific orality of the ghost tale translates not only into the written but also into the cinematic form. Singaporean ghost stories do not simply tell stories about ghosts, but rather stories about people who gather to tell and listen to stories about ghosts. K. K. Seet's collection *Death Rites* (1990) takes place during a wake for Fanny Gan, described in the prologue as "a true Occidentophile" who would have rather been sent off into eternity to the sounds of Mahler or Mozart playing discreetly "in the candle-lit, flower-scented cubicle of a modern, airconditioned funeral parlour."[3] Instead Fanny's corpse is treated to the clamor of gongs and cymbals, paper lanterns, shamanistic incantations, and a bunch of people who decide to remember her by telling ghost stories for three consecutive days. The stories of ghosts haunting office bathrooms, honeymoon suites, shops and restaurants, old mansions and cramped apartments, university campuses, and military training sites told with equal enthusiasm by ordinary people, shamans, radio DJs, army sergeants, and university professors proliferate in Singaporean ghost literature and movies, just as they are a part of everyday life.

Catherine Lim advised in *They Do Return* (1983): "Ghosts do return [...] but when they do, gently lead them back. Call them by their name, then tell them to go back quickly to their new home. If they refuse, be patient with them, and gently lead them back."[4] Indeed, like all things uncanny, ghosts have a habit of returning and they seem oblivious of cultural or geographic boundaries set by man, providing us with an opportunity to search for the Gothic outside its immediately visible territory. But without a clear understanding of how different instances of the supernatural inscribe themselves into the fabric of a particular culture, Asian supernatural Gothic faces the threat of being appreciated merely for its exoticism, which is certainly not its most remarkable quality. It is easy to read Asian ghosts as remnants of a colonial past or echoes of other traumatic events from the history of the continent, or as manifestations of individual guilt, but such readings depend heavily on methodologies developed outside Asia and do little for internalizing Gothic within the region. Dealing with the incredibly rich supernatural texture of Asia on its own terms is much more challenging for Western audiences, but it may prove a better strategy in the long run for actually understanding the Asian literature of ghosts.

The unspeakable: Asian nonsupernatural Gothic

Outside of the domain of the supernatural, Gothic themes of madness, disease and degeneration, violence and cruelty, impossibility and loss, trauma, grief and mourning, otherness, the grotesque, inequality, and oppression proliferate in Asian texts. Gothic motifs are frequently employed to deal with "unspeakable" issues, such as politicized violence, abuse of power, gender discrimination, or oppression of minority groups, commonly left untouched for political, religious, or cultural reasons. The human-centeredness of those motifs makes them particularly interesting for modernist-to-postmodern authors and opens them to psychologically oriented readings. Having said that, one has to remember that Western psychoanalytical theories were not developed with Asians in mind, relegated as they have been to the realm of the cultural Other, so they should be applied with caution. At the same time, the fact that Gothic theory has so far been informed exclusively by Western philosophies does not mean that it cannot benefit from exploring other systems of thought. If there is one thing we have learned about Gothic so far, it is that the concept is capable of great malleability and alteration.

Edmund Burke's very British insights into the French Revolution (published in 1790) revealed the Gothic dimension of political terror. Asia too has had its fair share of wars, revolutions, and territorial strife (between and within nations), the savagery of which has left deep wounds in individual and collective memories. Those conflicts have often been followed by prolonged periods of political repression and denial, which have made history an unmentionable subject and a potential breeding ground for stories resonating with Gothic sentiments. Recollections of wartime cruelty and violence haunt the protagonists of those stories, affecting their lives in profound ways, and crippling their ability to function in the new world, which is more eager to forget than to remember.

Many texts tackle the war trauma directly, describing its destructive power to turn victims into abusers. In Mo Yan's story "Man and Beast" (*Shifu, You'll Do Anything for a Laugh*, 1999), the narrator imagines his grandfather, a conscript Chinese laborer in Japan, in an act of attempted rape upon a Japanese countrywoman, which is justified in his mind by the "blood debt" between the two races: "Jap bastards! You raped and killed my women, bayoneted my daughter, enslaved my people, slaughtered my troops, trampled on my countrymen, and burned down our houses."[5] The rapist is caught by remorse at the sight of his victim's underwear uncannily reminding him of his wife. The victims of another displaced Chinese laborer, described by S. P. Somtow in "The Bird Catcher" (*Dragon's Fin Soup*, 1998), are not so lucky, since this character is based on See Uey Sae Ung, the cannibal killer who made headlines in 1958 and subsequently became immortalized in Thai nursery rhymes as a liver-eating ghoul. Somtow writes:

> [i]t's like the time I looked into Si Ui's eyes and saw the fire. I see a Chinese boy running through a field of dead people. It's sort of all in black and white and he's screaming and behind him a village is burning.
>
> At first it's the Chinese boy, but somehow it's me too, and I'm running, with my bare feet squishing into dead men's bowels, running over a sea of blood and shit. And I run into someone's arms. Hard. The comic-book Japanese villain face. A human heart, still beating in his hand.[6]

War turns men into monsters, and its memories can haunt the victors and the defeated. In Gothic renderings of such traumas, the return of the past can be just as devastating as the realization that it is impossible to turn back the clock. In Duong Thu Huong's *No Man's Land* (2005), a woman recoils at the touch of her first husband, a North Vietnamese war veteran, when his return home after having been thought dead for fourteen years tears her new family apart. In Bao Ninh's *The Sorrow of War* (1991), another Vietnamese soldier cannot recognize his teenage sweetheart in the hardened woman he finds after the war, her innocence lost on the night she was raped on a train during a bombardment. The good people of Blora, a small Javanese town described by Pramoedya Ananta Toer in his story "Acceptance" (*All That Is Gone*, 1952), replace their humanity with the desire for revenge. In Ha Jin's *War Trash* (2004), Chinese Korean War veterans, who upon their return to China after liberation from the POW camps become the living symbols of the past government's political failures, realize the historical inconvenience of their survival. Although the book's laconic memoir-style narrative may not appear particularly "Gothic," the haunting sense of abandonment and isolation, forced silences, masochistic guilt, and acceptance of one's fate as belonging to the "lost generation" are just some of its themes that invite a Gothic exploration.

Partly as a consequence of years of self-imposed censorship, Asian texts frequently turn to the Gothic grotesque to deliver social and political critique, a convenient habit picked up in times when authors risked persecution if they dared to disagree openly with the authorities. The stories of Ma Jian (*The Noodle Maker*, 1991), an absurd commentary on life in modern China, overflow with the bizarre: an entrepreneur who opens up a private crematorium, an elderly mother who reminds her son to pay the electricity bill while being cremated alive, an actress who chooses to be eaten by a tiger during the performance to make her lover suffer, or a three-legged talking dog that likes to engage in lengthy philosophical discussions. Chart Korbjitti introduces "The Personal Knife" (*An Ordinary Story*, 1983), which we find out is an instrument necessary for the Thai upper classes to cannibalize the poor. The grotesque seems an obvious choice for stories dealing with the themes of madness and disease, degeneration, corruption, social disorder, and perverse sexuality, all of which are by no means alien to Asian authors.

Madness, such authors claim, is often strangely liberating, even if this apparent freedom from the constraints of the rigid structures of Asian hierarchical societies comes at a price. Madness gives one the right to rave against the corrupt political system, to oppose the will of one's parents, to deny the expectations imposed on one's gender. It can be artistic inspiration, as in the case of Yoshihide painting his daughter's violent death in Ryonosuke Akutagawa's "Hell Screen" (1918), or turn a skeptic scientist into a believer, like when Edogawa Rampo's character Tanuma takes a look at himself reflected by a completely spherical mirror in "The Hell of Mirrors" (1926). The political dimension of madness is explored by Lu Xun in "Diary of a Madman" (1918) and Kim Sŏk-pŏm in *The Curious Tale of Mandogi's Ghost* (1970). Not surprisingly, madness is often seen as besetting women whose lives were broken by harsh living conditions, neglect, and abuse they suffered at the hands of their kin and the state (Su Tong, Mo Yan, Xinran).

Indeed, the plight of women in societies where their fate is decided by men is often given a Gothic treatment in Asian texts. Traditional gender roles are replayed in the Gothic romances of Catherine Lim (*The Bondmaid*, 1995; *The Teardrop Story Woman*, 1998; *Following the Wrong God Home*, 2001), where unhappy Chinese women are frequently driven into the arms of sympathetic foreigners, sealing their doom with these acts of transgression. Lisa See's exotic romances counteract the orientalist imagery of footbinding and female submission with tales of women's resistance to an endurance of gender bonds (*Snow Flower and the Secret Fan*, 2005; *Peony in Love*, 2007). Women's fatalistic determination is foregrounded in the novels of Xinran (*The Good Women of China*, 2002; *Sky Burial*, 2004), as well as those of Mo Yan (*Big Breasts and Wide Hips*, 1996) or Su Tong (*Binu and the Great Wall of China*, 2006).

Xinran's journalistic style of writing seems somewhat at odds with the Gothic sentiments punctuating her accounts of systematic cultural oppression of Chinese women and their inability to break from a life of silence. Mo Yan and Su Tong's dark politically critical fiction, awash with the grotesque and the fantastic, occasionally also comments on the horrors specifically, it seems, reserved for the female kind: rape, forced marriage, family servitude, marital abuse, or culturally sanctioned gendercide. Male authors are well aware of the tragic consequences of the gender status quo. Pramoedya Ananta Toer's story "Inem" (*All That Is Gone*, 1952, 2005) sympathizes with an 8-year-old girl sold into marriage, while Mo Yan's "Abandoned Child" (*Shifu*, 2000) discusses the Chinese preference for sons and the bleak fate of unwanted daughters. Last but not least, we find Gothic portrayals of independent, sexually aware new Asian women in search of their identity in the rapidly changing world (Xu Xi, Beth Yahp, Shirley Geok-Lin Lim, Mian Mian, Natsuo Kirino, Hitomi Kanehara, and Wendy Law-Yone).

Described as the continent of diversity, Asia is a land of extreme contrasts. Gothic seeps into the cracks, feeding off the fear of difference and animosity between religions, races, ethnicities, castes and classes, the old and the new. Racism isolates the characters of Kiran Desai's *The Inheritance of Loss* (2006): the judge, Jemubhai, who "worked at being English with the passion of hatred and for what he would become, he would be despised by absolutely everyone, English and Indians, both," Biju, who "possessed an awe of white people [. . .] and a lack of generosity regarding almost everyone else," or his boss who "had been kind enough to hire Biju, although he found him smelly."[7] Ethnic tensions escalate into a full-blown rebellion when the Nepalese nationalists demand the separation of Gorkhaland. Squatter encampments creep up on private property. The old world crumbles but the new one seems equally desolate.

The abundance of Gothic themes and motifs in Asian texts testifies to its ability to transgress cultural boundaries. At the same time, however, since most of the crucial methodologies that contributed to the development of Gothic theory are West-centric, they may seem alienating to native Asian readers. We may look for Catholic guilt in Filipino novels, we may wince at the descriptions of Chinese dysfunctional families, or gasp in terror at the exploits of feudal lords in old-time Japan, but we must not forget that each of these concepts was shaped by distinct cultural values and under specific historical circumstances – and so were the methods of their representation. Given the growing interest of Gothic scholars in Asian texts, Gothic theory has already proven beneficial in enhancing our understanding of Asian literatures. But if the Gothic is ever to truly take root in Asia, it needs to be relatable to and even spring from the indigenous systems of thought.

Buddhist concepts of impermanence and change, karma and fate, or the Asian cultural preoccupation with individual and collective "face" and its connection to shame are but a few examples of ideas that may help localize Gothic studies in Asia. In popular understanding, the laws of karma are often reduced to a crude expectation of divine retribution for one's sins and a reward for one's virtues. This notion translates into another simplification demanding that everyone accept their fate, which also means their gender, class, position, social status, wealth, and so on, unequivocally. The rich and beautiful are believed to be so because of the good karma they accumulated in their past lives. The sick and destitute are seen as suffering punishment for their past misdeeds. Humans should not interfere with the laws of karma. Indeed, in supernatural Asian narratives, vengeance is often left to spirits (themselves doomed to become spirits by their bad karma) which act as instruments of karmic retribution. In nonsupernatural texts, the unswerving devotion to fatalism and the resulting inertia can turn people into silent accomplices of evil, or prompt them to self-harm, both situations easily becoming a source of Gothic horror.

For Pira Sudham, karma is an instrument of political control: "I was gagged and blindfolded by the despotic regimes [...] taught and trained to become utterly obedient, subservient, unthinking, fearing the authorities."[8] In Chart Korbjitti's novels, it is a force of habit and a justification of the existing power structure. The protagonist of The Judgment (1981), Fak, left alone with his young mentally unstable stepmother, is shunned by his neighbors. His decision to resist the social order leads to his demise. Cheated, degraded, beaten, and unjustly arrested, Fak effectively drinks himself to death. In the final act of humiliation, his body is used to test a new furnace at the temple rather than be given a proper funeral. Korbjitti's characters frequently fall into a downward spiral and blame fate for their poverty (No Way Out, 1980), mundane existence (Carrion Floating By, 1987), or inability to adapt to the changing world (Mad Dogs & Co., 1988). Their emotional paralysis is further reinforced by the cultural expectation of collectivist conformity and the demand to maintain one's face at all times, leaving them vulnerable to exploitation and prone to melancholy, both familiar traits for Gothic fiction.

Asian theories of subjectivity can prove equally groundbreaking for the Gothic as those of Freud, Jung, or Lacan. Face-saving mechanisms produce polarizations worthy of Dr. Jekyll and Mr. Hyde. Oriental philosophies of time, space, or indeed the conceptualization of life, death, and the beyond can help naturalize the Gothic within Asia and enrich Gothic criticism. Buddhist concepts of change, flux, immaterialism, or detachment are pliable enough to merit a Gothic reading too. In Yasutaka Tsutsui's Hell (2003), the afterworld is in flux, there is no difference between days and years, people can slip in and out of time and space, and knowing each other's minds eliminates the need for reward or punishment. Tsutsui's nomadic characters, whether a telepathic maid (The Maid, 1972) or a cybernetically enhanced dream doctor (*Paprika*, 1993), are characterized as much by their unusual abilities as by their detachment from the world – a quality recognized in equal measure by Western psychoanalysis and Eastern philosophies.

Searching for Asian Gothic may not take us in the direction we originally intended, and it will certainly not leave us with easy or simple conclusions. Asian Gothic is not a forgotten category that needs rediscovering. On the contrary, it is still very much a label without a structure and in the process of becoming. Cultivating Gothic criticism in Asia is a task well worth attempting, given the existence of numerous texts that open themselves to Gothic interpretations. Such a search may change our current understanding of what the Gothic has been and can be. But the Gothic, as we know, has always been open to change. Who says it cannot rise to the challenge?

NOTES

1 Ian MacKinnon, "Briton Arrested with Roasted Human Foetuses for Use in Black Magic Ritual," *The Telegraph*, May 18, 2012.
2 Su Tong, "Raise the Red Lantern," in *Raise the Red Lantern: Three Novellas* (1990), trans. M. S. Duke (New York: Harper, 2004), pp. 11–99, pp. 53–54.
3 K. K. Seet, *Death Rites* (1990; Singapore: Times Books International, 1995), p. 9.
4 Catherine Lim, *They Do Return … But Gently Lead Them Back* (1983; Singapore: Times Books International, 2000), p. 106.
5 Mo Yan, *Shifu, You'll Do Anything for a Laugh* (1999), trans. Howard Goldblatt (New York: Arcade, 2001), p. 79.
6 S. P. Somtow, *Dragon's Fin Soup* (1998; Bangkok: Asia Books, 2002), p. 114.
7 Kiran Desai, *The Inheritance of Loss* (New York: Grove Press, 2006), pp. 231, 86, 26.
8 Pira Sudham, *Tales of Thailand* (1983; Bangkok: Shire Asia, 2002), p. 5.

14

LUCIE ARMITT

The Gothic and magical realism

We live today in a world of transparency and open-access information systems: global communication, transglobal travel, freedom of information requests, and twenty-four-hour digital communications. Such transparency is, for the Western world, redolent with democratic ideals. One might also argue that, in literary terms, clarity is associated most clearly with the transparency of literary realism, for in setting up a mirror to life, the realist text purports to eschew the dark corners in which secrets lurk. Our literary appetites, however, seem to move in the opposite direction to those of our politics. For it remains the case that the Gothic, a form of literature and culture wedded to anachronism, the interior and its claustrophobic secrets, the pathological and its sick desires, continues to enthrall ever new generations of Western readers. But is this because, given its emphasis upon the interior (including the interiority of psychology and pathology), we seal our Gothic reading away from our everyday political concerns? I think not. In this essay I look at the Gothic alongside its more overtly politicized sister form, magical realism – with which it is interacting increasingly – to consider to what extent the terrain that lies on the blurry boundary between these two modes of writing shifts in response to a larger political impetus that rejects the world of confidences and its political tricksters.

Magical realism comes to us first from Latin America, though it has also taken strong root elsewhere, and carries with it a particular ideological resonance that identifies it closely with postcolonial politics. Its relationship to realism is different from the Gothic's, in that the boundary markers between mimesis (Greek for "realistic imitation") and antimimesis in magical realism are far more fluid and permeable. At one moment a character is standing in a room in his or her own house; at the next moment, a specter arrives and engages in dialogue. Unlike the conventional ghost story, the result in literary terms is neither to eradicate the realism established beforehand in the text nor to dilute the unsettling effect of the ghost. Instead, by granting equal narrative presence to both, magical realism reveals that the extraordinary exists most absolutely *within* the quotidian real. Here, the specter usually bears a message or embodies political significance, for, in the cultures most closely associated with magical realism, politics is more frequently associated with the extraordinary than the ordinary. As Salman Rushdie tells us in the opening chapter of *Shame* (1982):

> The thin-eyed, rock-hard tribals who dwelt in the [Impossible Mountains] . . . also called the range, "the roof of Paradise". The mountains, in fact the whole region . . . suffered from periodic earthquakes; it was a zone of instability, and the tribals believed that the tremors were caused by the emergence of angels through fissures in the rocks.[1]

In the Gothic, by contrast, points of entry and exit between earth and hell are far more clear-cut. Once we have opened that creaking old door, hell takes over until the threshold is recrossed and the reader returns to the daylight world of order and reason. Magical realist literature never departs from the world of the everyday (and its politics). However, it does irrevocably challenge its "natural" association with order and reason, and it is through the introduction into it of ghosts and other apparitions from the afterlife that this challenge is mounted. This more continual means of engaging with the supernatural shatters any easy convictions that realism can be equated either with logic and order or with safe territory. Equally challenged is the easy claim that major global concerns can be explored only through political realism.

Though magical realism started in Latin America, its diaspora now populates most of the modern literary world. In their landmark volume of essays on *Magical Realism* (1995), Lois Parkinson Zamora and Wendy B. Faris bring together a series of essays focused on writing from North and South America, mainland Europe, Britain, the Caribbean, Japan, North Africa, and the Indian subcontinent. Since then, as we will see below, Brenda Cooper has extended our understanding of its reach to literature from South and West Africa. Despite this global span, it is in Anglo-American and British writing that magical realism most struggles to gain purchase, perhaps because of (or despite) the preeminence the Gothic enjoys in both cultures. One issue this essay explores is why this might be the case, beginning with questions connecting magical realism with "the foreign" in the English-speaking world.

Where magical realism embraces the foreign, whether spiritual or extraterritorial, the Gothic fights to keep the stranger at bay but fails, intimating a cultural failure which Western cultures have perhaps found it easier to identify with than to overcome. Roger Corman's film version of Poe's 1839 American Gothic tale *The Fall of the House of Usher* (1960) illustrates this trait neatly. The interloper arrives on horseback through a landscape of shrunken vegetation, resembling the magical realist writer Isabel Allende's description of her first trip to the North of Chile as a child: "Sun, baked rocks, kilometres and kilometres of ghostly solitudes [*sic*], from time to time an abandoned cemetery, ruined buildings of adobe and wood."[2] Arriving at the house, Poe's interloper knocks at the door, the scale of which no longer takes its frame of reference from the human body, such that he is as dwarfed by its architecture, as by the expanse of wilderness he has just crossed. Inside he finds Roderick, brother to his beloved Madeline. Roderick's hostility toward the unwelcome visitor is more than the usual familial resistance to intruders. He recoils from all sensory stimulus, embodying a cultural shrinkage from any miscegenation. Is this all just Gothic, or is there some magical realism here too?

To answer that, we need to look again at definitions of the Gothic and magical realism, noting that, for British and Anglo-American readers, each term immediately strikes us as "foreign." In a key definition of what is Gothic, this compulsion appears in Freud's landmark essay "The Uncanny," originally published in 1919 as "Das Unheimliche." Freud opens by acknowledging he is stepping on foreign soil, apologizing for intruding on the world of "aesthetics," before justifying his foray by asserting it to be an area neglected by "the specialist literature." As if to make himself more at home, he quickly turns to questions of etymology and dictionary defin-itions. The word uncanny (*unheimlich* in the original German) derives from the etymological root "home" (*Heim*) and, from that, derivations such as "homely" and "familiar." However, in examining the prefix "un-," Freud observes that it is too simplistic to suggest that it merely translates as what is "*not* known and familiar" (original italics), because "naturally not every-thing that is new and unfamiliar is frightening."[3] Instead, the *unheimlich* requires the ongoing trace of homeliness prior to a sudden or even a slight shift, having the effect of turning the familiar into the strange or, to put it another way, turning the cherished notion of privacy into the unsettling notion of secrecy.

Although Freud takes several detours on the road to understanding, the issue toward which he most strives leads us back in time and ultimately returns us to our birth:

> It often happens that neurotic men declare that they feel there is something uncanny about the female genital organs. This *unheimlich* place, however, is the entrance to the former Heim [home] of all human beings, to the place where each one of us lived once upon a time ... Whenever a man dreams of a place or a country and says to himself ... "this place is familiar to me, I've been here before" we may interpret the place as being his mother's genitals or her body.[4]

Identifying the vagina and womb as the origins of the uncanny seems far-fetched, but the concept of homesickness Freud also attaches to this identification is less so, for such an unsettling emotion may well prompt the intrusion of uncanny fears. It is also a better means of accessing another motif raised by Freud, namely the haunted house, which Freud downplays by comparison, speaking of it only in passing, as a subset of that category of the uncanny linked to "death and dead bodies . . . the return of the dead, and to spirits and ghosts." However, the haunted house is key, in my view, not only to the uncanny in general but to the connection between the Gothic and magical realism in particular, as is a further aspect of the uncanny identified by Freud, namely that "an uncanny effect is often and easily produced when the distinction between imagination and reality is effaced, as when something that we have hitherto regarded as imaginary appears before us in reality."⁵

The painstaking route Freud takes through the uncanny is mirrored by the way in which the origins and etymology of the term "magical realism" have reached Western readers. Anglo-American scholars take as their introduction to magical realism the definition provided by another German scholar, Franz Roh, who, six years after "The Uncanny," published the landmark essay "Nach-Expressionismus, Magischer Realismus: Probleme der neuesten Europäischen Malerei." This essay, though translated into Spanish by Fernando Vela in 1927, came to English translation only a couple of decades ago, when Wendy B. Faris translated it under the title "Magic Realism: Post-Expressionism" in her coedited collection of 1995. Arguably, the unavailability of this essay in English translation has contributed to magical realism's late arrival to the field of Anglo-American literary criticism and the perceived "foreignness" of it to "us" still. Moreover, the term is further complicated for literary scholars by the fact that Roh's essay is a contribution to a debate about art history, more specifically post-expressionist painting. Only subsequently does it become attached to literature and only then in a manner that appears to contradict Roh's initial coinage of the phrase. Hence, rather like Freud's tricky twisting between the terms *heimlich* and *unheimlich*, magical realism's own introduction to English-language literature has required a number of steps on the route to acceptance.

To rehearse this twist in more detail: Roh's *Magischer Realismus* documents a retreat from expressionism, a movement he associates with "an exaggerated preference for fantastic, extraterrestrial, remote objects" which, though it "resorts to the everyday and the commonplace for the purpose of distancing it, invest[s] it with a shocking exoticism." For Roh, such work is epitomized by the paintings of the Russian artist Marc Chagall (1887–1985) in which, he notes:

> animals walked in the sky; behind the transparent brain of the viewer, also present in the picture, appeared towns and villages; overly vehement and heated heads popped like corks from overflowing bottles; grandiose chromatic storms flared through all these beings; and the farthest reaches of the picture appeared mysteriously close to the foregrounds.[6]

Importantly, though the post-expressionism of magical realism turns away from these fantastic excesses, one must not assume, as a result, that a simple taste for mimesis returns. Roh continues: "this new world of [art] objects is still alien to the current idea of Realism." Instead, "when a piece of imitated 'reality' hangs on the wall it only makes sense if it starts from and then . . . transcends the representation of a window, that is, if it constitutes a magical gaze opening onto a piece of mildly transfigured 'reality.'"[7] Both Gothic and magical realism, then, come to us via a foreign etymology, not simply because they derive from languages that are not English, but because they reach us via disciplines that are not literary and, in the process of becoming applied to areas for which they were never intended, their origins become obscured, distorted, perhaps even corrupted.

To return briefly to Freud: His essay makes use of a series of journey motifs, from the uncanny effect of "accidental" returns on foot to the red-light district of a city to the similar effect of finding the number 62 repeated on everything one touches. Journeys are also a central theme of magical realism, where the traveler operates as the reader's key representative in the text. The Cuban writer Alejo Carpentier expounds at length on the relationship between travel and art, but in so doing argues that narrative fiction only offers a poor substitute for the "marvelous real" as it exists in our geographical encounters with the exotic:

> After having felt the undeniable spell of the lands of Haiti, after having found magical warnings along the red roads of the Central Meseta . . . I was moved to set this recently experienced marvelous reality beside the tiresome pretension of creating the marvelous that has characterized certain European literatures over the past thirty years.

Uncomfortably for us, examples cited of such "tiresome pretension" include "Lewis' monk, the horrifying machinery of the English Gothic novel: ghosts, immured priests, lycanthropes, hands nailed to a castle door."[8] Nevertheless, that both the uncanny and magical realism require an etymological journey before we can embrace them suggests, at least, their acceptance by those with an appetite for the "foreign" (in its widest sense), along with the fact that their strangeness emerges from that aforementioned common engagement with homesickness. Furthermore, pretentious or otherwise, our appetite for literary or cinematic ghosts remains wholly undimmed, even in this cynical postmodern age, a need as pertinent to magical realism as to the Gothic. Though magical realism requires "a strong *presence* of the phenomenal world" to succeed, because of its preoccupation with political injustice and the postcolonial legacy of European expansion, questions of presence immediately invoke specters.[9] As John Jervis observes in "Uncanny Presences," "history has to be understood as a stream of disappearing traces, each alienated in the very moment of its appearance."[10]

In *My Invented Country* (2003), Allende opens in characteristic magical realist mode, drawing attention to the importance of topography to imagination, but she soon slips into a more Gothic lexicon:

> I travelled to the North [of Chile] when I was a child, and I've never forgotten it ... In my memory, Antofagasta, which in Quecha means "town of the great salt lands," is not the modern city of today but a miserable, out-of-date port ... [A]s the nitrate companies began to close down ... the pampa became strewn with ghost towns. Those two words – "ghost town" – gave wings to my imagination on that first trip.[11]

Questions of haunting persist as she describes the house in which they lived:

> To go to the bathroom at night, you had to make an excursion with a flashlight, defying cold air and spiders and turning a deaf ear to the sounds of creaking wood and scurrying mice. That huge old house ... harbored a tribe of [family relations] and guests ... There was also an occasional ghost of dubious authenticity ... Some attest that souls in pain wandered within those walls, but one of my older relatives confessed to me that as a boy he dressed up in an ancient military uniform to frighten Tía Cupertina. That poor maiden lady hadn't the slightest doubt that her nocturnal visitor was the spirit of Don José Miguel Carrera ...[12]

Here truths and fictions are woven together into a tapestry of storytelling which begins with the Gothic in general (spiders spinning cobwebs; creaking boards at night) and shifts more precisely into the ghost story. Depending upon the reader's propensities, one can read this place either as a haunted house (one fake ghost does not explain away the attestations about "souls in pain wander[ing] within [the] walls") or as a house inhabited by tricksters and make-believe (Carpentier's pretenders). Either way, it is the kind of magic out of which true Gothic storytelling has been forged ever since Walpole's *The Castle of Otranto* (1764).

Compare Allende's house to the "high, fortress-like, gigantic residence which faced inwards to a well-like and lightless compound yard" depicted in Rushdie's *Shame*.[13] Here, three sisters, Chhunni, Munnee, and Bunny, are incarcerated. The catalyst for the story in this text is the conception of the central protagonist, Omar Khayyam Shakil, whose mother is one of the three (precisely who remains a mystery). To perpetuate the secret, an architectural solution, a dumbwaiter, is constructed such that "items could be winched by a system of motorized pulleys from the street into the upper stories of the house, or vice versa."[14] Thus obscured from the sight of the outside world, the individual identity of the pregnant mother cannot be ascertained publicly. In a conventional Gothic novel, such architectural mysteries would herald a claustrophobic narrowing of all horizons until the rude intrusion of an interloper, as in *House of Usher*, brings what "ought to have remained secret and hidden ... to light."[15] In the magically realist *Shame*, however, the relationship established between secrets and horizons is more complex. Here the very presence of secrets pushes against the confines of architectural, cultural, and rational limits, fueling the larger-than-life possibilities afforded by storytelling and "pulling out the rug" from under the reader's expectations:

> The dumb-waiter contained, then, many terrible secrets. The Mistri completed his work without once laying eyes on any of the three sisters Shakil, but when he died a few weeks later, clutching his stomach and rolling about in a gully, spitting blood on to the dirt, it got about that those shameless women had him poisoned to ensure his silence on the subject of his last and most mysterious commission. It is only fair to state, however, that the medical evidence in the case runs strongly against this version of events. Yakoob Balloch, who had been suffering for some time from sporadic pains in the region of the appendix, almost certainly died of natural causes ... Or some such thing.[16]

As in Allende's narrative, Rushdie's style shuttles, like a needle through cloth, toward and then away from witchcraft, sorcery, ghosts, and the occult. He evokes them only to apparently dismiss them but, in the act of seeming to dismiss them, he evokes them again ("Or some such thing"). For both writers, it is the possibility of belief in a form of dark magic that enables the story to be large enough to cross cultural horizons and extend its reach beyond the control of the implied author. Allende herself considers the role of the ghost to be directly connected to one's ability to write, as is revealed when she describes writing *The House of the Spirits* (1982):

> I wrote my first book by letting my fingers run over the typewriter keys, just as I am writing this, without a plan. I needed very little research because I had it all inside, not in my head but in that place in my chest where I felt a perpetual knot ... I wrote in a trance, as if someone was dictating to me, and I have

always attributed that favor to the ghost of my grandmother, who was whispering into my ear.[17]

The same thing happens later, she notes, when she writes her first memoir, *Paula* (1994), about which "I have no doubt that in writing that book I received help from the benign spirit of my daughter."[18] The key point to note, here, is that such hauntings, though they may be experienced on a personal level, in magical realism always take on application to a broader cultural or national narrative.

In an earlier novel, *Midnight's Children* (1981), Rushdie demonstrates the cultural application that haunting can have upon a nation. The midnight in question is August 15, 1947, the time and date of India's independence from British rule. As in Allende's writing, in *Midnight's Children* stories are handed down from generation to generation and, after an opening section detailing how the birth of his narrator, Saleem Sinai, coincides with this historical moment, we are plunged into the story of Saleem's grandfather, Doctor Aadam Aziz. As a young and newly qualified doctor, Aziz is called to the house of Ghani, a wealthy landowner, to attend his daughter. On entering the house of this blind widower who, the narrator tells us, is so unable to pay sufficient attention to its maintenance that the servants take advantage, Saleem notes that:

> There were cobwebs in corners and layers of dust on ledges ...
>
> In later years, Doctor Aadam Aziz swore that during those two moments of solitude in the gloomy spidery corridors ... he was gripped by an almost uncontrollable desire to turn and run away as fast as his legs would carry him ... A woman with the biceps of a wrestler was staring at him, beckoning him to follow her into the room ... Clutching his bag a fraction too tightly, he followed her through the dark teak door.[19]

The key aspect of such doorways, in both the Gothic and magical realism, is that they are necessary conduits for storytelling; unless the protagonist crosses that threshold, no story follows. Here, on the other side of the door, we find a shift from the Gothic into the larger-than-life arena of the magical real, where lurks a wholly more worldly kind of secret in which the fabulous aspect remains part of the realism. To be sure, in *Midnight's Children* Rushdie flirts with the uncanny, assuring us that this side of the door is "as ill-lit as the rest of the house," but he then establishes a more carnivalesque sense of the larger-than-life: "Two more women, also built like professional wrestlers, stood stiffly in the light, each holding one corner of an enormous white bedsheet."[20] As Aziz looks around, confusedly, for Ghani's daughter, it emerges that she is concealed behind the cloth, a small section of which has been cut away. Thus can Aziz examine the relevant part of her body while she maintains her modesty. It is from within these small snippets that the story gradually unfolds. Indeed, later on, Rushdie, in the guise of his narrator, will draw attention to the double meaning of the word "sheet" (bed linen and piece of paper) and, in the process, make a further connection between the ways in which the stories of different generations take shape: "Condemned by a perforated sheet to a life of fragments ... I have nevertheless done better than my grandfather; because while Aadam Aziz remained the sheet's victim, I [the writer] have become its master ..."[21]

One major difference between the storytelling technique of magical realism and the storytelling technique of the Gothic, in fact, resides in the respective roles adopted in both modes by the author/storyteller. In his work, Rushdie intrudes in a manner that can only be read as the implied author's rather than the narrator's voice, as this example from *Shame* demonstrates:

> Not so long ago, in the East End of London, a Pakistani father murdered his only child, a daughter, because by making love to a white boy she had brought such dishonor upon her family that only her blood could wash away the stain ... The story appalled me when I heard it, appalled me in a fairly obvious way. I had recently become a father myself and was therefore newly capable of estimating how colossal a force would be required to make a man turn a knife-blade against his own flesh and blood. But even more appalling was my realization that ... I, too, found myself understanding the killer.[22]

This is not a narrator subsumed by the magical enchantments of story, but one whose horror is rooted in the materiality and cultural assumptions of everyday realism. This is the same "bus stop" world with which Angela Carter's final novel, *Wise Children* (1991), opens:

> Once upon a time, you could make a crude distinction, thus: the rich lived amidst pleasant verdure in the North [of London] speedily whisked to exclusive shopping by abundant public transport while the poor eked out miserable existences in the South in circumstances of urban deprivation condemned to wait for hours at windswept bus-stops while sounds of marital violence, breaking glass and drunken song echoed around ...[23]

In a Gothic narrative, the author's voice must remain outside the text; otherwise the distancing of the terrible required by the narrative format will shatter. Magical realism revels in a form of narrative embroidery, within the terms of which the needle pulls the thread in and out of the woven cloth, perforating the "bedsheet" anew as in *Midnight's Children*, thus allowing the extraordinary to percolate through the everyday fabric of realism.

In an earlier essay on the Gothic and magical realism, I examined the role of "cryptonomy" in this coupling, bringing forward a notion from Nicholas Abraham and Maria Torok.[24] Understood as a form of "transgenerational haunting," cryptonomy is a particularly apposite concept for the exploration of those traumas that manifest themselves primarily in narrative form and that are handed down from generation to generation, expressed most clearly as "the gaps left within us by the secrets of others."[25] Family inheritances are a key characteristic of the Gothic tradition, epitomized by those ancestral portraits that peer down upon interlopers as they make their way up the imposing sweep of those staircases. A more whimsical instance of this phenomenon is depicted in *Wise Children*, in which the ghost of Grandma Chance reveals a truth to her 75-year-old granddaughters, Dora and Nora, as they stand in their late grandmother's bedroom in 49 Bard Road, Brixton, London, the house they inherited from her when she died. Reminiscing about the past, they turn to wistful daydreaming about never having been mothers:

> Then a funny thing happened. Something leapt off the shelf where the hats were. No, not leapt; "propelled itself," is better because it came whizzing out like a flying saucer, slicing across the room as if about to knock our heads off, so we ducked. It knocked against the opposite wall, bounced down to the ground, fluttered and was still.
>
> It was her hat, her little toque, with the spotted veil, that had spun out like a discus. And as we nervously inspected it, there came an avalanche of gloves – all her gloves, all slithery leather thumbs, and fingers, whirling around us as if inhabited by hands, pelting us, assaulting us, smacking our faces, so that we clutched hands for protection . . .
>
> "Grandma's trying to tell us something," said Nora, in an awed voice.[26]

Wise Children is a comparatively rare example of British magical realism, and its occasional ghosts hover around the allure of make-up and make-believe which party in the face of the ever-approaching Grim Reaper. In terms of its commentary on global politics, the particular combination, in *Wise Children*, of Shakespearean high art and popular storytelling revels in Shakespeare's global appeal. At the same time, it parodies the manner in which he has come to be established as an icon of British authenticity in an age of lost empire and the decreasing political influence of Britain on the world stage. Thus is it able to combine moments of ridicule at the expense of British imperialism with a profound love of the magic of performative storytelling and its ability to infuse pleasure into the everyday reality of those who live on "the wrong side of the tracks."[27]

As we have seen, magical realism is basically a form of storytelling that maximizes the political responsibility of story to connect with the everyday world, while reveling in the simultaneous presence of the extraordinary within that actuality. For Gothic writers, a very similar interest has taken them to the world of the folktale, and Carter belongs to this group too. Her collection of Gothic fairy tales, *The Bloody Chamber* (1979), is well known, but her overall influence over Anglo-American readings of the fairy tale has a broader reach. In her introduction to the first volume of the *Virago Book of Fairy Tales*, she makes this characteristically playful observation: "The history, sociology and psychology transmitted to us by fairy tales is unofficial – they pay even less attention to national and international affairs than do the novels of Jane Austen."[28] A lack of engagement with the high politics of international affairs, however, detracts neither from their internationalism, nor from their local, regional, or even national influence, and she selects, for this volume, stories from Europe, Asia, Africa, North and Central America, and the Middle East. Among them, she brings to the reader's attention one of the traditional opening phrases of Armenian folk tales: "There was and there was not, there was a boy ..." Of this she observes that it is "both utterly precise and absolutely mysterious."[29]

This combination of precision and mystery is equally characteristic of magical realism. Also clear in Carter's introduction is the way in which these tales evolve from everyday struggle and questions of identity politics, and yet the storytelling takes precedence over the locale enabling, again, this combination of precision (here of a cultural kind) and the transcendent potential of the enchanting tale:

> Although the content of the fairy tale may record the real lives of the anonymous poor with sometimes uncomfortable fidelity – the poverty, the hunger, the shaky family relationships, the all-pervasive cruelty and also, sometimes, the good humor, the vigor, the straightforward consolations of a warm fire and a full belly – the form of the fairy tale is not usually constructed so as to invite the audience to share a sense of lived experience.[30]

Furthermore, in its central focus on child/parent politics, the folktale instantly levels the political playing field in relation to global politics:

> Fairy-tale families are, in the main, dysfunctional units in which parents and step-parents are neglectful to the point of murder and sibling rivalry to the point of murder is the norm. A profile of the typical European fairy-tale family reads like that of a "family at risk" in a present-day inner-city social worker's casebook, and the African and Asian families represented here offer evidence that even widely different types of family structures still create unforgivable crimes between human beings too close together.[31]

One continent noticeably absent from Carter's first volume is South America, but, in case one might assume this omission derives from its more harmonious relationship between region and family, in *My Invented Country*, Allende connects larger-than-life storytelling directly to the traumas of childhood. Indeed, she cites folktales as one form of evidence of childhood trauma being "normal": "A happy childhood is a myth, and in order to understand that we have only to take a look at children's stories . . . Nothing is simple or humane in childhood . . . I wasn't whipped like my brothers, but I lived in fear, like all the other children I knew."[32]

One of the concerns voiced of certain modes of fantasy writing by politically orientated critics is that it fosters a type of readerly escapism which detracts from a sustained engagement with questions of material, social, or political inequality. It is an argument underlying Lynne Pearce's reading of Jeanette Winterson's *Sexing the Cherry* in her 1994 book, *Reading Dialogics*, and one that begins by noting the possibility that, in novels such as Winterson's, "by removing her characters to the realms of fantasy and history . . . Winterson [may have] left behind the question of what it is to be a woman and/or lesbian in any more material sense." Though Pearce gradually qualifies this early concern, ultimately noting that "In Winterson's defense . . . the characters in *Sexing the Cherry* never do 'transcend' their genders even though they may challenge their definition," she remains uneasy about Winterson's use of fantastic tropes and how they map on to the material reality of historical time and place.[33] This bone of contention is, similarly, at the root of Cooper's reading of magical realism as it applies to West African fiction, an approach she describes as "seeing with a third eye." In keeping with Pearce's reading of Winterson, Cooper identifies in the work of the Sierra Leone writer Syl Cheney-Coker, the Nigerian writer Ben Okri, and the Ghanaian writer Kojo Laing "the powerful, restless reincarnations of myth into magic and history into the universal." Adopting a different perspective from Pearce's, however, Cooper argues that this aspect of the writing enables rather than evades ongoing engagement with political and material realities. According to Cooper, magical realism is a mode of writing which "contests polarities" and "strives . . . to capture the paradox of the unity of opposites," including "history versus magic, the pre-colonial past versus the post-industrial present and life versus death."[34]

More recently, in "Women Dancing on Water," Cooper has turned her attention specifically toward questions of gender and, more particularly, the work of writers such as the Nigerian-born Helen Oyeyemi. This shift leads Cooper to a renewed examination of the nature of the relationship between magical realism and the Gothic. The houses at the center of novels such as Oyeyemi's *The Opposite House* (2007) and *White Is for Witching* (2009), she argues, are "redolent of gothic overtones," such that they form a type of "haunted house" structure. Furthermore, in following precisely the kind of cultural needlework we have identified in magical realist novels from other continents, their doorways are "exemplary of multiple belongings as they open out to more than one country." In the work of diasporic communities, the relationship between magical realism and the Gothic becomes an interrogative one, in that it exposes two different layers of storytelling: "the dominant tale of the unified nation," geographically rooted in its "enclosures, castles, and citadels," and the subversive stories of the silenced, whose ghostly echoes bounce off their walls.[35]

In *White Is for Witching*, Oyeyemi's own approach to family secrets leads to a scene which uncannily recalls the type of literary influence from the dead of which we have already witnessed Allende speak. Oyeyemi's schoolgirl protagonist Miranda suffers from an eating disorder and has already found, on opening her wardrobe, it is "full of clammy ghosts that hovered around her body when she put them [her clothes] on." Later, required to write an essay for school which explores the ethics of suicide, Miranda no sooner starts writing than she feels the presence of another hand on her work:

> she turned to a new page in her notebook and began writing questions. Beneath the questions she wrote answers, in a hand as different from the one the questions were written in as possible ... The answer unnerved her because the handwriting was truly different from her own. It was handwriting she'd seen before in Christmas and birthday cards, shaky but elegant, the "g"s and the "y"s straight-legged, rather than curled.[36]

While Miranda is writing, two additional things are taking place: She catches her elbow on the edge of the paper and receives a paper cut which bleeds onto the page, such that it becomes "red-spotted" and she throws the sheet away; at the same time, the two "hands" on the page begin to separate. The two-handed approach begins as a methodology for imitating a dialogue with suicide itself (a "devil's advocate" approach, perhaps). However, as the writing process takes over, the presence in the room takes the form of her dead great-grandmother, GrandAnna or Anna Good, who suffered from the same eating disorder as Miranda and from whom the family inherits the house. As a type of psychical conversation imprints itself on the page, Miranda's voice is inscribed in the more tentative font of italics, while GrandAnna's reply is written in bold:

> *Goodlady, are you really good?*
> **yes**
> *Even when no one is looking?*
> **of course**
> *But do you understand your nature?*
> **my nature?**
> *Did you choose to be good, or were you so created?*
> **i chose to be created**
> *Is that really an answer?*
> **yes.**[37]

The interspersing of different fonts upon the page (the "conversation" ends by these fonts being interleaved into the regular font in which the main narrative is written) fits well with the connection, made above, between narrative stitching and the shared phantoms which populate the magical real and the Gothic. In Gothic terms, haunting exists as a cryptonomy, the hiding of a spectral figure within another figure. In the magical real, it becomes a means of articulating the secrets of those whose cultural narratives have been erased by colonialism. At the same time, this scene between Miranda and her great-grandmother also resonates with what Cooper identifies as a form of cultural "code-switching":

> From the very beginning, African writers in English recognized the imperative to bend the language to their wills, to make it work as their slave and not their master. This was a gargantuan task; it is not merely a case of using a few proverbs and words from indigenous languages, or depicting African rituals in the mode of anthropological interpreters. Far more deeply concealed in the very intestines of the English language are its stories of conquest, its tropes and topoi of light and darkness, its multiple codes and maps and keys, which either barricade or unlock the citadels of power and knowledge.[38]

Borrowing from linguistics, Cooper identifies code-switching as the means by which Oyeyemi reworks the English language into which she has been assimilated, to the point that it becomes "visceral, poetic, and idiosyncratic."[39] In this more recent article, it is interesting to note how Cooper's position on the relationship between the Gothic and magical realism has shifted. In her earlier work on West African fiction, she notes:

> In the ideal magic realist plot, there is no gothic subtext, no dark space of the unconscious, no suppressed libidinous attic space, in which a madwoman is concealed. The mysterious, sensuous, unknown and unknowable are not in the subtext, as in realist writing, but rather share the fictional space with history. The alternative histories, the mysteries, dreams, pain, bewilderments and nightmare labyrinths, struggle to be visibly inscribed within the text's surfaces.[40]

In renegotiating a closer interaction between the two, in relation to women's writing of the West African diaspora, Cooper intimates that haunting takes on a more specifically Gothic aspect when situated within house and home and when such visible inscriptions are threaded, bodily, through a female storytelling tradition.

In her book *Ordinary Enchantments*, Wendy B. Faris describes magical realism as a form of writing in which "the marvelous seems to grow organically within the ordinary," but also in which are combined "the inclusion of different cultural traditions," such that it "reflects, in both its narrative mode and its cultural environment, the hybrid nature of much postcolonial society."[41] Like the magical real, the Gothic requires the coming together of otherwise divergent worlds (such as those of "romance" and "novel") to create a spillage of one into the other, without which, to paraphrase Freud's citation of Friedrich von Schelling, one could not reveal "everything that ought to have remained ... secret and hidden but has come to light."[42] One possible explanation for the increasing popularity of both the Gothic and magical realism might reside in the point with which this essay opened. We now live in a society that "contests" (to borrow Cooper's phrase) the existence of secrecy, whether on the level of familial and other forms of abuse "behind closed doors" (the realm of the Gothic) or on the level of unearthing the buried narratives and silenced, but still hovering, voices of the culturally and socially oppressed (the primary terrain of the magical real). The Gothic can only exist because a moment identifying itself as "modern" is intruded upon by another moment (through visitation) viewed as anachronistic. This essay suggests that such "modernity" and its open vistas might attach themselves equally to magical realism. Hence, those narratives (such as the ones with which this essay deals) that lie on the boundary between magical realism and the Gothic afford the possibility of a new rapprochement between literatures and their cultures. In removing from the "foreign" any fear of the unknown, even the ghosts of magical realism surrender their clanking chains. How might the ghosts of our history respond in the years to come?

NOTES

1 Salman Rushdie, *Shame* (New York: Vintage, 1995), p. 23.
2 Isabel Allende, *My Invented Country: A Memoir*, trans. Margaret Sayers Peden (New York: HarperCollins, 2004), p. 3.
3 Sigmund Freud, "The Uncanny," in *The Penguin Freud Library*, vol. XIV: *Art and Literature*, ed. Albert Dickson (London: Penguin, 1990), pp. 335–376, pp. 339–341.
4 Freud, "The Uncanny," p. 368.
5 Freud, "The Uncanny," pp. 364, 367.
6 Franz Roh, "Magic Realism: Post-Expressionism" (1925), in *Magical Realism: Theory, History, Community*, ed. Lois Parkinson Zamora and Wendy B. Faris (Durham, NC: Duke University Press, 1995), pp. 15–31, p. 17.
7 Roh, "Magic Realism," p. 20.
8 Alejo Carpentier, "On the Marvelous Real in America" (1949), in *Magical Realism*, ed. Zamora and Faris, pp. 75–88, pp. 84–85.
9 Wendy B. Faris, *Ordinary Enchantments: Magical Realism and the Remystification of Narrative* (Nashville, TN: Vanderbilt University Press, 2004), p. 14.
10 John Jervis, "Uncanny Presences," in *Uncanny Modernity: Cultural Theories, Modern Anxieties*, ed. Jo Collins and John Jervis (New York: Palgrave Macmillan, 2008), pp. 10–50, p. 11.

11 Allende, *My Invented Country*, p. 3.
12 Allende, *My Invented Country*, pp. 20–21.
13 Rushdie, *Shame*, p. 12.
14 Rushdie, *Shame*, p. 17.
15 Freud, "The Uncanny," p. 345.
16 Rushdie, *Shame*, pp. 17–18.
17 Allende, *My Invented Country*, p. 180.
18 Allende, *My Invented Country*, p. 180.
19 Salman Rushdie, *Midnight's Children* (New York: Vintage, 1995), pp. 21–22.
20 Rushdie, *Midnight's Children*, p. 22.
21 Rushdie, *Midnight's Children*, p. 121.
22 Rushdie, *Shame*, p. 115.
23 Angela Carter, *Wise Children* (London: Chatto and Windus, 1991), p. 1.
24 Lucie Armitt, "The Magical Realism of the Contemporary Gothic," in *A New Companion to the Gothic*, ed. David Punter (Oxford: Wiley-Blackwell, 2012), pp. 510–522.
25 Nicholas Abraham, "Notes on the Phantom: A Complement to Freud's Metapsychology," trans. Nicholas Rand, *Critical Inquiry*, 13 (1987), pp. 287–292, p. 287.
26 Carter, *Wise Children*, pp. 189–190.
27 Carter, *Wise Children*, p. 1.
28 *The Virago Book of Fairy Tales*, ed. Angela Carter, vol. 1 (London: Virago, 1991), p. x.
29 Carter, *The Virago Book of Fairy Tales*, p. xii.
30 Carter, *The Virago Book of Fairy Tales*, p. xi.
31 Carter, *The Virago Book of Fairy Tales*, p. xix.
32 Allende, *My Invented Country*, pp. xiii–xiv.
33 Lynne Pearce, *Reading Dialogics* (London: Edward Arnold, 1994), pp. 174, 185.
34 Brenda Cooper, *Magical Realism in West African Fiction: Seeing with a Third Eye* (London: Routledge, 1998), p. 1.
35 Brenda Cooper, "Women Dancing on Water: A Diasporic Feminist Fantastic?," *Contemporary Women's Writing*, 6 (2012), pp. 140–158, pp. 144–145.
36 Helen Oyeyemi, *White Is for Witching* (London: Picador, 2009), pp. 36, 67–68.
37 Oyeyemi, *White Is for Witching*, pp. 67–68.
38 Cooper, "Women Dancing on Water," p. 143.
39 Cooper, "Women Dancing on Water," p. 142.
40 Cooper, *Magical Realism*, p. 36.
41 Faris, *Ordinary Enchantments*, p. 1.
42 Freud, "The Uncanny," p. 345.

GUIDE TO FURTHER READING

Important primary writings of modern Gothic
(or largely Gothic) since 1900

Acker, Kathy. *Pussy, King of the Pirates*. New York: Grove Press, 1996.

Acosta, Oscar. *The Autobiography of a Brown Buffalo*. New York: Vintage Books, 1989.

The Revolt of the Cockroach People. New York: Vintage Press, 1989.

Allende, Isabel. *The House of the Spirits* (1982), trans. Maqda Bogin. New York: Dell, 2005.

My Invented Country: A Memoir, trans. Margaret Sayers Peden. New York: HarperCollins, 2004.

Atwood, Margaret. *The Blind Assassin*. New York: Random House, 2000.

Surfacing (1972). London: Bloomsbury, 2009.

Bakker, R. Scott. *Neuropath*. New York: Tom Doherty, 2008.

Banks, Iain. *The Wasp Factory*. London: Macmillan, 1984.

Banville, John. *The Sea*. London: Picador, 2005.

Bechdel, Alison. *Fun Home: A Family Tragicomic*, graphic memoir. New York: Mariner, 2007.

Beckett, Samuel. *Three Novels: Molloy, Malone Dies, The Unnamable*. New York: Grove Press, 2009.

Bloch, Robert. *Psycho*. New York: Simon and Schuster, 1959.

Bowen, Elizabeth. *Collected Stories*. New York: Vintage, 1981.

The Heat of the Day (1949). London: Penguin, 1962.

Brijs, Stefan. *The Angel Maker*, trans. Hester Velmens. London: Weidenfeld and Nicholson, 2008.

Brite, Poppy Z. *Lost Souls*. New York: Delacorte Press, 1992.

Brown, Rebecca. *The Haunted House*. San Francisco: City Lights, 2007.

The Terrible Girls. San Francisco: City Lights, 1992.

Butler, Octavia. *Fledgling*. New York: Seven Stories Press, 2005.

Campbell, Ramsey. *The Darkest Part of the Woods*. New York: Tor, 2003.

Carroll, Jonathan. *Bones of the Moon*. London: Century Press, 1987.

Voice of Our Shadow (1983). New York: Ace, 1985.

Carter, Angela. *The Bloody Chamber* (1979). New York: Penguin, 1981.

The Magic Toyshop. London: Heinemann, 1967.

Wise Children. London: Chatto and Windus, 1991.

Chandler, Raymond. *The Big Sleep.* New York: Knopf, 1939.

Clarke, Susanna. *Jonathan Strange & Mr. Norrell.* New York: Bloomsbury, 2004.

Cohen, Leonard. *Beautiful Losers* (1966). Melbourne: Text Publishing, 2011.

Collins, Nancy A. *Knuckles and Tales.* Forest Hills, MD: Cemetery Dance, 2002.

Cox, Michael. *The Meaning of Night: A Confession.* New York: Norton, 2006.

Crisp, Quentin. *Chog: A Gothic Fable.* New York: Methuen, 1979.

Danielewski, Mark Z. *House of Leaves.* New York: Pantheon, 2000.

Danticat, Edwidge. *Krik? Krak!* New York: Vintage, 1996.

Davidson, Andrew. *The Gargoyle.* New York: Doubleday, 2008.

Desai, Kiran. *The Inheritance of Loss.* New York: Grove Press, 2006.

Diaz, Junot. *The Brief Wondrous Life of Oscar Wao.* London: Faber and Faber, 2008.

Dick, Philip K. *Do Androids Dream of Electric Sheep?* (1968). London: HarperCollins, 1972.

Dinesen, Isak (Karen Blixen). *Seven Gothic Tales* (1934). New York: Random House, 1961.

Donoghue, Emma. *Kissing the Witch: Old Tales in New Skins.* New York: Harper, 1997.

Dowling, Terry. *Clowns at Midnight: A Tale of Appropriate Fear.* Hornsea: PS Publishing, 2010.

du Maurier, Daphne. *Don't Look Now and Other Stories.* Harmondsworth: Penguin, 1973.

  My Cousin Rachel. London: Gollancz, 1951.

  Rebecca. London: Gollancz, 1938.

Eagan, Jennifer. *The Keep.* New York: Knopf, 2006.

Ellis, Bret Easton. *American Psycho.* New York: Vintage, 1991.

  Lunar Park. London: Picador, 2005.

Ellison, Ralph. *Invisible Man* (1952). New York: Vintage, 1990.

Enright, Anne. *The Gathering.* London: Jonathan Cape, 2007.

Erdrich, Louise. *Four Souls.* New York: HarperCollins, 2004.

Faber, Michael. *The Crimson Petal and the White.* New York: Harcourt, 2002.

Faulkner, William. *Absalom, Absalom! The Corrected Text* (1936). New York: Vintage, 1986.

  Light in August (1932). New York: Random House, 1968.

  Sanctuary: The Original Text (1931), ed. Noel Polk. New York: Random House, 1981.

Gaimon, Neal. *The Graveyard Book.* New York: HarperCollins, 2008.

Garner, Alan. *Thursbitch.* London: Harvill, 2003.

Gibson, William. *Neuromancer.* London: Gollancz, 1984.

Gomez, Jewelle. *The Gilda Stories.* New York: Firebrand, 1991.

Gordimer, Nadine. *The Conservationist* (1974). London: Bloomsbury, 2005.

Grimsley, Jim. *Dream Boy.* New York: Scribner, 1997.

Groff, Lauren. *The Monsters of Templeton.* New York: Voice/Hyperion, 2008.

Hand, Elizabeth. *The Bride of Frankenstein: Pandora's Bride.* Milwaukee, OR: Dark Horse, 2007.

Harris, Charlaine. *The Southern Vampire Mysteries.* London: Ace Books, 2001–2013.

Harris, Thomas. *Red Dragon.* New York: G. P. Putnam, 1981.

  The Silence of the Lambs. New York: St. Martin's Press, 1988.

Harwood, John. *The Ghost Writer.* New York: Harcourt, 2004.

Heaney, William (Graham Joyce). *Memoirs of a Master Forger.* London: Gollancz, 2008.

Hill, Joe. *Heart-Shaped Box.* New York: William Morrow, 2007.

Holt, Victoria (Eleanor Hibbert). *The Captive.* New York: Doubleday, 1989.

  Mistress of Mellyn (1960). New York: St. Martin's Griffin, 2008.

  On the Night of the Seventh Moon (1972). New York: St. Martin's Griffin, 2010.

Ishiguro, Kazuo. *Never Let Me Go.* London: Faber and Faber, 2006.

Jackson, Shirley. *The Haunting of Hill House.* New York: Penguin, 1959.

James, M. R. *"Casting the Runes" and Other Ghost Stories* (1904–1925). Oxford University Press, 1987.

Kafka, Franz. *The Metamorphosis* (1915), trans. Stanley Appelbaum. Mineola, NY: Dover, 2009.

King, Stephen. *Bag of Bones.* New York: Scribner, 1998.

  Carrie. New York: Doubleday, 1974.

  The Dark Tower (1982–2004). New York: Signet, 2003–2006.

  'Salem's Lot. New York: Doubleday, 1975.

  The Shining. New York: Doubleday, 1977.

Kirino, Natsuo. *Real World*, trans. Phillip Gabriel. London: Vintage, 2008.

Kirkman, Robert, and Tony Moore. *The Walking Dead,* serial graphic novel. Berkeley, CA: Image Comics, 2003–.

Klein, Rachel. *The Moth Diaries.* Washington, DC: Counterpoint, 2002.

Kostova, Elizabeth. *The Historian.* New York: Little, Brown, 2005.

Lasdun, James. *The Horned Man.* New York: Norton, 2002.

Lee, Tanith. *Fatal Women.* Bexhill on Sea: Egerton House, 2004.

Lim, Catherine. *They Do Return . . . But Gently Lead Them Back.* Singapore: Times Books International, 2000.

Ling, Hong. "Fever," in *Red Is Not the Only Color: Contemporary Stories*, ed. Patricia Sieber. Lanham, MD: Rowman & Littlefield, 2001, pp. 149–152.

Livesey, Margaret. *Eva Moves the Furniture.* New York: Henry Holt, 2001.

Lovecraft, H. P. *H. P. Lovecraft: The Complete Fiction (1916–1936)*, ed. S. T. Joshi. New York: Barnes and Noble, 2011.

Lurie, Alison. *Women and Ghosts.* New York: Talese, 1995.

Mantel, Hilary. *Beyond Black.* London: Harper Perennial, 2005.

Maquire, Gregory. *Lost.* New York: Regan Books, 2001.

Matheson, Richard. *I Am Legend* (1954). London: Orion, 2006.

McCarthy, Cormac. *No Country for Old Men.* New York: Knopf, 2005.

McGahan, Andrew. *The White Earth.* Sydney: Allen & Unwin, 2004.

McGrath, Patrick. *Asylum.* New York: Random House, 1996.

  Blood and Water and Other Tales. New York: Poseidon, 1988.

  Ghost Town: Tales of Manhattan Then and Now. New York: Bloomsbury, 2005.

  Martha Peake: A Novel of the American Revolution. New York: Vintage, 2000.

  Spider. New York: Poseidon, 1991.

Meyer, Stephenie. *Twilight.* New York: Little, Brown, 2005–2008.

Miéville, China. *Kraken.* London: Macmillan, 2010.

  Perdido Street Station. London: Macmillan, 2000.

Mo Yan. *Shifu, You'll Do Anything for a Laugh*, trans. Howard Goldblatt. New York: Arcade, 2001.

Momaday, N. Scott. *House Made of Dawn*. New York: Harper & Row, 1968.

Montero, Maya. *In the Palm of Darkness*. New York: Harper Perennial, 1998.

Moore, Alan, and Eddie Campbell. *From Hell,* serial graphic novel. Marietta, GA: Top Shelf, 1989–1999.

Morrison, Toni. *Beloved* (1987). New York: Penguin, 1988.

A Mercy. New York: Knopf, 2009.

Morton, Kate. *The Forgotten Garden*. New York: Atria, 2009.

Naylor, Gloria. *Linden Hills* (1985). New York: Penguin, 1986.

Oates, Joyce Carol. *Beasts*. New York: Carroll and Graf, 2002.

The Bloodsmoor Romance. New York: Jonathan Cape, 1983.

Haunted: Tales of the Grotesque. New York: Penguin, 1994.

O'Connor, (Mary) Flannery. *The Complete Short Stories* (1953–1965). New York: Farrar, Straus and Giroux, 1971.

Mystery and Manners: Occasional Prose, ed. Sally and Robert Fitzgerald. New York: Farrar, Straus and Giroux, 1970.

Wise Blood. New York: Harcourt, 1952.

Oyeyemi, Helen. *The Opposite House*. London: Bloomsbury, 2007.

White Is for Witching. London: Picador, 2009.

Palahniuk, Chuck. *Fight Club*. New York: Norton, 1996.

Lullaby (2002). New York: Anchor, 2003.

Peattie, Elia Wilkinson. *The Shape of Fear, and Other Ghostly Tales*. New York: Macmillan, 1904.

Pineda, Cecile. *Bardo 99*. San Antonio, TX: Wings Press, 2002.

Face. San Antonio, TX: Wings Press, 2003.

Priest, Cherie. *The Eden Moore Trilogy* (starting with *Four and Twenty Blackbirds)*. New York: Tor, 2003–2007.

Purdy, James. *Mourners Below*. New York: Viking Press, 1981.

Reese, James. *The Dracula Dossier*. New York: HarperCollins, 2008.

Rhys, Jean. *Wide Sargasso Sea* (1966). London: Penguin, 1997.

Rice, Anne. *Interview with the Vampire*. New York: Knopf, 1976.

The Vampire Lestat. New York: Knopf, 1985.

The Witching Hour. New York: Knopf, 1990.

Rivera, Tomás. . . . *y no se lo tragó la tierra /* . . . *and the Earth Did Not Devour Him* (1971), trans. Evangelina Vigil-Piñón. Houston, TX: Arte Público, 1987.

Robinson, Eden. *Monkey Beach*. New York: Knopf Canada, 2000.

Roy, Arundhati. *The God of Small Things*. London: Flamingo, 1997.

Rushdie, Salman. *Midnight's Children*. New York: Vintage, 1995.

Shame. New York: Vintage, 1995.

Sebold, Alice. *The Lovely Bones*. New York: Little, Brown, 2002.

Seet, K. K. *Death Rites*. Singapore: Times Books International, 1995.

Self, Will. *Dorian*. New York: Grove Press, 2004.

Setterfield, Diane. *The Thirteenth Tale*. London: Orion, 2006.

Silko, Leslie Marmon. *Ceremony*. New York: Penguin, 1986.

Simmons, Dan. *The Terror*. New York: Little, Brown, 2007.

Somtow, S. P. *Dragon's Fin Soup*. Bangkok: Asia Books, 2002.

Soucy, Gaétan. *The Little Girl Who Was Too Fond of Matches*. London: Flamingo, 2002.

Straub, Peter. *A Dark Matter*. New York: Doubleday, 2010.

Ghost Story. New York: Cower, McGann, 1979.

Shadowland. New York: Cower, McGann, 1980.

Sudham, Pira. *Tales of Thailand.* Bangkok: Shire Asia, 2002.

Suzuki, Koji. *Ring* (1991), trans. Robert B. Rohmer and Glynne Walley, New York: Vertical, 2004.

Tong, Su. *Raise the Red Lantern: Three Novellas,* trans. M. S. Duke. New York: Harper, 2004.

Trevor, William. *The Story of Lucy Gault.* London: Penguin, 2002.

Tritt, Donna. *The Little Friend.* New York: Random House, 2002.

Updike, John. *The Witches of Eastwick* (1984). New York: Penguin, 1985.

Vinge, Vernor. *Rainbows End: A Novel with One Foot in the Future.* New York: Tom Doherty, 2006.

Viramontes, Helena Maria. *Under the Feet of Jesus.* New York: Plume, 1995.

Walker, Alice. *Meridian.* New York: Pocket Books, 1976.

Waters, Sarah. *Affinity.* New York: Riverhead, 2000.

Fingersmith. New York: Riverhead, 2002.

Wynne, Madeleine Yale. *The Little Room and Other Stories.* Chicago: W. M. Hill, 1906.

Zafón, Carlos Ruiz. *The Shadow of the Wind* (2001). New York: Penguin, 2004.

Zuzak, Markus. *The Book Thief.* New York: Knopf, 2006.

Collections of modern Gothic or of essays on modern Gothic and its foundations

Bienstock Anolik, Ruth, and Douglas L. Howard, eds. *The Gothic Other: Racial and Social Constructions in the Literary Imagination.* Jefferson, NC: McFarland, 2004.

Bloom, Clive, ed. *Gothic Horror: A Reader's Guide from Poe to King and Beyond.* New York: St. Martin's Press, 1998.

Botting, Fred, ed. *Essays and Studies 2001: The Gothic.* Cambridge: Brewer, 2001.

Brabon, Benjamin A., and Stéphanie Genz, eds. *Postfeminist Gothic: Critical Interventions in Contemporary Culture.* Basingstoke: Palgrave Macmillan, 2007.

Bruhm, Steven, Reynold Humphries, Dale Townshend, Gary Rhodes, and Michael Lee, eds. *Horror Studies.* Bristol: Intellect, 2010–.

Byron, Glennis, ed. *Globalgothic. International Gothic.* Manchester University Press, 2013.

and David Punter, eds. *Spectral Readings: Towards a Gothic Geography.* London: Macmillan, 1999.

and Dale Townshend, eds. *The Gothic World.* London: Routledge, 2014.

Carter, Angela, ed. *The Virago Book of Fairy Tales,* vol. 1. London: Virago, 1991.

Cherry, Brigid, ed. *True Blood: Investigating Vampires and Southern Gothic.* New York: I. B. Tauris, 2012.

Collins, Jo, and John Jervis, eds. *Uncanny Modernity: Cultural Theories, Modern Anxieties.* Houndmills: Palgrave Macmillan, 2008.

Crow, Charles L., ed. *American Gothic: From Salem Witchcraft to H.P. Lovecraft, An Anthology.* 2nd edn. Oxford: Wiley-Blackwell, 2013.

A Companion to American Gothic. Oxford: Wiley-Blackwell, 2014.

Danticat, Edwidge, ed. *Haiti Noir.* New York: Akashic Books, 2011.

Dunn, George A., and Rebecca Housel, eds. *True Blood and Philosophy*. Oxford: Wiley-Blackwell, 2011.

Duperray, Max, ed. *Gothic N.E.W.S.*, 2 vols. Paris: Houdiard, 2009.

Edwards, Justin D., and Agnieska Soltysik Monnet, eds. *The Gothic in Contemporary Literature and Popular Culture: Pop Goth*. London: Routledge, 2012.

Gelder, Ken, and Jane M. Jacobs, eds. *Uncanny Australia: Sacredness and Identity in a Postcolonial Nation*. Melbourne University Press, 1998.

Gordon, Jan, and Veronica Hollinger, eds. *Blood Read: The Vampire in Contemporary Culture*. Philadelphia, PA: University of Pennsylvania Press, 1997.

Grant, Barry Kieth, ed. *The Dread of Difference: Gender and the Horror Film*. Austin, TX: University of Texas Press, 1996.

Gray, Chris Hables, ed. *The Cyborg Handbook*. London: Routledge, 1995.

Hoeveler, Diane Long, and Tamar Heller, eds. *Approaches to Teaching Gothic Fiction: The British and American Traditions*. New York: Modern Language Association of America, 2003.

Hogle, Jerrold E., ed. *The Cambridge Companion to Gothic Fiction*. Cambridge University Press, 2002.

Horner, Avril, ed. *European Gothic: A Spirited Exchange 1760–1960*. Manchester University Press, 2002.

and Sue Zlosnik, eds. *Le Gothic: Influences and Appropriations in Europe and America*. New York: Palgrave Macmillan, 2008.

Hughes, William, ed. *Gothic Studies*, the journal of the International Gothic Association. University of Manchester Press, 1999–.

and Andrew Smith, eds. *Queering the Gothic*. Manchester University Press, 2009.

Hurley, Kelly, ed. *Genre and Affect,* special issue of *English Language Notes*, 48:1 (spring/summer 2010), pp. 1–190.

Jackson, Anna, Karen Coats, and Roderick McGillis, eds. *The Gothic in Children's Literature: Haunting the Borders*. New York: Routledge, 2008.

Khair, Tabish, and Johan Höglund, eds. *Transnational and Postcolonial Vampires: Dark Blood*. London: Palgrave, 2012.

Lacefield, Kristen, ed. *The Scary Screen: Media Anxiety in* The Ring. Farnham: Ashgate, 2010.

Lloyd Smith, Allan, and Victor Sage, eds. *Gothick Origins and Innovations*. Amsterdam: Rodopi, 1994.

Magistrale, Tony, and Michael A. Morrison, eds. *A Dark Night's Dreaming: Contemporary American Horror Fiction*. Columbia, SC: University of South Carolina Press, 1996.

Mittman, Asa Simon, and Peter Dendle, eds. *The Ashgate Research Companion to Monsters and the Monstrous*. Farnham: Ashgate, 2012.

Morrow, Bradford, and Patrick McGrath, eds. *The New Gothic: A Collection of Contemporary Fiction*. New York: Vintage, 1992.

Mulvey-Roberts, Marie, ed. *The Handbook to the Gothic*, 2nd edn. New York University Press, 2009.

Mutch, Deborah, ed. *The Modern Vampire and Human Identity*. New York: Palgrave Macmillan, 2013.

Ng, A. H. S., ed. *Asian Gothic*. Jefferson, NC: McFarland, 2008.

Oates, Joyce Carol, ed. *American Gothic Tales*. New York: Penguin, 1996.

Olsen, Danel, ed. *Exotic Gothic: Forbidden Tales from Our Gothic World.* Ashcroft, BC: Ash-Tree Press, 2007.

21st Century Gothic: Great Gothic Novels since 2000. Toronto: Scarecrow Press, 2011.

Perron, Bernard, ed. *Horror Video Games: Essays on the Fusion of Fear and Play.* Jefferson, NC: McFarland, 2009.

Powell, Anna, and Andrew Smith, eds. *Teaching the Gothic. Teaching the New English.* New York: Palgrave, 2006.

Punter, David, ed. *A New Companion to the Gothic.* Oxford: Wiley-Blackwell, 2012.

Riquelme, John Paul, ed. *Gothic and Modernism: Essaying Dark Literary Modernity.* Baltimore, MD: The Johns Hopkins University Press, 2008.

Sage, Victor, and Allan Lloyd Smith, eds. *Modern Gothic: A Reader.* Manchester University Press, 1996.

Smith, Andrew, Diane Mason, and William Hughes, eds. *Fictions of Unease: The Gothic from* Otranto *to* The X-Files. Newton Park: Sulis Press, 2002.

Smith, Andrew, and William Hughes, eds. *EcoGothic. International Gothic.* Manchester University Press, 2013.

Empire and the Gothic: The Politics of Genre. Basingstoke: Palgrave Macmillan, 2003.

Smith, Andrew, and Jeff Wallace, eds. *Gothic Modernisms.* New York: Palgrave, 2001.

Spooner, Catherine, and Emma McEvoy, eds. *The Routledge Companion to Gothic.* London: Routledge, 2007.

Straub, Peter, ed. *Poe's Children: The New Horror.* New York: Doubleday, 2008.

Taddeo, Julie Ann, and Cynthia J. Miller, eds. *Steaming into a Victorian Future: A Steampunk Anthology.* Lanham, MD: Scarecrow, 2012.

VanderMeer, Ann, and Jeff VanderMeer, eds. *The New Weird.* San Francisco: Tachyon, 2008.

The Weird: A Compendium of Strange and Dark Stories. New York: Tor Books, 2012.

Wallace, Diana, and Andrew Smith, eds. *The Female Gothic: New Directions.* New York: Palgrave Macmillan, 2009.

Wasson, Sara, and Emily Alder, eds. *Gothic Science Fiction, 1980–2010.* Liverpool University Press, 2011.

Williams, Gilda, ed. *The Gothic: Documents of Contemporary Art.* London: Whitechapel, 2007.

Zamora, Lois Parkinson and Wendy B. Faris, eds. *Magical Realism: Theory, History, Community.* Durham, NC: Duke University Press, 1995.

Key secondary monographs and essays about modern Gothic,
including important influences on it

Aaron, Jane. *Welsh Gothic. Gothic Literary Studies.* Cardiff: University of Wales Press, 2013.

Abraham, Nicholas. "Notes on the Phantom: A Complement to Freud's Metapsychology," trans. Nicholas Rand. *Critical Inquiry*, 13 (1987), pp. 287–292.

Aiken, Susan Hardy. *Isak Dinesen and the Engendering of Narrative.* University of Chicago Press, 1990.

Anzaldúa, Gloria. *Borderlands/La Frontera: The New Mestiza* (1987), 5th edn. San Francisco: Aunt Lute Books, 2012.

Armitt, Lucie. *Contemporary Women's Fiction and the Fantastic.* Basingstoke: Palgrave, 2000.

Fantasy Fiction. New York: Continuum, 2005.

History of the Gothic: Twentieth Century Gothic. Gothic Literary Studies. Cardiff: University of Wales Press, 2011.

Atwood, Margaret. *Strange Things: The Malevolent North in Canadian Literature.* Oxford: Clarendon Press, 1995.

Survival: A Thematic Guide to Canadian Literature. Toronto: House of Anansi, 1972.

Auerbach, Nina. *Our Vampires, Ourselves.* University of Chicago Press, 1995.

Badiou, Alain. *Ethics: An Essay on the Understanding of Evil*, trans. Peter Hallward. New York: Verso, 2001.

Baudrillard, Jean. *Simulacra and Simulation* (1981), trans. Sheila Glaser. Ann Arbor, MI: University of Michigan Press, 1994.

The Transparency of Evil: Essays on Extreme Phenomena, trans. James Benedict. London: Verso, 1993.

Becker, Susanne. *Gothic Forms of Feminine Fictions.* Manchester University Press, 1999.

Benshof, Harry M. *Monsters in the Closet: Homosexuality and the Horror Film.* Manchester University Press, 1997.

Beville, Maria. *Gothic Post-Modernism: Voicing the Terrors of Postmodernity.* Amsterdam: Rodopi, 2009.

Bishop, Kyle William. *American Zombie Gothic: The Rise and Fall (and Rise) of the Walking Dead in Popular Culture.* Jefferson, NC: McFarland, 2010.

Botting, Fred. *Gothic*, 2nd edn. *New Critical Idioms.* London: Routledge, 2013.

Gothic Romanced: Consumption, Gender, and Technology in Contemporary Fictions. London: Routledge, 2008.

Limits of Horror: Technology, Bodies, Gothic. Manchester University Press, 2008.

Sex, Machines, and Navels: Fiction, Fantasy, and History in the Future Present. Manchester University Press, 1999.

Bradford, Clare, Kerry Mallan, John Stephens, and Robyn McCallum. *New World Orders in Contemporary Children's Literature: Utopian Transformations.* Basingstoke: Palgrave Macmillan, 2008.

Brantlinger, Patrick. *Rule of Darkness: British Literature and Imperialism, 1830–1914.* Ithaca, NY: Cornell University Press, 1988.

Bronfen, Elisabeth. *Night Passages: Philosophy, Literature, Film.* New York: Columbia University Press, 2013.

Bruhm, Steven. *Reflecting Narcissus: A Queer Aesthetic.* Minneapolis, MN: University of Minnesota Press, 2001.

Campany, R. F. "Ghost Matter: The Culture of Ghosts in Six Dynasties Zhiguai." *Chinese Literature*, 13 (1991), pp. 15–34.

Case, Sue-Ellen. "Tracking the Vampire," *Differences: A Journal of Feminist Cultural Studies*, 3 (1991), pp. 1–19.

Castricano, Jodey. *Cryptomimesis: The Gothic and Jacques Derrida's Ghost Writing.* London: McGill-Queens University Press, 2001.

Cavallaro, Dani. *The Gothic Vision: Three Centuries of Horror, Terror and Fear.* London: Continuum, 2002.

Cavell, Stanley. *The World Viewed: Reflections on the Ontology of Film.* Cambridge, MA: Harvard University Press, 1979.

Chaplin, Sue. *The Gothic and the Rule of Law.* London: Palgrave, 2007.

"From Blood Bonds to Brand Loyalties: Poppy Z. Brite's *Lost Souls* and Alan Ball's *True Blood*." *Horror Studies*, 3:1 (2012), pp. 71–86.

Cheah, Pheng. *Spectral Nationality: Passages of Freedom from Kant to Postcolonial Literatures of Liberation.* New York: Columbia University Press, 2003.

Clemens, Valdine. *The Return of the Repressed: Gothic Horror from* The Castle of Otranto *to* Alien. State University of New York Press, 1999.

Coetzee, J. M. *White Writing: On the Culture of Letters in South Africa.* New Haven, CT: Yale University Press, 1988.

Cooper, Brenda. *Magical Realism in West African Fiction: Seeing with a Third Eye.* London: Routledge, 1998.

Dayan, Joan (Colin). *Haiti, History, and the Gods.* Berkeley, CA: University of California Press, 1996.

Dolar, Mladen. " 'I Shall Be with You on Your Wedding-Night': Lacan and the Uncanny." *October*, 58 (1991), pp. 5–23.

Dunker, Patricia. "Queer Gothic: Angela Carter and the Lost Narratives of Sexual Subversion." *Critical Survey*, 8:1 (1996), pp. 58–68.

Edmundson, Mark. *Nightmare on Main Street: Angels, Sadomasochism, and the Culture of Gothic.* Cambridge, MA: Harvard University Press, 1997.

Edwards, Justin D. *Gothic Canada: Reading the Spectre of a National Literature.* Edmonton: University of Alberta Press, 2005.

Gothic Passages: Racial Ambiguity and the American Gothic. University of Iowa Press, 2003.

Faris, Wendy B. *Ordinary Enchantments: Magical Realism and the Remystification of Narrative.* Nashville, TN: Vanderbilt University Press, 2004.

Fiedler, Leslie A. *Love and Death in the American Novel*, rev. edn. New York: Stein and Day, 1966.

Forlini, Stephania. "Technology and Morality: The Stuff of Steampunk." *Neo-Victorian Studies*, 3 (2010), pp. 72–98.

Freud, Sigmund. "Mourning and Melancholia" (1915–17)," in *The Standard Edition of the Complete Psychological Works of Sigmund Freud*, ed. and trans. James Strachey, vol. xiv. London: Hogarth, 1937, pp. 243–258.

"The Uncanny" (1919), in *Collected Papers*, trans. Joan Riviere, vol. v. London: Hogarth, 1949, pp. 368–407.

Frye, Northrop. *The Bush Garden: Essays on the Canadian Imagination.* Toronto: House of Anansi, 1971.

Gelder, Ken. *New Vampire Cinema.* London: British Film Institute, 2012.

Reading the Vampire. Oxford: Routledge, 1994.

Haggerty, George E. *Queer Gothic.* Urbana, IL: University of Illinois Press, 2006.

Halberstam, Judith. *Skin Shows: Gothic Horror and the Technology of Monsters.* Durham, NC: Duke University Press, 1995.

Hanson, Ellis. "Lesbians Who Bite," in *Out Takes: Essays on Queer Theory and Film*, ed. Ellis Hanson. Durham, NC: Duke University Press, 1999, pp. 183–222.

"Undead," in *Inside/Out: Lesbian Theories, Gay Theories*, ed. Diana Fuss. New York: Routledge, 1991, pp. 324–340.

Hayles, Katherine. *How We Became Posthuman: Virtual Bodies in Cybernetics, Literature, and Informatics*. University of Chicago Press, 1999.

Heiland, Donna. *Gothic and Gender: An Introduction*. Oxford: Blackwell, 2004.

Hendershot, Cyndy. *The Animal Within: Masculinity and the Gothic*. Ann Arbor, MI: University of Michigan Press, 1998.

Hennelly, Mark M. "Framing the Gothic: From Pillar to Post-Structuralism." *College Literature*, 28 (2001), pp. 68–87.

Hirsch, Foster. *The Dark Side of the Screen: Film Noir*. Cambridge, MA: Da Capo Press, 2001.

Hodkinson, Paul. *Goth: Identity, Style and Subculture. Dress, Body, Culture*. Oxford: Berg, 2002.

Hogle, Jerrold E. *The Undergrounds of* The Phantom of the Opera: *Sublimation and the Gothic in Leroux's Novel and Its Progeny*. New York: Palgrave, 2002.

Horner, Avril, and Sue Zlosnik. *Daphne du Maurier: Writing, Identity, and the Gothic Imagination*. Basingstoke: Macmillan, 1998.

Gothic and the Comic Turn. New York: Palgrave Macmillan, 2005.

Hughes, H. J. "Familiarity of the Strange: Japan's Gothic Tradition." *Criticism*, 41 (2000), pp. 59–89.

James, Kathryn. *Death, Gender and Sexuality in Contemporary Adolescent Literature*. New York: Routledge, 2009.

Jameson, Fredric. "Historicism in *The Shining*" (1981), in *Signatures of the Visible*. London: Routledge, 1990, pp. 82–98.

Postmodernism, or the Cultural Logic of Late Capitalism. Durham, NC: Duke University Press, 1991.

Jayamanne, Laleen. *Toward Cinema and Its Double: Cross-Cultural Mimesis*. Bloomington, IN: Indiana University Press, 2001.

Joshi, S. T. *The Modern Weird Tale: A Critique of Horror Fiction*. Jefferson, NC: McFarland, 2001.

Juul, Jesper. *Half-Real: Video Games between Real Rules and Fictional Worlds*. Cambridge, MA: MIT Press, 2005.

Kaes, Anton. *Shell Shock Cinema: Weimar Culture and the Wounds of War*. Princeton University Press, 2009.

Khair, Tabish. *The Gothic, Postcolonialism and Otherness: Ghosts from Elsewhere*. New York: Palgrave Macmillan, 2009.

King, Stephen. *Dance Macabre* (1982). New York: Berkeley, 1987.

Kratter, Matthew. "Twilight of the Vampires: History and the Myth of the Undead." *Contagion*, 5 (1998), pp. 30–45.

Kristeva, Julia. *Powers of Horror: An Essay on Abjection*, trans. Leon S. Roudiez. New York: Columbia University Press, 1982.

Lloyd Smith, Allan. *American Gothic Fiction: An Introduction*. New York: Continuum, 2004.

Lovecraft, H. P. *Supernatural Horror in Literature* (1927–1935). New York: Dover, 1973.

Magistrale, Tony. *Abject Terrors: Surveying the Modern and Postmodern Horror Film*. New York: Peter Lang, 2005.

Massé, Michelle. *In the Name of Love: Women, Masochism, and the Gothic*. Ithaca, NY: Cornell University Press, 1992.

McDaniel, J. T. *The Lovelorn Ghost and the Magical Monk: Practicing Buddhism in Modern Thailand*. New York: Columbia University Press, 2011.

Miéville, China. "M. R. James and the Quantum Vampire: Weird; Hauntological: Versus and/or and and/or or?," *Collapse*, 4: *Concept Horror* (2000), pp. 105–128.

Morgan, Jack. *The Biology of Horror: Gothic Literature and Film*. Carbondale, IL: Southern Illinois University Press, 2002.

Mulvey, Laura. *Fetishism and Curiosity*. London: BFI Publishing, 1996.

Nelson, Victoria. *Gothicka: Vampire Heroes, Human Gods, and the New Supernatural*. Cambridge, MA: Harvard University Press, 2012.

Palmer, Paulina. *The Queer Uncanny: New Perspectives on the Gothic. Gothic Literary Studies*. Cardiff: University of Wales Press, 2012.

Perry, Dennis, and Carl H. Sederholm. *Poe, "The House of Usher," and the American Gothic*. New York: Palgrave Macmillan, 2009.

Punter, David. *Gothic Pathologies: The Text, the Body and the Law*. London: Macmillan, 1998.

The Literature of Terror, 2nd edn., 2 vols. Vol. I: *The Gothic Tradition*. Vol. II: *The Modern Gothic*. London: Longman, 1996.

Postcolonial Imaginings. Edinburgh University Press, 2000.

Punter, David, and Glennis Byron. *The Gothic*. Oxford: Blackwell, 2004.

Rabinowitz, Paula. *Black and White & Noir: America's Pulp Modernism*. New York: Columbia University Press, 2002.

Radway, Janice A. *Reading the Romance: Women, Patriarchy, and Popular Literature*. Chapel Hill, NC: University of North Carolina Press, 1984.

Reider, N. T. "The Emergence of Kaidan-shū: The Collection of Tales of the Strange and Mysterious in the Edo Period." *Asian Folklore Studies*, 60 (2001), pp. 79–99.

Rigby, Mair. "Uncanny Recognition: Queer Theory's Debt to the Gothic." *Gothic Studies*, 11 (2009), pp. 46–58.

Rudd, Alison. *Postcolonial Gothic Fictions from the Caribbean, Canada, Australia and New Zealand. Gothic Literary Studies*. Cardiff: University of Wales Press, 2010.

Ryan, Marie-Laure. *Possible Worlds, Artificial Intelligence, and Narrative Theory*. Bloomington, IN: Indiana University Press, 1991.

Said, Edward. *Culture and Imperialism*. London: Vintage, 1994.

Sconce, Jeffrey. *Haunted Media: Electronic Presence from Telegraphy to Television*. Durham, NC: Duke University Press, 2000.

Sears, John. *Stephen King's Gothic. Gothic Literary Studies*. Cardiff: University of Wales Press, 2012.

Sedgwick, Eve Kosofsky. *Between Men: English Literature and Male Homosocial Desire*. New York: Columbia University Press, 1985.

Sheehan, Jonathan. "Sacrifice before the Secular." *Representations*, 105:1 (2009), pp. 12–36.

Showalter, Elaine. *Sexual Anarchy: Gender and Culture at the Fin de Siecle*. London: Bloomsbury, 1991.

Women, Madness, and English Culture, 1830–1980. New York: Penguin, 1987.

Skal, Robert J. *The Monster Show: A Cultural History of Horror*. New York: Norton, 1993.

Smith, Andrew. *The Ghost Story, 1840–1920: A Cultural History.* Manchester University Press, 2010.

Gothic Literature, 2nd edn. *Edinburgh Critical Guides.* Edinburgh University Press, 2013.

Spencer, Kathleen L. "Purity and Danger: Dracula, the Urban Gothic and the Late-Victorian Degeneracy Crisis." *ELH*, 59 (1992), pp. 197–225.

Spivak, Gayatri. *A Critique of Postcolonial Reason.* Cambridge, MA: Harvard University Press, 1999.

Spooner, Catherine. *Contemporary Gothic. Focus on Contemporary Issues.* London: Reaktion, 2006.

Fashioning Gothic Bodies. Manchester University Press, 2004.

Taylor, Charles. *A Secular Age.* Cambridge, MA: Harvard University Press, 2007.

Todorov, Tzvetan. *The Fantastic: A Structural Approach to a Literary Genre* (1971), trans. Richard Howard. Cleveland, OH: Press of Case Western Reserve University, 1973.

Tropp, Martin. *Images of Fear: How Horror Stories Helped Shape Modern American Culture, 1818–1919.* Jefferson, NC: McFarland, 1990.

Twitchell, James B. *Dreadful Pleasures: An Anatomy of Modern Horror.* Oxford University Press, 1985.

van Elferen, Isabella. "Dances with Specters: Theorising the Cybergothic." *Gothic Studies*, 11 (2009), pp. 99–112.

Gothic Music: The Sounds of the Uncanny. Gothic Literary Studies. Cardiff: University of Wales Press, 2012.

Vincent, J. Keith. *Two-Timing Modernity: Homosocial Narrative in Modern Japanese Fiction.* Cambridge, MA: Harvard University Press, 2012.

Vinge, Vernor. "The Coming Technological Singularity: How to Survive in the Post-Human Era." *Whole Earth Review*, 81 (1993), pp. 88–95.

Wallace, Diana. *Female Gothic Histories: Gender, History, and the Gothic. Gothic Literary Studies.* Cardiff: University of Wales Press, 2013.

Wasson, Sara. *Urban Gothic of the Second World War: Dark London.* New York: Palgrave Macmillan, 2010.

Watkiss, Joanne. *Gothic Contemporaries: The Haunted Text. Gothic Literary Studies.* Cardiff: University of Wales Press, 2012.

Weinstock, Jeffrey Andrew. *Scare Tactics: Supernatural Fiction by American Women.* New York: Fordham University Press, 2008.

Wester, Maisha L. *African American Gothic: Screams from Shadowed Places.* New York: Palgrave Macmillan, 2012.

Wheatley, Helen. *Gothic Television.* Manchester University Press, 2007.

Williamson, Milly. *The Lure of the Vampire: Gender, Fiction and Fandom from Bram Stoker to Buffy.* London: Wallflower Press, 2005.

Yi, Dongshin. *A Genealogy of Cyborgothic: Aesthetics and Ethics in the Age of Posthumanism.* Abingdon: Ashgate, 2010.

Žižek, Slavoj. *Living in the End Times.* London: Verso, 2011.

The Parallax View. Cambridge, MA: MIT Press, 2009.

The Plague of Fantasies. London and New York: Verso, 1997.

The Sublime Object of Ideology. London: Verso, 1989.

GUIDE TO FURTHER VIEWING

Important primary Gothic works of film since 1918

Alfredson, Tomas, dir. *Let the Right One In* (Swedish). Sandrew Metronome, 2008.
Amenábar, Alejandro, dir. *The Others*. Dimension, 2001.
Anderson, Paul W. S., dir. *Resident Evil*. Screen Gems, 2002.
Argento, Dario, dir. *Suspiria*. Seda Septtacoli, 1977.
Bates, Richard, Jr., dir. *Suburban Gothic*. New Normal Films, 2014.
Bayona, J. A., dir. *The Orphanage* (Spanish). Esta Vivo!/Warner Bros., 2007.
Bigelow, Kathryn, dir. *Near Dark*. F/M Entertainment/DeLaurentiis Entertainment, 1987.
Browning, Tod, dir. *Dracula*. Universal Pictures, 1931.
Burton, Tim, dir. *Edward Scissorhands*. 20th Century Fox, 1990.
　Sleepy Hollow. Mandelay-Zoetrope, 1999.
　Sweeney Todd: The Demon Barber of Fleet Street. Dreamworks/Warner Bros., 2007.
Cameron, James, dir. *The Terminator*. Orion/Hemdale/Pacific Western, 1984.
Castle, William, dir. *House on Haunted Hill*. Castle Productions/Allied Artists, 1959.
Clayton, Jack, dir. *The Innocents*. 20th Century Fox, 1961.
Coppola, Francis Ford, dir. *Bram Stoker's Dracula*. Columbia/Zoetrope, 1992.
Corman, Roger, dir. *House of Usher*. American International, 1960.
Craven, Wes, dir. *A Nightmare on Elm Street*. New Line Cinema, 1984.
Cronenberg, David, dir. *Dead Ringer*. 20th Century Fox/Rank, 1988.
　eXistenZ. Dimension/Momentum, 1999.
　Videodrome. Universal, 1983.
Cukor, George, dir. *Gaslight*. MGM, 1944.
de Palma, Brian, dir. *Carrie*. MGM, 1976.
del Toro, Guillermo, dir. *The Devil's Backbone (El espinazo del diablo)*. El Deseo S.A., 2001.
　Pan's Labyrinth (El laberinto del fauno). Estudios Picasso, 2006.
Dreyer, Carl Theodor, dir. *Vampyr*. Vereinigte Star-Film, 1932.
Fincher, David, dir. *Fight Club*. Fox 2000 Pictures, 1999.
Fisher, Terence, dir. *The Curse of Frankenstein*. Hammer/Warner Bros., 1957.
　Horror of Dracula. Hammer/Warner Bros., 1958.
Freund, Karl, dir. *The Mummy*. Universal, 1932.

Friedkin, William, dir. *The Exorcist*. Warner Bros, 1973.
Goddard, Drew, dir. *The Cabin in the Woods*. Mutant Enemy/Lionsgate, 2012.
Halperin, Victor, dir. *White Zombie*. United Artists, 1932.
Hawks, Howard, dir. *The Big Sleep*. Warner Bros., 1946.
Hitchcock, Alfred, dir. *Psycho*. Paramount/Universal, 1960.
 Rebecca. Selznik-United Artists, 1940.
 Spellbound. Selznik-United Artists, 1945.
Houston, John, dir. *The Maltese Falcon*. Warner Bros., 1941.
Jordon, Neil, dir. *Interview with the Vampire*. Warner Bros., 1994.
Julian, Rupert, dir. *The Phantom of the Opera*. Universal, 1925.
Kubrick, Stanley, dir. *The Shining*. Warner Bros., 1980.
Lang, Fritz, dir. *Metropolis*. UFA, 1927.
LeRoy, Mervyn, dir. *The Bad Seed*. Warner Bros., 1956.
Lewin, Albert, dir. *The Picture of Dorian Gray*. MGM, 1945.
Lynch, David, dir. *Blue Velvet*. De Laurentiis Entertainment Group, 1986.
 Mulholland Drive. Universal, 2001.
Mamoulian, Rouben, dir. *Dr. Jekyll and Mr. Hyde*. Paramount, 1931.
Murnau, F. W., dir. *Nosferatu: A Symphony of Horror*. Film Arts Guild, 1922.
Polanski, Roman, dir. *Chinatown*. Paramount, 1974.
 Rosemary's Baby. Paramount, 1968.
Reed, Carol, dir. *The Third Man*. Selznick-London, 1949.
Rodriguez, Robert, dir. *The Faculty*. Dimension Films, 1998.
 From Dusk till Dawn. Dimension, 1996.
Roeg, Nicholas, dir. *Don't Look Now*. Casey/Eldorado/British Lion Films, 1973.
Romero, George, dir. *Dawn of the Dead*. United Film, 1978.
 Day of the Dead. United Film, 1985.
 Land of the Dead. Universal, 2005.
 Night of the Living Dead. Continental Distribution, 1968.
Russell, Ken, dir. *The Devils*. Warner Bros., 1971.
 Gothic. Virgin Films, 1986.
 The Lair of the White Worm. Vestron Pictures, 1988.
Sánchez, Eduardo, and Daniel Myrick, dirs. *The Blair Witch Project*. Hexen Films, 1999.
Scorcese, Martin, dir. *Hugo*. GK Films/Infinitum Nihil, 2011.
Scott, Ridley, dir. *Alien*. 20th Century Fox, 1979.
 Blade Runner. Warner Bros., 1982.
Sharman, Jim, dir. *The Rocky Horror Picture Show*. 20th Century Fox, 1975.
Shyamalan, M. Night, dir. *The Sixth Sense*. Spyglass/Buena Vista, 1999.
Siodmark, Robert, dir. *The Killers*. Universal, 1946.
Tourneur, Jacques, dir. *The Cat People*. RKO, 1942.
 I Walked with a Zombie. RKO, 1943.
Verbinski, Gore, dir. *The Ring*. Dreamworks, 2002.
Waggner, George, dir. *The Wolf Man*. Universal, 1941.
Wan, James, dir. *The Conjuring*. Warner Bros./New Line, 2013.
Weine, Robert, dir. *The Cabinet of Dr. Caligari* (1920). Decla-Bioscop/Goldwyn, 1921.
Welles, Orson, writer/dir. *Citizen Kane*. RKO Radio, 1941.
 Touch of Evil. Universal, 1958.

Whale, James, dir. *The Bride of Frankenstein*. Universal, 1935.
Frankenstein. Universal, 1931.
The Old Dark House. Universal, 1932.
Wilder, Billy, dir. *Double Indemnity*. Paramount, 1944.
Sunset Boulevard. Paramount, 1950.
Wise, Robert, dir. *The Haunting*. MGM, 1963.

Important Gothic series made for television since 1950

Addams, Charles, and David Levy, creators. *The Addams Family*. MGM-TV/ABC, 1964–1966.
Ball, Alan, creator/dir. *True Blood*. HBO, 2008–.
Burns, Alan, and Chris Hayward, creators. *The Munsters*. Universal/MCA-TV, 1964–1966.
Carter, Chris, creator/dir. *Millennium*. FOX-TV, 1996–1999.
The X-Files. FOX-TV, 1993–2002.
Cassidy, Shaun, creator. *American Gothic*. CBS, 1995–1996.
Clark, Lawrence Gordon, creator/dir. *Ghost Stories for Christmas*. BBC 1, 1971–1978.
Curtis, Dan, and Art Wallace, creators. *Dark Shadows*. ABC, 1966–1971.
Darabont, Frank, creator/dir. *The Walking Dead*. AMC, 2010–.
Fuller, Bryan, creator. *Hannibal*. NBC, 2013–.
Hitchcock, Alfred, creator/host. *Alfred Hitchcock Presents*. Revue/Universal-TV, 1955–1965.
ITV Network, creators. *Mystery and Imagination*. ABC/Thames TV, 1966–1970.
Lynch, David, and Mark Frost, creators/dirs. *Twin Peaks*. CBS, 1990–1991.
Murphy, Ryan, and Brad Fulchik, creators. *American Horror Story*. 20th Century Fox/FX-TV, 2011–.
Serling, Rod, creator/writer/host. *The Twilight Zone* (frequently Gothic). CBS, 1959–1964.
Whedon, Joss, creator/dir. *Buffy the Vampire Slayer*. WB Network, 1997–2003.

Major Gothic video games

Bytes, Piranha, creator. *Gothic*. Spellbound Entertainment, 2001–2012.
Gray, Christopher, creator. *Call of Cthulhu: Dark Corners of the Earth*. Bethesda Softworks, 2005.
Grip, Thomas, Jens Nilsson, and Mikhail Hedberg, creators. *Amnesia: The Dark Descent*. Frictional Games, 2010–2011.
Hall, Tom, Sandy Peterson, John Romero, and Shawn Green, creators. *Doom*. idSoftware, 1993–2004.
Mikami, Shinji, creator. *Resident Evil*. Capcom, 1996–2012.
Toyama, Keiichiro, creator. *Silent Hill*. Konami, 1999–2012.

INDEX

Cambridge companions to ...

AUTHORS